George Henry Lewes

The Biographical History of Philosophy

George Henry Lewes

The Biographical History of Philosophy

ISBN/EAN: 9783744664424

Printed in Europe, USA, Canada, Australia, Japan

Cover: Foto ©Thomas Meinert / pixelio.de

More available books at **www.hansebooks.com**

THE BIOGRAPHICAL HISTORY OF PHILOSOPHY,

FROM ITS ORIGIN IN GREECE DOWN TO THE PRESENT DAY.

BY

GEORGE HENRY LEWES.

"Man is not born to solve the mystery of Existence; but he must nevertheless attempt it, in order that he may learn how to keep within the limits of the Knowable."—GOETHE.

"For I doubt not through the ages one increasing purpose runs,
And the thoughts of men are widened by the process of the suns."
TENNYSON.

LIBRARY EDITION,

MUCH ENLARGED AND THOROUGHLY REVISED.

VOL. I.

NEW YORK:
D. APPLETON AND COMPANY,
1, 3, AND 5 BOND STREET.
1890.

PREFACE.

This new edition may almost be considered as a new work, so many are the additions and so extensive the alterations. Seven new names have been added to the list of philosophers,—ABELARD, ALGAZZALI, GIORDANO BRUNO, HARTLEY, DARWIN, CABANIS, and GALL. An Introduction, setting forth the distinguishing characteristics of Philosophy and Science, replaces the original Introduction. Under the heads of SOCRATES, the SOPHISTS, ARISTOTLE, BACON, SPINOZA, HUME, CONDILLAC, KANT, and ECLECTICISM, considerable additions and alterations will be found; and, throughout, the revision has been such that scarcely a paragraph remains unaltered.

The work was written ten years ago, and was addressed to a popular audience. Ten years have not been without their influence on the historian; and moreover, the success of the work has so greatly exceeded any thing that could reasonably have been anticipated—not only in respect to sale, but in the directions of its influence—that on undertaking this Library Edition I felt the necessity of modifying both the aim and scope of the work. A graver audience was to be addressed, a graver tone adopted. Without forgetting the general public, I had now to think also of what students would require. Many polemical passages, many extracts, and some digressions, have been removed; and the space thus gained has prevented the new matter from swelling the work to an inconvenient size. Many references and other bibliographical details have been added, although the principle of abstinence from unnecessary citation has still been preserved.

The labor bestowed on this Edition will, I hope, render it more worthy of public acceptance. To my friend, the Rev. W. G. Clark, of Trinity College, Cambridge, an acknowledgment is due for the kindness with which he permitted me to profit by his accomplished scholarship and taste, in the revision of the proofs; but while thanking him publicly for his many suggestions and corrections, I must exonerate him from every iota of responsibility either as to the opinions or the statements in this volume.

The Introduction explains the purpose of this History and the principles of its composition; let me therefore only add here that, although availing myself of the labors of other historians and critics, I have not restricted myself to them. The works of the various philosophers, with rare exceptions, have been studied at first hand, and have furnished the extracts and abstracts; that is to say, I have either collected the passages myself, or have verified them by reference to the originals, in almost all cases. While, therefore, this History makes no pretension to a place beside the many erudite and comprehensive Histories previously published, it claims to be regarded as something very different from a mere compilation. The novelty of its conception made direct acquaintance with the originals indispensable. Having to exhibit the Biography of Philosophy in its rise, growth, and development, I could not always have drawn my material from writers who had no such aim; many of the passages most significant for my purpose being totally disregarded by my predecessors.

In another respect also I have innovated, namely, in the constant interweaving of criticism with exposition. This was necessary to my purpose of proving that no metaphysical system has had in it a principle of vitality; none has succeeded in establishing itself, because none deserved to succeed. In this way I have been led to express every conclusion to which the study of metaphysical problems has led me; in some places—especially in the refutation of Sensationalism, and in the physiological discussion of psychological questions—I have been forced to content myself with a brief and imperfect exposition of my own views; and the reader is requested to regard them rather in their bearing as criticisms, than as expressing what I have to say on such difficult topics.

The following list comprises some of the many general Histories which the student will find useful, should he desire ampler detail than was consistent with the size and plan of this volume:

> *In English.*—Ritter, *History of Philosophy*, 3 vols.; Tennemann, *Manual of the History of Philosophy*, 1 vol.; Victor Cousin, *Introduction to the History of Philosophy*, 1 vol.; Morell, *History of Speculative Philosophy in the Nineteenth Century*, 2 vols. (2d edition, much improved).
>
> *In French.*—Degérando, *Histoire Comparée des Systèmes de Philosophie*, 4 vols. (2d edition); Renouvier, *Manuel de la Philosophie Ancienne*, 2 vols., and *Manuel de la Philosophie Moderne*, 1 vol.; Damiron, *Histoire de la Philosophie en France au*

XIX Siècle, 1 vol.; Galuppi, *Lettres Philosophiques*, 1 vol.

In German.—Ritter, *Geschichte der Philosophie*, 9 vols.; Tennemann, *Geschichte der Philosophie*, 11 vols.; Hegel, *Geschichte der Philosophie*, 3 vols.; Zeller, *Die Philosophie der Griechen*, 2 vols.; Brandis, *Geschichte der Griechisch-Römischen Philosophie*, 2 vols.

CONTENTS.

PART I.—ANCIENT PHILOSOPHY.

INTRODUCTION xi

FIRST EPOCH.
Speculations on the Nature of the Universe.

CHAPTER I. THE PHYSICISTS.—Thales.—Anaximenes.—Diogenes of Apollonia.. 1

CHAPTER II. THE MATHEMATICIANS.—Anaximander of Miletus.—Pythagoras.—Philosophy of Pythagoras.—Translations from Aristotle's *Metaphysics* 10

CHAPTER III. THE ELEATICS.—Xenophanes.—The Philosophy of Xenophanes.—Parmenides.—Zeno of Elea........................ 37

SECOND EPOCH.
Speculations on the Creation of the Universe, and on the Origin of Knowledge.

Heraclitus.—Anaxagoras.—Empedocles.—Democritus 63

THIRD EPOCH.

Intellectual Crisis.—The Insufficiency of all Attempts towards a Solution of the Problem of Existence, as well as that of Knowledge, produces the Sophists.

THE SOPHISTS.—What were they?—Protagoras 109

FOURTH EPOCH.
A New Era opened by the Invention of a New Method.

SOCRATES.—The Life of Socrates.—Philosophy of Socrates............ 122

FIFTH EPOCH.
Partial Adoption of the Socratic Method.

The Megaric School.—Euclid.—The Cyrenaic School.—Aristippus.—The Cynics.—Antisthenes and Diogenes 169

SIXTH EPOCH.

Complete Adoption and Application of the Socratic Method.

PLATO.—Life of Plato.—Plato's Writings; their Character, Object, and Authenticity.—Plato's Method.—Plato's Ideal Theory.—Plato's Psychology.—Summary of Plato's Dialectics.—Plato's Theology and Cosmology.—Plato's View of the Beautiful and the Good.—Plato's Ethics 186

SEVENTH EPOCH.

Philosophy again reduced to a System: Close of the Socratic Movement.—Aristotle.

CHAPTER I. ARISTOTLE.—Life of Aristotle.—Aristotle's Method.—Aristotle's Logic.—Aristotle's Metaphysics 241

CHAPTER II. SUMMARY OF THE SOCRATIC MOVEMENT 266

EIGHTH EPOCH.

Second Crisis of Greek Philosophy: the Skeptics, Epicureans, Stoics, and the New Academy.

CHAPTER I. THE SKEPTICS.—Pyrrho 268
CHAPTER II. THE EPICUREANS.—Epicurus 274
CHAPTER III. THE STOICS.—Zeno................................ 281
CHAPTER IV. THE NEW ACADEMY.—Arcesilaus and Carneades 293
CHAPTER V. SUMMARY OF THE EIGHTH EPOCH 305

NINTH EPOCH.

Philosophy allies itself with Faith: the Alexandrian Schools.

CHAPTER I. RISE OF NEO-PLATONISM.—Alexandria.—Philo......... 307
CHAPTER II. ANTAGONISM OF CHRISTIANITY AND NEO-PLATONISM.—Plotinus.—The Alexandrian Dialectics.—The Alexandrian Trinity.—The Doctrine of Emanation 314
CHAPTER III. PROCLUS 332
CONCLUSION OF ANCIENT PHILOSOPHY 339

PART II.—MODERN PHILOSOPHY.

TRANSITION PERIOD.

FROM PROCLUS TO BACON.—Scholasticism.—Life of Abelard.—Philosopny of Abelard.—Algazzâli.—Revival of Learning.—Giordano Bruno .. 843

CONTENTS.

FIRST EPOCH
Foundation of the Inductive Method.

The Life of Bacon.—Bacon's Method.—The Spirit of Bacon's Method — Was the Method New and Useful? 398

SECOND EPOCH.
Foundation of the Deductive Method.

CHAPTER I. DESCARTES.—Life of Descartes.—The Method of Descartes.—Application of the Method.—Is the Method True? 435

CHAPTER II. SPINOZA.—Spinoza's Life.—Spinoza's Doctrine........ 456

CHAPTER III. FIRST CRISIS IN MODERN PHILOSOPHY 493

THIRD EPOCH.
Philosophy reduced to a Question of Psychology.

CHAPTER I. HOBBES...................................... 495

CHAPTER II. LOCKE.—Life of Locke.—On the Spirit of Locke's Writings.—Locke's Method.—The Origin of our Ideas.—Elements of Idealism and Skepticism in Locke.—Locke's Critics.............. 506

CHAPTER III. LEIBNITZ.................................... 541

CHAPTER IV. SUMMARY OF THE THIRD EPOCH..................... 546

FOURTH EPOCH.
The Subjective Nature of Knowledge leads to Idealism.

BERKELEY.—The Life of Berkeley.—Berkeley and Common Sense.— Idealism... 548

FIFTH EPOCH.
The Arguments of Idealism carried out into Skepticism.

HUME.—Life of Hume.—Hume's Skepticism.—Hume's Theory of Causation 570

SIXTH EPOCH.
The Origin of Knowledge reduced to Sensation by the confusion of Thought with Feeling: the Sensational School.

CHAPTER I. CONDILLAC.—Life of Condillac.—Condillac's System . 589

CHAPTER II. HARTLEY.—Life of Hartley.—Hartley's System........ 603

CHAPTER III. DARWIN.. 60f

SEVENTH EPOCH.
Second Crisis: Idealism, Skepticism, and Sensationalism producing the Reaction of Common Sense.

REID 618

EIGHTH EPOCH.

Recurrence to the Fundamental Question respecting the Origin of Knowledge.

KANT.—Life of Kant.—Kant's Historical Position.—Kant's Psychology.—Consequences of Kant's Psychology.—Examination of Kant's Fundamental Principles 630

NINTH EPOCH.

Ontology reasserts its Claim.—The Demonstration of the Subjectivity of Knowledge once more leads to Idealism.

CHAPTER I. FICHTE.—Life of Fichte.—Fichte's Historical Position.—Basis of Fichte's System.—Fichte's Idealism.—Application of Fichte's Idealism 675

CHAPTER II. SCHELLING.—Life of Schelling.—Schelling's Doctrines.. 705

CHAPTER III. HEGEL.—Life of Hegel.—Hegel's Method.—Absolute Idealism.—Hegel's Logic.—Application of the Method to Nature and History, Religion and Philosophy 715

TENTH EPOCH.

Psychology seeking its Basis in Physiology.

CHAPTER I. CABANIS 740

CHAPTER II. PHRENOLOGY.—Life of Gall.—Gall's Historical Position.—Cranioscopy.—Phrenology as a Science 749

ELEVENTH EPOCH.

Philosophy finally relinquishing its Place in favor of Positive Science.

CHAPTER I. ECLECTICISM 769
CHAPTER II. AUGUSTE COMTE 776
CONCLUSION 788
INDEX 791

INTRODUCTION.

§ I. ON THE DISTINCTION BETWEEN PHILOSOPHY AND SCIENCE.

PHILOSOPHY is everywhere in Europe fallen into discredit. Once the pride and glory of the greatest intellects, and still forming an important element of liberal culture, its present decadence is attested no less by the complaints of its few followers than by the thronging ranks of its opponents. Few now believe in its large promises; still fewer devote to it that passionate patience which is devoted by thousands to Science. Every day the conviction gains strength that Philosophy is condemned, by the very nature of its impulses, to wander forever in one tortuous labyrinth within whose circumscribed and winding spaces weary seekers are continually finding themselves in the trodden tracks of predecessors, who, they know, could find no exit.

Philosophy has been ever in movement, but the movement has been circular; and this fact is thrown into stronger relief by contrast with the linear progress of Science. Instead of perpetually finding itself, after years of gigantic endeavor, returned to the precise point from which it started, Science finds itself year by year, and almost day by day, advancing step by step, each accumulation of power adding to the momentum of its progress; each evolution, like the evolutions of organic development, bringing with it a new functional superiority, which in its turn becomes the agent of higher developments. Not a fact is discovered but has its bearing on the whole body of doctrine; not a mechanical improvement in the construction of instruments but opens fresh sources of discovery. Onward, and forever onward, mightier and forever mightier, rolls this wondrous tide of discovery, and the "thoughts of men are widened by the process of the suns." While the first principles of Philosophy are to this day as much a matter of dispute as they were two thousand years ago, the first principles of Science are securely established, and form the guiding lights of European progress. Precisely the same questions are agitated in Germany at the present moment that were agitated in ancient Greece; and with no more certain Methods of solving them, with no nearer hopes of ultimate success. The History of Philosophy presents the spectacle of thousands of intellects—some the greatest that have made our race illustrious—steadily concentrated on problems believed to be of vital importance, yet producing no other result than a conviction of the extreme facility of error, and the remoteness of any probability that Truth can be reached.* The only conquest has been *critical*, that is to say, psychological. Vainly do some argue that Philosophy has made no progress hitherto, because its problems are so complex, and require more effort than the simpler problems of Science; vainly are we warned not to conclude from the past to the future, averring that no progress will be made because no progress has been made. Perilous as it must ever be to set absolute limits to the future of human capacity, there can be no peril in averring that Philosophy never will achieve its aims, because those aims lie beyond all human scope. The difficulty is impossibility. No progress can be made because no certainty is possible. To aspire to the knowledge of more than phenomena,—their resemblances, co-existences, and successions,—is to aspire to transcend the inexorable limits of human faculty. To *know* more, we must *be* more.

The reader will have perceived that I use the word Philosophy in some restricted sense; and as this is the sense which will be attached to it throughout the present History, an explanation becomes requisite. In all countries the word Philosophy has come to be used with large latitude, designating indeed any and every kind of speculative inquiry; nay, in England, as Hegel notices with scorn,† microscopes, telescopes, barometers, and balances, are freely baptized "philosophical instruments;"—New-

---

* Compare Kant in the Preface to the 2d ed. of the *Kritik der reinen Vernunft:* "Der Metaphysik . . . ist das Schicksal bisher noch so günstig nicht gewesen dass sie den sichern Gang einer Wissenschaft einzuschlager vermogt hätte; ob sie gleich älter ist als alle übrige. . . . Es ist also kein Zweifel dass ihr Verfahren bisher ein blosses Herumtappen, und, was das Schlimmste ist, unter blossen Begriffen gewesen sey."

† *Geschichte der Philosophie,* i. 72.

ton is called a philosopher; and even Parliamentary proceedings get named philosophical;—so wide a range is given to this word. Such expressions may be criticised, but no criticism will root them out of our language; and it is futile to argue against whatever has become thus familiar and extensive. Nevertheless, when any one undertakes to write a History of Philosophy, he must define the limits of his undertaking; and as I have not the slightest intention of including either microscopic inquiries, or Parliamentary debates, within my narrative, but of rigorously limiting it to such topics as are comprised in other Histories of Philosophy, it is indispensable to define the word "Philosophy," by limiting it exclusively to Metaphysics, in direct antithesis to Science. This is the sense it bears in all other Histories; except that the demarcation from Science is not always rigorously made.

In the early days of speculation all Philosophy was essentially metaphysical, because Science had not distinctly emerged. The particular sciences then cultivated, no less than the higher generalities on Life, Destiny, and the Universe, were studied on one and the same Method; but in the course of human evolution a second Method grew up, at first timidly and unconsciously, gradually enlarging its bounds as it enlarged its powers, and at last separating itself into open antagonism with its parent and rival. The child then destroyed its parent; as the mythic Zeus, calling the Titans to his aid, destroyed Saturn and usurped his throne. Observation and Experiment were the Titans of the new Method.

There are many who deplore the encroachment of Science, fondly imagining that Philosophy would respond better to the wants of man. This regret is partly unreasoning sentiment, partly ignorance of the limitations of human faculty. Even among those who admit that Philosophy is an impossible attempt, there are many who think it should be persevered in, because of the lofty views it is supposed to open to us. This is as if a man desirous of going to America should insist on walking there, because journeys on foot are more poetical than journeys by rail and steam; in vain is he shown the impossibility of crossing the Atlantic on foot; he admits that grovelling fact, but his lofty soul has visions of some mysterious overland route by which he will pass. He dies without reaching America, but to the last gasp he maintains that he has discovered the route on which others may reach it.

O Reader! let us hear no more of the lofty views claimed as the exclusive privilege of Philosophy. Ignorant indeed must the man be who nowadays is unacquainted with the grandeur and sweep of scientific speculation in Astronomy and Geology, or who has never been thrilled by the revelations of the Telescope and Microscope. The heights and depths of man's nature, the heights to which he aspires, the depths into which he searches, and the grander generalities on Life, Destiny, and the Universe, find as eminent a place in Science as in Philosophy, with the simple difference that they are less vague and are better founded. And even were we compelled to acknowledge that the lofty views of Philosophy were excluded from Science, the earnest mind would surely barter such loftiness for Truth. Our struggle, our passion, our hope, is for Truth, not for loftiness; for sincerity, not for pretence. If we cannot reach certain heights, let us acknowledge them to be inaccessible, and not deceive ourselves and others by phrases which pretend that these heights are accessible. Bentham warns us against "question-begging epithets;" and one of these is the epithet "lofty," with which Philosophy allures the unwary student. As a specimen of the sentiment so inappropriately dragged in to decide questions not of sentiment but of truth, consider the following passage delivered from the professorial chair to students whose opinions were to be formed:

"A spirit of most misjudging contempt has for many years become fashionable towards the metaphysical contemplations of the elder sages. Alas! I cannot understand on what principles. Is it, then, a matter to be exulted in that we have at length discovered that our faculties are only formed for earth and earthly phenomena? Are we to rejoice at our own limitations, and delight that we can be cogently demonstrated to be prisoners of sense and the facts of sense? In those early struggles after a higher and more perfect knowledge, and in the forgetfulness of every inferior science through the very ardor of the pursuit, there is at least a glorious, an irresistible testimony to the loftier destinies of man; and it might almost be pronounced that in *such* a view, their very errors evidence a truth higher than all our discoveries can disclose! When Lord Bacon, with his clear and powerful reasonings, led our thinkers from these ancient regions of thought (then newly opened to the modern world) to the humbler but more varied and extensive department of inductive inquiry, I represent to myself that angel-guide, all light and grace, who is pictured by our great poet as slowly conducting the first of our race from Paradise, to leave him in a world, vast, indeed, and varied, but where thorns and thistles abounded, and food—often uncertain and often perilous—was to be gained only by the sweat of the brow and in the downcast attitude of servile toil."*

It would be an insult to the reader's understanding to answer the several absurdities and " question-begging" positions of this passage, which however is a typical specimen of much that may be met in modern writers; all that I feel called upon to notice is the opening sentence. Contempt for the metaphysical speculations of the elder sages is the last feeling I should acknowledge, however erroneous I may believe them to be. They were the precursors of modern Science. Without them we should have been in darkness. The forlorn hope of Humanity can never be an object of contempt. We follow the struggles of the early thinkers with intense interest, because we trace in their defeats the causes of future victory.

The historical connection of Science with Philosophy, and the essential differences between them, which led to their separation and the final neglect of Philosophy, will be understood better when the characteristics of the two are clearly set forth. The object of both is the same, namely, Explanation of all phenomena. Their characteristic differences, therefore, do not lie in the thing sought, so much as in the Method of search. I have met with no satisfactory statement of these characteristic differences; and the readiest way I can think of to make them intelligible, will be to exhibit the Metaphysical and Scientific Methods in

---

* Archer Butler, *Lectures on the Hist. of Ancient Philosophy*, ii. 109. The varied and accurate erudition of Mr. W. H. Thompson's notes to these lectures gives these volumes their chief value.

operation on the search after the causes of the same phenomenon; for instance, that of "Table-turning."*

A few persons stand round a table, gently resting their hands on it, but sedulously careful not to push in any direction. In a little while the table moves, at first slowly, afterwards with growing velocity. The persons are all of the highest respectability, above suspicion of wilful deceit. The phenomenon is so unexpected, so unprecedented, that an explanation is imperiously demanded. We have here an illustration of the origin of Philosophy. In presence of unusual phenomena, men are unable to remain without some explanation which shall render intelligible to them how the unusual event is produced. They are spectators merely; condemned to witness the event, unable to penetrate directly into its causes, unable to get behind the scenes and *see* the strings which move the puppets, they *guess* at what they cannot see. In this way Man is *interpres Naturæ*. Whether he be metaphysician or man of science, his starting-point is the same; and they are in error who say that the metaphysician differs from the man of science in drawing his explanation from the recesses of his own mind in lieu of drawing it from the observation of facts. Both observe facts, and both draw their interpretations from their own minds. Nay, strictly considered, there is necessarily, even in the most familiar fact, the annexation of mental inference—something added by the mind, suggested by, but not given in, the immediate observation. Facts are the registration of direct observation and indirect inference, congeries of particulars partly sensational, partly ideal. The scientific value of facts depends on the validity of the inferences bound up with them; and hence the profound truth of Cullen's paradox, that there are more false facts than false theories current.

The facts comprised in the phenomenon of "Table-turning"

---

* There is difficulty in selecting a suitable illustration, because if an undisputed scientific truth be chosen, the reader may not be able to place himself at the metaphysical point of view; whereas if a disputed point be chosen he may perhaps himself adopt the metaphysical explanation, and refuse to acknowledge the scientific explanation. "Table-turning" escapes both objections. The mania is sufficiently recent to permit our vividly realizing the mental condition of the theorists; and the error is sufficiently exploded to admit of being treated as an error.

are by no means so simple as they have been represented. Let us however reserve all criticism, and fix our attention solely on the phenomenon, which, expressed in rigorous terms, amounts to this:—the table turns; the cause of its turning unknown. To explain this, one class of metaphysical minds refers it to the agency of an unseen spirit: connecting this spiritual manifestation with others which have been familiar to him, the interpreter finds no difficulty in believing that a spirit moved the table; for the movement assuredly issued from no human agency; the respectable witnesses declare they did not push. Unless the table moved itself, therefore, the conclusion must be that it was moved by a spirit.

Minds of another class gave another explanation, one equally metaphysical, although its advocates scornfully rejected the spiritual hypothesis. These minds were indisposed to admit the existence of Spirits as agents in natural phenomena; but their interpretation, in spite of its employing the language of science, was as utterly removed from scientific induction as the spiritual interpretation they despised. They attributed the phenomenon to Electricity.* Connecting this supposed electrical manifestation with some other facts which seemed to warrant the belief of nervous action being identical with electricity, they had no hesitation in affirming that electricity streamed from the tips of the fingers; and it was even suggested by one gentleman that "the nervous fluid had probably a rotatory action, and a power of throwing off some of its surplus force."

Each of these explanations was very widely accepted by the general public, although few persons of any reasoning power now accept them. The obvious defect in both lies in the utter absence of any guarantee. We ought to be satisfied with no explanation which is without its valid guarantee. Before we purchase silver spoons we demand to see the mark of Silversmiths' Hall, to be assured that the spoons are silver, and not plated only. The test of the assayer dispels our misgivings. In like manner when the motion of a table is explained by spiritual agency, instead of debating whether the spirit bring airs from heaven or blasts from hell, we suffer our skepticism to fall on the preliminary assumption of the spirit's presence. Prove the pres ence of the spirit, before you ask us to go further. We may admit that, *if present*, the spirit is capable of producing this motion of the table; but we cannot permit you to assume such a presence merely to explain such a movement; for if the fact to be explained is sufficient proof of the explanation, we might with equal justice assume that the movement was caused by an invisible dragon who turned the table by the fanning of his awful wings.

A similar initial error is observable in the electrical hypothesis. Electricity may be a less intrinsically improbable assumption, but its presence requires proof. After that step had been taken, we should require proof that electricity could comport itself with reference to tables and similar bodies in this particular manner. We have various tests for the presence of electricity; various means of ascertaining how it would act upon a table. But seeing that the gentleman who spoke so confidently of " currents issuing from the tips of the fingers" never once attempted to prove that there were currents; and knowing moreover that these currents, if present, would *not* make a table turn, all men of true scientific culture dismissed the explanation with contempt.

Such were the metaphysical Methods of explaining the phenomenon. Let us now watch the scientific Method. The point sought is the unknown cause of the table's movement. To reach the unknown we must pass through the avenues of the known; we must not attempt to reach it through the unknown. Is there any known fact with which this movement can be allied? The first and most obvious suggestion is, that the table was pushed by the hands which rested on it. There is a difficulty in the way of this explanation, namely, that the persons declare solemnly they did *not* push; and, as persons of the highest respectability, we are bound to believe them. Is this statement of any value? The whole question is involved in it. But the philosophical mind is very little affected by guarantees of respectability in matters implicating sagacity rather than integrity. The Frenchman assured his friend that the earth did turn round the sun, and offered his *parole d'honneur* as a guarantee; but in the delicate and difficult questions of science *paroles d'honneur* have a quite inappreciable weight. We may therefore set aside

the respectability of the witnesses, and, with full confidence in their integrity, estimate the real value of their assertion, which amounts to this: they were *not conscious* of pushing. We now see that the fact, which was imagined to be simple, namely, that " the persons did not push," turns out to be excessively dubious, namely, " they were not conscious of pushing." If we come to examine such a case, we find Physiology in possession of abundant examples of muscular action accompanied by no distinct consciousness, and some of these examples are very similar to those of the unconscious pushing, which may have turned the table; and we are thus satisfied of three important points:—
1. Pushing is an adequate cause, and will serve to explain the movement of the table, as well as either the supposed spirit or electricity. 2. Pushing *may* take place without any distinct consciousness on the part of those who push. 3. Expectant attention is known to produce such a state of the muscles as would occasion this unconscious pushing.

Considered therefore as a mere hypothesis, this of unconscious pushing is strictly scientific; it may not be true, but it has fulfilled the preliminary conditions. Unlike the two hypotheses it opposes, it assumes nothing previously unknown, or not easily demonstrable; every position has been verified; whereas the metaphysicians have not verified one of their positions: they have not proved the presence of their agents, nor have they proved that these agents, if present, would act in the required manner. Of spirit we know nothing, consequently can predicate nothing. Of electricity we know something, but what is known is *not* in accordance with the table-turning hypothesis. Of pushing we know that it can and does turn tables. All then that is required to convert this latter hypothesis into scientific certainty, is to prove the presence of the pushing in this particular case. And it is proved in many ways, positive and negative, as I showed when the phenomenon first became the subject of public investigation. Positive, because if the hands rest on a loose tablecloth, or on substances with perfectly smooth surfaces which will glide easily over the table, the cloth or the substances will move, and not the table. Negative, because if the persons are duly *warned* of their liability to unconscious pushing, and are told to keep vigilant guard over their sensations, they do not move the table, although previously they have moved it frequently. When we have thus verified the presence of unconscious pushing, all the links in the chain have been verified, and certainty is complete.

Reviewing the three explanations which the phenomenon of table-turning called forth, we elicit one characteristic as distinguishing the scientific Method, namely, the *verification* of each stage in the process, the guaranteeing of each separate point, the cultivated caution of proceeding to the unknown solely through the avenues of the known. The *germinal* difference, then, between the metaphysical and scientific Methods, is not that they draw their explanations from a different source, the one employing Reasoning where the other employs Observation, but that the one is content with an explanation which has no further guarantee than is given in the logical explanation of the difficulty; whereas the other imperatively demands that every assumption should be treated as provisional, hypothetical, until it has been confronted with fact, tested by acknowledged tests, in a word, *verified*. The guarantee of the metaphysician is purely logical, subjective: it is the *intellectus sibi permissus;* the guarantee of the other is derived from a correspondence of the idea with experience. As Bacon says, all merely logical explanations are valueless, the subtlety of nature greatly surpassing that of argument: "Subtilitas naturæ subtilitatem argumentandi multis partibus superat;" and he further says, with his usual felicity, "Sed axiomata à particularibus ritè et ordine abstracta nova particularia rursus facilè indicant et designant." It is these "new particulars" which are reached through those already known, and complete the links of the causal chain.

Open the history of Science at any chapter you will, and its pages will show how all the errors which have gained acceptance gained it because this important principle of verification of particulars was neglected. Incessantly the mind of man leaps forward to "anticipate" Nature, and is satisfied with such anticipations if they have a logical consistence. When Galen and Aristotle thought that the air circulated in the arteries, causing the pulse to beat, and *cooling* the temperature of the blood, they were content with this plausible anticipation; they did not verify the facts of the air's presence, and its cooling effect; when they said that the "spirituous blood" nourished the delicate organs, such as the lungs, and the "venous blood" nourished the coarser organs, such as the liver; when they said that the "spirit," which was the purer element of the blood, was formed in the left ventricle, and the venous blood in the right ventricle, they contented themselves with unverified assumptions. In like manner, when in our own day physiologists of eminence maintain that in the organism there is a Vital Force which suspends chemical actions, they content themselves with a metaphysical unverified interpretation of phenomena. If they came to rigorous confrontation with fact, they would see that so far from chemical action being "suspended" it is incessantly at work in the organism; the varieties observable being either due to a difference of conditions (which will produce varieties out of the organism), or to the fact that the action is masked by other actions.

If the foregoing discussion has carried with it the reader's assent, he will perceive that the distinguishing characteristic of Science is its Method of graduated Verification, and not, as some think, the employment of Induction in lieu of Deduction. All Science is deductive, and deductive in proportion to its separation from ordinary *knowledge*, and its co-ordination into systematic Science. "Although all sciences tend to become more and more deductive," says a great authority, "they are not therefore the less inductive; every step in the deduction is still an induction. The opposition is not between the terms Inductive and Deductive, but between Deductive and Experimental."* Experiment is the great instrument of Verification. The difference between the ancient and modern philosophies lies in the facility with which the one accepted axioms and hypotheses as the basis for its deductions, and the cultivated caution with which the other insists on verifying its axioms and hypotheses before

---

* Mill's *System of Logic:* perhaps the greatest contribution to English speculation since Locke's *Essay.* Had Mr. Mill invented a new terminology and expressed himself with less clearness, he would assuredly have gained that reputation for profundity which, by a thorough misconception of the nature of thought, is so often awarded to obscurity.

deducing conclusions from them. We guess as freely as the ancients; but we know that we are guessing; and if we chance to forget it, our rivals quickly remind us that our guess is not evidence. Without guessing, Science would be impossible. We should never discover new islands, did we not often venture seawards with intent to sail beyond the sunset. To find new land, we must often quit sight of land. As Mr Thompson admirably expresses it:—"Philosophy proceeds upon a system of credit, and if she never advanced beyond her tangible capital, our wealth would not be so enormous as it is."* While both metaphysician and man of science trade on a system of credit, they do so with profoundly different views of its aid. The metaphysician is a merchant who speculates boldly, but without that convertible capital which can enable him to meet his engagements. He gives bills, yet has no gold, no goods to answer for them; these bills are not representative of wealth which exists in any warehouse. Magnificent as his speculations seem, the first obstinate creditor who insists on payment makes him bankrupt. The man of science is also a venturesome merchant, but one fully alive to the necessity of solid capital which can on emergency be produced to meet his bills; he knows the risks he runs whenever that amount of capital is exceeded; he knows that bankruptcy awaits him if capital be not forthcoming.

The contrast therefore between Philosophy and Science, or Metaphysics and Positive Philosophy, is a contrast of Method; but we must not suppose that the Method of the one is Deduction, while that of the other is Observation. Nothing can be more erroneous than the vulgar notion of the "Inductive Method," as one limited to the observation of facts. Every instructed thinker knows that facts of observation are particular theories; that is to say, every fact which is registered as an observation is constituted by a synthesis of sensation and inference. We shall see this illustrated presently. To it must be added the truth that Science is constantly making discoveries by Reasoning alone, aloof from any immediate exercise of Observation, aloof indeed from the very phenomena it classifies; for when facts are regis-

---

* *Outlines of the Laws of Thought*, p. 312.

tered in formulas, we resign ourselves to the manipulation of these formulas as symbols or equations, assured that the result will accord with Nature. Fresnel predicted the change in polarization from no observation of facts immediately lying before him, but from a happy elucidation of algebraic symbols. Astronomy is more studied on paper than through the telescope, which however is called upon to verify the results figured on paper. So that if we compare our astronomical and geological theories with the cosmical speculations of a Plato or a Hegel, we shall not find them deficient in the speculative daring which outruns the slow process of observation, but we shall find the difference to lie initially in the rigor with which our deductive formulas are established, and in the different estimates we form of what is valid evidence.

Galileo made Astronomy a science when he began to seek the unknown through the known, and to interpret celestial phenomena by those laws of motion which were recognized on the surface of the earth. Geology became possible as a science when its principal phenomena were explained by those laws of the action of water, visibly operating in every river, estuary, and bay. Except in the grandeur of its sweep, the mind pursues the same course in the interpretation of geological facts which record the annals of the universe, as in the interpretation of the ordinary incidents of daily life. To read the pages of the great Stone-book, and to perceive from the wet streets that rain has recently fallen, are the same intellectual processes. In the one case the mind traverses immeasurable spaces of time, and infers that the phenomena were produced by causes similar to those which have produced similar phenomena within recent experience; in the other case, the mind similarly infers that the wet streets and swollen gutters have been produced by the same cause we have frequently observed to produce them. Let the inference span with its mighty arch a myriad of years, or span but a few minutes, in each case it rises from the ground of certain familiar indications, and reaches an antecedent known to be capable of producing these indications. Both inferences may be wrong: the wet streets may have been wetted by a water-cart, or by the bursting of a pipe. We cast about for some other indication of rain besides the wetness of the streets and the turbid rush of gutters, which might equally have been produced by the bursting of a water-pipe. If we see passers-by carrying wet umbrellas, some still held above the head, our inference is strengthened by this indication, that rain, and no other cause, produced the phenomena. In like manner, the geologist casts about for other indications besides those of the subsidence of water, and as they accumulate, his conviction strengthens.

While this is the course of Science, the course of Philosophy is very different. Its inferences start from no well-grounded basis; the arches they throw are not from known fact to unknown fact, but from some unknown to some other unknown. Deductions are drawn from the nature of God, the nature of Spirit, the essences of Things, and from what Reason can postulate. Rising from such mists, the arch so brilliant to look upon is after all a rainbow, not a bridge.

To make his method legitimate, the Philosopher must first prove that a co-ordinate correspondence exists between Nature and his Intuitional Reason,* so that whatever is true of the one must be true of the other. The geologist, for example, proceeds on the assumption that the action of waters was essentially the same millions of years ago as it is in the present day; so that whatever can be positively proved of it *now*, may be confidently asserted of it *then*. He subsequently brings evidence to corroborate his assumption by showing that the assumption is necessary and competent to explain facts not otherwise to be consistently explained. But does the Philosopher stand in a similar position? Does he show any validity in his preliminary assumption? Does he produce any evidence for the existence of a nexus between his Intuitional Reason and those noumena or essences, about which he reasons; does he show the probability of there being such a correspondence between the two, that what

---

* By Intuitional Reason I here wish to express what the Germans call *Vernunft*, which they distinguish from *Verstand*, as Coleridge tried to make Englishmen distinguish between Reason and Understanding. The term Reason is too deeply rooted in our language to be twisted into any new direction; and I hope by the unusual "Intuitional Reason" to keep the reader's attention alive to the fact that by it is designated the process of the mind engaged in transcendental inquiry.

is true of the one may be accepted as probable of the other? Nothing of the kind. He assumes that it is so. He assumes, as a preliminary to all Philosophy, that Intuitional Reason is competent to deliver verdicts, even when the evidence is entirely furnished by itself. He assumes that Intuitions are face to face with Existences, and have consequently immediate knowledge of them. But this immense assumption, this gratuitous begging of the whole question, can only be permitted after a demonstration that the *contrary* assumption must be false. Now it is certain that we can assume the contrary, and assume it on evidence as cogent as that which furnishes his assumption. I can assume that Intuitions are not face to face with Existences; indeed this assumption seems to me by far the most probable; and it is surely as valid as the one it opposes? I call upon the metaphysician to prove the validity of his assumption, or the invalidity of mine. I call upon him for some principle of verification. He may tell me (as in past years the Hegelians used to tell me, not without impatience) that "Reason must verify itself;" but unhappily Reason has no such power; for if it had, Philosophy would not be disputing about first principles; and when it claims the power, who is to answer for its accuracy, *quis custodiet ipsos custodes?* If Philosophy is possible, its only basis rests on the correspondence between Nature and Intuitional Reason. But a correct analysis of our intellectual processes will furnish a solvent which will utterly destroy the last shred of organic basis out of which Philosophy grows.

Reasoning, if I rightly apprehend it, is the same intellectual process as Perception, with this difference, that Perception is inferential respecting objects *present*, and Reasoning is inferential respecting objects *absent*. In the laxity of current language, sensations and perceptions are almost convertible terms; but if we rigorously separate from our perceptions all those elements not actually given in the momentary sensations, it will be evident that Perception is distinguished from Sensation by the addition of certain inferences: as when we perceive a substance to be hard, square, odorous, sweet, etc., from certain inferences rising out of its form, color, etc., although we do not actually touch, smell, or taste the object. What is this process of inference? It is a presentation before the consciousness of something which has been formerly observed in conjunction with the object, and is therefore supposed to be now actually present in fact, although not present in sensation. I have no sensation of sweetness when I see the lump of sugar; but the sight of the sugar brings before my consciousness the sweetness, which the sugar will bring to my sensibility when in contact with my tongue. I perceive the sweetness; and I do this by making present to my mind what is absent from sense. I *infer* that the lump of white substance before me is sugar, as I infer that it rains when I see, from my window, water falling on the streets. In both cases the inference may be wrong. The white substance may be salt; the falling water may be the spray of the garden-hose. But in each and every case of Perception, a something is added to the Sensation, and that something is inferential, or the assumption of some quality present in fact which is not present in sense.

Reasoning is likewise inferential, but about objects which, although they were formerly given in sense, are now absent altogether. Reasoning is the presentation before the consciousness, of objects which, if actually present, would affect the consciousness in a similar way. It mentally supplies their existence. Thus, when from the wet streets and turbulent gutters I conclude, or infer, that it *has* rained, I make present to myself the phenomena of falling water in somewhat the same order as the falling water would follow *if* present. On closely attending to any chain of Reasoning we shall find that if it were possible to realize all the links in the chain, *i. e.* so to place the actual objects in their connected series that we could *see* them, this mental series would become a visible series, and, in lieu of reasonings, would afford direct perceptions. Good reasoning is the ideal assemblage of facts, and their re-presentation to the mind in the order of their actual series. It is seeing with the mind's eye. Bad reasoning will always be found to depend on some of the objects not being mentally *present;* some links in the chain are dropped or overlooked; some objects instead of being re-presented are left absent, or are presented so imperfectly that the inferences from them are as erroneous as the inferences from imperfect vision are erroneous. Bad reasoning is imperfect re-presentation

This explanation of the intellectual operations is, I believe, novel; should it be accepted, it will light up many obscure questions. But for the present we must only notice its bearing on Philosophy. When the table-turners concluded that electricity was the cause of the table's movement, they did not make present to their minds the real facts of electricity and its modes of operations; otherwise they would have seen that electricity would not turn the table round, and they would have seen this almost as vividly as if a battery had been then and there applied to the table. Faraday, on the contrary, did make these facts mentally present, so as not to need the actual presence of a battery; and his correct reasoning might not be owing to any greater general vigor of ratiocination, but to his greater power of making these particular facts mentally present. Describe an invention to Dr. Neil Arnott, and he will be able to reason on its practicability almost as well as if he saw the machine in operation: because he can mentally make present to himself all the details of structure, and from these infer all the details of action, just as his direct inferences would follow the actual presentation of the objects. There are two modes of detecting false logic, and there are but two: either we must reduce the argument to a series of sensations—make the facts in question visible to sense, and show that the sequences and co-existences of these facts are not what the reasoner asserted them to be; or we must mentally supply the place of this visible demonstration, and by re-presenting the objects before the mind, see where their sequences and co-existences differ from what the reasoner asserted them to be.

If all Reasoning be the re-presentation of what is now absent but formerly was present, and can again be made present,—in other words, if the test of accurate reasoning is its reduction to fact,—then is it evident that Philosophy, dealing with transcendental objects which *cannot* be present, and employing a Method which admits of no verification (or reduction to the test of fact) must be an impossible attempt. And if I am asked how it is that philosophers have reasoned at all on transcendental subjects, since according to my statement they could only reason by making such subjects present to their minds, the reply is that they could not, and did not, make present to their minds any such subjects at all; the Infinite was really conceived by them as Finite, the Unconditioned as Conditioned, Spirit as Body, Noumenon as Phenomenon; for only thus were these things conceivable at all. Thus it is only possible to take the first step in Philosophy by bringing transcendental subjects within the sphere of experience, *i. e.* making them no longer transcendental. Thus, and thus only, is it possible for us to reason on such topics.

All this will doubtless be utterly denied by metaphysicians. They proceed on the assumption that Intuitional Reason, which is independent of experience, is absolute and final in its guarantee. The validity of its conclusions is self-justified. Hegel boldly says, "Whatever is rational is real, and whatever is real is rational,—*das Vernünftige ist wirklich und das Wirkliche vernünftig.*" And writers of less metaphysical rigor frequently avow the axiom, and always imply it. Thus in a remarkable article on Sir W. Hamilton, which appeared in the *Prospective Review* (understood to be by Mr. James Martineau), we read that Philosophy in England has dwindled down to mere Psychology and Logic, whereas its proper business is with the notions of Time, Space, Substance, Soul, God; "to pronounce upon the validity of these notions as revelations of real Existence, and, if they be reliable, use them as a bridge to cross the chasm from relative Thought to absolute Being. Once safe across, and gazing about it in that realm, the mind stands in presence of the objects of Ontology."

"Once safe across;" this is indeed the step which constitutes the whole journey; unhappily we have no means of getting safe across; and in this helplessness we had better hold ourselves aloof from the attempt. If a man were to discourse with amplitude of detail and eloquence of conviction respecting the inhabitants of Sirius, setting forth in explicit terms what they were like, what embryonic forms they passed through, what had been the course of their social evolution and what would be its ultimate stage, we should first ask, And pray, Sir, what *evidence* have you for these particulars? what guarantee do you offer for the validity of these conclusions? If he replied that Intuitional Reason assured him these things must be so from the inherent necessities of the case, he having logically evolved these conclusions from the data of Reason; we should suppose him to be either attempting to mystify us, or to be hopelessly insane. Nor would this painful impression be removed by his proceeding to affirm that he never thought of trusting to such fallacious arguments as could be furnished by observation and experiment—tests wholly inapplicable to objects so remote from all experience, objects accessible only by Reason.

In the present day, speculations on Metaphysics are not, intrinsically, more rational than speculations on the development of animated beings peopling Sirius; nay, however masked by the ambiguities of language and old familiarities of speculation, which seem to justify Metaphysics, the attempt of the Philosopher is really less rational, the objects being even less accessible. Psychology has taught us one lesson at least, namely, that we cannot know causes and essences, because our experience is limited to sequences and phenomena. Nothing is gained by despising Experience, and seeking refuge in Intuition. The senses may be imperfect channels, but at any rate they are in direct communication with their objects, and are true up to a certain point. The error arising from one sense may be corrected by another; what to the eye appears round, the hand feels to be square. But Intuition has no such safeguard. It has only itself to correct its own errors. Holding itself aloof from the corroborations of Sense, it is aloof from all possible verification, because it cannot employ the test of confrontation with fact.

This conviction has been growing slowly. It could never have obtained general acceptance until Philosophy had proved its incapacity by centuries of failure. In the course of our History we shall see the question of Certitude continually forced upon philosophers, always producing a crisis in speculation, although always again eluded by the more eager and impatient intellects. Finally, these repeated crises disengage the majority of minds from so hopeless a pursuit, and set them free to follow Science which *has* Certitude. If our History has any value, it is in the emphatic sanction it thus gives to the growing neglect of Philosophy, the growing preference for Science. In the former edition I adopted the common view which regards the distinction between Philosophy and Science as lying in the pursuit of different objects. "Philosophy aspires to the knowledge of *essences* and *causes*. Positive Science aspires only to the knowledge of *Laws*. The one pretends to discover *what things are*, in themselves, apart from their appearances to sense; and *whence they came*. The other only wishes to discover their *modus operandi*, observing the constant *co-existences and successions* of phenomena among themselves, and generalizing them into some one *Law*." But this I no longer regard as the whole truth. It does not discriminate between scientific and metaphysical speculation on subjects within the scope of Science; such for instance as the phenomena of life, or such as table-turning. The vital and fundamental difference between the two orders of speculation does not lie in their objects, but in their methods. *A priori*, indeed, we might conclude that such a circumscription of the aims of speculation as is implied in Science would necessarily bring about a corresponding change in Method; in other words, that men having once relinquished the pursuit of essences and causes would have been forced to adopt the Method of Verification, because that alone was competent to lead to certitude. But History tells a different tale. Men did not adopt the Method of Verification because they had previously relinquished all attempts to penetrate into causes; but they relinquished all attempts to penetrate into causes because they found that the only Method which could lead to certainty was the Method of Verification, which was not applicable to causes. Hence a gradual elimination followed the gradual rise of each particular science; till at last, in the doctrine of Auguste Comte, all inquiry is limited to such objects as admit of verification, in one way or another.

The Method of Verification, let us never forget, is the one grand characteristic distinguishing Science from Philosophy, modern inquiry from ancient inquiry. Of the ancients, Fontenelle felicitously says: "Souvent de faibles convenances, de petites similitudes, des discours vagues et confus, passent chez eux pour des preuves: *aussi rien ne leur coûte à prouver*." The proof is, with us, the great object of solicitude. We demand certainty; and as the course of human evolution shows certainty to be attainable on no other Method than the one followed by Science, the condemnation of Metaphysics is inevitable.

Grand, indeed, has been the effort of Philosophy; great the part it has played in the drama of civilization; but the part is played out. It has left the legacy bequeathed by every great effort. It has enriched all succeeding ages, but its work is accomplished. Men have grown less presumptuous in speculation, and inconceivably more daring in practice. They no longer attempt to penetrate the mystery of the universe, but they explore the universe, and yoke all natural forces to their splendid chariot of Progress. The marvels of our age would have seemed more incredible to Plato, than were the *Arabian Nights* to Bentham; but while Science thus enables us to realize a wonderland of fact, it teaches us to regard the unhesitating temerities of Plato and Plotinus as we regard the efforts of a child to grasp the moon.

Philosophy was the great initiator of Science. It rescued the nobler part of man from the dominion of brutish apathy and helpless ignorance, nourished his mind with mighty impulses, exercised it in magnificent efforts, gave him the unslaked, unslakable thirst for knowledge which has dignified his life, and enabled him to multiply tenfold his existence and his happiness. Having done this, its part is played. Our interest in it now is purely historical.

The purport of this history is to show how and why the interest in Philosophy has become purely historical. In this purport lies the principal novelty of the work. There is no other History of Philosophy written by one disbelieving in the possibility of metaphysical certitude.

§ II. Limits of the Work.

Having explained what is the final purpose of this History and makes it subservient to the general History of Humanity rather than to any philosophical system, I will now briefly indicate the reasons which, apart from the limitations of my own knowledge, have determined the selection of the illustrative types. Brucker, having no purpose beyond that of accumulating materials, includes in his History the speculations of Antediluvian, Scythian, Persian, and Egyptian thinkers. Mr. Maurice, who has a purpose, also includes Hebrew, Egyptian, Hindoo,

Chinese, and Persian philosophies.* Other historians vary in their limits, upon not very intelligible grounds. I begin with Greece, because in the history of Grecian thought all the epochs of speculative development are distinctly traceable; and as I write the Biography of Philosophy, it is enough for my purpose if anywhere I can find a distinct filiation of ideas. Rome never had a philosophy of its own; it added no new idea to the ideas borrowed from Greece. It occupies no place therefore in the development of Philosophy, and is omitted from this Biography.

The omission of the East, so commonly believed to have exercised extensive and profound influence on Greece, will to many readers seem less excusable. But to unfold the arguments which justify the omission here, would require more space than can be spared in this Introduction. It is questionable whether the East had any Philosophy distinct from its Religion; and still more questionable whether Greece borrowed its philosophical ideas.† True it is that the Greeks themselves supposed their early teachers to have drunk at the Eastern fount. True it is that modern orientalists, on first becoming acquainted with the doctrines of the Eastern sages, recognized strong resemblances to the doctrines of the Greeks; and a Röth‡ finds Aristotle to be the first independent thinker, all his predecessors having drawn their speculations from the Egyptian; while a Gladisch§ makes it quite obvious (to himself) that the Pythagorean system is nothing but an adoption of the Chinese, the Heraclitic system an adoption of the Persian, the Eleatic of the Indian, the Empedoclean of the Egyptian, the Anaxagorean of the Jewish. But neither the vague tradition of the Greeks, nor the fallacious ingenuity of moderns, weigh heavy in the scale of historical criticism. It is true that coincidences of thought are to be found between Grecian and many other systems; but coincidences are no evi-

---

* *Moral and Metaphysical Philosophy*, part i., second edition, 1850: a work of singular fascination and great ingenuity.

† I have elsewhere stated reasons for this belief.—*Edinburgh Review*, April, 1847, p. 352 *sq*.

‡ *Geschichte unserer abendländischen Philosophie*, i. p. 228 *sq*.

§ *Die Religion und die Philosophie in ihrer weltgesch. Entwickelung.*

dence of direct filiation; and he has studied the history of speculation to little purpose who is not thoroughly familiar with the natural tendency of the mind to sweep into the same tracks, where others have been before, where others will find themselves afterwards. Moreover, many of these coincidences, upon which historical theories are based, turn out, on close inspection, to be merely verbal, or at the best, approximative. Thus the physical speculations of the Greeks often coincide in expression with those of modern science. Does this prove that the moderns borrowed their science from the ancients? M. Dutens thought so, and has written an erudite but singularly erroneous book to prove it. Democritus asserted the Milky Way to be only a cluster of stars; but the assertion was a mere guess, wholly without proof, and gained no acceptance. It was Galileo who *discovered* what Democritus *guessed*. Thus also Empedocles, Pythagoras, and Plato, are said to have been perfectly acquainted with the doctrine of gravitation; and this absurdity is made delusive by dint of forced translations, which elicit something like coincidence of expression, although every competent person detects the want of coincidence in the ideas.*

Waiving all discussion of disputable and disputed points, it is enough that in Greece from the time of Thales, and in Europe from the time of Descartes, a regular development of Philosophy is traceable, quite sufficient for our purpose, which is less that of narrating the lives and expounding the opinions of various thinkers, than of showing how the course of speculation necessarily brought about that radical change in Method which distinguishes Philosophy from Science. In pursuance of such an aim it was perfectly needless to include any detailed narrative of the speculations which, under the name of Scholasticism, occupied the philosophical activity of the Middle Ages. Those speculations were either subordinate to Theology, or were only instrumental in perfecting philosophical language; and in this latter respect the historian of Philosophy is no more called upon to notice them, than a writer on the art of War would be called upon to

---

* Karsten expresses the distinction well: " Empedocles poeticè *adumbravit* idem quod tot seculis postea *mathematicis rationibus demonstratum est* à Newtono."—*Philos. Græcorum Operum Reliquiæ*, p. xii.

give a history of the armorers of Milan or the sword-manufacturers of Toledo.

The same principle which determines the selection of Epochs also determines the selection of the points of doctrine to be expounded. It is obvious that in nothing like the space to which this work is limited could even the barest outline of all the opinions held by all the philosophers be crowded; nor would ten times the space suffice for an exposition of those opinions with any thing like requisite detail. Brucker's vast compilation, and Ritter's laborious volumes, are open for any student desirous of more detailed knowledge; but even they are imperfect. My purpose is different; I write the Biography, not the Annals of Philosophy, and I am more concerned about the doctrines peculiar to each thinker than about those held by him in common with others. If I can ascertain and make intelligible the doctrines which formed the *additions* of each thinker to the previous stock, and which helped the evolution of certain germs of philosophy, collateral opinions will need only such mention as is necessary to make the whole course of speculation intelligible. Thus limited in scope, I may find myself more at ease in the discussion of those points on which attention should be fastened. More space can be given to fundamental topics. In restricting myself to Descartes, Spinoza, and Kant, without noticing Cartesians, Spinozists, and Kantians, I also on the same principle restrict myself to what is in each thinker peculiar to him, and directly allied to the course of philosophical development. The student who needs the Pandects of Philosophy will have to look elsewhere: this work only pretends to be a Summary

A BIOGRAPHICAL

HISTORY OF PHILOSOPHY.

PART I.

ANCIENT PHILOSOPHY.

FIRST EPOCH.

SPECULATIONS ON THE NATURE OF THE UNIVERSE.

CHAPTER I.

THE PHYSICISTS.

§ I. THALES.

ALTHOUGH the events of his life, no less than the precise doctrines of his philosophy, are shrouded in mystery, and belong to the domain of fable, nevertheless Thales is very justly considered as the father of Greek Speculation. He made an epoch. He laid the foundation-stone of Greek philosophy. The step he took was small, but it was decisive. Accordingly, although nothing but a few of his tenets remain, and those tenets fragmentary and incoherent, we know enough of the general tendency of his doctrines to speak of him with some degree of certitude.

Thales was born at Miletus, a Greek colony in Asia Minor. The date of his birth is extremely doubtful; but the first year of the 36th Olympiad (B. C. 636) is generally accepted as correct. He belonged to one of the most illustrious families of Phœnicia, and took a conspicuous part in all the political affairs of his country,—a part which earned for him the highest esteem of his fellow-citizens. His immense activity in politics has been denied by later writers, as inconsistent with the tradition, countenanced by Plato, of his having spent a life of solitude and meditation; while on the other hand his affection for solitude has been questioned on the ground of his political activity. It seems to us that the two things are perfectly compatible. Meditation does not necessarily unfit a man for action; nor does an active life absorb all his time, leaving him none for meditation. The wise man will strengthen himself by meditation before he acts; and he will act, to test the truth of his opinions.

Miletus was one of the most flourishing Greek colonies; and at the period we are now speaking of, before either a Persian or a Lydian yoke had crushed the energies of its population, it was a fine scene for the development of mental energies. Its commerce both by sea and land was immense. Its political constitution afforded the finest opportunities for individual development. Thales both by birth and education would naturally be fixed there, and would not travel into Egypt and Crete for the prosecution of his studies, as some maintain, although upon no sufficient authority. The only ground for the conjecture is the fact of Thales being a proficient in mathematical knowledge; and from very early times, as we see in Herodotus, it was the fashion to derive the origin of almost every branch of knowledge from Egypt. So little consistency is there however in this narrative of his voyages, that he is said to have astonished the Egyptians by showing them how to measure the height of their pyramids by their shadows. A nation so easily astonished by one of the simplest of mathematical problems could have had little to teach. Perhaps the strongest proof that he never travelled into Egypt— or that, if he travelled there, he never came into communication with the priests—is the absence of all trace, however slight, of any Egyptian doctrine in the philosophy of Thales which he might not have found equally well at home.

The distinctive characteristic of the Ionian School, in its first period, was its inquiry into the constitution of the universe. Thales opened this inquiry. It is commonly said: "Thales taught that the principle of all things was water." On a first glance, this will perhaps appear a mere extravagance. A smile of pity may greet it, accompanied by a reflection on the smiler's part, of the unlikenhood of *his* ever believing such an absurdity. But the serious student will be slow to accuse his predecessors of sheer and transparent absurdity. The history of Philosophy may be the history of errors; it is not a history of follies. All the systems which have gained acceptance have had a pregnant meaning, or they would not have been accepted. The meaning was proportionate to the opinions of the epoch, and as such is worth penetrating. Thales was one of the most extraordinary men that ever lived, and produced an extraordinary revolution. Such a man was not likely to have enunciated a philosophical thought which any child might have refuted. There was deep meaning in the thought, to him at least. Above all, there was deep meaning in the attempt to discover the origin of things. Let us endeavor to penetrate the meaning of his thought; let us see if we cannot in some shape trace its rise and growth in his mind.

It is characteristic of philosophical minds to reduce all imaginable diversities to one principle. As it is the inevitable tendency of religious speculation to reduce polytheism to monotheism,—to generalize all the supernatural powers into one expression,—so also was it the tendency of early philosophical speculation to reduce all possible modes of existence into one generalization of Existence itself.

Thales, speculating on the constitution of the universe, could not but strive to discover the one principle—the primary Fact—the *substance*, of which all special existences were but the *modes*. Seeing around him constant transformations—birth and death, change of shape, of size, and of mode of existence—he could not regard any one of these variable states of existence as Existence itself. He therefore asked himself, What is that *invariable Existence* of which these are the *variable states?* In a word, What is the *beginning* of things?

To ask this question was to open the era of philosophical inquiry. Hitherto men had contented themselves with accepting the world as they found it; with believing what they saw; and with adoring what they could not see.

Thales felt that there was a vital question to be answered relative to the beginning of things. He looked around him, and the result of his meditation was the conviction that Moisture was the Beginning.

He was impressed with this idea by examining the constitution of the earth. There also he found moisture everywhere. All things he found nourished by moisture; warmth itself he declared to proceed from moisture; the seeds of all things are moist. Water when condensed becomes earth. Thus convinced of the universal presence of water, he declared it to be the beginning of things.

Thales would all the more readily adopt this notion from its harmonizing with ancient opinions; such for instance as those expressed in Hesiod's Theogony, wherein Oceanus and Thetis are regarded as the parents of all such deities as had any relation to Nature. "He would thus have performed for the popular religion that which modern science has performed for the Book of Genesis: explaining what was before enigmatical."*

It is this which gives Thales his position in Philosophy. Aristotle calls him ὁ τῆς τοιαύτης ἀρχηγὸς φιλοσοφίας, the man who made the first attempt to establish a physical Beginning, without the assistance of myths. He has consequently been accused of Atheism by modern writers; but Atheism is the growth of a much later thought, and one under no pretence to be attributed to Thales, except on the negative evidence of Aristotle's silence, which we conceive to be directly counter to the supposition, since it is difficult to believe Aristotle would have been silent had he thought Thales believed or disbelieved in the existence of any thing deeper than Water, and *prior* to it. Water was the ἀρχή, the beginning of all. When Cicero, following and followed by writers far removed from the times of Thales,† says that he "held water to be the beginning of things, but that God was the mind which created things out of the water," he does violence to the chronology of speculation. We

---

* Benj. Constant, *Du Polythéisme Romain*, i. 167.

† And uncritically followed by many moderns who feel a difficulty in placing themselves at the point of view of ancient speculation.

agree with Hegel that Thales could have had no conception of God as Intelligence, since *that* is the conception of a more advanced philosophy. We doubt whether he had any conception of a Formative Intelligence or of a Creative Power. Aristotle* very explicitly denies that the old Physicists made any distinction between Matter (ἡ ὕλη καὶ τὸ ὑποκείμενον) and the Moving Principle or Efficient Cause (ἡ ἀρχὴ τῆς κινήσεως); and he further adds that Anaxagoras was the first who arrived at a conception of a Formative Intelligence.† Thales believed in the Gods and in the *generation* of the Gods: they, as all other things, had their origin in water. This is not Atheism, whatever else it may be. If it be true that he held all things to be living, and the world to be full of demons or Gods, there is nothing inconsistent in this with his views about Moisture as the origin, the starting-point, the primary existence.

It is needless however to discuss what were the particular opinions of a thinker whose opinions have only reached us in fragments of uncritical tradition; all we certainly know is that the step taken by Thales was twofold in its influence:—first, to discover the Beginning, the *prima materia* of all things (ἡ ἀρχή); secondly, to select from among the elements that element which was most potent and omnipresent. To those acquainted with the history of the human mind, both these notions will be significant of an entirely new era.

§ II. ANAXIMENES.

Anaximander is by most historians placed after Thales. We agree with Ritter in giving that place to Anaximenes. The reasons on which we ground this arrangement are, first, that in so doing we follow our safest guide, Aristotle; secondly, that the doctrines of Anaximenes are the development of those of Thales; whereas Anaximander follows a totally different line of speculation. Indeed, the whole ordinary arrangement of the Ionian

---

* Arist. *Metaph.* i. 3.
† It will presently be seen that Diogenes was the first to conceive this.

School seems to have proceeded on the conviction that each disciple not only contradicted his master, but also returned to the doctrines of his master's teacher. Thus Anaximander is made to succeed Thales, though quite opposed to him; whereas Anaximenes, who only carries out the principles of Thales, is made the disciple of Anaximander. When we state that 212 years, *i. e.* six or seven generations, are taken up by the lives of the four individuals said to stand in the successive relations of teacher and pupil, Thales, Anaximander, Anaximenes, and Anaxagoras, the reader will be able to estimate the value of the traditional relationship.

The truth is, only the names of the great leaders in philosophy were thought worth preserving; all those who merely applied or extended the doctrine were very properly consigned to oblivion. This is also the principle upon which the present history is composed. No one will therefore demur to our placing Anaximenes second to Thales: not as his disciple, but as his historical successor; as the man who, taking up the speculation where Thales and his disciples left it, transmitted it to his successors in a more developed form.

Of the life of Anaximenes nothing further is known than that he was born at Miletus, probably in the 63d Olympiad (B. C. 529), others say in the 58th Olympiad (B. C. 548), but there is no possibility of accurately fixing the date. He is said to have discovered the obliquity of the Ecliptic by means of the gnomon.

Pursuing the method of Thales, he could not satisfy himself of the truth of his doctrine. Water was not to him the most significant element. He felt within him a something which moved him he knew not how, he knew not why; something higher than himself; invisible, but ever-present: this he called his life. His life he believed to be air. Was there not also without him, no less than within him, an ever-moving, ever-present, invisible air? The air which was within him, and which he called Life, was it not a part of the air which was without him? and, if so, was not this air the Beginning of things?

He looked around him and thought his conjecture was confirmed. The air seemed universal.* The earth was as a broad leaf resting upon it. All things were produced from it; all things were resolved into it. When he breathed, he drew in a part of the universal life. All things were nourished by air, as he was nourished by it.

To Anaximenes, as to most of the ancients, Air breathed and expired seemed the very stream of life, holding together all the heterogeneous substances of which the body was composed, giving them not only unity, but force, vitality. The belief in a living world—that is to say, of the universe as an organism—was very ancient, and Anaximenes, generalizing from the phenomena of individual life to universal life, made both dependent on Air. In many respects this was an advance on the doctrine of Thales, and the reader may amuse himself by finding its coincidence with some speculations of modern science. A grave chemist like Dumas can say, "Les Plantes et les Animaux dérivent de l'air, ne sont que de l'air condensé, ils *viennent de l'air et y retournent;*" and Liebig, in a well-known passage of the *Chemical Letters*, eloquently expresses the same idea.

§ III. Diogenes of Apollonia.

Diogenes of Apollonia is the proper successor to Anaximenes, although, from the uncritical arrangement usually adopted, he is made to represent no epoch whatever. Thus, Tennemann places him after Pythagoras. Hegel, by a strange oversight, says that we know nothing of Diogenes but the name.

Diogenes was born at Apollonia, in Crete. More than this we are unable to state with certainty; but as he is said to have been a contemporary of Anaxagoras, we may assume him to have flourished about the 80th Olympiad (B. C. 460). His work *On*

---

* When Anaximenes speaks of Air, as when Thales speaks of Water, we must not understand these elements as they appear in *this* or *that* determinate form on earth, but as Water and Air pregnant with vital energy and capable of infinite transmutations.

Nature was extant in the time of Simplicius (the sixth century of our era), who extracted some passages from it.

Diogenes adopted the tenet of Anaximenes respecting Air as the origin of things; but he gave a wider and deeper signification to the tenet by attaching himself more to its analogy with the Soul.* Struck with the force of this analogy, he was led to push the conclusion to its ultimate limits. What is it, he may have asked himself, which constitutes Air the origin of things? Clearly its vital force. The air is a Soul; therefore it is living and *intelligent*. But this Force or Intelligence is a higher thing than the Air, through which it manifests itself; it must consequently be prior in point of time; it must be the ἀρχή philosophers have sought. The Universe is a living being, spontaneously evolving itself, deriving its transformation from its own vitality.

There are two remarkable points in this conception, both indicative of very great progress in speculation. The first is the attribute of Intelligence, with which the ἀρχή is endowed. Anaximenes considered the primary substance to be an animated substance. Air was Life, in his system, but the Life did not necessarily imply Intelligence. Diogenes saw that Life was not only Force, but Intelligence; the air which stirred within him not only *prompted*, but *instructed*. The Air, as the origin of all things, is necessarily an eternal, imperishable substance; but as soul, it is also necessarily endowed with consciousness. "It knows much," and this knowledge is another proof of its being the primary substance; "for without Reason," he says, "it would be impossible for all to be arranged duly and proportionately; and whatever object we consider will be found to be arranged and ordered in the best and most beautiful manner." Order can result only from Intelligence; the Soul is therefore the first (ἀρχή). This conception was undoubtedly a great one; but that the

---

* By Soul (ψυχή) we must understand Life in its most general meaning, rather than Mind in the modern sense. Thus the treatise of Aristotle περὶ ψυχῆς is a treatise on the Vital Principle, *including* Mind, not a treatise on Psychology.

reader may not exaggerate its importance, nor suppose that the rest of Diogenes' doctrines were equally reasonable and profound, we must for the sake of preserving historical truth advert to one or two of his applications of the conception. Thus:

The world, as a living unity, must like other individuals derive its vital force from the Whole: hence he attributed to the world a set of respiratory organs, which he fancied he discovered in the stars. All creation and all material action were but respiration and exhalation. In the attraction of moisture to the sun, in the attraction of iron to the magnet, he equally saw a process of respiration. Man is superior to brutes in intelligence because he inhales a purer air than brutes who bow their heads to the ground.

These *naïve* attempts at the explanation of phenomena will suffice to show that although Diogenes had made a large stride, he had accomplished very little of the journey.

The second remarkable point indicated by his system is the manner in which it closes the inquiry opened by Thales. Thales, starting from the conviction that one of the four elements was the origin of the world, and Water that element, was followed by Anaximenes, who thought that not only was Air a more universal element than Water, but that, being life, it must be the universal Life. To him succeeded Diogenes, who saw that not only was Air Life, but Intelligence, and that Intelligence must have been the First of Things.

We concur therefore with Ritter in regarding Diogenes as the last philosopher attached to the *Physical* method; and that in his system the method receives its consummation. Having thus traced one great line of speculation, we must now cast our eyes upon what was being contemporaneously evolved in another direction.

CHAPTER II.
THE MATHEMATICIANS.

§ I. Anaximander of Miletus.

" As we now, for the first time in the history of Greek Philosophy, meet with contemporaneous developments, the observation will not perhaps be deemed superfluous that in the earliest times of philosophy, historical evidences of the reciprocal influence of the two lines either entirely fail or are very unworthy of credit; on the other hand, the internal evidence is of very limited value, because it is impossible to prove a complete ignorance in one, of the ideas evolved and carried out in the other; while any argument drawn from an apparent acquaintance therewith is far from being extensive or tenable, since all the olden philosophers drew from one common source—the national habit of thought. When indeed these two directions had been more largely pursued, we shall find in the controversial notices sufficient evidence of an active conflict between these very opposite views of nature and the universe. In truth, when we call to mind the inadequate means at the command of the earlier philosophers for the dissemination of their opinions, it appears extremely probable that their respective systems were for a long time known only within a very narrow circle. On the supposition, however, that the philosophical impulse of these times was the result of a real national want, it becomes at once probable that the various elements began to show themselves in Ionia nearly at the same time, independently and without any external connection."*

---

* Ritter, i. 265.

ANAXIMANDER OF MILETUS.

The chief of the school we are now about to consider was Anaximander of Miletus, whose birth may be dated in the 42d Olympiad (B. C. 610). He is sometimes called the friend and sometimes the disciple of Thales. We prefer the former relation; the latter is at any rate not the one in which this history can regard him. His reputation, both for political and scientific knowledge, was very great; and many important inventions are ascribed to him, amongst others that of the sun-dial and the sketch of a geographical map. His calculations of the size and distance of the heavenly bodies were committed to writing in a small work, which is said to be the earliest of all philosophical writings. He was passionately addicted to mathematics, and framed a series of geometrical problems. He was the leader of a colony to Apollonia; and he is also reported to have resided at the court of the tyrant Polycrates, in Samos, where also lived Pythagoras and Anacreon.

No two historians are agreed in their interpretation of Anaximander's doctrines; few indeed are agreed as to the historical position he is to occupy.

Anaximander is stated to have been the first to use the term ἀρχή for the Beginning of things. What he meant by this term *principle* is variously interpreted by the ancient writers; for, although they are unanimous in stating that he called it the *infinite* (τὸ ἄπειρον), what he understood by the infinite is yet undecided.*

On a first view, nothing can well be less intelligible than this tenet: "The Infinite is the origin of all things." It either looks like the monotheism of a far later date,† or like the word-jugglery of mysticism. To our minds it is neither more nor less

---

* Ritter, i. 267.
† Which it certainly could not have been. To prevent any misconception of the kind, we may merely observe that the Infinite here meant, was not even the Limitless Power, much less the Limitless Mind, implied in the modern conception. In Anaxagoras, who lived a century later, we find τὸ ἄπειρον to be no more than vastness.—See Simplicius, *Phys.* 33, *b*, quoted in Ritter.

difficult of comprehension than the tenet of Thales, that "Water is the origin of all things." Let us cast ourselves back in imagination into those early days, and see if we cannot account for the rise of such an opinion.

On viewing Anaximander side by side with his great predecessor and friend, Thales, we cannot but be struck with the exclusively abstract tendency of his speculations. Instead of the meditative Metaphysician, we see a Geometrician. Thales, whose famous maxim, "Know thyself," was essentially concrete, may serve as a contrast to Anaximander, whose axiom, "The Infinite is the origin of all things," is the ultimate effort of abstraction. Let us concede to him this tendency; let us see in him the geometrician rather than the moralist or physicist; let us endeavor to understand how all things presented themselves to his mind in the abstract form, and how mathematics was the science of sciences, and we shall then perhaps be able to understand his tenets.

Thales, in searching for the origin of things, was led, as we have seen, to maintain water to be that origin. But Anaximander, accustomed to view things in the abstract, could not accept so concrete a thing as Water: something more ultimate in the analysis was required. Water itself, which in common with Thales, he held to be the material of the universe, was it not subject to *conditions?* What were those conditions? This Moisture, of which all things are made, does it not cease to be moisture in many instances? And can that which is the origin of all, ever change, ever be confounded with individual things? Water itself is a thing; but a Thing cannot be All Things.

These objections to the doctrine of Thales caused him to reject, or rather to modify, that doctrine. The ἀρχή, he said, was not Water; it must be the Unlimited All, τὸ ἄπειρον.

Vague and profitless enough this theory will doubtless appear. The abstraction "All" will seem a mere distinction in words. But in Greek Philosophy, as we shall repeatedly notice, *distinctions in words* were generally equivalent to *distinctions in things.*

And if the reader reflects how the mathematician, by the very nature of his science, is led to regard abstractions as entities,—to separate *form*, and treat of it as if it alone constituted *body*,— there will be no difficulty in conceiving Anaximander's distinction between all Finite Things and the Infinite All.

It is thus only we can explain his tenet; and this explanation seems borne out by the testimony of Aristotle and Theophrastus, who agree, that by the Infinite he understood the multitude of elementary parts out of which individual things issued by separation. "*By separation:*" the phrase is significant. It means the passage from the abstract to the concrete,—the All realizing itself in the Individual Thing. Call the Infinite by the name of Existence, and say, "There is existence *per se*, and Existence *per aliud;* the former is *Existence*, the ever-living fountain whence flow the various *existing Things*." In this way we may, perhaps, make Anaximander's meaning intelligible.

Let us now hear Ritter. Anaximander "is represented as arguing that the primary substance must have been infinite to be all-sufficient for the limitless variety of produced things with which we are encompassed. Now, although Aristotle especially characterizes this infinite as a mixture, we must not think of it as a mere multiplicity of primary material elements; for to the mind of Anaximander it was a Unity immortal and imperishable —an ever-producing energy. This production of individual things he derived from an eternal *motion of the Infinite.*"

The primary Being, according to Anaximander, is unquestionably a Unity. It is One yet All. It comprises within itself the multiplicity of elements from which all mundane things are composed; and these elements only need to be separated from it to appear as separate phenomena of nature. Creation is the *decomposition of the Infinite.* How does this decomposition originate? By the eternal motion which is the condition of the Infinite. "He regarded," says Ritter, "the Infinite as being in a constant state of incipiency, which, however, is nothing but a constant secretion and concretion of certain immutable elements: so that we might well say, the parts of the whole are constantly changing, while the whole is unchangeable."

The idea of elevating an abstraction into a Being—the origin of all things—is baseless enough; it is as if we were to say, "There are numbers 1, 2, 3, 20, 80, 100; but there is also *Number* in the abstract, of which these individual numbers are but the concrete realization: without *Number* there will be no numbers." Yet so difficult is it for the human mind to divest itself of its own abstractions, and to consider them as no more than as abstractions, that this error lies at the root of the majority of philosophical systems. It may help the reader to some tolerance of Anaximander's error to learn that celebrated philosophers of modern times, Hegel and others, have maintained precisely the same tenet, though somewhat differently worded: they say, that Creation is God passing into activity, but not exhausted by the act; in other words, *Creation is the mundane existence of God;* finite Things are but the eternal motion, the *manifestation* of the All.

Anaximander separated himself from Thales by regarding the abstract as of higher significance than the concrete: and in this tendency we see the origin of the Pythagorean school, so often called the mathematical school. The speculations of Thales tended towards discovering the material constitution of the universe; they were founded, in some degree, upon an induction from observed facts, however imperfect that induction might be. The speculations of Anaximander were *wholly deductive;* and, as such, tended towards mathematics, the science of pure deduction.

As an example of this mathematical tendency we may allude to his physical speculations. The central point in his cosmopœia was the earth; for, being of a cylindrical form, with a base in the ratio 1 : 3 to its altitude, it was retained in its centre by the aid and by the equality of its distances from all the limits of the world.

From the foregoing exposition the Reader may judge of the propriety of that ordinary historical arrangement which places

Anaximander as the successor of Thales. It is clear that he originated one of the great lines of speculative inquiry, and that one, perhaps, the most curious in all antiquity. By Thales, Water, the origin of things, was held to be a real physical element, which in the hands of his successors became gradually transformed into a merely *representative* emblem of something wholly different (Life or Mind); and the element which lent its name as the representative was looked upon as a secondary phenomenon, derived from that primary force of which it was the emblem. Water was the real primary element with Thales; with Diogenes, Water (having previously been displaced for Air) was but the emblem of Mind. Anaximander's conception of the All, though abstract, is nevertheless to a great degree physical: it is *All Things*. His conception of the Infinite was not ideal; it had not passed into the state of a symbol; it was the mere *description* of the primary fact of existence. Above all, it involved no conception of intelligence except as a mundane finite thing. His τὸ ἄπειρον was the Infinite Existence, but not the Infinite Mind. This later development we shall meet with hereafter in the Eleatics.

§ II. Pythagoras.

The life of Pythagoras is enshrouded in the dim magnificence of legends, from which the attempt to extricate is hopeless. Certain general indications are doubtless to be trusted; but they are few and vague.

As a specimen of the trouble necessary to settle any one point in this biography, we will here cite the various dates given by ancient authors and modern scholars as the results of their inquiries into his birth. Diodorus Siculus says 61st Olympiad; Clemens Alex., 62d Ol.; Eusebius, 63d or 64th Ol.; Stanely, 53d Ol.; Gale, 60th Ol.; Dacier, 47th Ol.; Bentley, 43d Ol.; Lloyd, 43d Ol.; Dodwell, 52d Ol.; Ritter, 49th Ol.; Thirlwall, 51st Ol.: so that the accounts vary within the limits of eighty-four years. If we must make a choice, we should decide with Bentley; not only from respect for that magnificent scholar, but because it agrees with the probable date of the birth of one known to have been Pythagoras's friend and contemporary, Anaximander.

Pythagoras is usually classed amongst the great founders of Mathematics; and this receives confirmation from what we know of the general scope of his labors, and from the statement that he was chiefly occupied with the determination of extension and gravity, and measuring the ratios of musical tones. His science and skill are of course absurdly exaggerated, as indeed is every portion of his life. Fable assigns him the place of a saint, a worker of miracles, and a teacher of more than human wisdom. His very birth was marvellous, some accounts making him the son of Hermes, others of Apollo: in proof of the latter, he is said to have exhibited a golden thigh. With a word he tamed the Daunian bear, which was laying waste the country; with a whisper he restrained an ox from devouring beans. He was heard to lecture at different places, such as Metapontum and Taurominium, on the same day and at the same hour. As he crossed the river, the river-god saluted him with "Hail, Pythagoras!" and to him the harmony of the Spheres was audible music.

Fable enshrines these wonders. But that they could exist, even as legendary lore, is significant of the greatness of Pythagoras. It is well said by Sir Lytton Bulwer that "not only all the traditions respecting Pythagoras, but the certain fact of the mighty effect that in his single person he afterwards wrought in Italy, prove him also to have possessed that nameless art of making a personal impression upon mankind, and creating individual enthusiasm, which is necessary to those who obtain a moral command, and are the founders of sects and institutions. It is so much in conformity with the manners of the time and the objects of Pythagoras, to believe that he diligently explored the ancient religious and political systems of Greece, from which he had been long a stranger, that we cannot reject the traditions

(however disfigured with fable) that he visited Delos, and affected to receive instructions from the pious ministrants of Delphi."*
It is no ordinary man whom Fable exalts into its poetical region. Whenever you find romantic or miraculous deeds attributed, be certain that the hero was great enough to sustain the weight of this crown of fabulous glory.

But the fact thus indicated is a refutation of the ordinary tradition of his having borrowed all his learning and philosophy from the East. Could not so great a man dispense with foreign teachers? Assuredly he could, and did. But his countrymen, by a very natural process of thought, looked upon his greatness as the result of his Eastern education. No man is a prophet in his own country; and the imaginative Greeks were peculiarly prone to invest the distant and the foreign with striking attributes. They could not believe in wisdom springing up from amongst them; they turned to the East as to a vast and unknown region, whence all novelty, even of thought, must come.

When we consider, as Ritter observes, how Egypt was peculiarly the wonder-land of the olden Greeks, and how, even in later times, when it was so much better known, it was still, as it is to this day, so calculated to excite awe by the singular character of its people, which, reserved in itself, was always obtruding on the observer's attention through the stupendous structures of national architecture, we can easily imagine how the Greeks were led to establish some connection between this mighty East and their great Pythagoras.

But, although we can by no means believe that Pythagoras was much indebted to Egypt for his doctrines, we are not skeptical as to the account of his having travelled there. Samos was in constant intercourse with Egypt. If Pythagoras had travelled into Egypt, or indeed listened to the relations of those who had done so, he would have thereby obtained as much knowledge of Egyptian customs as appears in his system; and that without

---

* *Athens, its Rise and Fall,* ii. 412.

having had the least instruction from the Priesthood. The doctrine of metempsychosis was a public doctrine with the Egyptians; though, as Ritter says, he might not have been indebted to them even for that. Funeral customs and abstinence from particular kinds of food were things to be noticed by any traveller. But the fundamental objection to Pythagoras having been instructed by the Egyptian Priests, is to be sought in the constitution of the priestly caste itself. If the priests were so jealous of instruction as not to bestow it even on the most favored of their countrymen unless belonging to their caste, how unreasonable to suppose that they would bestow it on a stranger, and one of a different religion!

The ancient writers were sensible of this objection. To get rid of it they invented a story which we shall give as it is given by Brucker. Polycrates was in friendly relations with Amasis, King of Egypt, to whom he sent Pythagoras, with a recommendation to enable him to gain access to the Priests. The king's authority was not sufficient to prevail on the Priests to admit a stranger to their mysteries: they referred Pythagoras therefore to Thebes, as of greater antiquity. The Theban Priests were awed by the royal mandate, but were loth to admit a stranger to their rites. To disgust the novice, they forced him to undergo several severe ceremonies, amongst which was circumcision. But he could not be discouraged. He obeyed all their injunctions with such patience that they resolved to take him into their confidence. He spent two-and-twenty years in Egypt, and returned perfect master of all science. This is not a bad story: but there is one objection to it—it is not substantiated.

To Pythagoras the invention of the word Philosopher is ascribed. When he was in Peloponnesus he was asked by Leontius, what was his art. "I have no art; I am a philosopher," was the reply. Leontius never having heard the name before, asked what it meant. Pythagoras gravely answered, "This life may be compared to the Olympic games: for as in this assembly some seek glory and the crowns; some by the purchase or by the sale of merchandise seek gain; and others, more noble than either, go there neither for gain nor for applause, but solely to enjoy this wonderful spectacle, and to see and know all that passes. We, in the same manner, quit our country, which is Heaven, and come into the world, which is an assembly where many work for profit, many for gain, and where there are but few who, despising avarice and vanity, study nature. It is these last whom I call Philosophers; for as there is nothing more noble than to be a spectator without any personal interest, so in this life the contemplation and knowledge of nature are infinitely more honorable than any other application." It is necessary to observe that the ordinary interpretation of Philosopher, as Pythagoras meant it, a "lover of wisdom," is only accurate where the utmost extension is given to the word "lover." Wisdom must be the "be-all and the end-all here" of the philosopher, and not simply a taste or a pursuit. It must be his mistress, to whom a life is devoted. This was the meaning of Pythagoras. The word which had before designated a wise man was σοφός. But he wished to distinguish himself from the *Sophoi*, or philosophers of his day, by name, as he had done by system. What was the meaning of *Sophos?* Unquestionably what we mean by a wise man, as distinct from a philosopher; one whose wisdom is *practical*, and turned to practical purposes; one who loves wisdom not for its own sake so much as for the sake of its uses. Now Pythagoras loved wisdom for its own sake. Contemplation was to him the highest exercise of humanity: to bring wisdom down to the base purposes of life was desecration. He called himself therefore a Philosopher—a Lover of Wisdom—to demarcate himself from those who sought Wisdom only as a power to be used for ulterior ends.

This interpretation of the word Philosopher may explain some of his opinions. Above all, it explains the constitution of his Secret Society, into which no one was admitted except after a severe initiation. For five years the novice was condemned to silence. Many relinquished the task in despair; they were unworthy of the contemplation of pure wisdom. Others, in whom the tendency to loquacity was observed to be less, had the period commuted. Various humiliations had to be endured; various experiments were made of their powers of self-denial. By these Pythagoras judged whether they were worldly-minded, or whether they were fit to be admitted into the sanctuary of science. Having purged their souls of the baser particles by purifications, sacrifices, and initiations, they were admitted to the sanctuary, where the higher part of the soul was purged by the knowledge of truth, which consists in the knowledge of immaterial and eternal things. For this purpose he commenced with Mathematics, because, as they just preserve the medium between corporeal and incorporeal things, they can alone draw off the mind from Sensible things and conduct them to Intelligibles.

Shall we wonder, then, that he was venerated as a God? He who could transcend all earthly struggles, and the great ambitions of the greatest men, to live only for the sake of wisdom, was he not of a higher stamp than ordinary mortals? Well might later historians picture him as clothed in robes of white, his head crowned with gold, his aspect grave, majestical, and calm; above the manifestation of any human joy, of any human sorrow; enwrapt in contemplation of the deeper mysteries of existence; listening to music and the hymns of Homer, Hesiod, and Thales, or listening to the harmony of the spheres. And to a lively, talkative, quibbling, active, versatile people like the Greeks, what a grand phenomenon must this solemn, earnest, silent, meditative man have appeared!

From Sir Lytton Bulwer's *Athens* we borrow the following account of the political career of Pythagoras:—" Pythagoras arrived in Italy during the reign of Tarquinius Superbus, according to the testimony of Cicero and Aulus Gellius, and fixed his residence in Croton, a city in the bay of Tarentum, colonized by Greeks of the Achæan tribe. If we may lend a partial credit to the extravagant fables of later disciples, endeavoring to extract from florid super-addition some original germ of simple truth, it

would seem that he first appeared in the character of a teacher
of youth, and, as was not unusual in those times, soon rose from
the preceptor to the legislator. Dissensions in the city favored
his objects. The Senate (consisting of a thousand members,
doubtless of a different race from the body of the people—the
first the posterity of the settlers, the last the native population)
availed itself of the arrival and influence of an eloquent and renowned philosopher. He lent himself to the consolidation of
aristocracies, and was equally inimical to democracy and tyranny.
But his policy was that of no vulgar ambition. He refused, at
least for a time, ostensible power and office, and was contented
with instituting an organized and formidable society, not wholly
dissimilar to that mighty Order founded by Loyola in times com-
paratively recent. The disciples admitted into this society un-
derwent examination and probation : it was through degrees that
they passed into its higher honors, and were admitted into its
deeper secrets. Religion made the basis of the fraternity, but
religion connected with human ends of advancement and power.
He selected the three hundred who at Croton formed his Order,
from the noblest families, and they were professedly reared to
know themselves, that so they might be fitted to command the
world. It was not long before this society, of which Pythagoras
was the head, appears to have supplanted the ancient Senate and
obtained the legislative administration. In this Institution Pythagoras stands alone ; no other founder of Greek philosophy resembles him. By all accounts he also differed from the other
sages of his time in his estimation of the importance of women.
He is said to have lectured to, and taught them. His wife was
herself a philosopher, and fifteen disciples of the softer sex rank
among the prominent ornaments of his school. An Order based
upon so profound a knowledge of all that can fascinate or cheat
mankind could not fail to secure a temporary power. His influence was unbounded in Croton : it extended to other Italian
cities ; it amended or overturned political constitutions ; and had
Pythagoras possessed a more coarse and personal ambition, he

might perhaps have founded a mighty dynasty, and enriched our social annals with the result of a new experiment. But his was the ambition not of a hero, but a sage. He wished rather to establish a system than to exalt himself. His immediate followers saw not all the consequences that might be derived from the fraternity he founded; and the political designs of his gorgeous and august philosophy, only for awhile successful, left behind them but the mummeries of an impotent freemasonry, and the enthusiastic ceremonies of half-witted ascetics.

"It was when this power, so mystic and so revolutionary, had, by the means of branch societies, established itself throughout a considerable portion of Italy, that a general feeling of alarm and suspicion broke out against the sage and his sectarians. The anti-Pythagorean risings, according to Porphyry, were sufficiently numerous and active to be remembered long generations afterwards. Many of the sage's friends are said to have perished, and it is doubtful whether Pythagoras himself fell a victim to the rage of his enemies, or died a fugitive amongst his disciples at Metapontum. Nor was it until nearly the whole of Lower Italy was torn by convulsions, and Greece herself drawn into the contest as pacificator and arbiter, that the ferment was allayed. The Pythagorean institutions were abolished, and the timocratic democracies of the Achæans rose upon the ruins of those intellectual but ungenial oligarchies.

"Pythagoras committed a fatal error when, in his attempt to revolutionize society, he had recourse to aristocracies for his agents. Revolutions, especially those influenced by religion, can never be worked out but by popular emotions. It was from this error of judgment that he enlisted the people against him; for by the account of Neanthes, related by Porphyry, and indeed from all other testimony, it is clearly evident that to popular not party commotion his fall must be ascribed. It is no less clear that after his death, while his philosophical sect remained, his political code crumbled away. The only seeds sown by philosophers which spring up into great States, are those that, whether for good or evil, are planted in the hearts of the Many."

We cannot omit the story which so long amused the world, respecting his discovery of the musical chords. Hearing one day, in the shop of a blacksmith, a number of men striking successively a piece of heated iron, he remarked that all the hammers, except one, produced harmonious chords, viz. the octave, the fifth, and the third; but the sound between the fifth and the third was discordant. On entering the workshop, he found the diversity of sounds was owing to the difference in the *weight* of the hammers. He took the exact weights, and on reaching home suspended four strings of equal dimensions, and hanging a weight at the end of each of the strings equal to the weight of each hammer, he struck the strings, and found the sounds correspond with those of the hammers. He then proceeded to the formation of a musical scale.

On this, Dr. Burney, in his *History of Music*, remarks: "Though both hammers and anvil have been swallowed by ancients and moderns with most ostrich-like digestion, yet upon examination and experiment it appears that hammers of different size and weight will no more produce different tones upon the same anvil, than bows or clappers of different size will from the same string or bell."

We close here our account of the life of Pythagoras, reminding the reader that one great reason for the fabulous and contradictory assertions collected together in histories and biographies arises from the uncritical manner in which the "authorities" have been used. To take only one "authority" as an example: Iamblicus wrote his Life of Pythagoras with a view of combating the rising doctrine of Christianity, and of opposing by implication a Pagan philosopher to Christ. The miracles that were attributed to Pythagoras have no better source than this.

§ III. PHILOSOPHY OF PYTHAGORAS.

There is no system in the whole course of our history more difficult to seize and represent accurately than that commonly known as the Pythagorean. It has made prodigious noise in the world; so much so as to be often confounded with its distant echoes. An air of mystery, always inviting to a large class, surrounds it. The marvellous relations concerning its illustrious founder, the supposed assimilation it contains of various elements of Eastern speculation, and the supposed symbolical nature of its doctrines, have all equally combined to render it attractive and contradictory. Every dogma in it has been traced to some prior philosophy. Not a vestige will remain to be called the property of the teacher himself, if we restore to the Jews, Indians, Egyptians, Chaldeans, Phœnicians, nay even Thracians, those various portions which he is declared to have borrowed from them.

All this pretended plagiarism we incline to think extremely improbable: Pythagoras was a consequence of Anaximander; and his doctrines, in as far as we can gather from their leading tendency, were but a continuation of that abstract and deductive philosophy of which Anaximander was the originator.

At the outset we must premise, that whatever interest there may be in following out the particular opinions recorded as belonging to Pythagoras, such a process is quite incompatible with our plan. The greatest uncertainty still exists, and must forever exist amongst scholars, respecting the genuineness of those opinions. Even such as are recorded by trustworthy authorities are always vaguely attributed by them to "the Pythagoreans," not to Pythagoras. Modern criticism has clearly shown that the works attributed to Timæus and Archytas are spurious; and that the supposed treatise of Ocellus Lucanus on the "Nature of the All" cannot even have been written by a Pythagorean. Plato and Aristotle, the only ancient writers who are to be trusted in this matter, do not attribute any peculiar doctrines to Pythagoras. The reason is simple. Pythagoras taught in secret; and never wrote. What he taught his disciples it is impossible accurately to learn from what those disciples themselves taught. His influence over their minds was unquestionably immense; and this influence would communicate to his school a distinctive *tendency*, but not one accordant doctrine; for each scholar would carry out that tendency in the direction which best suited his tastes and powers.*

The extreme difficulty of ascertaining accurately what Pythagoras thought, or even what his disciples thought, will not embarrass us if we can but ascertain the general tendency of their speculations, and, above all, the peculiarity of their method. For this difficulty—which, to the critical historian insuperable, only affects us indirectly—renders indeed our endeavor to seize the characteristic method and tendency more hazardous and more liable to contradiction; but it does not compel us to interrupt our march for the sake of storming every individual fortress of opinion we may encounter on our way. We have to trace out the map of the philosophical world; we must be careful to ascertain the great outlines of each country: this we may be enabled to do without absolutely being acquainted with the *internal* varieties of that country, for geographers are not bound to be also geologists.

What were the method and tendency of the Pythagorean school? The method, purely deductive; the tendency, wholly towards the consideration of abstractions as the only true materials of science. Hence the name not unfrequently given to that school, of "the Mathematical." The list of Pythagoreans embraces the greatest names in mathematics and astronomy,— Archytas and Philolaus, and subsequently Hipparchus and Ptolemy.†

---

* We assume this to be the case; but we do not assume it groundlessly. We are guided by the striking analogy afforded by the celebrated Saint-Simon. Like Pythagoras, the Frenchman published no complete account of his system. He communicated it to his disciples; and, as his influence over their minds was almost unparalleled, the *tendency* of his philosophy took deep root, though producing very different fruits in different minds. Those moderately acquainted with French writers will appreciate this when we simply enumerate MM. Augustin Thierry, Auguste Comte, Pierre Leroux, Michel Chevalier, Le Père Enfantin, and M. Bazard, all disciples of Saint-Simon

† Æschylus, a disciple of Pythagoras, makes his Titan boast of having discovered for men, Number, the highest of the sciences; Καὶ μὴν ἀριθμὸν, ἔξοχον σοφισμάτων, ἐξεῦρον αὐτοῖς.—*Prom.*, 459.

We may now perhaps, in some sort, comprehend what Pythagoras meant when he taught that *Numbers* were the *principles of Things:* τοὺς ἀριθμοὺς αἰτίους εἶναι τῆς οὐσίας,* or, to translate more literally, "Numbers are the cause of the material existence of Things;" οὐσία being here evidently the expression of concrete existence. This is confirmed by the wording of the formula given elsewhere by Aristotle, that Nature is *realized* from Numbers: τὴν φύσιν ἐξ ἀριθμῶν συνιστᾶσι,† Or again: Things are but the *copies* of Numbers: μίμησιν εἶναι τὰ ὄντα τῶν ἀριθμῶν.‡ What Pythagoras meant was, that numbers were the *ultimate nature* of things. Anaximander saw that things in themselves are not final; they are constantly changing both position and attributes; they are variable, and the principle of existence must be *invariable;* he called that invariable existence THE ALL.

Pythagoras saw that there was an invariable existence lying beneath these varieties; but he wanted some more definite expression for it, and he called it Number. Thus each individual thing may change its position, its mode of existence; all its peculiar attributes may be destroyed except one, namely, its numerical attribute. It is always "*One*" thing; nothing can destroy that numerical existence. Combine the Thing in every possible variety of ways, and it still remains "One;" it cannot be less than "one," it cannot be made more than "one." Resolve it into its minutest particles, and each particle is one. Having thus found that numerical existence was the only invariable existence, he was easily led to proclaim all Things to be but copies of Numbers. "All phenomena must originate in the simplest elements," says Sextus Empiricus, "and it would be contrary to reason to suppose the Principle of the Universe to participate in the nature of sensible phenomena. The *Principia* are consequently not only invisible and intangible, but also incorporeal."

As numerical existence is the ultimate state at which analysis can arrive with respect to finite Things, so also is it the ultimate

---

* Aristot. *Metaph.* i. 6.   † *De Cælo,* iii. 1.   ‡ *Metaph.* i. 6

state at which we can arrive with respect to the Infinite, or Existence in itself. The Infinite, therefore, must be *One*. One is the absolute number; it exists in and by itself; it has no need of any relation with any thing else, not even with any other number; *Two* is but the relation of One to One. All modes of existence are but finite aspects of the Infinite; so all numbers are but numerical relations of the One. In the original One all numbers are contained, and consequently the elements of the whole world.

Observe, moreover, that One is necessarily the ἀρχή—the beginning of things so eagerly sought by philosophers, since, wherever you begin, you must begin with One. Suppose the number be three, and you strike off the initial number to make two, the second then will be *One*. In a word, One is the Beginning of all things.

The verbal quibble on which this, as indeed the whole system reposes, need not excite any suspicion of the sincerity of Pythagoras. The Greeks were unfortunately acquainted with no language but their own: and, as a natural consequence, mistook distinctions in language for distinctions in things. It has been well said by Dr. Whewell, that "all the first attempts to comprehend the operations of Nature led to the introduction of abstract conceptions, vague indeed, but not therefore unmeaning. And the next step in philosophizing necessarily was to make those vague abstractions more clear and fixed, so that the logical faculty should be able to employ them securely and coherently. But there were two ways of making this attempt; the one, by examining the words only, and the thoughts which they call up; the other, by attending to the facts and things which bring these abstract terms into use. The Greeks followed the *verbal* or *notional* course, and failed."*

It is only by means of the above explanation that we can any way credit the belief in distinctions so wire-drawn as those of

---

* *History of the Inductive Sciences*, I. 84.

Pythagoras; it is only thus that we can understand how he could have held that Numbers were Beings. Aristotle attributes this philosophy to the fondness of Pythagoras for mathematics, which concerns itself with the abstract, not with the material existence of sensible things; but surely this is only half the explanation? The mathematicians in our day not only reason entirely with symbols, which stand as the representatives of things, without having the least affinity or resemblance to the things (being wholly arbitrary *marks*), but very many of these men never trouble themselves at all with inspecting the things about which they reason by means of symbols. Much of the science of Astronomy is carried on by those who never use a telescope; it is carried on by figures upon paper, and calculations of those figures. Because, however, astronomers use numbers as symbols, they do not suppose that numbers are more than symbols. Pythagoras was not able to make this distinction. He believed that numbers were things in reality, not merely in symbol. When therefore Ritter says that the Pythagorean formula "can only be taken symbolically," he appears to us to commit a great anachronism, and to antedate by several centuries a mode of thought at variance with all we know of Greek Philosophy; at variance also with the express testimony of Aristotle, who says, "The Pythagoreans did not separate Numbers from Things. They held number to be the Principle and Material of things, no less than their essence and power."*
The notion that because we, in the present state of philosophy, cannot conceive Numbers otherwise than as symbols, therefore Pythagoras must have conceived them in the same way, is one

---

* *Metaph*. i. 5. Perhaps it would be more accurate to say, "Numbers are the beginning of things, the *cause of their material existence* (ὕλην τοῖς οὖσι: Aristotle has before defined ὕλη as *causa materialis*, cap. 3) and *of their modifications* (ὡς πάθη τε καὶ ἕξεις)."

The whole chapter should be consulted by those who believe in the symbolical use of numbers; a belief Aristotle had certainly no suspicion of. I have translated all the passages bearing on this point at the close of this Section.

which has been very widely spread, but which we hold to be as great an anachronism as Shakespeare's Hector quoting Aristotle, or Racine exhibiting the etiquette of Versailles in the camp of Aulis. And Ritter himself, after having stated with considerable detail the various points in this philosophy, admits that the essential doctrine rests on "the derivation of all in the world from mathematical relations, and on the resolution of the relations of space and time into those of units or numbers. All proceeds from the original one, or primary number, or from the plurality of units or numbers into which the one in its life-development divides itself." Now, to suppose that this doctrine was simply mathematical, and not mathematico-cosmological, is to violate all principles of historical philosophy; for it is to throw the opinions of our day into the period of Pythagoras. For a final proof, consider the formula, $\mu i\mu\eta\sigma\iota\nu$ $\varepsilon\tilde{\iota}\nu\alpha\iota$ $\tau\grave{\alpha}$ $\check{o}\nu\tau\alpha$ $\tau\tilde{\omega}\nu$ $\dot{\alpha}\rho\iota\theta\mu\tilde{\omega}\nu$, "Things are the copies of Numbers." This formula, which of all others is the most favorable to the notion we are combating, will on a close inspection exhibit the real meaning of Pythagoras to be directly the reverse of symbolical. Symbols are arbitrary marks, bearing no resemblance to the things they represent; a, b, c, x are but letters of the alphabet; the mathematician makes them the symbols of quantities, or of things; but no one would call x the *copy* of an unknown quantity. But what is the meaning of Things being copies of Numbers, if they are Numbers in essence? The meaning we must seek in anterior explanations. We shall there find that Things are *the concrete existences of abstract Existence;* and that when numbers are said to be the *principia*, it is meant that the *forms* of material things, the original essences, which remain invariable, are Numbers.* Thus a stone is One stone; as such it is a copy of One; it is the realization of the abstract One into a concrete

---

* Hence we must caution against supposing Pythagoras to have anticipated the theory of "definite proportions." Numbers are not the laws of combination, nor the expression of those laws, but the essences which remain invariable under every variety of combination.

stone. Let the stone be ground to dust, and the particle of dust is still a copy, another copy of the One.

The reader will bear in mind that we have only a few mystical expressions, such as, "Number is the principle of Things," handed down to us as the doctrines of a Thinker who created a considerable school, and whose influence on philosophy was undeniably immense. We have to interpret these expressions as we best can. Above all, we have to give them some appearance of plausibility; and this not so much an appearance of plausibility to modern thinkers as what would have been plausible to the ancients. Now, as far as we have familiarized ourselves with the antique modes of thought, our interpretation of Pythagoras is one which, if not the true, is at any rate very analogous to it; by such a logical process he *might* have arrived at his conclusions, and for our purpose this is almost the same as if he had arrived at them by it.

This history has but to settle two questions respecting Pythagoras: first, did he regard Numbers as symbols merely, or as entities? Second, if he regarded them as entities, how could he have arrived at such an opinion? The second of these questions has been answered in a hypothetical manner in the remarks just made; but of course the explanation is worthless if the first question be negatived, and to that question therefore we now turn. If we are to accept the authority of Aristotle, the question is distinctly and decisively answered, as we have seen, in favor of the *reality* of Numbers. It is true that doubts are thrown on the authority of Aristotle, who is said to have misunderstood or misrepresented the Pythagorean doctrine; but when we consider the comprehensiveness and exactness of Aristotle's mighty intellect; when we consider further that he had paid more than his usual attention to the doctrines of the Pythagoreans, having written a special treatise thereon, we shall be slow to reject any statement he may make unless *better* evidence is produced; and where can better evidence be sought? Either we must accept Aristotle, or be silent on the whole matter; unless, indeed, we prefer—as many prefer—our own sagacity to his authority. It may be stated as a final consideration, that the view taken by the Stagirite is in perfect conformity with the opinions of Anaximander; so that given, the philosophy of the master, we might *à priori* deduce the opinions of the pupil.

The nature of this Work forbids any detailed account of the various opinions attributed to Pythagoras on subsidiary points. But we may instance his celebrated theory of the music of the spheres as a good specimen of the deductive method employed by him. Assuming that every thing in the great Arrangement (κόσμος), which he called the world, must be harmoniously arranged, and, assuming that the planets were at the same proportionate distances from one another as the divisions of the monochord, he concluded that in passing through the ether they must make a sound, and that this sound would vary according to the diversity of their magnitude, velocity, and relative distance. Saturn gave the deepest tone, as being the furthest from the earth; the Moon gave the shrillest, as being nearest to the earth.

It may be necessary just to state that the attempt to make Pythagoras a Monotheist is utterly without solid basis, and unworthy of detailed refutation.

His doctrine of the Transmigration of Souls has been regarded as symbolical; with very little reason, or rather with no reason at all. He defined the soul to be a Monad (unit) which was self-moved.* Of course the soul, inasmuch as it was a number, was One, *i. e.* perfect. But all perfection, in as far as it is moved, must pass into imperfection, whence it strives to regain its state of perfection. Imperfection he called a departure from unity; *two* therefore was accursed.

The soul in man is in a state of comparative imperfection.†
It has three elements, Reason (νοῦς), Intelligence (φρήν), and

---

* Aristot., *De Animâ*, i. 2.
† Thus Aristotle expresses himself when he says that the Pythagoreans maintained the soul and intelligence to be a certain combination of numbers, τὸ ἰδὶ τοιονδὶ (sc. τῶν ἀριθμῶν πάθος) ψυχὴ καὶ νοῦς.—*Metaph.*, i. 5.

Passion (θυμός): the two last man has in common with brutes; the first is his distinguishing characteristic. It has hence been concluded that Pythagoras could not have maintained the doctrine of transmigration, his distinguishing man from brutes being a refutation of those who charge him with the doctrine.* The objection is plausible, and points out a contradiction; but there is abundant evidence for the belief that transmigration was taught.† The soul, being a self-moved monad, is One, whether it connect itself with two or with three; in other words, the *essence* remains the same whatever its *manifestations*. The One soul may have two aspects, Intelligence and Passion, as in brutes; or it may have the three aspects, as in man. Each of these aspects may predominate, and the man will then become eminently rational, or able, or sensual. He will be a philosopher, a man of the world, or a beast. Hence the importance of the Pythagorean initiation, and of the studies of Mathematics and Music.

"This soul, which can look before and after, can shrink and shrivel itself into an incapacity of contemplating aught but the present moment, of what depths of degeneracy is it capable! What a beast it may become! And if something lower than itself, why not something higher? And if something higher and lower, may there not be a law accurately determining its elevation and descent? Each soul has its peculiar evil tastes, bringing it to the likeness of different creatures beneath itself; why may it not be under the necessity of abiding in the condition of that thing to which it had adapted and reduced itself?"‡

In closing this account of a very imperfectly known doctrine, we have only further to exhibit its relation to the preceding philosophy. It is clearly an offshoot of Anaximander's doctrine,

---

* Pierre Leroux, *De l'Humanité*, i. 390-426.
† Plato distinctly mentions the transmigration into beasts.—*Phædrus*, p. 45. And **the** Pythagorean Timæus, in his statement of the doctrine, also **ex** pressly includes beasts.—*Timæus*, p. 45.
‡ Maurice, *Moral and Metaphysical Philosophy*.

which it develops in a more logical manner. In Anaximander there remained a trace of physical inquiry; in Pythagoras science is frankly mathematical. Assuming that number is the real invariable essence of the world, it was a natural deduction that the world is regulated by numerical proportions; and from this all the rest of his system followed as a consequence. Anaximander's system is but a rude and daring sketch of a doctrine which the great mathematical genius of Pythagoras developed. The Infinite of Anaximander became the One of Pythagoras. Observe that in neither of these systems is Mind an attribute of the Infinite. It has been frequently maintained that Pythagoras taught the doctrine of "a soul of the world." But there is no solid ground for the opinion, any more than for that of his Theism, which later writers anxiously attributed to him. The conception of an Infinite Mind is much later than Pythagoras. He only regarded Mind as a phenomenon; as the peculiar manifestation of an essential number; and the proof of this assertion we take to lie in his very doctrine of the soul. If the Monad, which is self-moved, can pass into the state of a brute or of a plant, in which state it successively loses its Reason ($νοῦς$) and its Intelligence ($φρήν$) to become merely sensual and concupiscible, does not this abdication of Reason and Intelligence distinctly prove them to be only variable manifestations (phenomena) of the invariable Essence? Assuredly; and those who argue for the Soul of the World as an Intelligence in the Pythagorean doctrine, must renounce both the doctrine of transmigration and the central doctrine of the system, the invariable Number as the Essence of things.

Pythagoras represents the second epoch of the second Branch of Ionian Philosophy; he is parallel with Anaximenes.

Translations from the 5th Chapter of Book I. of Aristotle's Metaphysics.

"In the age of these philosophers [the Eleats and Atomists], and even before them, lived those called Pythagoreans, who at first applied themselves to mathematics, a science they improved; and, having been trained exclusively in it, they fancied that the principles of mathematics were the principles of all things.

"Since numbers are by nature *prior* to all things, in Numbers they thought they perceived greater analogies with that which exists and that which is produced (ὁμοιώματα πολλὰ τοῖς οὖσι καὶ γιγνομένοις), than in fire, earth, or water. So that a certain combination of Numbers was justice; and a certain other combination of Numbers was Reason and Intelligence; and a certain other combination of Numbers was opportunity (καιρός); and so of the rest.

"Moreover, they saw in Numbers the combinations of harmony. Since therefore all things seemed formed similarly to Numbers, and Numbers being by nature anterior to things, they concluded that the elements (στοιχεῖα) of Numbers are the elements of things, and that the whole heaven is a harmony and a Number. Having indicated the great analogies between Numbers and the phenomena of heaven and its parts, and with the phenomena of the whole world (τὴν ὅλην διακόσμησιν), they formed a system; and if any gap was apparent in the system, they used every effort to restore the connection. Thus, since Ten appeared to them a perfect number, potentially containing all numbers, they declared that the moving celestial bodies (τὰ φερόμενα κατὰ τὸν οὐρανόν) were ten in number; but because only nine are visible they imagined (ποιοῦσι) a tenth, the *Anticthone*.

"We have treated of all these things more in detail elsewhere But the reason why we recur to them is this—that we may learn from *these* philosophers also what they lay down as their first principles, and by what process they hit upon the causes aforesaid.

"They maintained that Number was the Beginning (Principle, ἀρχή) of things, the cause of their material existence, and of their modifications and different states. The elements (στοιχεῖα) of Number are Odd and Even. The Odd is finite, the Even infinite. Unity, the One, partakes of both these, and is both Odd and Even. All number is derived from the One. The heavens, as we said before, are composed of numbers. Other Pythagoreans say there are ten Principia, those called co-ordinates:

    The finite and the infinite.
    The odd and the even.
    The one and the many.
    The right and the left.
    The male and the female.
    The quiescent and the moving.
    The right line and the curve.
    Light and darkness.
    Good and evil.
    The square and the oblong.

" . . . All the Pythagoreans considered the elements as material; for the elements are in all things, and constitute the world. . . .

" . . . The finite, the infinite, and the One they maintained to be not separate existences, such as are fire, water, etc.; but the abstract Infinite and the abstract One are respectively the substance of the things of which they are predicated, and hence, too, Number is the substance of all things (αὐτὸ τὸ ἄπειρον, καὶ αὐτὸ τὸ ἕν, οὐσίαν εἶναι τούτων). They began by attending only to the *Form*, and began to define it; but on this subject they were very imperfect. They define superficially; and that which suited their definition they declared to be the essence (*causa materialis*) of the thing defined; as if one should maintain that the double and the number two are the same thing, because the double is first found in the two. But two and the double are not equal (in essence), or if so, then the one would be many; a consequence which follows from their (the Pythagorean) doctrine."

(*We add also a passage from the 7th Chapter of the same Book.*)

"The Pythagoreans employ the Principia and Elements more strangely than even the Physiologists; the cause of which is that they do not take them from sensible things (αὐτὰς οὐκ ἐξ αἰσθητῶν). However, all their researches are physical; all their systems are physical. They explain the production of heaven, and observe that which takes place in its various parts, and its revolutions; and thus they employ their Principles and Causes, as if they agreed with the Physiologists, that whatever *is* is *material* (αἰσθητόν), and is that which contains what we call heaven.

"But their Causes and Principles we should pronounce sufficient (ἱκανάς) to raise them up to the conception of Intelligible things,—of things above sense (ἐπαναβῆναι καὶ ἐπὶ τὰ ἀνωτέρω τῶν ὄντων); and would accord with such a conception much better than with that of physical things."

This criticism of Aristotle's is a perfect refutation of those who see in Pythagoras the traces of symbolical doctrine. Aristotle sees how much more rational the doctrine would have been had it been symbolical; but this very remark proves that it was not so.

CHAPTER III.

THE ELEATICS.

§ I. XENOPHANES.

THE contradictory statements which so long obscured the question of the date of Xenophanes' birth, may now be said to be satisfactorily cleared up. M. Victor Cousin's essay on the subject will leave few readers unconvinced.* We may assert therefore with some probability, that Xenophanes was born in the 40th Olympiad (B. C. 620-616), and that he lived nearly a hundred years. His birthplace was Colophon, an Ionian city of Asia Minor; a city long famous as the seat of elegiac and gnomic poetry, and ranking the poet Mimnermus among its celebrated men. Xenophanes cultivated this species of poetry from youth upwards; it was the joy of his youth, the consolation of his manhood, and support of his old age. Banished from his native city, he wandered over Sicily as a Rhapsodist;† a profession he exercised apparently till his death, though, if we are to credit Plutarch, with very little pecuniary benefit. He lived poor, and died poor. But he could dispense with riches, having within him treasures inexhaustible. He whose whole soul was enwrapt in the contemplation of grand ideas, and whose vocation was the poetical expression of those ideas, needed but little worldly grandeur. He seems to have been one of the most remarkable men of anti-

---

* *Nouveaux Fragmens Philosophiques.*—The critical reader will observe some misstatements in this essay, but on the whole it is well worthy of perusal. Karsten's *Xenophanis Carminum Reliquiæ* is of great value.

† The Rhapsodists were the Minstrels of antiquity. They learned poems by heart, and recited them to assembled crowds on the occasions of feasts Homer was a rhapsodist, and rhapsodized his own verses.

quity, and also one of the most fanatical. He had no pity for the idle and luxurious superstitions of his time; he had no tolerance for the sunny legends of Homer, defaced as they were by the errors of polytheism. He, a poet, was fierce in the combat he perpetually waged with the first of poets: not from petty envy; not from petty ignorance; but from the deep sincerity of his heart, from the holy enthusiasm of his reverence. He who believed in one God, supreme in power, goodness, and intelligence, could not witness without pain the degradation of the Divine in the common religion. He was not dead to the poetic beauty of the Homeric fables, but keenly alive to their religious falsehood. Plato, whom none will accuse of wanting poetical taste, made the same objection. The latter portion of the second and the beginning of the third books of Plato's *Republic* are but expansions of these verses of Xenophanes:

> "Such things of the Gods are related by Homer and Hesiod
> As would be shame and abiding disgrace to any of mankind;
> Promises broken, and thefts, and the one deceiving the other."

He who firmly believed in

> "One God, of all beings divine and human the greatest,
> Neither in body alike unto mortals, neither in spirit,"*

could not but see, "more in sorrow than in anger," the gross anthropomorphism of his fellows:

> "But men foolishly think that Gods are born like as men are,
> And have too a dress like their own, and their voice and their figure:
> But if oxen and lions had hands like ours, and fingers,
> Then would horses like unto horses, and oxen to oxen,
> Paint and fashion their god-forms, and give to them bodies
> Of like shape to their own, as they themselves too are fashioned."†

---

* This is too important a position to admit of our passing over the original:

Εἷς θεὸς ἔν τε θεοῖσι καὶ ἀνθρώποισι μέγιστος
Οὔτε δέμας θνητοῖσιν ὁμοίιος οὔτε νόημα.—*Fragm.* i., ed. *Karsten.*

Wiggers, in his *Life of Socrates*, expresses his surprise that Xenophanes was allowed to speak so freely respecting the State Religion in Magna Græcia, when philosophical opinions much less connected with religion had proved so fatal to Anaxagoras in Athens. But the apparent contradiction is perhaps reconciled when we remember that Xenophanes was a poet, and poets have in all ages been somewhat privileged persons.

† Fragments v. and vi. are here united, as in Ritter; the sense seems

In confirmation of which satire he referred to the Ethiopians, who represent their gods with flat noses and black complexion; while the Thracians give them blue eyes and ruddy complexions.

Having attained a clear recognition of the unity and perfection of the Godhead, it became the object of his life to spread that conviction abroad, and to tear down the thick veil of superstition which hid the august countenance of truth. He looked around him, and saw mankind divided into two classes: those who speculated on the nature of things, endeavoring to raise themselves up to a recognition of the Divine; and those who yielded an easy unreflecting assent to the superstitions which composed religion. The first class speculated; but they kept their speculations to themselves, and to a small circle of disciples. If they sought truth, it was not to communicate it to all minds: they did not work for humanity, but for the few. Even Pythagoras, earnest thinker as he was, could not be made to believe in the fitness of the multitude for truth. He had two sorts of doctrine to teach: one for a few disciples, whom he chose with extreme caution; the other for those who pleased to listen. The former doctrine was what he believed the truth; the latter was what he thought the masses were fitted to receive. Xenophanes recognized no such distinction. Truth was for all men; to all men he endeavored to present it; and for three-quarters of a century he, the great Rhapsodist of Truth, emulated his countryman Homer, the great Rhapsodist of Beauty, and wandered into many lands, uttering the thought which was working in him. What a contrast is presented by these two Ionian singers! contrast in purpose, in means, and in fate. The rhapsodies of the philosopher, once so eagerly listened to and affectionately preserved in traditionary fragments, are now only extant in briefest extracts contained in ancient books, so ancient and so uninteresting as to be visited only by some rare old scholars and a few

---

to demand this conjunction. But Clemens Alexandrinus quotes the second Fragment as if it occurred in another part of the poem; introducing it with καὶ πάλιν φησι, "and again he says."—*Karsten*, p. 41.

dilettanti spiders; while the rhapsodies of the blind singer are living in the brain and heart of thousands and thousands, who go back to them as the fountain-source of poetry, the crystal mirror of an antique world.

The world presented itself to Homer in pictures, to Xenophanes in problems. The one saw Nature, enjoyed it, and painted it. The other also saw Nature, but questioned it, and wrestled with it. Every trait in Homer is sunny clear; in Xenophanes there is indecision, confusion. In Homer there is a resonance of gladness, a sense of manifold life, activity, and enjoyment. In Xenophanes there is bitterness, activity of a spasmodic sort, infinite doubt, and infinite sadness. The one was a poet singing as the bird sings, carolling for very exuberance of life; the other was a Thinker, and a fanatic. He did not sing, he recited:

"Ah! how unlike
To that large utterance of the early Gods!"

That the earnest philosopher should have opposed the sunny poet, opposed him even with bitterness, on account of the degraded actions and motives which he attributed to the Gods, is natural; but we must distinguish between this opposition and satire. Xenophanes was bitter, not satirical. The statement derived from Diogenes, that he wrote satires against Homer and Hesiod, is erroneous.* Those who think otherwise are referred to the excellent essay of Victor Cousin, before mentioned, or to Ritter.

Rhapsodizing philosophy, and availing himself, for that purpose, of all that philosophers had discovered, he wandered from place to place, and at last came to Elea, where he settled. Hegel questions this: he says he finds no distinct mention of such a fact in any of the ancient writers; on the contrary, Strabo, in his

---

* Γέγραφε δὲ καὶ ἐν ἔπεσιν, καὶ ἐλεγείας, καὶ ἰάμβους κατὰ Ἡσιόδου καὶ Ὁμήρου. Here, says M. Cousin, the word ἰάμβους is either an interpolation of a copyist, as Feurlin and Rossi conjecture, or else it is a misstatement by Diogenes. There is not a single iambic verse of his remaining. But in his hexameters he opposes Homer and Hesiod, as we have seen.

sixth book, when describing Elea, speaks of Parmenides and Zeno as having lived there, but is silent respecting Xenophanes, which Hegel holds to be suspicious. Indeed the words of Diogenes Laertius are vague. He says, "Xenophanes wrote two thousand verses on the foundation of Colophon, and on a colony sent to Elea." This by no means implies that he lived there. Nevertheless we concur with the modern writers who, from the various connections with the Eleatics observable in his fragments, maintain that he must actually have resided there. The reader is again referred to M. Cousin on this point. Be that as it may, Xenophanes terminated a long and active life without having solved the great problem. The indecision of his acute mind sowed the seeds of that skepticism which was hereafter to play so large a part in philosophy. All his knowledge enabled him only to know how little he knew. His state of mind is finely described by Timon the sillograph, who puts into the mouth of Xenophanes these words:

"Oh that mine were the deep mind, prudent and looking to both sides!
Long, alas! have I strayed on the road of error, beguiled,
And am, now, hoary of years, yet exposed to doubt and distraction
Manifold, all-perplexing, for whithersoever I turn me
I am lost in the *One and All.*"—(εἰς ἓν ταὐτά τε πᾶν ἀνελέσθαι.)*

It now remains for us to state some of the conclusions at which this great man arrived. They will not, perhaps, answer to the reader's expectation; as with Pythagoras, the reputation for extraordinary wisdom seems ill justified by the fragments of that wisdom which have descended to us. But although to modern philosophy the conclusions of these early thinkers may appear trivial, let us never forget that it is to these early thinkers that we owe our modern philosophy. Had there not been many a

"Gray spirit yearning in desire
To follow knowledge, like a sinking star,
Beyond the utmost bound of human thought,"†

---

* Preserved by Sextus Empiricus, *Hypot. Pyrrhon.* i. 224; and quoted also by Ritter, i. 443.
† Tennyson

we should not have been able to travel on the secure terrestrial path of slow inductive science. The impossible has to be proved impossible, before men will consent to limit their endeavors to the compassing of the possible. And it was the cry of despair which escaped from Xenophanes, the cry that nothing can be certainly known, which first called men's attention to the nothingness of knowledge, *as knowledge was then conceived.* Xenophanes opens a series of thinkers, which attained its climax in Pyrrho. That he should thus have been at the head of the monotheists, and at the head of the skeptics, is sufficient to entitle his speculations to an extended consideration here.

§ II. The Philosophy of Xenophanes.

The great problem of existence had early presented itself to his mind; and the resolution of that problem by Thales and Pythagoras had left him unsatisfied. Neither the physical nor the mathematical explanation could still the doubts which rose within him. On all sides he was oppressed with mysteries, which these doctrines could not penetrate. The state of his mind is graphically painted in that one phrase of Aristotle's: "Casting his eyes upwards at the immensity of heaven, he declared that *The One* is God." Overarching him was the deep blue, infinite vault, immovable, unchangeable, embracing him and all things; *that* he proclaimed to be God. As Thales had gazed abroad upon the sea, and felt that he was resting on its infinite bosom, so Xenophanes gazed above him at the sky, and felt that he was encompassed by it. Moreover it was a great mystery, inviting yet defying scrutiny. The sun and moon whirled to and fro through it; the stars were

"Pinnacled dim in its intense inane."

The earth was constantly aspiring to it in the shape of vapor, the souls of men were perpetually aspiring to it with vague yearnings. It was the centre of all existence; it was Existence itself. It was The One,—the Immovable, on whose bosom the Many were moved.

Is not this the explanation of that opinion universally attributed to him, but always variously interpreted, "God is a sphere?" The Heaven encompassing him and all things, was it not The One Sphere which he proclaimed to be God?

It is very true that this explanation does not exactly accord with his physics, especially with that part which relates to the earth being a flat surface, whose inferior regions are infinite, by which he explained the fixity of the earth. M. Cousin, in consequence of this discrepancy, would interpret the phrase as metaphorical. "The epithet *spherical* is simply a Greek locution, to indicate the perfect equality and absolute unity of God, and of which a sphere may be an image. The σφαιρικός of the Greeks is the *rotundus* of the Latins. It is a metaphorical expression, such as that of *square*, meaning *perfect;* an expression which, though now become trivial, had at the birth of mathematical science something noble and elevated in it, and is found in most elevated compositions of poetry. Simonides speaks of a 'man square as to his feet, his hands, and his mind,' meaning an accomplished man; and the metaphor is also used by Aristotle. It is not, therefore, surprising that Xenophanes, a poet as well as a philosopher, writing in verse, and incapable of finding the metaphysical expression which answered to his ideas, should have borrowed from the language of imagination the expression which would best render his idea."

We should be tempted to adopt this explanation, could we be satisfied that the Physics of Xenophanes were precisely what it is said they were, or that they were such at the epoch in which he maintained the sphericity of God. This latter difficulty is insuperable, but has been unobserved by all critics. A man who lives a hundred years, necessarily changes his opinions on such subjects; and when opinions are so lightly grounded, as were those of philosophers at that epoch, it is but natural to admit that the changes may have been frequent and abrupt. In this special instance, scholars have been aware of the very great and irreconcilable contradictions existing between certain opinions equally authentic; showing him to have been decidedly Physical (Ionian) in one department, and as decidedly Mathematical (Pythagorean) in another.

As to the case in point, Aristotle's express statement of Xenophanes having "looked up at heaven, and pronounced The One to be God," is manifestly at variance with any belief in the infinity of the lower regions of the earth. The One must be the Infinite.

To return, however, to his Monotheism, or more properly Pantheism, which is the greatest peculiarity of his doctrine: he not only destroyed the notion of a multiplicity of Gods, but he proclaimed the Self-existence and Intelligence of The One.

God must be Self-existent; for to conceive Being as incipient is impossible. Nothing can be produced from Nothing. Whence, therefore, was Being produced? From itself? No; for then it must have been already in existence to produce itself, otherwise it would have been produced from nothing. Hence the primary law: Being is self-existent. If self-existent, consequently eternal.

As in this it is implied that God is all-powerful and all-wise and all-existent, a multiplicity of Gods is inconceivable.

It also follows that God is immovable, when considered as The All:

"Wholly unmoved and unmoving it ever remains in the same place,
  Without change in its place when at times it changes appearance."

The All must be unmoved; there is nothing to move it. It cannot move itself; for to do so it must be external to itself.

We must not suppose that he denied motion to finite things because he denied it to the Infinite. He only maintained that The All was unmoved. Finite things were moved by God: "without labor, he ruleth all things by reason and insight." His monotheism was carefully distinguished from anthropomorphism, as the verses previously quoted have already exemplified. Let us only further remark on the passage in Diogenes Laertius, wherein he is said to have maintained that "God did not resemble man, for he heard and saw all things without *respira-*

tion." This is manifestly an allusion to the doctrine of Anaximenes that the soul was *air*. The intelligence of God, being utterly unlike that of man, is said to be independent of respiration.*

It is necessary to caution the reader against the supposition that by the One God Xenophanes meant a Personal God, distinct from the universe. He was a monotheist in contradistinction to his polytheistical contemporaries; but his monotheism was pantheism. Indeed this point would never have been doubted, notwithstanding the ambiguity of language, if moderns had steadily kept before their minds the conceptions held by the Greeks of their Gods as personifications of the Powers of Nature. When Xenophanes argued against the polytheism of his contemporaries, he argued against their *personifying* as distinct deities the various aspects of The One; he was wroth with their degradation of the divine nature by assimilating it to human nature, by making these powers *persons*, and independent existences,—conceptions irreconcilable with that of the unity of God. He was a monotheist therefore, but his monotheism was pantheism; he could not separate God from the world, which was merely the manifestation of God; he could not conceive God as the One Existent, and admit the existence of a world *not* God. There could be but One Existence with many modes; that one was God.

There is another tenet of almost equal importance in his system, and one which marks the origin of that skeptical philosophy which we shall see henceforward running through all the evolutions of this history, always determining a crisis in speculation. Up to the time of Xenophanes philosophy was unsuspectingly dogmatical: it never afterwards recovered that simple position. He it was who began to doubt, and to confess the in-

---

* Only by thus connecting one doctrine with another can we hope to understand ancient philosophy. It is in vain that we puzzle ourselves with the attempt to penetrate the meaning of these antique fragments of thought unless we view them in relation to the opinions of their epoch.

competence of Reason to solve doubts and compass the exalted aims of philosophy. Yet the doubt was moral rather than psychological. It was no systematic skepticism: an earnest spirit struggling after Truth, whenever he obtained, or thought he obtained, a glimpse of her celestial countenance, he proclaimed his discovery, however it might contradict what he had before announced. Long travel, various experience, examination of different systems, new and contradictory glimpses of the problem he was desirous of solving,—these working together produced in his mind a skepticism of a noble, somewhat touching sort, wholly unlike that of his successors. It was the combat of contradictory opinions in his mind, rather than disdain of knowledge. His faith was steady, his opinions vacillating. He had a profound conviction of the existence of an eternal, all-wise, infinite Being; but this belief he was unable to reduce to a consistent formula. There is deep sadness in these verses:

"Surely never hath been, nor ever shall be a mortal
Knowing both well the Gods and the All, whose nature we treat of;
For when by chance he at times may utter the true and the perfect,
He wists not unconscious; *for error is spread over all things.*"

In vain M. Cousin attempts to prove that these verses are not skeptical; many of the recorded opinions of Xenophanes are of the same tendency. The man who had lived to find his most cherished convictions turn out errors, might well be skeptical of the truth of any of his opinions. But this skepticism was vague; it did not prevent his proclaiming what he held to be the truth; it did not prevent his search after truth.

For although Truth could never be compassed in its totality by man, glimpses could be caught. Ἀλλὰ χρόνῳ ζητοῦντες ἐφευρίσκουσιν ἄμεινον: we cannot indeed be certain that our knowledge is absolute; we can only strive our utmost, and believe our opinions to be probable. This is not scientific skepticism; it does not ground itself on an investigation of the nature of Intelligence and the sources of our knowledge: it grounds itself solely on the perplexities into which philosophy is thrown. Thus reason (*i. e.* the logic of his day) taught him that God the Infinite could not be infinite, neither could he be finite. Not infinite, because *non-being* alone, as having neither beginning, middle, nor end, is unlimited (infinite). Not finite, because one thing can only be limited by another, and God is one, not many.

In like manner did logic teach him that God was neither moved nor unmoved. Not moved, because one thing can only be moved by another, and God is one, not many; not unmoved, because *non-being* alone is unmoved, inasmuch as it neither goes to another, nor does another come to it.

With such verbal quibbles as these did this great thinker darken his conception of the Deity. They were not quibbles to him; they were the real conclusions involved in the premises from which he reasoned. To have doubted their validity would have been to doubt the possibility of philosophy. He was not quite prepared for that; and Aristotle in consequence calls him "somewhat clownish," ἀγροικότερος (*Met.* i. 5); meaning that his conceptions were rude and undigested, instead of being systematized.

Although in the indecision of Xenophanes we see the germs of later skepticism, we are disposed to agree with M. Cousin in discrediting his absolute skepticism—resting on the incomprehensibility of all things—ἀκαταληψία πάντων. Nevertheless some of M. Cousin's grounds appear to us questionable.*

The reader will, perhaps, have gathered from the foregoing, that Xenophanes was too much in earnest to believe in the incomprehensibility of all things, however the contradictions of his logic might cause him to suspect his and other people's conclusions. Of course, if carried out to their legitimate consequences, his principles lead to absolute skepticism; but he did not so

---

* *E. g.* He says: "It appears that Sotion, according to Diogenes, attributed to Xenophanes the opinion, all things are incomprehensible; but Diogenes adds that Sotion was wrong on that point." (*Fragmens*, p. 89.) Now this is altogether a misstatement. Diogenes says: "Sotion pretends that *no one before Xenophanes* maintained the incomprehensibility of all things; but he is wrong." Diogenes here does not deny that Xenophanes held the opinion, but that any one held it before him.

carry them out, and we have no right to charge him with consequences which he himself did not draw. Indeed, it is one of the greatest and commonest of critical errors, to charge the originator or supporter of a doctrine with consequences which he did not see, or would not have accepted had he seen them. Because they may be contained in his principles, it by no means follows that he saw them. A man would be ridiculed if he attributed to the discoverer of any law of nature the various discoveries which the *application* of that law might have produced; nevertheless these applications were all potentially existing in the law; but as the discoverer of the law was not aware of them, he does not get the credit. Why, then, should a man have the *dis*-credit of conseqences contained, indeed, in his principles, but which he himself could not see? On the whole, although Xenophanes was not a clear and systematic thinker, it cannot be denied that he exercised a very remarkable influence on the progress of speculation; as we shall see in his successors.

§ III. Parmenides.

The readers of Plato will not forget the remarkable dialogue in which he pays a tribute to the dialectical subtlety of Parmenides; but we must at the outset caution them against any belief in the genuineness of the opinions attributed to him by Plato. If Plato could reconcile to himself the propriety of altering the sentiments of his beloved master, Socrates, and of attributing to him such as he had never entertained; with far greater reason could he put into the mouth of one long dead, sentiments which were the invention of his own dramatic genius. Let us read the *Parmenides*, therefore, with extreme caution; let us prefer the authority of Aristotle and the verses of Parmenides which have been preserved.

Parmenides was born at Elea, somewhere about the 61st Olympiad (B. C. 536). This date does not contradict the rumor which, according to Aristotle, asserted him to have been a disciple of Xenophanes, whom he might have listened to when that great rhapsodist was far advanced in years. The most positive statement, however, is that by Sotion, of his having been taught by Amcinias and Diochœtes the Pythagorean. But both may be true.

Born to wealth and splendor, enjoying the esteem and envy which always follow splendor and talents, it is conjectured that his early career was that of a dissipated voluptuary; but Diochœtes taught him the nothingness of wealth (at times, perhaps, when satiety had taught him the nothingness of enjoyment), and led him from the dull monotony of noisy revelry to the endless variety and excitement of philosophic thought. He forsook the feverish pursuit of enjoyment, to contemplate "the bright countenance of Truth, in the quiet and still air of delightful studies." *
But this devotion to study was no egoistical seclusion. It did not prevent his taking an active share in the political affairs of his native city. On the contrary, the fruits of his study were shown in a code of laws which he drew up, and which were deemed so wise and salutary, that the citizens at first yearly renewed their oath to abide by the laws of Parmenides.

> "And something greater did his worth obtain,
> For fearless virtue bringeth boundless gain."

The first characteristic of his philosophy, is the decided distinction between Truth and Opinion: in other words, between the ideas obtained through the Reason and those obtained through Sense. In Xenophanes we noticed a vague glimmering of this notion; in Parmenides it attained to something like clearness. In Xenophanes it contrived to throw an uncertainty over all things; which, in a logical thinker, would become absolute skepticism. But he was saved from skepticism by his faith. Parmenides was saved from it by his philosophy. He was perfectly aware of the deceitful nature of opinion; but he was also aware that within him there was certain ineradicable convictions, in which, like Xenophanes, he had perfect faith, but which he wished to explain by reason. Thus was he led in some sort to

---

* Milton.

anticipate the celebrated doctrine of *innate ideas*. These ideas were concerning necessary truths; they were true knowledge: all other ideas were uncertain.

The Eleatics, as Ritter remarks, believed that they recognized and could demonstrate that the truth of all things is one and unchangeable; perceiving, however, that the human faculty of thought is constrained to follow the appearance of things, and to apprehend the changeable and the many, they were forced to confess that we are unable fully to comprehend the divine truth in its reality, although we may rightly apprehend a few general principles. Nevertheless, to suppose, in conformity with human thought, that there is actually both a plurality and a change, would be but a delusion of the senses. While, on the other hand, we must acknowledge, that in all that appears to us as manifold and changeable, including all particular thought as evolved in the mind, the Godlike is present, unperceived indeed by human blindness, and become, as it were beneath a veil, indistinguishable.

We may make this conception more intelligible if we recall the mathematical tendency of the whole of this school. Their knowledge of Physics was regarded as contingent—delusive. Their knowledge of Mathematics eternal—self-evident. Parmenides was thus led by Xenophanes on the one hand, and Diochœtes on the other, to the conviction of the duality of human thought. His Reason, *i. e.* the Pythagorean logic, taught him that there is naught existing but The One (which he did not, with Xenophanes, call God; he called it Being). His Sense, on the other hand, taught him that there were Many Things, because of his manifold sensuous impressions. Hence he maintained two Causes and two Principles: the one to satisfy the Reason; the other to accord with the explanations of Sense. His work on "Nature" was therefore divided into two parts: in the first is expounded the absolute Truth, as Reason proclaims it; in the second, human Opinion, accustomed to

"Follow the rash eye, and ears with singing sounds confused, and tongue,"

which is but a mere *seeming* (δόξα, appearance): nevertheless there is a cause of this seeming; there is also a principle, consequently there is a doctrine appropriate to it.

It must not be imagined, that Parmenides had a mere vague and general notion of the uncertainty of human knowledge. He maintained that thought was delusive because dependent upon organization. He had as distinct a conception of this celebrated theory as any of his successors, as may be seen in the passage preserved by Aristotle in the 5th chapter of the 4th book of his *Metaphysics*, where, speaking of the materialism of Democritus, in whose system sensation was thought, he adds, that others have shared this opinion, and proceeds thus: "Empedocles affirms, that a change in our condition (τὴν ἕξιν) causes a change in our thought:

" 'Thought grows in men according to the impression of the moment;'*

and, in another passage, he says:

" 'It is always according to the changes which take place in men
That there is change in their thoughts.' "

Parmenides expresses himself in the same style:

"Such as to each man is the nature of his many-jointed limbs,
Such also is the intelligence of each man; for it is
The nature of limbs (organization) which thinketh in men,
Both in one and in all; for the highest degree of organization
gives the highest degree of thought."†

Now, as thought was dependent on organization, and as each

---

* Πρὸς παρεὸν γὰρ μῆτις ἀέξεται ἀνθρώποισι.

† The last sentence, "for the highest degree of organization gives the highest degree of thought," is a translation which, differing from that of every other we have seen, and being, as we believe, of some importance in the interpretation of Parmenides' system, it is necessary to state at full our reasons. Here is the origina of the verses in the text:

'Ως γὰρ ἕκαστος ἔχει κρᾶσιν μελίων πολυκάμπτων,
Τὼς νόος ἀνθρώποισι παρίστηκεν. Τὸ γὰρ αὐτὸ
Ἔστιν ὅπερ φρονέει μελίων φύσις ἀνθρώποισι,
Καὶ πᾶσιν, καὶ παντί· τὸ γὰρ πλέον ἐστὶ νόημα.

The last sentence Ritter translates—

"For thought is the fulness."

Objecting to Hegel's version of τὸ πλέον, "the most," and to that of Brandis, organization differed in degree from every other, so would the opinions of men differ. If thought be sensation, it requires but little reflection to show, that, as sensations from the same object differ according to the senses of different persons, and indeed differ at different times with the same person, therefore one opinion is not more true than another, and all are equally false. But Reason is the same in all men: that alone is the fountain of certain knowledge. All thought derived from sense is but a

---

"the mightier," Ritter says the meaning is "the full." But we shall then want an interpretation of "the full." What is it? He elsewhere slightly alters the phrase thus:

"The fulness of all being is thought."

We speak with submission, but it appears to us that Ritter's assertion respecting τὸ πλέον meaning "the full," or "the fulness," is unwarrantable. The ordinary meaning is certainly "the more" or "the most," and hence used occasionally to signify *perfection*, as in Theocritus:

Καὶ τὰς βωκολικὰς ἐπὶ τὸ πλέον ἵκεο μώσας.—*Idy.* i. 20.

When Parmenides, therefore, uses the phrase τὸ πλέον ἐστὶ νόημα, he seems to us to have the ordinary meaning in view; he speaks of τὸ πλέον as a necessary consequence of the πολυκάμπτος. Man has many-jointed limbs, *ergo* many sensations; if he had more limbs he would have more sensations; the highest degree of organization gives the highest degree of thought. This explanation is in conformity with what Aristotle says on introducing the passage; is in conformity with the line immediately preceding:

Ἔστιν ὅπερ φρονέει μελέων φύσις ἀνθρώποισι;

is in conformity with the explanation of the scholiast Asclepias, τὸ πλέον ἐστὶ νόημα, προσγίγνεται ἐκ τῆς πλείονος αἰσθήσεως καὶ ἀκριβεστέρας; and, finally, is in conformity with the opinion attributed to Parmenides by Plutarch, that "sentir et penser ne lui paraissaient choses distinctes, ni entre elles ni de l'organisation."[1]

It is on this account we reject the reading of πολυπλάγκτων, "far-wandering," in place of πολυκάμπτων, "many-jointed," suggested by Karsten. The change is arbitrary and for the worse; πολυπλάγκτων having reference only to the feet, whereas the simile in Parmenides is meant to apply to the whole man.

The meaning of the verses is, therefore, that the intelligence of man is formed according to his many-jointed frame, *i. e.* dependent on his organization.

---

[1] Ch. Renouvier, *Manuel de la Philosophie Ancienne*, i. 152, who cites Plutarch, *Opin. des Philos.* iv. 5.

seeming (δόξα); but thought derived from Reason is absolutely true. Hence his antithesis to δόξα is always πίστις, *faith*.

This is the central point in his system. He was thereby enabled to avert absolute skepticism, and at the same time to admit the uncertainty of ordinary knowledge. He had therefore two distinct doctrines, each proportioned to the faculty adapted to it. One doctrine, of Absolute Knowledge (Metaphysics, μετὰ τα φυσικά), with which the faculty of pure Reason was concerned, a doctrine called in the language of that day, the "science of Being." The other doctrine, of Relative Knowledge, or Opinion (Physics, τὰ φυσικά), with which the faculty of Intelligence, or Thought, derived from Sense, was concerned, and which may be called the Science of Appearance.

On the science of Being, Parmenides did not differ much from his predecessors, Xenophanes and Pythagoras. He taught that there was but one Being; non-Being was impossible. The latter assertion amounts to saying that non-existence cannot exist; a position which may appear extremely trivial to the reader not versed in metaphysical speculations; but which we would not have him despise, inasmuch as it is a valuable piece of evidence respecting the march of human opinion. It is only one of the many illustrations of the tendency to attribute positive qualities to words, as if they were *things*, and not simply *marks* of things; a tendency admirably exposed by James Mill, and subsequently by his son.* It was this tendency which so greatly puzzled the early thinkers, who, when they said that "a thing *is* not," believed that they nevertheless predicated existence, viz. the existence of non-existence. A thing *is*, and a thing *is not* ; these

---

* "Many volumes might be filled with the frivolous speculations concerning the nature of Being (τὸ ὂν, οὐσία, *Ens*, *Entitas*, *Essentia*, and the like), which have arisen from overlooking this double meaning of the words *to be*, from supposing that when it signifies *to exist*, and when it signifies *to be* some specified thing, as to *be* a man, to *be* Socrates, to *be* seen, to *be* a phantom, or even to *be* a nonentity, it must still at the bottom answer to the same idea; and that a meaning must be found for it which shall suit all these cases."—*John Mill, System of Logic*, i. 4, *first ed.*

two assertions seemed to be affirmations of two different states of existence; an error from which, under some shape or other, later thinkers have not always been free.

Parmenides, however, though affirming that Being alone existed and that non-Being was impossible, did not see the real ground of the sophism. He argued that Non-Being could not be, because Nothing can come out of Nothing (as Xenophanes taught him); if therefore Being existed, it must embrace all existence.

Hence he concluded that The One was all Existence, identical, unique, neither born nor dying, neither moving nor changing. It was a bold step to postulate the finity of the One, Xenophanes having declared it to be necessarily infinite. But there is abundant evidence to prove that Parmenides regarded The One as finite. Aristotle speaks of it as the distinction between Parmenides and Melissus: "The unity of Parmenides was a *rational* unity (τοῦ κατὰ λόγον ἑνός); that of Melissus was a *material* unity (τοῦ κατὰ τὴν ὕλην). Hence the former said that The One was finite (πεπερασμένον), but the latter said it was infinite (ἄπειρον)." From which it appears that the ancients conceived the Rational unity as limited by itself; a conception it is difficult for us to understand. Probably it was because they held The One to be spherical: all the parts being equal: having neither beginning, middle, nor end: and yet self-limited.

The conception of the identity of thought and existence is expressed in some remarkable verses by Parmenides, of which, as a very different interpretation has been drawn from them, we shall give a literal translation:

"Thought is the same thing as the cause of thought:
For without the thing in which it is announced
You cannot find the thought; for there is nothing, nor shall be—
Except the existing."

Now, as the only Existence was The One, it follows that The One and Thought are identical; a conclusion which by no means contradicts the opinion before noticed of the identity of human thought and sensation, both of these being merely transitory modes of Existence.

Respecting the second or physical doctrine of Parmenides, we may briefly say that, believing it necessary to give a science of Appearances, he sketched out a programme according to the principles reigning in his day. He denied motion in the abstract, but admitted that *according to appearance* there was motion.

Parmenides represents the logical and more rigorous side of the doctrine of Xenophanes, from which the physical element is almost banished, by being condemned to the region of uncertain Sense, Knowledge. The ideal element alone was really nourished by the speculations of Parmenides. Although he preserved himself from skepticism, as we saw, nevertheless the tendency of his doctrine was to forward skepticism. In his exposition of the uncertainty of knowledge, he retained a saving clause,—that, namely, of the certainty of Reason. It only remained for successors to apply the same skepticism to the ideas of Reason, and Pyrrhonism was complete.

§ IV. Zeno of Elea.

Zeno, by Plato called the Palamedes of Elea, must not be confounded with Zeno the Stoic. He was on all accounts one of the most distinguished of the ancient philosophers; as great in his actions as in his works; and remarkable in each for a strong, impetuous, disinterested spirit. Born at Elea about the 70th Olympiad (B. C. 500), he became the pupil of Parmenides, and, as some say, his adopted son.

The first period of his life was spent in the calm solitudes of study. From his beloved friend and master he had learned to appreciate the superiority of intellectual pleasures—the only pleasures that do not satiate. From him also he had learned to despise the splendors of rank and fortune, without becoming misanthropical or egoistical. He worked for the benefit of his fellowmen, but declined the recompense of rank, or worldly honors, with which they would have repaid those labors. His recompense was the voice of his own heart, beating calmly in the consciousness of its integrity. The absence of ambition in so intrepid and exalted a mind, might well have been the wonderment of antiquity; for it was no skeptical indifference, no disdain for the opinions of his fellow-men, which made him shun office. He was a delicate no less than an impetuous man, extremely sensitive to praise and blame; as may be seen in his admirable reply to one who asked him why he was so hurt by blame : "If the blame of my fellow-citizens did not cause me pain, their approbation would not cause me pleasure." In timid minds, shrinking from the coarse ridicule of fools and knaves, this sensitiveness is fatal; but in those brave spirits who fear nothing but their own consciences, and who accept no approbation but such as their consciences can ratify, this sensitiveness lies at the root of much heroism and noble endeavor. One of those men was Zeno. His life was a battle, but the battle was for Truth; it ended tragically, but it was not fought in vain.

Perhaps of all his moral qualities his patriotism has been the most renowned. He lived at the period of Liberty's awakening, when Greece was everywhere enfranchising herself, everywhere loosening the Persian yoke, and endeavoring to found national institutions on Liberty. In the general effervescence and enthusiasm Zeno was not cold. His political activity we have no means of judging; but we learn that it was great and beneficial. Elea was but a small colony; but Zeno preferred it to the magnificence of Athens, whose luxurious, restless, quibbling, frivolous, passionate, and unprincipled citizens he contrasted with the provincial modesty and honesty of Elea. He did, however, occasionally visit Athens, and there promulgated the doctrines of his master, as we see by the opening of Plato's dialogue, the *Parmenides*. There he taught Pericles.

On the occasion of his last return to Elea, he found it had fallen into the hands of the tyrant Nearchus (or Diomedon or Demylos: the name is differently given by ancient writers). He, of course, conspired against him, failed in his project, and was captured. It was then, as Cicero observes, that he proved the excellence of his master's doctrines, and proved that a courageous soul fears only that which is base, and that fear and pain are for women and children, or men who have feminine hearts. When Nearchus interrogated him as to his accomplices, he threw the tyrant into an agony of doubt and fear by naming all the courtiers: a master-stroke of audacity, and in those days not discreditable. Having thus terrified his accuser, he turned to the spectators, and exclaiming, " If you can consent to be slaves from fear of what you see me now suffer, I can only wonder at your cowardice." So saying, he bit his tongue off, and spat it in the face of the tyrant. The people were so roused that they fell upon Nearchus and slew him.

There are considerable variations in the accounts of this story by ancient writers, but all agree in the main narrative given above. Some say that Zeno was pounded to death in a huge mortar. We have no trustworthy account of his death.

As a philosopher, Zeno's merits are peculiar. He was the inventor of that logic so celebrated as *Dialectics*. This, which, in the hands of Socrates and Plato, became a powerful weapon of offence, is, by the universal consent of antiquity, ascribed to Zeno. It may be defined as " A refutation of error by the *reductio ad absurdum* as a means of establishing the truth." The truth to be established in Zeno's case was the system of Parmenides; we must not, therefore, seek in his arguments for any novelty beyond the mere exercise of dialectical subtlety. He brought nothing new to the system; but he invented a great method of polemical exposition. The system had been conceived by Xenophanes, precision had been given to it by Parmenides; and there only remained for Zeno the task of fighting for and defending it; which task he admirably fulfilled. " The destiny of Zeno was altogether polemical. Hence, in the external world, the impetuous existence and tragical end of the patriot; and, in the internal world, the world of thought, the laborious character of Dialectician." *

It was this fighter's destiny which caused him to perfect the

---

* Cousin, *Fragmens Philosophiques*, art. *Zénon d'Elée*.

art of offence and defence. He very naturally wrote in *prose*, of which he set the first example: for, as the wild and turbulent enthusiasm of Xenophanes would instinctively express itself in poetry, so would the argumentative subtlety of Zeno naturally express itself in prose. The great Rhapsodist wandered from city to city, intent upon earnest and startling enunciation of the mighty thoughts stirring confusedly within him; the great Logician was more intent upon a convincing exposition of the futility of the arguments alleged against his system, than upon any propagande of the system itself; for he held that the truth must be accepted when once error is exposed. "Antiquity," says M. Cousin, "attests that he wrote not poems, like Xenophanes and Parmenides, but treatises, and treatises of an eminently prosaic character: that is to say, refutations."

The reason of this may be easily guessed. Coming as a young man to Athens, to preach the doctrine of Parmenides, he must have been startled at the opposition which that doctrine met with from the subtle, quick-witted, and empirical Athenians, who had already erected the Ionian philosophy into the reigning doctrine. Zeno, no doubt, was at first stunned by the noisy objections which on all sides surrounded him; but, being also one of the keenest of wits, and one of the readiest, he would soon have recovered his balance, and in turn assailed his assailers. Instead of teaching dogmatically, he began to teach dialectically. Instead of resting in the domain of pure science, and expounding the ideas of Reason, he descended upon the ground occupied by his adversaries—the ground of daily experience and sense-knowledge—and turning their ridicule upon themselves, forced them to admit that it was more easy to conceive The Many as a produce of The One, than to conceive The One on the assumption of the existing Many.

"The polemical method entirely disconcerted the partisans of the Ionian philosophy," says M. Cousin, "and excited a lively curiosity and interest for the doctrines of the Italian (Pythagorean) school; and thus was sown, in the capital of Greek civiliration, the fruitful germ of a higher development of philosophy."

Plato has succinctly characterized the difference between Parmenides and Zeno by saying, that the master established the existence of The One, and the disciple proved the non-existence of The Many.

When he argued that there was but One thing really existing, all the others being only modifications or appearances of that One, he did not deny that there were *many appearances*, he only denied that these appearances were real existences. So, in like manner, he denied motion, but not the appearance of motion. Diogenes the Cynic, who, to refute his arguments against motion, rose and walked, entirely mistook the argument; his walking was no more a refutation of Zeno, than Dr. Johnson's kicking a stone was a refutation of Berkeley's denial of matter. Zeno would have answered: Very true; you walk: according to Opinion (τὸ δοξαστόν) you are in motion; but according to Reason you are at rest. What you call motion is but the *name* given to a series of similar conditions, each of which, separately considered, is *rest*. Thus, every object filling space equal to its bulk is necessarily at rest in that space; motion from one spot to another is but a name given to the *sum-total* of all these *intermediate spaces* in which *the object at each moment is at rest*. Take the illustration of the circle: a circle is composed of a number of individual points, or straight lines; not one of these lines can individually be called a circle; but all these lines, considered as a totality, have one general name given them, viz. a circle. In the same way, in each individual point of space, the object is at rest; the sum-total of a number of these states of rest is called motion.

The original fallacy is in the supposition that Motion is a thing superadded, whereas, as Zeno clearly saw, it is only a *condition*. In a falling stone there is not the "stone" and a thing called "motion;" otherwise there would be also another thing called "rest." But both motion and rest are names given to express conditions of the stone. Even rest is a positive exertion of *force* Rest is force resistant, and Motion is force triumphant. It follows that matter is always in motion; which amounts to the same as Zeno's saying, there is no such thing as motion.

The other arguments of Zeno against the possibility of Motion (and he maintained four, the third of which we have above explained,) are given by Aristotle; but they *seem* more like the ingenious puzzles of dialectical subtlety than the real arguments of an earnest man. It has, therefore, been asserted, that they were only brought forward to ridicule the unskilfulness of his adversaries. We must not, however, be hasty in rescuing Zeno from his own logical net, into which he may have fallen as easily as others. Greater men than he have been the dupes of their own verbal distinctions.

Here are his two first arguments:

1. Motion is impossible, because before that which is in motion can reach the end, it must reach the middle point; but this middle point then becomes the end, and the same objection applies to it—since to reach it the object in motion must traverse a middle point; and so on *ad infinitum*, seeing that matter is infinitely divisible. Thus, if a stone be cast four paces, before it can reach the fourth it must reach the second; the second then becomes the end, and the first pace the middle; but before the object can reach the first pace, it must reach the half of the first pace, and before the half it must reach the half of that half; and so on *ad infinitum*.

2. This is his famous Achilles puzzle. We give both the statement and refutation as we find it in Mill's *Logic* (ii. 453).

The argument is, let Achilles run ten times as fast as a tortoise, yet, if the tortoise has the start, Achilles will never overtake him; for, suppose them to be at first separated by an interval of a thousand feet; when Achilles has run these thousand feet, the tortoise will have run a hundred, and when Achilles has run those hundred, the tortoise will have got on ten, and so on forever: therefore Achilles may run forever without overtaking the tortoise.

Now the "forever" in the conclusion means, for any length of time that can be supposed; but in the premises, "forever" does not mean any *length* of time—it means any *number of subdivisions of time*. It means that we may divide a thousand feet by ten, and that quotient again by ten, and so on as often as we please; that there never need be an end to the subdivisions of the distance, nor, consequently, to those of the time in which it is performed. But an unlimited number of subdivisions may be made of that which is itself limited. The argument proves no other infinity of duration than may be embraced within five minutes. As long as the five minutes are not expired, what remains of them may be divided by ten, and again by ten, as often as we like, which is perfectly compatible with their being only five minutes altogether. It proves, in short, that to pass through this finite space requires *a time which is infinitely divisible*, but not an *infinite time;* the confounding of which distinction Hobbes had already seen to be the gist of the fallacy.

Although the credit of seeing the ground of the fallacy is given by Mill to Hobbes, we must also observe that Aristotle had clearly seen it in the same light. His answer to Zeno, which Bayle thinks "pitiable," was, that a foot of space being only *potentially infinite*, but *actually finite*, it could be easily traversed in a *finite time*.

We have no space to follow Zeno in his various arguments against the existence of a multitude of things. His position may be briefly summed up thus:—There is but one Being existing, necessarily indivisible and infinite. To suppose that The One is divisible, is to suppose it finite. If divisible, it must be infinitely divisible. But, suppose two things to exist, then there must necessarily be an interval between those two; something separating and limiting them. What is that something? It is some *other* thing. But then, if not the *same* thing, *it also* must be separated and limited; and so on *ad infinitum*. Thus only One thing can exist as the *substratum* for all manifold appearances.

7

Zeno closes the second great line of independent inquiry, which, opened by Anaximander, and continued by Pythagoras, Xenophanes, and Parmenides, we may characterize as the Mathematical or Absolute system. Its opposition to the Ionian, Physical or Empirical system was radical and constant. But, up to the coming of Zeno, these two systems had been developed almost in parallel lines, so little influence did they exert upon each other. The two systems clashed together on the arrival of Zeno at Athens. The result of the conflict was the creation of a new method—Dialectics. This method created the Sophists and the Skeptics. It also greatly influenced all succeeding schools, and may be said to have constituted one great peculiarity of Socrates and Plato, as will be shown.

We must, however, previously trace the intermediate steps which philosophy took, before the crisis of Sophistry, which preceded the era of Socrates.

SECOND EPOCH.

SPECULATIONS ON THE CREATION OF THE UNIVERSE, **AND** ON THE ORIGIN OF KNOWLEDGE.

CHAPTER I.

§ I. Heraclitus.

"Life is a comedy to those who think, a tragedy to those who feel." This, Horace Walpole's epigram, may be applied to Democritus and Heraclitus, celebrated throughout antiquity as the laughing and the weeping philosophers:

> "One pitied, one condemn'd the woeful times;
> One laugh'd at follies, and one wept o'er crimes."

Modern criticism has indeed pronounced both these characteristics to be fabulous; but fables themselves are often only exaggerations of truth, and there must have been something in each of these philosophers which formed the nucleus round which the fables grew. Of Heraclitus it has been well said, "The vulgar notion of him as the crying philosopher must not be wholly discarded, as if it meant nothing, or had no connection with the history of his speculations. The thoughts which came forth in his system are like fragments torn from his own personal being, and not torn from it without such an effort and violence as must needs have drawn a sigh from the sufferer. If Anaximenes discovered that he had within him a power and principle which ruled over all the acts and functions of his bodily frame, Heraclitus found that there was a life within him which he could not call his own, and yet it was, in the very highest sense, *himself*, so that without it he would have been a poor, helpless, isolated creature;—a universal life, which connected him with his fellow-men,—with the absolute source and original fountain of life."*

Heraclitus was the son of Blyson, and was born at Ephesus, about the 69th Olympiad (B. C. 503). Of a haughty, melancholy temper, he refused the supreme magistracy which his fellow-citizens offered him, on account, according to Diogenes Laertius, of their dissolute morals; but as he declined the offer in favor of his brother, we are disposed to think his rejection was grounded on some other cause. Is not his rejection of magistracy in perfect keeping with what else we know of him? For instance: playing with some children near the temple of Diana, he answered those who expressed surprise at seeing him thus occupied, " Is it not better to play with children, than to share with you the administration of affairs?" The contempt which pierces through this reply, and which subsequently grew into confirmed misanthropy, may have been the result of morbid meditation, rather than of virtuous scorn. Was it because the citizens were corrupt, that he refused to exert himself to make them virtuous? Was it because the citizens were corrupt, that he retired to the mountains, and there lived on herbs and roots, like an ascetic? If Ephesus was dissolute, was there not the rest of Greece for him to make a home of? He fled to the mountains, that he might there, in secret, prey on his own heart. He was a misanthrope, and misanthropy is madness, not virtuous indignation; misanthropy issues from the morbid consciousness of self, not from the sorrowful opinion formed of others. The aim of his life had been to explore the depths of his own nature. This has been the aim of all ascetics, as of all philosophers: but in the former it is *morbid* anatomy; in the latter it is science.

The contemptuous letter in which he declined the courteous

---

* Maurice, *Moral and Metaphysical Philosophy.*

invitation of Darius to spend some time at his court, will best explain his character:

"*Heraclitus of Ephesus to the King Darius, son of Hystaspes, health!*

"All men depart from the paths of truth and justice. They have no attachment of any kind but avarice; they only aspire to a vain-glory with the obstinacy of folly. As for me, I know not malice; I am the enemy of no one. I utterly despise the vanity of courts, and never will place my foot on Persian ground. Content with little, I live as I please."

Misanthropy was the nucleus of the fable of Heraclitus as a weeping philosopher, who refused the magistracy because the citizens were corrupt. The story of his attempting to cure himself of a dropsy by throwing himself on a dunghill, hoping that the heat would cause the water within him to evaporate, is apocryphal.

The Philosophy of Heraclitus was, and is, the subject of dispute. He expressed himself in such enigmatical terms, that he was called "the Obscure." A few fragments have been handed down to us.* From these it would be vain to hope that a consistent system could be evolved; but from them, and from other sources, we may gather the general tendency of his doctrines.

The tradition which assigns him Xenophanes as a teacher, is borne out by the evident relation of their systems. Heraclitus is somewhat more Ionian than Xenophanes: that is to say, in him the physical explanation of the universe is more prominent. At the same time, Heraclitus is neither frankly Ionian nor Italian; he wavers between the two. The pupil of Xenophanes would naturally regard human knowledge as a mist of error, through which the sunlight only gleamed at intervals. But the inheritor of the Ionian doctrines would not adopt the conclusion of the

---

* Schleiermacher has collected, and endeavored to interpret them, in Wolf and Buttmann's *Museum der Alterthumswissenschaften*, vol. i. part iii.

Mathematical school, namely, that the cause of this uncertainty of knowledge is the uncertainty of sensuous impressions; and that consequently Reason is the only fountain of truth. Heraclitus was not mathematician enough for such a doctrine: he was led to maintain a doctrine directly opposed to it. He maintained that the senses are the sources of all true knowledge, for they drink in the universal intelligence. The senses deceive only when they belong to barbarian souls: in other words, the ill-educated sense gives false impressions, the rightly-educated sense gives truth. Whatever is common is true; whatever is remote from the common, *i. e.* the exceptional, is false. The True is the Unhidden.* Those whose senses are open to receive the Unhidden, the Universal, attain truth.

As if to mark the distinction between himself and Xenophanes more forcibly, he says: "Inhaling through the breath the Universal Ether, which is Divine Reason, we become conscious. In sleep we are unconscious, but on waking we again become intelligent; for in sleep, when the organs of sense are closed, the mind within is shut out from all sympathy with the surrounding ether, the universal Reason; and the only connecting medium is the breath, as it were a root, and by this separation the mind loses the power of recollection it before possessed. Nevertheless on awakening the mind repairs its memory through the senses, as it were through inlets; and thus, coming into contact with the surrounding ether, it resumes its intelligence. As fuel when brought near the fire is altered and becomes fiery, but on being removed again becomes quickly extinguished; so too the portion of the all-embracing which sojourns in our body becomes more irrational when separated from it; but on the restoration of this connection, through its many pores or inlets, it again becomes similar to the whole."

Can any thing be more opposed to the Eleatic doctrine? That system rests on the certitude of pure Reason; this declares that

---

* Ἀληθές τὸ μὴ λῆθον. This kind of play upon words is very characteristic of metaphysical thinkers in all ages.

Reason left to itself, *i. e.* the mind when it is not nourished by the senses, can have no true knowledge. The one system is exclusively rational, the other exclusively material; but both are pantheistical, for in both it is the universal Intelligence which becomes conscious in man,—a conception pushed to its ultimate limits by Hegel. Accordingly Hegel declares that there is not a single point in the Logic of Heraclitus which he, Hegel, has not developed in his Logic.

The reader will remark how in Heraclitus, as in Parmenides, there is opened the great question which for so long agitated the schools, and which still agitates them,—the question respecting the origin of our ideas. He will also remark how the two great parties, into which thinkers have divided themselves on the question, are typified in these two early thinkers. In Parmenides the idealist school, with its contempt of sense; in Heraclitus the materialist school, with its contempt of every thing not derived from sensation.

With Xenophanes, Heraclitus agreed in denouncing the perpetual delusion which reigned in the mind of man; but he placed the cause of that delusion in the imperfection of human Reason, not, as Xenophanes had done, in the imperfection of Sense. He thought that man had too little of the Divine Ether (soul) within him. Xenophanes thought that the senses clouded the intellectual vision. The one counselled man to let the Universal mirror itself in his soul through the senses; the other counselled him to shut himself up within himself, to disregard the senses, and to commune only with ideas.

It seems strange that so palpable a contradiction between two doctrines should ever have been overlooked. Yet such is the fact. Heraclitus is said to have regarded the world of Sense as a perpetual delusion: and this is said in the very latest and not the least intelligent of Histories, to say nothing of former works. Whence this opinion? Simply from the admitted skepticism of both Heraclitus and Xenophanes with respect to Phenomena (appearances). It is true they both denied the certainty of human knowledge, but they denied this on different grounds. "Man has no certain knowledge," said Heraclitus, "but God has; and vain man learns from God just as the boy from the man." In his conception, human intelligence was but a portion of the Universal Intelligence; but a part can never be otherwise than imperfect. Hence it is that the opinion of all mankind upon any subject (common sense) must be a nearer approximation to the truth than the opinion of any individual; because it is an accumulation of parts, making a nearer approach to the whole.

While therefore he maintained the uncertainty of all knowledge, he also maintained its certainty. Its origin was Sense; being sensuous and individual, it was imperfect, *because* individual; but it was true as far as it went. The ass, he scornfully said, prefers thistles to gold. To the ass gold is *not* so valuable as thistle. The ass is at once right and wrong. Man is equally right and wrong in all positive affirmations; for nothing truly *is*, about which a positive affirmation can be made. "All is," he said, "and all is not; for though in truth it does come into being, yet it forthwith ceases to be."

We are here led to his celebrated doctrine of all things as a "perpetual flux and reflux;" which Hegel declares to be an anticipation of his own celebrated dogma, *Seyn und Nichtseyn ist dasselbe:* "Being and Non-Being is the same."* Heraclitus conceived the principle—ἀρχή—of all things to be Fire. To him Fire was the type of spontaneous force and activity; not flame, which was only an intensity of Fire, but a warm, dry vapor—an Ether; this was the beginning. He says: "The world was made neither by God† nor man; and it was, and is,

---

* Much of the ridicule which this logical canon has excited, especially in England, has been prompted by the blindest misunderstanding. The laughers, misled by verbal ambiguity, have understood Hegel to say that Existence and Non-Existence was one and the same, as if by *Nichtseyn* he meant Nothing. He meant by Nothing No Thing—no *phenomenon*. The position is perhaps absurd, but it is not for metaphysicians to say so.

† This is the translation given in Ritter: it is not however exact; οὔτε τις θεῶν is the original, *i. e.* "neither one of the Gods," meaning of course one of the polytheistic Deities.

and ever shall be, an ever-living fire in due measure self-enkindled and in due measure self-extinguished." That this is but a modification of the Ionian system, the reader will at once discern. The Fire, which here stands as the semi-symbol of Life and Intelligence, because of its spontaneous activity, is but a modification of the Water of Thales and the Air of Anaximenes; moreover, it is only semi-symbolical. Those who accept it as a pure symbol overlook the other parts of the system. The system which proclaims the senses as the source of all knowledge necessarily attaches itself to a material element as the primary one. At the same time this very system is in one respect a deviation from the Ionian; in the distinction between sense-knowledge and reflective knowledge. Hence we placed Diogenes of Apollonia as the last of the pure Ionians; although chronologically he came some time after Heraclitus, and his doctrine is in many respects the same as that of Heraclitus.

This Fire which is forever kindling into flame, and passing into smoke and ashes; this restless, changing flux of things which never *are*, but are ever *becoming;* this he proclaimed to be God, or the One.

Take his beautiful illustration of a river: "No one has ever been twice on the same stream; for different waters are constantly flowing down; it dissipates its waters and gathers them again—it approaches and it recedes—it overflows and falls." This is evidently but a statement of the flux and reflux, as in his aphorism that "all is in motion; there is no rest or quietude." Let us also add here what Ritter says:

"The notion of life implies that of alteration, which by the ancients was generally conceived as motion. The Universal Life is therefore an eternal motion, and therefore tends, as every motion must, towards some end, even though this end, in the course of the evolution of life, present itself to us as a mere transition to some ulterior end. Heraclitus on this ground supposed a certain longing to be inherent in Fire, to gratify which it constantly transformed itself into some determinate form of being, without, however, any wish to maintain it, but in the mere desire of transmuting itself from one form into another. Therefore, to make worlds is Jove's pastime."

He explained phenomena as the concurrence of opposite tendencies and efforts in the motion of the ever-living Fire, out of which results the most beautiful harmony. All is composed of contraries, so that the good is also evil, the living is dead, etc. The harmony of the world is one of conflicting impulses, like that of the lyre and the bow. The strife between opposite tendencies is the parent of all things: πόλεμος πάντων μὲν πατήρ ἐστί πάντων δὲ βασιλεὺς, καὶ τοὺς μὲν θεοὺς ἔδειξε τοὺς δὲ ἀνθρώπους, τοὺς μὲν δούλους ἐποίησε τοὺς δὲ ἐλευθέρους. Nor is this simple metaphor: the strife here spoken of is the splitting in two of that which is in essence one; the contradiction which necessarily lies between the particular and the general, the result and the force, Being and Non-Being. All life is change, and change is strife.

Heraclitus was the first to proclaim the absolute vitality of Nature, the endless change of matter, the mutability and perishability of all individual things, in contrast with the eternal Being, the supreme Harmony which rules over all.

The view we have taken of his doctrines will at once explain the position in which we have placed them. He stands with one foot on the Ionian path, and with the other on the Italian; but his attempt is not to unite these two: his office is negative; he has to criticize both.

§ II. ANAXAGORAS.

Anaxagoras is generally said to have been born at Clazomenæ in Lydia, not far from Colophon. Inheriting from his family a splendid patrimony, he seemed born to figure in the State; but, like Parmenides, he disregarded all such external greatness, and placed his ambition elsewhere. Early in life, so early as his twentieth year, the passion for philosophy engrossed him. Like all young ambitious men, he looked with contempt upon the intellect exhibited in his native city. His soul panted for the capital. The busy activity, and the growing importance of Athens, solicited him. He yearned towards it, as the ambitious youth in a provincial town yearns for London; as all energy longs for a fitting theatre on which to play its part.

He came to Athens. It was a great and stirring epoch. The countless hosts of Persia had been scattered by a handful of resolute men. The political importance of Greece, and of Athens, the Queen of Greece, was growing to a climax. The Age of Pericles, one of the most glorious in the long annals of mankind, was dawning. The Poems of Homer formed the subject of literary conversation, and of silent enjoyment. The early triumphs of Æschylus had created a Drama, such as still remains the wonder and delight of scholars and critics. The young Sophocles, that perfect flower of antique art, was then in his bloom, meditating on that Drama which he was hereafter to bring to perfection in the *Antigone* and the *Œdipus Rex*. The Ionian philosophy had found a home at Athens; and the young Anaxagoras shared his time with Homer and Anaximenes.*

Philosophy soon obtained the supreme place in his affections. The mysteries of the universe tempted him. He yielded himself to the fascination, and declared that the aim and purpose of his life was to contemplate the heavens. All care for his affairs was given up. His estates ran to waste, whilst he was solving problems. But the day he found himself a beggar, he exclaimed, "To Philosophy I owe my worldly ruin, and my soul's prosperity." He commenced teaching, and he had illustrious pupils in Pericles, Euripides, and Socrates.

He was not long without paying the penalty of success. The

---

* By this we no more intimate that he was a *disciple* of Anaximenes (as some historians assert) than that he was a friend of Homer. But in some such ambiguous phrase as that in the text, must the error of calling him the disciple of Anaximenes have arisen. Brucker's own chronology is strangely at variance with his statement: for he places the birth of Anaximenes, 56th Olympiad; that of Anaxagoras, 70th Olympiad: thus making the master fifty-six years old at the birth of the pupil; and the pupil only became such in the middle of his life.

envy and uncharitableness of some, joined to the bigotry of others, caused an accusation of impiety to be brought against him. He was tried, and condemned to death, but owed the mitigation of his sentence into banishment, to the eloquence of his friend and pupil, Pericles. Some have supposed that the cause of his persecution was this very friendship of Pericles; and that the statesman was struck at through the unpopular philosopher. The supposition is gratuitous, and belongs rather to the ingenuity of modern scholarship, than to the sober facts of history. In the persecution of Anaxagoras there is nothing but what was very natural; it occurred afterwards in the case of Socrates, and it has subsequently occurred a thousand times in the history of mankind, as the simple effect of outraged convictions. Anaxagoras attacked the religion of his time: he was tried and condemned for his temerity.

After his banishment he resided in Lampsacus, and there preserved tranquillity of mind until his death. "It is not I who have lost the Athenians; it is the Athenians who have lost me," was his proud reflection. He continued his studies, and was highly respected by the citizens, who, wishing to pay some mark of esteem to his memory, asked him on his death-bed in what manner they could do so. He begged that the day of his death might be annually kept as a holiday in all the schools of Lampsacus. For centuries this request was fulfilled. He died in his seventy-third year. A tomb was erected to him in the city, with this inscription:

> "This tomb great Anaxagoras confines,
> Whose mind explored the heavenly paths of Truth."

His philosophy contains so many contradictory principles, or perhaps it would be more correct to say, so many contradictory principles are attributed to him, that it would be vain to attempt a systematic view of them. We shall, as usual, confine ourselves to leading doctrines.

On the great subject of the origin and certainty of our knowledge, he differed from Xenophanes and Heraclitus. He thought, with the former, that all sense-knowledge is delusive; and, with the latter, that all knowledge comes through the senses. Here is a double skepticism brought into play. It has usually been held that these two opinions contradict each other; that he could not have maintained both. Yet both opinions are tenable. His reason for denying certainty to the senses, was the incapacity of distinguishing all the real objective elements of which things are made. Thus the eye discerns a complex mass which we call a flower; but discerns nothing of that *of which* the flower is composed. In other words, the senses perceive *phenomena*, but do not, and cannot observe *noumena*,*—an anticipation of the greatest discovery of modern psychology, though seen dimly and confusedly by Anaxagoras. Perhaps the most convincing proof of his having so conceived knowledge is in the passage quoted by Aristotle: "Things are to each according as they seem to him" (ὅτι τοιαῦτα αὐτοῖς τὰ ὄντα, οἷα ἂν ὑπολάβωσι). What is this but the assertion of all knowledge being confined to phenomena? It is further strengthened by the passage in Sextus Empiricus, that "phenomena are the criteria of our knowledge of things beyond sense," *i. e.*, things inevident are evident in phenomena (τῆς τῶν ἀδήλων καταλήψεως, τὰ φαινόμενα).

It must not, however, be concluded from the above, that Anaxagoras regarded sense as the sole origin of knowledge. He held that the Reason (λόγος) was the regulating faculty of the mind, as Intelligence (νοῦς) was of the universe. The senses are accurate in their reports; but their reports are not accurate *copies of Things*. They reflect objects; but they reflect them as these objects appear to Sense. Reason has to control these impressions, to verify these reports.

---

* *Noumenon* is the antithesis to *Phenomenon*, which means *Appearance; Noumenon* means the *Substratum*, or, to use the scholastic word, the *Substance*. Thus, as matter is recognized by us only in its manifestations (phenomena), we may logically distinguish those manifestations from the thing manifested (noumenon). And the former will be the *materia circa quam*; the latter, the *materia in quâ*. Noumenon is therefore equivalent to the *Essence*; Phenomenon to the *Manifestation*.

Let us now apply this doctrine to the explanation of some of those apparently contradictory statements which have puzzled all the critics. For instance, Anaxagoras says that snow is not white but black, because the water of which it is composed is black. Now, in this he could not have meant that snow did not *appear* to our senses white; his express doctrine of sense-knowledge forbids such an interpretation. But reason told him that the Senses gave inaccurate reports; and, in this instance, Reason showed him how their report was contradictory, since the water was black, yet the snow white. Here, then, is the whole theory of knowledge exemplified: Sense asserting that snow is white; Reflection asserting that snow being made from black water could not be white. He had another illustration—Take two liquids, white and black, and pour the one into the other drop by drop: the eye will be unable to discern the actual change as it is gradually going on; it will only discern it at certain marked intervals.

Thus did he separate himself at once from Xenophanes and Heraclitus. From the former, because admitting Sense to be the only criterion of things, the only source of knowledge, he could not regard the λόγος as the unfailing source of truth, but merely as the reflective power, whereby the reports of sense were controlled. From the latter, because reflection convinced him that the reports of the senses were *subjectively* true, but *objectively* false.* (Heraclitus maintained that the reports of the senses were alone certain.) Both Xenophanes and Heraclitus had principles of absolute certitude; the one proclaimed Reason, the other Sense, to be that principle. Anaxagoras annihilated the one by showing that the Reason was dependent on the senses for materials; and

---

* Subjective and objective are now almost naturalized: it may not be superfluous, nevertheless, to explain them. The *subject* means the "Mind of the Thinker" (*Ego*), the *object* means the "Thing thought of" (*Non-Ego*). In the above passage "the reports of the senses being subjectively true," means that the senses truly inform us of their *impressions;* but these impressions are not at all like the actual *objects* (as may be shown by the *broken appearance* of a stick, half of which is dipped in water), and therefore the reports are "objectively false."

he annihilated the other by showing that the materials were fallacious.

Having thus, not without considerable difficulty, brought his various opinions on human knowledge under one system, let us endeavor to do the same for his cosmology. The principle of his system is thus announced: "Wrongly do the Greeks suppose that aught begins or ceases to be; for nothing comes into being or is destroyed; but all is an aggregation or secretion of pre-existent things; so that all becoming might more correctly be called becoming-mixed, and all corruption becoming separate." What is the thought here? It is that instead of there being a Creation, there was only an arrangement; instead of one first element, there was an infinite number of elements. These elements are the celebrated *homœomeriæ*:

> "Ex aurique putat micis consistere posse
> Aurum, et de terris terram concrescere parvis;
> Ignibus ex ignem, humorem ex humoribus esse;
> Cætera consimili fingit ratione putatque."*

This singular opinion which maintains that flesh is made of molecules of elementary flesh, and bones of elementary bones, and so forth, is intelligible when we remember his theory of knowledge. The Sense discerns elementary differences in matter, and reflection confirms the truth of this observation. If Nothing can proceed from Nothing, all things can be only an arrangement of existing things; but when in this Arrangement certain things are discovered to be radically distinguished from each other, gold from blood for example,—either the distinction observed by the Senses is altogether false, or else the things distinguished must be elements. But the first horn of the dilemma is avoided by

---

* Lucretius, i. 839.—

> "That gold from parts of the same nature rose,
> That earths do earth, fires fire, airs air compose,
> And so in all things else alike to those."—CREECH.

There seems to be good reason to believe that not Anaxagoras, but Aristotle was the originator of the word *homœomeriæ*. See Ritter, i. 286.

the sensuous nature of all knowledge ; if the Senses deceive us in this respect, and Reason does not indicate the deception, then is knowledge all a delusion; therefore, unless we adopt skepticism, we must abide by the testimony of the Senses, as to the distinction of things. But, having granted the distinction, we must grant that the things distinguished are elements ; if not, whence the distinction ? Nothing can come of Nothing ; blood can only become blood, gold can only become gold, mix them how you will ; if blood can become bone, then does bone become something out of nothing, for it was not bone before, and it is bone now. But, as blood can only be blood, and bone only be bone, whenever they are mingled it is a mingling of two elements, *homœomeriæ*.

In the beginning therefore there was the infinite composed of *homœomeriæ*, or elementary seeds of infinite variety. So far from The All being The One, as Parmenides and Thales equally taught, Anaxagoras proclaimed The All to be The Many. But the mass of elements were as yet unmixed. What was to mix them ? What power caused them to become arranged in one harmonious all-embracing system ?

This power Anaxagoras declared to be Intelligence (νοῦς), the moving force of the Universe. He had, on the one hand, rejected Fate, as an empty name ; on the other, he rejected Chance, as being no more than the Cause unperceived by human reasoning (τὴν τύχην, ἄδηλον αἰτίαν ἀνθρωπίνῳ λογισμῷ). This is another remarkable glimpse of what modern philosophy was to establish. Having thus disclaimed these two powers, so potent in early speculation, Fate and Chance, he had no other course left than to proclaim Intelligence the Arranging Power.*

This seems to us, on the whole, the most remarkable speculation of all the pre-Socratic epoch ; and indeed is so very near the philosophic precision of modern times, that it is with difficulty we

---

* We have his own words reported by Diogenes, who says that his work opened thus : "Formerly all things were a confused mass ; afterwards, Intelligence coming, arranged them into worlds."

preserve its original simplicity. We will cite a portion of the fragment preserved by Simplicius, wherein Intelligence is spoken of:—" Intelligence (νοῦς) is infinite, and autocratic; it is mixed up with nothing, but exists alone in and for itself. Were it otherwise, were it mixed up with any thing, it would participate in the nature of all things; for in all there is a part of all; and so that which was mixed with intelligence would prevent it from exercising power over all things."*—In this passage we have an expression of the modern conception of the Deity acting through invariable laws, but in no way mixed up with the matter acted on.

Will not the foregoing remarks enable us to meet Aristotle's objection to Anaxagoras, that "he uses Intelligence as a machine,† in respect to the formation of the world; so that, when he is embarrassed how to explain the cause of this or that, he introduces Intelligence; but in all other things it is any cause but Intelligence which produces things?" Now, surely this is a very unfair criticism, and could only be valid against one who, like Malebranche, saw God everywhere. Anaxagoras assigned to Intelligence the great Arrangement of the *homœomeriæ*; but of course he supposed that subordinate arrangements were carried on by themselves. The Christian thinker some centuries back believed that the Deity created and ordained all things; nevertheless when he burnt his finger, the cause of the burn he attributed to fire, and not to God; but when the thunder muttered in the sky he attributed that to no cause but God. Is not this similar to the conception formed by Anaxagoras? What he *can* explain, he does explain by natural causes; whatever he is embarrassed to explain, whatever he does not understand, he attrib-

---

* This passage perfectly accords with what Aristotle says, *De Animâ*, i. 2, and *Metaph.* i. 7.

† This is an allusion to the theatrical artifice of bringing down a God from Olympus, to solve the difficulty of the *dénouement*,—the *Deus ex machinâ* of Horace. We make this remark to caution the reader against supposing that the objection is to a mechanical intelligence.

utes to God. It is here we see the force of Anaxagoras's opinion respecting Chance as an unascertained cause: what others called the effect of Chance, he called the effect of the universal Intelligence.

On the same grounds we object to the reasoning of Plato. Those who have read the *Phædo*,—and who has not read it in some shape or other, either in the original diction, or in the dim and misty version of some translator?—those who have read the *Phædo*, we say, will doubtless remember the passage in which Socrates is made to express his poignant disappointment at the doctrine of Anaxagoras, to which he had at first been so attracted. This passage has an air of authenticity. It expresses a real disappointment, and the disappointment of Socrates, not merely of Plato. We believe firmly that Socrates is here expressing his own opinion; and it is rarely that we can say this of opinions promulgated by Plato under the august name of his master. Here is the passage in the misty version of Thomas Taylor: we make no alterations, otherwise we should hold ourselves responsible for the whole:

"But having once heard a person reading from a certain book, composed as he said by Anaxagoras, when he came to that part in which he says that intellect orders and is the cause of all things, I was delighted with this cause, and thought that in a certain respect it was an excellent thing for intellect to be the cause of all; and I considered if this was the case, disposing intellect would adorn all things, and place every thing in that situation in which it would subsist in the best manner. If any one therefore should be willing to discover the cause through which every thing is generated or corrupted, or is, he ought to discover how it may subsist in the best manner, or suffer, or perform any thing else. In consequence of this, therefore, it is proper that a man should consider nothing else, either about himself or about others, except that which is the most excellent and the best; but it is necessary that he who knows this should also know that which is subordinate, since there is one and the same science of both. But thus reasoning with myself, I rejoiced, thinking that I had found a preceptor in Anaxagoras who would instruct me in the causes of things agreeable to my own conceptions; and that he would inform me in the first place whether the earth is flat or round, and afterwards explain the cause of its being so, adducing for this purpose that which is better, and showing that it is better for the earth to exist in this manner. And if he should say that it is situated in the middle, that he would besides this show that it was better for it to be in the middle—and if he should render all this apparent to me, I was so disposed as not to require any other species of cause; for I by no means thought, after he had said that all these were orderly disposed by intellect, he would introduce any other cause for their subsistence except that which shows that it is better for them to exist in this manner. Hence I thought that in rendering the cause common to each particular and to all things, he would explain that which is best for each, and is the common good of all. And indeed I would not have exchanged these hopes for a mighty gain! But having obtained his books with prodigious eagerness, I read them with great celerity, that I might with great celerity know that which is best and that which is base.

"But from this admirable hope, my friend, I was forced away, when in the course of my reading I saw him make no use of intellect, nor employ certain causes for the purpose of orderly disposing particulars, but assign air, ether, and water, and many other things equally absurd, as the causes of things. And he appeared to me to be affected in a manner similar to him who should assert that all the actions of Socrates are produced by intellect; and afterwards, endeavoring to relate the causes of each particular action, should say that I now sit here because, in the first place, my body is composed of bones and nerves, and that the bones are solid and are separated by intervals from each other; but that the nerves, which are by nature capable of intension and remission, cover the bones together with the skin in which they are contained. The bones therefore, being suspended from their joints, the nerves, by straining and relaxing them, enable me to bend my limbs as at present; and through this cause I here sit in an inflected position. And again, should assign other such like causes of my now conversing with you, namely, voice, and air, and hearing, and a thousand other particulars, neglecting the true cause, that since it appeared to the Athenians better to condemn me on this account, it also appeared to me better and more just to sit here, and thus abiding, sustain the punishment which they have ordained me; for otherwise, by the dog, as it appears to me, these bones and nerves would have been carried long ago either into Megara or Bœotia through an opinion of that which is best, if I had not thought it more just and becoming to sustain the punishment ordered by my country, whatever it might be, than to withdraw myself and run away. But to call things of this kind causes is extremely absurd. Indeed, if any one should say that without possessing such things as bones and nerves I could not act as I do, he would speak the truth; but to assert that I act as I do at present through these, and that I operate with this intellect, and not from a choice of what is best, would be an assertion full of extreme negligence and sloth: for this would be the consequence of not being able to collect by division that the true cause of a thing is very different from that without which a cause would not be a cause."

Now this reasoning we take to be an *ignoratio elenchi*. The illustration made use of is nothing to the purpose, and would be admitted by Anaxagoras as true, without in the least impugning his argument.

The Intelligence, which Anaxagoras conceived, was in no wise a moral Intelligence: it was simply the *primum mobile*, the all-knowing and motive force by which the arrangement of the elements was affected. Hence from a passage in Aristotle, some have inferred that the νοῦς was only a physical principle, the sole office of which was to set matter in motion. This is an error easy of explanation. Men are still so accustomed to conceive the divine Intelligence as only a more perfect and exalted human

Intelligence, that where they see no traces of the latter they are prone to question the existence of the former. When Anaxagoras says that *Nous* was the creative principle, men instantly figure to themselves a *Nous* similar to human intelligence. On examination, they find that *such* an intelligence as they conceive has no place in the doctrine, whereupon they declare that Intelligence has no place there; the *Nous*, they aver, means no more than Motion, and might have been called Motion.

But fortunately Simplicius has preserved a long passage from the work of Anaxagoras; we have already quoted a portion of it, and shall now select one or two sentences in which the *Nous*, as a cognitive power, is distinctly set forth; and we quote these the more readily because Ritter, to whom we are indebted for the passage, has not translated it:—" Intelligence is, of all things, the subtlest and purest, and has entire knowledge of all. Every thing which has a soul, whether great or small, is governed by the Intelligence (νοῦς κρατεῖ). Intelligence knows all things (πάντα ἔγνω νοῦς), both those that are mixed and those that are separated; and the things which ought to be, and the things which were, and those which now are, and those which will be; all are arranged by Intelligence (πάντα διεκόσμησε νοῦς*)." Here the creative, or rather disposing, faculty is not more distinctly expressed than the cognitive. The *Nous* both *knows* and *acts:* this is its duplicate existence. A grand conception: one seldom rivalled in ancient speculation; one so far in advance of the epoch as to be a puzzle to all critics.

The relation in which the system of Anaxagoras stands to other systems may be briefly characterized. The Infinite Matter of the Ionians became in his hands the *homœomeriæ*. Instead of one substance, such as Water, Air, or Fire, he saw the necessity of admitting Many substances. At the same time, he carried out

---

* It would be needless after this to refer to the numerous expressions of Aristotle in confirmation. The critical reader will do well to consult *Trendelenburg, Comment. Aristot. de Anim.*, p. 466 *et seq.* Plato, in speaking of the νοῦς, adds καὶ ψυχή.—*Craty.*, p. 400.

the Pythagorean and Eleatic principle of The One; thus avoiding the dialectical thrusts of Zeno against the upholders of The Many. Hegel and M. Cousin would call this eclecticism; and in one sense they would be correct; but inasmuch as Anaxagoras was led to his doctrine by the development which the Ionian and the Eleatic principles had taken, and was not led to it by any eclectical method, we must protest against the application of such a name. There was a truth dimly recognized by the Ionians, namely, that the material phenomena are all reducible to some *noumenon* or *noumena*, some ἀρχή. What that Beginning was, they variously sought. Anaxagoras also sought it; and his doctrine of perception convinced him that it could not be One principle, but Many; hence his *homœomeriæ*. So far he was an Ionian. But there was also a truth dimly seen by the Eleatics, namely, that The Many could never be resolved into One; and as without One there could not be Many, and with the Many only there could not be One; in other words, as God must be The One from whom the multiplicity of things is derived, the necessity of admitting The One as The All and the Self-existent was proved. This reasoning was accepted by Anaxagoras. He saw that there were Many things; he saw also the necessity for The One. In so far he was an Eleatic.

Up to this point the two doctrines had been at variance: a chasm of infinite depth yawned between them. Zeno's invention of Dialectics was a result of this profound difference. It was reserved for Anaxagoras to bridge over the chasm which could not be filled up. He did so with consummate skill. He accepted both doctrines, with some modifications, and proclaimed the existence of the Infinite Intelligence (The One) who was the Architect of the Infinite Matter (*homœomeriæ*, the Many). By this means he escaped each horn of the dilemma; he escaped that which gored the Ionians, namely, as to *how* and *why* the Infinite Matter became fashioned into worlds and beings; since Matter by itself can only be Matter. He escaped that which gored the Eleatics, as to *how* and why the Infinite One, who was pure and unmixed, became the Infinite Many, impure and mixed; since one thing could never be more than one thing. It must have some one thing on which to act, for it cannot act upon itself. Anaxagoras escaped both by his dualistic theory of Mind fashioning, and Matter fashioned.

A similar bridge was thrown by him over the deep chasm separating the Sensualists from the Rationalists, with respect to the origin of knowledge. He admitted both Sense *and* Reason; others had only admitted either Sense *or* Reason.

These two points entitle Anaxagoras to a very high rank in the history of Philosophy; and we regret to see that Aristotle uniformly speaks disparagingly of him, but we believe that the great Stagirite did not clearly apprehend the force of the doctrine he was combating.

§ III. Empedocles.

We are forced to differ from all historians we have consulted, except De Gerando, who hesitates about the matter, respecting the place occupied by Empedocles. Brucker classes him among the Pythagoreans; Ritter, amongst the Eleatics; Zeller and Hegel, as the precursor of the Atomists, who precede Anaxagoras; Renouvier, as the precursor of Anaxagoras; Tennemann placing Diogenes of Apollonia between Anaxagoras and Empedocles, but making Democritus precede them. When we come to treat of the doctrines of Empedocles, we shall endeavor to show the filiation of ideas from Anaxagoras. Meanwhile it is necessary to examine the passage in Aristotle, on which very contradictory opinions have been grounded.

In the 3d chapter of the 1st book of Aristotle's *Metaphysics*, after a paragraph on the system of Empedocles, occurs this passage: "But Anaxagoras of Clazomenæ being superior to him (Empedocles) in respect of age, but inferior to him in respect of opinions, said that the number of principles was infinite." By "*superior*" and "*inferior*" we preserve the antithesis of the original; but it would be more intelligible to say, "*older*" and "*inferior.*"

There are two other interpretations of this passage. One of them is that of M. Cousin (after Hegel), who believes that the antithesis of Aristotle is meant to convey the fact of Anaxagoras, although older in point of time, being more recent in point of published doctrine than Empedocles, having written after him. This is his translation: "Anaxagoras, qui naquit avant ce dernier, mais qui écrivit après lui."

The second is that adopted by M. Renouvier from M. Ravaisson, who interprets it as meaning that the doctrine of Anaxagoras, though more ancient in point of publication, is more recent in point of thought; *i. e.* more developed philosophically, although historically earlier.

Now we believe both these interpretations to be erroneous. There is no ground for them except the antithesis of Aristotle; and the original of this disputed passage is, Ἀναξαγόρας δὲ ὁ Κλαζομένιος τῇ μὲν ἡλικίᾳ πρότερος ὢν τούτου, τοῖς δ' ἔργοις ὕστερος; which is rendered by MM. Pierron and Zévort: "Anaxagore de Clazomène, l'aîné d'Empédocle, *n'était pas arrivé à un système aussi plausible.*"*

This agrees with our version. We confess however that on a first glance M. Cousin's version better preserves the force of the antithesis τῇ μὲν ἡλικίᾳ πρότερος—τοῖς δ' ἔργοις ὕστερος. But other reasons prevent a concurrence in this interpretation. MM. Pierron and Zévort, in their note on the passage, remark: "Mais les mots ἔργῳ, ἔργοις, dans une opposition, ont ordinairement une signification vague, comme *re, revera*, chez les Latins, et, chez nous, *en fait, en réalité.*" The force of the objection does not strike us. If Anaxagoras was *in fact, in reality*, posterior to Empedocles, we can only understand this in the sense M. Cousin has understood Aristotle; and moreover, MM. Pierron and Zévort here contradict their translation, which says that, in point

---

* *La Métaphysique d'Aristote*, i. 238.

of fact, the system of Anaxagoras was not so plausible as that of Empedocles.

More weight must be laid on the meaning of ὕστερος, which certainly cannot be exclusively taken to mean posterior in point of time. In the 11th chapter of Aristotle's 5th book he treats of all the significations of πρότερος and ὕστερος. One of these significations is superiority and inferiority. In the sense of inferiority ὕστερος is often used by the poets. Thus Sophocles:

>'Ὦ μιαρὸν ἦθος, καὶ γυναικὸς ὕστερον!
>
>"O shameful character, below a woman!"

"Inferior" is the primitive meaning; in English we say, "second to none," for "inferior to none."

This meaning of ὕστερος, namely, of inferiority, is the one always understood by the old commentators on the passage in question; none of them understood a chronological posteriority. Πρότερος indicates priority in point of time; ὕστερος inferiority in point of merit. Thus Philoponus: "Prior quidem tempore, sed posterior et mancus secundum opinionem" (fol. 2 a); and the anonymous scholiast of the Vatican MS.: πρότερος γοῦν τῷ χρόνῳ, ἀλλ' ὕστερος καὶ ἐλλείπων κατὰ τὴν δόξαν—"first indeed in time, but second *and inferior* in point of doctrine."

The only question which now remains to be answered in order to establish the truth of the foregoing interpretation of ὕστερος, is this: Did Aristotle regard the system of Anaxagoras as *inferior* to that of Empedocles?

This question we can answer distinctly in the affirmative. The reader will remember our citation of the passage in which Aristotle blames Anaxagoras for never employing his First Cause (Intelligence) except upon emergencies. Aristotle continues thus: "Empedocles *employs his causes more abundantly*, though not indeed sufficiently,—Καὶ Ἐμπεδοκλῆς ἐπὶ πλέον μὲν τούτῳ χρῆται τοῖς αἰτίοις, οὐ μὴ οὔτε ἱκανῶς.—*Met.* i. 4.

Chronology is moreover in favor of our view. Anaxagoras was born about the 70th Olympiad; Empedocles, by general consent, is said to have flourished in the 84th Olympiad; this would make Anaxagoras at least fifty-six years old at the time when Empedocles published his doctrine, after which age it is barely probable that Anaxagoras would have begun to write; and even this probability vanishes when we look upon the life of Anaxagoras, who was teaching in Athens about the 76th or 77th Olympiad, and who died at Lampsacus, in exile, in the 88th Olympiad, viz. sixteen years after the epoch in which Empedocles is said to have flourished.

Trusting that the above point was not unworthy of brief discussion, we will now commence the narrative.

Empedocles was born at Agrigentum, in Sicily, and flourished about the 84th Olympiad (B. C. 444). Agrigentum was at that period at the height of its splendor, and was a formidable rival to Syracuse. Empedocles, descended from a wealthy and illustrious family, acquired a high reputation by his resolute espousal of the democratic party. Much of his wealth is said to have been spent in a singular but honorable manner: namely, in bestowing dowries on poor girls, and marrying them to young men of rank and consequence. Like most of the early philosophers, he is supposed to have been a great traveller, and to have gathered in distant lands the wondrous store of knowledge which he displayed. It was assumed that only in the far East could he have learned the potent secrets of Medicine and Magic; only from the Egyptian Magi could he have learned the art of prophecy.

It is probable, however, that he did travel into Italy, and to Athens. But in truth we can mention little of his personal history that is not open to question. His name rivals that of Pythagoras in the regions of fable. The same august majesty of demeanor and the same marvellous power over nature are attributed to both. Miracles were his pastimes. In prophecy, in medicine, in power over the winds and rains, his wonders were so numerous and so renowned, that when he appeared at the Olympic Games all eyes were reverentially fixed upon him. His dress and demeanor accorded with his reputation. Haughty impassioned, and eminently disinterested in character, he refused the government of Agrigentum when freely offered him by the citizens; but his love of distinction showed itself in priestly garments, a golden girdle, the Delphic crown, and a numerous train of attendants. He proclaimed himself to be a God whom men and women reverently adored. But we must not take this literally: he probably only "assumed by anticipation an honor which he promised all soothsayers, priests, physicians, and princes of the people."

Fable has also taken advantage of the mystery which overhangs his death, to create out of it various stories of marvel. One relates that, after a sacred festival, he was drawn up to heaven in a splendor of celestial effulgence. Another, and more popular one is, that he threw himself headlong into the crater of Mount Ætna, in order that he might pass for a God, the cause of his death being unknown; but one of his brazen sandals, thrown out in an eruption, revealed the secret.

A similar uncertainty exists as to his Teachers and his Writings. Pythagoras, Parmenides, Xenophanes, and Anaxagoras have all been positively named as his Teachers. Unless we understand the word Teachers in a figurative sense, we must absolutely reject these statements. Diogenes Laertius, who reports them, does so in his dullest manner, with an absence of criticism remarkable even in him.* Considering that there was, at least, one hundred and forty years between Pythagoras and Empedocles, we need no further argument to disprove any connection between them.

Diogenes, on the authority of Aristotle (as he says), attributes to Empedocles the invention of Rhetoric; and Quinctilian (iii. c. 1) has repeated the statement. We have no longer the work of Aristotle; but, as Ritter says, the assertion must have arisen from a misunderstanding, or have been said in jest by Aristotle, because Empedocles was the teacher of Gorgias: most likely

---

* Diogenes is one of the stupidest of the stupid race of compilers. His work is useful, because containing occasional extracts, but can rarely be relied on for any thing else.

from a misunderstanding, since Sextus Empiricus mentions Aristotle as having said that Empedocles first *incited*, or *gave an impulse* to Rhetoric.* Aristotle, in his *Rhetoric*, declares that Corax and Tisias were the first to publish a written Treatise on Eloquence. We feel the less hesitation in rejecting the statement of Diogenes, because in the very passage which succeeds he is guilty of a very gross misquotation of Aristotle, who, as he says, "in his book of *The Poets* speaks of Empedocles as Homeric, powerful in his eloquence, rich in metaphors, and other poetical figures."† Now this work of Aristotle on the Poets is fortunately extant, and it proclaims the very reverse of what Diogenes alleges. Here is the passage:—"Custom, indeed, connecting the *poetry* or *making* with the *metre*, has denominated some elegiac poets, others epic poets: thus distinguishing poets, not according to the nature of their imitation, but according to that of their metre only; for even they who composed treatises of Medicine, or Natural Philosophy in verse, are denominated *Poets: yet Homer and Empedocles have nothing in common except their metre;* the former, therefore, justly merits the name of *Poet;* the other should rather be called a *Physiologist* than a Poet."‡

It is, indeed, quite possible that Diogenes may have had before him a book περὶ ποιητῶν, perhaps one of the many spurious treatises current under Aristotle's name; but it is not probable that Aristotle would have expressed an opinion so contrary to the one given in his authentic work.

The diversity of opinion, with respect to the position of Empedocles, indicated at the opening of this Chapter, is not without significance. That men such as Hegel, Ritter, Zeller, and Tennemann should see reasons for different classification, cannot be without importance to the Historian. Their arguments destroy each other; but it does not therefore follow that they all build upon false grounds. Each view has a certain truth in it; but, not being the whole truth, it cannot prevail. The cause of the

---

* Πρῶτον κεκινηκέναι.—*Adv. Mat.* vii.
† *Diog. Laert.* lib. viii. c. ii. § 2, p. 57. ‡ *De Poet.* c. i.

difference seems to be this: Empedocles has something of the Pythagorean, Eleatic, Heraclitic, and Anaxagorean systems in his system; so that each historian, detecting one of these elements, and omitting to give due importance to the others, has connected Empedocles with the system to which that one element belongs. Ritter and Zeller have, however, been aware of some of the complex relations of the doctrine, but failed, we think, in giving it its true position.

Respecting human knowledge, Empedocles belongs partly to the Eleatics. With them, he complained of the imperfection of the Senses; and looked for truth only in Reason, which is partly human and partly divine: it is partly clouded by the senses. The divine knowledge is opposed to sensuous knowledge; for men cannot approach the divine, neither can he seize it with the hand nor the eye. Hence Empedocles conjoined the duty of contemplating God in the mind. But he appears to have proclaimed the existence of this divine knowledge without attempting to determine its relation to human knowledge. In this respect he resembles rather Xenophanes than Parmenides.*

We have no clear testimony of his having studied the works of Anaxagoras; but, if we had, it might not be difficult to explain his inferior theory of knowledge; for, in truth, the theory of Anaxagoras was too far in advance of the age to be rightly apprehended. Empedocles, therefore, adhered to the Eleatic theory. With Xenophanes, he bewailed the delusion of the senses and experience. Listen to his lament:

> "Swift-fated and conscious, how brief is life's pleasureless portion!
> Like the wind-driven smoke, they are carried backwards and forwards,
> Each trusting to naught save what his experience vouches,
> On all sides distracted; yet wishing to find out the whole truth,
> In vain; neither by eye nor ear perceptible to man,
> *Nor to be grasped by mind:* and thou, when thus thou hast wandered,
> Wilt find that no further reaches the knowledge of mortals."

---

* Having quoted Aristotle's testimony of the sensuous nature of knowledge in the Empedoclean theory, we need only here refer to it; adding that, in this respect, Empedocles ranks with Parmenides rather than with Xenophanes.

These verses seem to indicate a skepticism of Reason as well as of the Senses; but other passages show that he upheld the integrity of Reason, which he thought was only prevented from revealing the whole truth because it was imprisoned in the body. Mundane existence was, in his system, the doom of such immortal souls as had been disgraced from Heaven. The Fall of Man he thus distinctly enunciated:

> "This is the law of Fate, of the Gods an olden enactment,
> If with guilt or murder a Dæmon* polluteth his members,
> Thrice ten thousand years must he wander apart from the blessed.
> Hence, doomed I stray, a fugitive from Gods and an outcast,
> To raging strife submissive."

But he had some more philosophical ground to go upon when he wished to prove the existence of Reason and of the Divine Nature. He maintained that like could only be known by like: through earth we learn the earth, through fire we learn fire, through strife we learn strife, and through love we learn love. If, therefore,† like could only be known by like, the Divine could only be known by Divine Reason; and, inasmuch as the Divine is recognized by man, it is a proof that the Divine exists. Knowledge and Existence mutually imply each other.

Empedocles resembles Xenophanes also in his attacks on anthropomorphism. God, he says, has neither head adjusted to limbs, like human beings, nor legs, nor hands:

> "He is, wholly and perfectly, mind ineffable, holy,
> With rapid and swift-glancing thought pervading the whole world."

We may compare these verses with the line of Xenophanes—

> "Without labor he ruleth all things by reason and insight."

---

* An immortal soul.

† We are here thinking for Empedocles; we have no other authority for this statement, than that something of the kind is wanting to make out a plausible explanation of what is only implied in the fragments extant. The fragments tell us that he believed in Reason as the transcendent faculty; and also that Reason did in some way recognize the Divine. All we have done is to supply the link wanting.

Thus far Empedocles belonged to the Eleatics. The traces of Pythagoras are fewer; for we cannot regard as such all those analogies which the ingenuity of some critics has detected.* In his life, and in his moral precepts, there is a strong resemblance to Pythagoras; but in his philosophy we see none beyond metempsychosis, and the consequent abstinence from animal food.

Heraclitus had said there was nothing but a perpetual flux of things, that the whole world of phenomena was as a flowing river, ever-changing yet apparently the same. Anaxagoras had also said that there was no creation of elements, but only an arrangement. Empedocles was now to amalgamate these views. "Fools!" he exclaims,

"Who think aught can begin to be which formerly was not,
Or, that aught which is, can perish and utterly decay.†
Another truth I now unfold: no natural birth
Is there of mortal things, nor death's destruction final;
Nothing is there but *a mingling, and then a separation of the mingled,*
Which are called a birth and death by ignorant mortals."‡

So distinct a relationship as these verses manifest towards both Heraclitus and Anaxagoras will account for the classification adopted by Hegel, Zeller, and Renouvier; at the same time it gives greater strength to our opinion of Empedocles as the successor of these two.

The differences are, however, as great as the resemblances. Having asserted that all things were but a mingling and a separation, he must have admitted the existence of certain primary elements, which were the materials mingled.

Heraclitus had affirmed Fire to be both the principle and the element; both the moving, mingling force, and the mingled matter. Anaxagoras, with great logical consistency, affirmed that the primary elements were *homœomeriæ*, since nothing could

---

* See them noticed in Zeller, *Philos. der Griechen*, pp. 169–173 (1845).

† Compare Anaxagoras, as quoted above: "Wrongly do the Greeks suppose that aught begins or ceases to be."

‡ Compare Anaxagoras: "So that all-becoming might more properly be called becoming mixed, and all-corruption becoming separate."

proceed from nothing, and whatever was arranged must, therefore, be an arrangement of primary elements. Empedocles affirmed that the primary elements were four, viz. Earth, Air, Fire, and Water: out of these all other things proceed; all things are but the various minglings of these four.

Now, that this is an advance on both the preceding conceptions will scarcely be denied; it bears indubitable evidence of being a later conception, and a modification of its antecedents. Nevertheless, although superior as a physiological view, it has not the logical consistency of the view maintained by Anaxagoras; for, as Empedocles taught that like can only be known by like, *i. e.* that existence and knowledge were identical and mutually implicative, he ought to have maintained that whatever is recognized by the mind as distinct, must be distinct *in esse*.

With respect to the Formative Power, we see the traces of Heraclitus and Anaxagoras in about the same proportion. Heraclitus maintained that Fire was impelled by *irresistible Desire* to *transform itself* into some determinate existence. Anaxagoras maintained that the infinite Intelligence was the great Architect who arranged all the material elements, the Mind that controlled and fashioned Matter. The great distinction between these two systems is, that the Fire transforms itself, the *Nous* transforms something which is radically different from itself. Both these conceptions were amalgamated by Empedocles. He taught that Love was the creative power. Wherever there is a mixture of different elements, Love is exerted.

Here we see the Desire of Heraclitus sublimed into its highest expression, and the *Nous* of Anaxagoras reduced to its moral expression, Love. The difficulties of the Heraclitean doctrine, namely, as to how Fire can ever become any thing *different* from Fire, are avoided by the adoption of the Anaxagorean dualism; while the difficulties of the Anaxagorean doctrine, namely, as to how the great Arranger was moved and incited to arrange the primary elements, are in some measure avoided by the natural desire of Love (Aphrodite).

But there was a difficulty still to be overcome. If Love was the creator, that is, the Mingler, what caused separation? To explain this, he had recourse to Hate. As the perfect state of supramundane existence was Harmony, the imperfect state of mundane existence was Discord. Love was, therefore, the Formative Principle, and Hate the Destructive. Hence he said that

"All the members of God war together, one after the other."

This is but the phrase of Heraclitus, "Strife is the parent of all things." It is nevertheless most probable that Empedocles regarded Hate as only a mundane power, as only operating on the theatre of the world, and nowise disturbing the abode of the Gods.* For, inasmuch as man is a fallen and perverted God, doomed to wander on the face of the earth, sky-aspiring, but sense-clouded; so may Hate be only perverted Love, struggling through space. Does not this idea accord with what we know of his opinions? His conception of God, that is, of the One, was that of a "sphere in the bosom of harmony fixed, in calm rest, gladly rejoicing." This quiescent sphere, which is Love, exists above and around the moved World. Certain points are loosened from the combination of the elements, but the unity established by Love continues. Ritter is convinced that "Hate has only power over the smaller portion of existence, over that part which, disconnecting itself from the whole, contaminates itself with crime, and thereby devolves to the errors of mortals."

Our account of Empedocles will be found to vary considerably from that in Aristotle; but our excuse is furnished by the great Stagirite himself, who is constantly telling us that Empedocles gave no reasons for his opinions. Moreover, Aristotle makes us aware that his own interpretation is open to question; for he says, that this interpretation can only be obtained by pushing the premises of Empedocles to their legitimate conclusions; a process which destroys all historical integrity, for what thinker *does* push his premises to their utmost limits?

---

* An opinion subsequently put forth by Plato in the *Phædrus*.

§ IV. Democritus.

The laughing Philosopher, the traditional antithesis to Heraclitus, was born at Abdera (the new settlement of the Teians after their abandonment of Ionia), in the 80th Olympiad (B. C. 460) His claim to the title of Laugher, ὁ γελασῖνος, has been disputed, and by moderns generally rejected. Perhaps the native stupidity of his countrymen, who were renowned for abusing the privilege of being stupid, afforded him incessant matter for laughter. Perhaps he was by nature satirical, and thought ridicule the test of truth. He was of a noble and wealthy family, so wealthy that it entertained Xerxes at Abdera. Xerxes in recompense left some of his Magi to instruct the young Democritus. Doubtless it was their tales of the wonders of their native land, and the deep unspeakable wisdom of their priests, which inspired him with the passion for travel. "I, of all men," he says, "of my day, have travelled over the greatest extent of country, exploring the most distant lands; most climates and regions have I visited, and listened to the most experienced and wisest of men; and in the calculations of line-measuring no one hath surpassed me, not even the Egyptians, amongst whom I sojourned five years." In travel he spent his patrimony; but he exchanged it for an amount of knowledge which no one had previously equalled.

The Abderites, on his return, looked on him with vague wonder. The sun-burnt traveller brought with him knowledge which, to them, must have appeared divine. He exhibited a few samples of his lore, foretold unexpected changes in the weather, and was at once exalted to the summit of that power to which it is a nation's pride to bow. He was offered political supremacy, but wisely declined it.

It would be idle to detail here the various anecdotes which tradition hands down respecting him. They are mostly either impossible or improbable. That, for instance, of his having put out his eyes with a burning-glass, in order that he might be more perfectly and undisturbedly acquainted with his reason, is in violent contradiction to his theory of the eye being one of the great inlets to the soul. Tradition is less questionable in its account of his having led a quiet, sober life, and of his dying at a very advanced age. More we cannot credit.

Respecting his Philosophy there is some certain evidence; but it has been so variously interpreted, and is in many parts so obscure, that historians have been at a loss to give it its due position in relation to other systems. Reinhold, Brandis, Marbach, and Hermann view him as an Ionian; Buhle and Tennemann, as an Eleatic; Hegel, as the successor of Heraclitus, and the predecessor of Anaxagoras; Ritter, as a Sophist; and Zeller, as the precursor of Anaxagoras. Of all these attempts at classification, that by Ritter seems to me the worst. Because Democritus has an occasional phrase implying great vanity—and those mentioned by Ritter seem to us to imply nothing of the kind—he is said to be a Sophist!

Democritus is distinguished from the Ionians by the denial of all sensible *quality* to the primary elements; from the Eleatics by his affirmation of the existence of a multiplicity of elements; from Heraclitus on the same ground; from Anaxagoras, as we shall see presently; and from Empedocles, by denying the Four Elements, and the Formative Love. All these differences are radical. The resemblances, such as they are, may have been coincidences, or derived from one or two of the later thinkers: Parmenides and Anaxagoras, for example.

What did Democritus teach? This question we will endeavor to answer somewhat differently from other historians; but our answer shall be wholly grounded on precise and certain data, with no other originality than that of developing the system from its central principles.

To commence with Knowledge, and with the passage of Aristotle, universally accredited, though variously interpreted: "Democritus says, that either nothing is true, or what is true is not evident to us. Universally in his system, the sensation constitutes the thought, and as at the same time it is but a change [in the sentient being], the sensible phenomena (*i. e. sensations*) are of necessity true."* This pregnant passage means, I think, that sensation, inasmuch as it is sensation, must be true: that is, true *subjectively;* but sensation, inasmuch as it is sensation, cannot be true *objectively.* M. Renouvier thinks that Democritus was the first to introduce this distinction; but our readers will remember that it was the distinction established by Anaxagoras. Sextus Empiricus quotes the very words of Democritus: "The sweet exists only *in form*, the bitter *in form*, the hot *in form*, the cold *in form*, color *in form;* but in *causal reality* (αἰτίη)† only atoms and space exist. The sensible things which are supposed by opinion to exist have no real existence, but only atoms and space exist."‡ When he says that sweetness, heat, color, etc., exist *in form* only, he means that they are *sensible images constantly emanating from things;* a notion we shall explain presently. A little further on, Sextus reports the opinion, that we only perceive that *which falls in upon us* according to the disposition of our bodies; all else is hidden from us.

Neither Condillac nor Destutt de Tracy has more distinctly identified sensation and thought, than in the above passages. But Democritus does so in the spirit of Kant rather than that of Condillac; for, although with the latter he would say, "Penser, c'est sentir," yet he would with the former draw the distinction between phenomenal and noumenal perception.

But did sensation constitute all knowledge? Was there nothing to guide man but the reports of his senses? Democritus said there was *Reflection.*§

This Reflection was not the source of absolute truth, but ful-

---

* 'Ήτοι οὐθὲν εἶναι ἀληθὲς ἢ ἡμῖν γ' ἄδηλον. *Ὅλως δὲ διὰ τὸ ὑπολαμβάνειν φρόνησιν μὲν τὴν αἴσθησιν ταύτην δ' εἶναι ἀλλοίωσιν, τὸ φαινόμενον κατὰ τὴν αἴσθησιν ἐξ ἀνάγκης ἀληθὲς εἶναι.—Metaph.* iv. 5.

† Modern editors read ἐτεῇ, "in reality." We are inclined however to preserve the old reading, as more antithetical to νόμῳ.

‡ *Adv. Mathem.* vii. 163.

§ Διάνοια: etymology, no less than psychology, justifies this translation.

filled a *controlling* office, and established certitude, as far as there could be certitude in human knowledge. And the existence of this Reflection was asserted very much in the style of the celebrated addition to the aphorism, "Nothing is in the Mind which was not previously in the Senses," when Leibnitz added, "except the Mind itself." Democritus, aware that most of our conceptions are derived through the senses, was also aware that many of them were utterly independent, and in defiance of the Senses. Thus the "infinitely small" and the "infinitely great" escape Sense, but are affirmed by Reflection. So also the *atoms* which his Reason told him were the primary elements of things, he could never have known by Sense.

Thus far we have seen Democritus only as the inheritor of Anaxagoras; but the epoch we are now considering was distinguished by the greater attention bestowed on the origin of knowledge, and we may reasonably expect that Democritus had devoted considerable thought to the subject, and had originated some view of his own.

He was not content with the theory of Anaxagoras. There were difficulties which remained unsolved by it; which, indeed, had never been appreciated. This was the grand problem Democritus set himself to solve: *How do we perceive external things?* It is no answer to say that we perceive them by the senses. This is no better an explanation than that of the occult quality of opium, given by Molière's physician: "L'opium endormit parce qu'il a une vertu soporifique." The question arises—*How is it that the senses perceive?*

No one had asked this question; to have asked it, was to form an era in the history of Philosophy. Men began by reasoning on the reports of the senses, unsuspicious of error; when they saw any thing, they concluded that what they saw existed, and existed *as* they saw it. Afterwards came others who began to question the accuracy of the senses. Lastly, came those who denied that accuracy altogether, and pronounced the reports to be mere delusions. Thus the question forced itself on the mind of Democritus—In what manner could the senses perceive external things? Once settle the *modus operandi*, and then the real efficacy of the senses may be estimated.

The hypothesis by which he attempted to explain perception was both ingenious and bold; and many centuries elapsed before a better one was suggested. He supposed that all things were constantly throwing off images of themselves (εἴδωλα,) which, after assimilating to themselves the surrounding air, enter the soul by the pores of the sensitive organ. The eye, for example, is composed of aqueous humors; and water sees. But how does water see? It is diaphanous, and receives the image of whatever is presented to it.

This is a very rude and material hypothesis; but did not philosophers, for centuries, believe that their senses received *impressions* of things? and did they not suppose that *images* of things were reflected in the mind? This latter hypothesis is, perhaps, less obviously fantastic and gratuitous; but it is also less tenable; for how is it that the mind becomes a mirror reflecting the images? The hypothesis stands as much in need of explanation as the phenomenon it pretends to explain.

The hypothesis of Democritus, once admitted, serves its purpose; at least, to a considerable extent. Only the external surface of a body is thrown off in the shape of an εἴδωλον or *image*, and even that only imperfectly and obscurely. The figure thrown off is not a perfect image of the object throwing it off. It is only an image of the external form, and is subject to variations in its passage to the mind. This being the case, the strictly *phenomenal* nature of all knowledge is accurately exhibited. The idols or images, being themselves imperfect, our knowledge is necessarily imperfect.

With this theory of knowledge how could he answer the other, greater, question of Creation? It is said that he rejected The One of the Eleatics, The four of Empedocles, and the *Ho-*

homœomeriæ of Anaxagoras, and declared *Atoms*, invisible and intangible, to be the primary elements; and that all things were but modes of one of the triple arrangements, namely, *configuration, combination,* and *position.* The atom, being indivisible, is necessarily *one;* and, being one, is necessarily self-existent. By this hypothesis, therefore, Democritus satisfied the demands of those who declared that the self-existent must be One; and of those who declared that there were many things existing, and that the One could never be more than the One, never become the Many. He amalgamated the Ionian and Eleatic schools in his speculation, correcting both. He, doubtless, derived this idea from the *homœomeriæ* of Anaxagoras; or, as those who place Anaxagoras later than Democritus would say, originated this idea. It becomes a question, therefore, which of these speculations bears the impress of greater maturity. On this question we cannot hesitate to pronounce. The idea of *homœomeriæ* betrays its more primitive nature in this—it attributes *positive* qualities to atoms, which qualities are not changed or affected by combination or arrangement. The idea of the *atom* divested of all quality, and only assuming that quality as phenomenal when in combination with other atoms, and changing its quality with every change of combination, is indubitably a far more scientific speculation; it is also obviously later in point of development.

From the axiom that only "like can act upon like," Anaxagoras formed his *homœomeriæ*. Democritus accepted the axiom, but gave it a wider application. If only like can act upon like, said he, then must all things be alike *in esse;* and the only differences are those of phenomena, *i. e.* of manifestation; these depend on combination and arrangement.

Atomism is homœomerianism stripped of qualities. It is therefore the system of Anaxagoras greatly improved.

The Atomism of Democritus has not been sufficiently appreciated as a speculation. It is one of the profoundest yet reached by human subtlety. Leibnitz, many centuries afterwards, was led to a doctrine essentially similar; his celebrated "Monadologie" is but Atomism, with a new terminology. Leibnitz called his Monad a *force*, which to him was the *prima materia*. So also Democritus denied that atoms had any weight; they had only force, and it was the impulsion given by superior force which constituted weight. It is worthy of remark that not only did these thinkers concur in their doctrine of atomism, but also, as we have seen, in their doctrine of the origin of knowledge: a coincidence which gives weight to the supposition that in both minds one doctrine was dependent on the other.

From what has already been said, the reader may estimate Ritter's assertion, that it would be in vain to seek for any profounder view in the theory of Democritus than that common to all mechanical physicists who sought to reduce every thing to mathematical conceptions: an assertion as preposterous as that which follows it, namely, that Democritus arrived at his atomic theory in the same way as modern physicists,—from a bias for the mechanical consideration of Nature. Ritter here contradicts himself. Having first declared that there was nothing in the Democritian theory but what the Ionians had previously discovered, he next declares that this theory is the same as that of the modern atomic theory. We are puzzled to which decision we shall award the palm of historical misconception. The modern atomic theory is the *law of definite proportions;* the ancient theory is merely the *affirmation of indefinite combinations.* Between these two conceptions there is precisely the difference between Positive Science and Philosophy. Instead of being similar conceptions, they were neither arrived at in the same way, nor have they the same signification.

Attempts have been made, from certain expressions attributed to Democritus, to deduce an Intelligence, somewhat similar to that in the Anaxagorean doctrine, as the Formative Principle. But the evidence is so small and so questionable, that we refrain from pronouncing on it. Certain it is that he attributed the formation of things to Destiny; but whether that Destiny was intelligent or not is uncertain.

In conclusion, we may observe that his system was an advance on that of his predecessors. In the two great points of psychology and physics, which we have considered at length, it is impossible to mistake a very decided progress, as well as the opening of a new line in each department.

THIRD EPOCH.

INTELLECTUAL CRISIS.—THE INSUFFICIENCY OF ALL ATTEMPTS TOWARDS A SOLUTION OF THE PROBLEM OF EXISTENCE, AS WELL AS THAT OF KNOWLEDGE, PRODUCES THE SOPHISTS.

CHAPTER I.

THE SOPHISTS.

§ I. WHAT WERE THEY?

THE Sophists are a much calumniated race. That they should have been so formerly is not surprising; that they should be so still, is an evidence that historical criticism is yet in its infancy. In raising our voices to defend them we are aware of the paradox; but looked at nearly, the paradox is greater on the side of those who credit and repeat the traditional account. In truth, we know of few charges so unanimous, yet so paradoxical, as that brought against the Sophists.* It is as if mankind had consented to judge of Socrates by the representation of him in *The Clouds*. The caricature of Socrates by Aristophanes is quite as near the

---

* It is proper to state that the novel view of the position and character of the Sophists advanced in this Chapter was published five years before the admirable Chapter of Mr. Grote's *History of Greece*, wherein that erudite and thoughtful writer brings his learning and sagacity to the most thorough elucidation of the question it has yet received. In claiming priority in this point of historical criticism, it is right for me to acknowledge that Mr. Grote substantiates his view with overwhelming force of argument and citation; and in revising the present Chapter, I have been much indebted to his criticisms and citations.

truth as the caricature of the Sophists by Plato;* with this difference, that in the one case it was inspired by political, in the other by speculative antipathy.

On the Sophists we have only the testimony of antagonists; and the history of mankind clearly proves that the enmities which arise from difference of race and country are feeble compared with the enmities which arise from difference of creed: the former may be lessened by contact and intercourse; the latter are only aggravated. Plato had every reason to dislike the Sophists and their opinions; he therefore lost no occasion of ridiculing the one and misrepresenting the other. And it is worthy of especial remembrance that this hostility was peculiarly Platonic, and *not* Socratic; for, as Mr. Grote reminds us, there is no such marked antithesis between Socrates and the Sophists in the biographical work of Xenophon. Plato, however, and those who followed Plato, misrepresented the Sophists, as in all ages antagonists have misrepresented each other.

The Sophists were wealthy; the Sophists were powerful; the Sophists were dazzling, rhetorical, and not profound. Interrogate human nature—above all, the nature of philosophers—and ask what will be the sentiment entertained respecting these Sophists by their rivals. Ask the solitary thinker what is his opinion of the showy, powerful, but shallow rhetorician who usurps the attention of the world. The man of convictions has at all times a superb contempt for the man of mere oratorical or dialectical display. The thinker knows that the world is ruled by Thought; yet he sees Expression gaining the world's attention. He knows, perhaps, that he has within him thoughts pregnant with human welfare; yet he sees the giddy multitude intoxicated with the enthusiasm excited by some plausible fallacy, clothed in enchanting language. He sees through the fallacy, but cannot make others as clear-sighted. His warning is unheeded; his wisdom is spurned; his ambition is frustrated: the popular Idol is carried

---

* See in particular that amusing dialogue, the *Euthydemus*, which is quite as exaggerated as Aristophanes.

onward in triumph. The neglected thinker would not be human if he bore this with equanimity. He does not. He is loud and angry in lamenting the fate of a world that can so be led; loud and angry in his contempt of one who could so lead it. Should he become the critic or historian of his age, what exactness ought we to expect in his account of the popular idol?

Somewhat of this kind was the relation in which the Sophists and Philosophers stood to each other.

The Sophists were hated by some because they were powerful, by others because shallow; and were misrepresented by all. In later times their antagonism to Socrates has brought them ill-will; and this ill-will was strengthened by the very prejudice of the name. Could a Sophist be other than a cheat and a liar? As well ask, could a Devil be other than Evil? In the name of Sophist all odious qualities are implied, and this implication perverts our judgment. Call the Sophists Professors of Rhetoric, which is their truest designation, and then examine their history; it will produce a very different impression.

Much discussion has been devoted to the meaning of the word Sophist, and to the supposed condemnation it everywhere carried " A Sophist, in the genuine sense of the word, was a wise man, a clever man, one who stood prominently before the public as distinguished for intellect or talent of some kind. Thus Solon and Pythagoras are both called Sophists; Thamyras, the skilful bard, is called a Sophist; Socrates is so denominated, not merely by Aristophanes, but by Æschines. Aristotle himself calls Aristippus, and Xenophon calls Antisthenes, both of them disciples of Socrates, by that name. Xenophon, in describing a collection of instructive books, calls them the writings of the old poets and Sophists. Plato is alluded to as a Sophist even by Isocrates; Isocrates himself was harshly criticised as a Sophist, and defends both himself and his profession. Lastly, Timon, who bitterly satirized all the philosophers, designated them all, including Plato and Aristotle, by the general name of Sophists."* This proves

---

* Grote, viii. 480.

the vagueness with which the term was employed: a like discrepancy might be detected in the modern use of the word "metaphysician," which is a term of honor or reproach, according to the speaker. Zeller says that the specific name of Sophist at first merely designated one who taught philosophy for pay. The philosophy might be good or bad; the characteristic designated by the epithet Sophistical was its demand of money-fees. The narrower meaning was given it by Plato and Aristotle.* It matters little, however, what was the meaning attached to the name. Even were it proved that "Sophist" was as injurious in those days as "Socialist" in our own, it would no more prove that the Sophists really taught the doctrines attributed to them, than the mingled terror and detestation with which "Socialist doctrines" are described in almost all modern journals, pamphlets, speeches, and reviews, prove that the Socialists really teach what is there imputed to them.

We said it was a paradox to maintain that the Sophists really promulgated the opinions usually attributed to them; and by this we mean that not only are some of those opinions nothing but caricatures of what was really maintained, but also that, in our interpretation of the others, we grossly err, by a confusion of Christian with Heathen views of morality. Moderns cannot help regarding as fearfully immoral, ideas which by the Greeks were regarded as moral, or at least as not disreputable. For instance: the Greek orators are always careful to impress upon their audience, that in bringing a charge against any one they are actuated by the strongest personal motives; that they have been injured by the accused; that they have good honest hatred as a motive for accusing him. Can any thing be more opposite to Christian feeling? A Christian accuser is just as anxious to extricate himself from any charge of being influenced by personal considerations, as the Greek was of making the contrary evident. A Christian seeks to place his motive to the account of abstract justice; and his statement would be received with great suspicion

---

* *Philosophie der Griechen*, erster Theil, 1856, p. 750.

were it known that a personal feeling prompted it. The reason of this difference is, that the Christian Ethics do not countenance vengeance; the Greek Ethics not only countenanced vengeance, but very much reprobated *informers:* consequently, whoever made an accusation had to clear himself from the ignominy of being an informer, and to do so he showed his personal motives.

This example will prepare the reader to judge, without precipitancy, the celebrated boast attributed to the Sophists, that they could "make the worse appear the better reason." This was said to be the grand aim of their endeavors. This was called their avowed object. To teach this art, it is said, they demanded enormous sums; and to learn it enormous sums were readily given, and given by many.

These assertions are severally false. We will take the last first. It is not true that enormous sums were demanded. Isocrates affirms that their gains were never very high, but had been maliciously exaggerated, and were very inferior to the gains of dramatic actors. Plato, a less questionable authority on such a point, makes Protagoras describe his system of demanding remuneration: "I make no stipulation beforehand; when a pupil parts from me, I ask from him such a sum as I think the time and the circumstances warrant; and I add, that if he deems the demand too great, he has only to make up his own mind what is the amount of improvement which my company has procured to him, and what sum he considers an equivalent for it. I am content to accept the sum so named by himself, only requiring him to go into a Temple and make oath that it is his sincere belief." Plato objects to this, and to every other mode of "selling wisdom;" but, as Mr. Grote remarks, "such is not the way in which the corrupters of mankind go to work."

But let us waive the question of payment, to consider the teaching paid for. The Sophists, it is said, and believed, boasted that they could teach the art of making the worse appear the better reason; and in one sense this is true; but understanding this art *as moderns have understood it*, and thereby forming our notion of the Sophists, let us ask, Is it credible that such an art should have been avowed, and, being avowed, should be rewarded, in a civilized state? Let us think, for an instant, of what are its moral, or rather immoral, consequences. Let us reflect how utterly it destroys all morality; how it makes the very laws but playthings for dialectical subtlety. Then let us ask whether, as we understand it, any State could have allowed such open blasphemy, such defiance of the very fundamental principle of honesty and integrity, such demolition of the social contract.

Could any State do this? and was Athens that State? We ask the reader to realize for himself some notion of the Athenians as citizens, not merely as statues; to think of them as human beings, full of human passions, not simply as architects, sculptors, poets, and philosophers. Having done this, we ask him whether he can believe that these Athenians would have listened to a man proclaiming all morality a farce, and all law a quibble—proclaiming that for a sum of money he could instruct any one how to make an unjust cause appear a just one? Would not such a proclamation be answered with a shout of derision, or of execration, according to the belief in his sincerity? Could any charlatan, in the corruptest age, have escaped lapidation for such effrontery? Yet the Sophists were wealthy, by many greatly admired, and were selected as ambassadors on very delicate missions. They were men of splendid talents, of powerful connections. Around them flocked the rich and noble youth of every city they entered. They were the intellectual leaders of their age. If they had been what their adversaries describe them, Greece could only have been an earthly Pandemonium, where Belial was King.

To believe this is beyond our power. Indeed such a paradox it would be frivolous to refute, had it not been maintained for centuries. Some have endeavored to escape it by maintaining that the Sophists were held in profound contempt; and certain passages are adduced from Plato in proof thereof. But the fact appears to us to be the reverse of this. The wealth and power of the Sophists—the very importance implied in Plato's constant polemic against them—prove that they were not objects of contempt. Objects of aversion they might be to one party: the successful always are. Objects of contempt they might be, to some sincere and profound thinkers. The question here, however, is not one relating to individuals, but to the State. It is not whether Plato despised Gorgias, but whether Athens allowed him to teach the most unblushing and undisguised immorality. There have been daring speculators in all times. There have been men shameless and corrupt. But that there has been any speculator so daring as to promulgate what he knew to be grossly immoral, and so shameless as to avow it, is in such contradiction to our experience of human nature as at once to be rejected.*

It is evident, therefore, that in teaching the art of "making the worse appear the better reason," the Sophists were not guilty of any thing held to be reprehensible; however serious thinkers, such as Plato and Aristotle, might detest the shallow philosophy from which it sprang.

But if this art was not reprehensible, except to severe minds, such as Plato and Aristotle, it is clear that it could not have been the art which its antagonists and defamers have declared it to be. If, as we have shown, universal human nature would have rebelled against a teaching which was avowedly immoral, the fact that the Sophists were not stoned, but were highly considered and well paid, is proof that their teaching was either not what we are told it was, or that such teaching was not considered immoral by the Greeks. Both of these negatives will be found true. The teaching of the Sophists was demonstrably *not* what

---

* We are told by Sextus that Protagoras was condemned to death by the Athenians, because he professed himself unable to say whether the Gods existed, or what they were, owing to the insufficiency of knowledge. Yet the Athenians are supposed to have tolerated the Sophists as they are understood by moderns!

is usually attributed to them, and what they *did* teach was very far from being considered as immoral. Let us consider both these points.

In the first place, Mr. Grote has shown beyond dispute that the Sophists had *no* doctrine in common; they formed no sect or school of thought, such as modern Germans indicate under the name of *Die Sophistik*. There never was a *Sophistik*. Each teacher had his own doctrinal views, and was not more bound to the opinions of the others than a modern Barrister is bound to share the theology of the Bar, or than a modern teacher of Elocution is bound to vote on the same side with all other professors. No sooner is this fact apprehended, than the absurdity of attributing to "the Sophists" opinions expressed by one Sophist, and that too in a caricature by Plato, is at once apparent. Moreover, the absurdity of talking of the "sophistical *doctrine*" becomes apparent, and we are forced to speak only of the "sophistical *art*," reserving for any special animadversion the special name of the offending sinner.

The Sophists taught the art of disputation. The litigious quibbling nature of the Greeks was the soil on which an art like that was made to flourish. Their excessive love of lawsuits is familiar to all versed in Grecian history. The almost farcical representation of a lawsuit given by Æschylus in his otherwise awful drama, *The Eumenides*, shows with what keen and lively interest the audience witnessed even the very details of litigation. For such an appetite food would not long be wanting. Corax and Tisias wrote precepts of the art of disputation. Protagoras followed with dissertations on the most remarkable points of law; and Gorgias composed a set accusation and apology for every case that could present itself. People, in short, were taught to be their own advocates.

This was by no means an immoral art. If it *might* or *did* lead to immorality, few Greeks would have quarrelled with an art so necessary. "Without some power of persuading or confuting, or defending himself against accusations, or, in case of need, accusing others, no man could possibly hold an ascendant position. He had probably not less need of this talent for private informal conversations to satisfy his own political partisans, than for addressing the public assembly formally convoked. Even commanding an army or a fleet, without any laws of war or habit of discipline, his power of keeping up the good-humor, confidence, and prompt obedience of his men, depended not a little on his command of speech. Nor was it only to the leaders in political life that such an accomplishment was indispensable. In all democracies, and probably in several Governments which were not democracies but oligarchies of an open character, the courts of justice were more or less numerous, and the procedure oral and public; in Athens especially the Dicasteries were both very numerous and were paid for attendance. Every citizen had to go before them in person, without being able to send a paid advocate in his place, if he either required redress for wrong offered to himself, or was accused of wrong by another. There was no man therefore who might not be cast or condemned, or fail in his own suit, even with right on his side, unless he possessed some power of speech to unfold his case to the Dicasts, as well as to confute the falsehoods and disentangle the sophistry of an opponent. To meet such liabilities, from which no citizen, rich or poor, was exempt, a certain training in speech became not less essential than a certain training in arms."* Thus was it that even quibbling ingenuity, " making the worse appear the better reason," became a sort of virtue, because it was obtained only by that mastery over argument which was the Athenian's ambition and necessity. *We* can send a paid advocate to quibble for us, and do not therefore need such argumentative subtlety. But let us ask, are barristers pronounced the " corruptors of mankind," and is their art called the art of " making the worse appear the better reason," as if that, and that alone, were the purport of all pleading? Yet, in defending a criminal, does not every bar-

---

* Grote, viii. 468–4.

rister exert his energy, eloquence, subtlety, and knowledge "to make the worse appear the better reason?" Do we reprobate Sergeant Talfourd or Sir Frederick Thesiger, if they succeed in gaining their client's cause, although that cause be a bad one? On the contrary, the badness of the cause makes the greatness of the triumph.

Now let us suppose Sergeant Talfourd to give lessons in forensic oratory; suppose him to announce to the world, that for a certain sum he would instruct any man in the whole art of exposition and debate, of the interrogation of witnesses, of the tricks and turning-points of the law, so that the learner might become his own advocate: this would be contrary to legal etiquette; but would it be immoral? Grave men might, perhaps, object that Mr. Talfourd was offering to make men cheats and scamps, by enabling them to make the worse appear the better reason. But this is a consequence foreseen by grave men, not acknowledged by the teacher. It is doubtless true that owing to oratory, ingenuity, and subtlety, a scamp's cause is sometimes gained; but it is also true that many an honest man's cause is gained, and many a scamp frustrated, by the same means. If forensic oratory does sometimes make the worse appear the better reason, it also makes the good appear in all its strength. The former is a necessary evil, the latter is the very object of a court of justice. "If," says Callicles, in defence of Gorgias, to Socrates, "any one should charge you with some crime which you had not committed, and carry you off to prison, you would gape and stare, and would not know what to say; and, when brought to trial, however contemptible and weak your accuser might be, if he chose to indict you capitally, you would perish. Can this be wisdom, which, if it takes hold of a gifted man, destroys the excellence of his nature, rendering him incapable of preserving himself and others from the greatest dangers, enabling his enemies to plunder him of all his property, and reducing him to the situation of those who, by a sentence of the Court, have been deprived of all their rights?"

If it be admitted that Sergeant Talfourd's instruction in forensic oratory would not be immoral, however unusual, we have only to extend the sphere and include politics, and represent to ourselves the democratic state of Athens, where demagogues were ever on the alert, and we shall be fully persuaded that the art of the Sophists was not considered immoral; and, as further proof, we select the passage in Plato's *Republic*, as coming from an unexceptionable source.

Socrates, speaking of the mercenary teachers whom the people call Sophists, says: "These Sophists teach them only the *things which the people themselves profess in assemblies;* yet this they call wisdom. It is as if a man had observed the instincts and appetites of a great and powerful beast, in what manner to approach it, how or why it is ferocious or calm, what cries it makes, what tones appease and what tones irritate it; after having learnt all this, and calling it wisdom, commenced teaching it without any knowledge of what is good, just, shameful and unjust among these instincts and appetites; but calling that good which flatters the animal, and that bad which irritates it; because he knows not the difference between what is good in itself and that which is only relatively good."*

There is the usual vein of caricature in this description (which is paraphrased in the *Quarterly Review*,† and there given as if the undoubted and unexaggerated doctrines of the Sophists); but it very distinctly sets forth the fact that the Sophists did not teach any thing contrary to public morals, however their art may have offended abstract morality. Indeed the very fact of their popularity would prove that they did but respond to a public want; and because they responded to this want they were paid by the public in money. Plato constantly harps upon their being mercenaries; but he was wealthy, and could afford such sarcasms. The Greeks paid their Musicians, Painters, Sculptors, Physicians, Poets, and Teachers in Schools; why therefore

---

* Plato, *Rep.* vi. 291.   † No. xlii. p. 288.

should they not pay their Philosophers? Zeno of Elea was paid; so was Democritus; but both of these have been sometimes included amongst the Sophists. We see nothing whatever more derogatory in the acceptance of money by Philosophers than by Poets; and we know how the latter stipulated for handsome payment.

Having done our best to show that the "Sophistical art"—that alone which the Sophists had in common—was not immoral, or at any rate was not regarded as immoral by the Greeks, we will now see how the case stands with respect to the old accusation of their having corrupted the Athenian youth, and of their doctrines being essentially corrupting.

That the Athenians did not consider the Sophists as corruptors of youth is unequivocally shown in two facts: they did not impeach the Sophists, and they *did* impeach Socrates. When Anaxagoras and Protagoras "sapped the foundations of morality" by expressing opinions contrary to the religion of Athens, they were banished; but who impeached Gorgias, or Hippias, or Prodicus?

The art however may have been essentially corrupting, although to contemporaries it did not appear so. We believe it was so, if it is to be made responsible for all the consequences which can logically be deduced from it. But "logical consequences" are unjust standards. Men are not responsible for what others may consider their doctrines "lead to." It was on the ground of such remote deduction that Socrates was put to death; and on such grounds the Sophists have been the byword of reproach. Mr. Grote grapples directly with the fact, where he declares Athens at the close of the Peloponnesian war was not more corrupt than Athens in the days of Miltiades and Aristides; and had it been more corrupt, we should demand quite other evidence than that usually alleged, before believing the corruption due to the Sophists.

Why then did Plato speak of the Sophists with so much asperity? Why did he consider their teaching so dangerous?

Because he differed from them *in toto*. He hated them for the same reason that Calvin hated Servetus; but having a more generous nature than Calvin, his hatred of their doctrines did not assume so disgraceful a form. If his allegations are to condemn the Sophists, they must equally condemn all the public men of that day. "Whoever will read either the *Gorgias* or the *Republic*, will see in how sweeping and indiscriminate a manner he passes the sentence of condemnation. Not only the Sophists and all the Rhetors, but all the Musicians and either Dithyrambic or Tragic Poets, all the Statesmen past as well as present, not excepting even the great Pericles, receive from his hand one common stamp of dishonor."* But so far is he from considering the Sophists as peculiar corruptors of Athenian morality, "that he distinctly protests against that supposition in a remarkable passage of the *Republic*. It is, he says, the whole people or the society, with its established morality, intelligence, and tone of sentiment, which is intrinsically vicious; the teachers of such a society must be vicious also, otherwise their teaching would not be received; and even if their private teaching were ever so good, its effect would be washed away, except in some few privileged natures, by overwhelming influences."†

The truth is that, in as far as the Sophists taught any doctrine at all, their doctrine was ethical; and to suppose men teaching immoral ethics, *i. e.* systems of morality known by them to be immoral, is absurd. To clear up this point we must endeavor to ascertain what that doctrine was.

Plato's account is on the face of it a caricature, since it is impossible that any man should have seriously entertained such a doctrine. What Protagoras and Gorgias thought is not given, but only a misrepresentation of what they thought. Plato seizes hold of one of their doctrines, and, *interpreting* it in his own

---

* Grote, viii. 537.
† *Ibid.* p. 59. The passage referred to is *Repub.* vi. 492 (page 388, ed Bekker), and the Sophists are mentioned by name as the teachers of whom it treats.

way, makes it lead to the most outrageous absurdity and immorality. This is as if Berkeley's doctrine had been transmitted to us by Beattie. Berkeley, it is well known, denied the existence of the external world, resolving it into a simple world of ideas. Beattie taunted him with not having followed out his principles, and with not having walked over a precipice. This was a gross misrepresentation; an *ignoratio elenchi;* Beattie misunderstood the argument, and drew conclusions from his misunderstanding. Now suppose him to have written a dialogue on the plan of those of Plato: suppose him making Berkeley expound his argument in the way he (Beattie) interpreted it, with a flavor of exaggeration for the sake of effect, and of absurdity for the sake of easy refutation: how would he have made Berkeley speak? Somewhat thus: "Yes, I maintain that there is no such external existence as that which men vulgarly believe in. There is no world of matter, but only a world of ideas. If I were to walk over a precipice, I should receive no injury; it is only an ideal precipice."

This is the interpretation of a Beattie; how true it is most men know: it is, however, quite as true as Plato's interpretation of the Sophists. From Berkeley's works we can convict Beattie. Plato we can convict from experience of human nature: experience tells us that no man, far less any set of men, could seriously, publicly, and constantly broach doctrines thought to be subversive of all morality, without incurring the heaviest penalties. To broach immoral doctrines with the faintest prospect of success, a man must do so in the name of rigid Morality. To teach immorality, and openly to avow that it is immoral, was, according to Plato, the office of the Sophists;* a statement which carries with it its own contradiction.

---

* This passage in the *Protagoras* is often referred to as a proof of the shamelessness of the Sophists, and sometimes of the ill-favor with which they were regarded. It is to us only a proof of Plato's tendency to caricature.

§ II. Protagoras.

Nothing can be more erroneous than to isolate the Sophists from previous teachers, as if they were no direct product of the speculative efforts which preceded them. They illustrate the crisis at which philosophy had arrived. They took the *negative*, as Socrates took the *positive* issue out of the dilemma.

Protagoras, the first who is said to have avowed himself a Sophist, was born at Abdera, where Democritus first noticed him as a porter, who showed great address in inventing the knot.* The consequence was that Democritus gave him instructions in Philosophy. The story is apocryphal, but indicates a connection to have existed between the speculations of the two thinkers. Let us suppose Protagoras to have accepted the doctrine of Democritus; with him to have rejected the unity of the Eleatics and to have maintained the existence of the Many. With this he also learned that thought is sensation, and that all knowledge is therefore phenomenal. There were two theories in the Democritean system which he could not accept, viz. the *Atomic* and *Reflective*. These two imply each other. Reflection is necessary for the idea of Atoms; and it is from the idea of Atoms not perceived by the sense, that the existence of Reflection is proved. Protagoras rejected the Atoms, and could therefore reject Reflection. He said that Thought was Sensation, and all knowledge consequently individual.

Did not the place of his birth no less than the traditional story lead one to suppose some connection with Democritus, we might feel authorized to adopt certain expressions of Plato, and consider Protagoras to have derived his doctrine from Heraclitus. He certainly resembles the last-named in the main results to which his speculations led him. Be that as it may, the fact is unques-

---

* What the precise signification of $τόλη$ is we are unable to say. A porter's knot, such as is now used, is the common interpretation. Perhaps Protagoras had contrived a sort of wooden machine such as the glazier's use, and which is used by the porters in Greece and Italy to this day.

tionable, that he maintained the doctrine of Thought being identical with and limited by Sensation. Now, this doctrine implies that every thing is true *relatively*—every sensation is a true sensation; and, as there is nothing but sensation, knowledge is inevitably fleeting and imperfect. In a melancholy mind, as in that of Heraclitus, such a doctrine would deepen sadness, till it produced despair. In minds of greater elasticity, in men of greater confidence, such a doctrine would lead to an energetic skepticism. In Protagoras it became the formula: "Man is the measure of all things."

Sextus Empiricus gives the psychological doctrine of Protagoras very explicitly; and his account may be received without suspicion. We translate a portion of it:

"Matter," says Protagoras, "is in a perpetual flux;* whilst it undergoes augmentations and losses, the senses also are modified, according to the age and disposition of the body." He said, also, that the reasons of all phenomena (*appearances*) resided in matter as *substrata* (τοὺς λόγους πάντων τῶν φαινομένων ὑποκεῖσθαι ἐν τῇ ὕλῃ); so that matter, in itself, might be whatever it appeared to each. But men have different perceptions at different times, according to the changes in the thing perceived. Whoever is in a healthy state perceives things such as they appear to all others in a healthy state, and *vice versâ*. A similar course holds with respect to different ages, as well as in sleeping and waking. Man is therefore the criterion of that which exists; all that is perceived by him exists, that which is perceived by no man does not exist"†

Now, conceive men conducted by what they thought irresistible arguments to such a doctrine as the above, and then see how naturally all the skepticism of the Sophists flows from it. The difference between the Sophists and the Skeptics was this: they

---

* Τὴν ὕλην ῥευστὴν εἶναι, an expression which, if not borrowed by Sextus from Plato, would confirm the conjecture above respecting Heraclitus, as the source of Protagoras's system.

† *Hypot. Pyrrhon.* p. 44.

were both convinced of the insufficiency of all knowledge, but the Skeptics contented themselves with the conviction, while the Sophists, satisfied with the vanity of all endeavor to penetrate the mysteries of the universe, began to consider their relations to other men: they devoted themselves to politics and rhetoric.* If there was no possibility of Truth, there only remained the possibility of Persuasion. If one opinion was as true as another—that is, if neither were true,—it was nevertheless desirable, for the sake of Society, that certain opinions should prevail; and, if Logic was powerless, Rhetoric was efficient. Hence Protagoras is made to say, by Plato, that the wise man is the physician of the soul: he cannot indeed induce truer thoughts into the mind, since all thoughts are equally true; but he can induce healthier and more profitable thoughts. He can in the same way heal Society, since by the power of oratory he can introduce good useful sentiments in the place of those base and hurtful.†

This doctrine may be false; but is it not a natural consequence of the philosophy of the epoch? It may be immoral; but is it necessarily the bold and shameless immorality attributed to the Sophists? To us it appears to be neither more nor less than the result of a sense of the radical insufficiency of knowledge. Protagoras had spent his youth in the study of philosophy; he had found that study vain and idle; he had utterly rejected it, and had turned his attention elsewhere. A man of practical tendencies, he wanted a practical result. Failing in this, he sought another path, firmly impressed with the necessity of having something more definite wherewith to enter the world of action. Plato could see no nobler end in life than that of contemplating Being,—than that of familiarizing the mind with the eternal Good, the Just, and the Beautiful,—of which all goodness, justice, and beautiful things were the images. With such a view of life it was natural that he should despise the skepticism of the

---

* See Plato's definition of the sophistical art, *Sophista*, p. 146.
† *Theætetus*, p. 223.

Sophists. This skepticism is clearly set forth in the following passage from the speech of Callicles, in Plato's *Gorgias*:

"Philosophy is a graceful thing when it is moderately cultivated in youth; but, if any one occupies himself with it beyond the proper age, it ruins him; for, however great may be his natural capacity, if he philosophizes too long he must of necessity be inexperienced in all those things which one who would be great and eminent must be experienced in. He must be unacquainted with the laws of his country, and with the mode of influencing other men in the intercourse of life, whether private or public, and with the pleasures and passions of men; in short, with human characters and manners. And when such men are called upon to act, whether on a private or public occasion, they expose themselves to ridicule, just as politicians do when they come to your conversation, and attempt to cope with you in argument; for every man, as Euripides says, occupies himself with that in which he finds himself superior; that in which he is inferior he avoids, and speaks ill of it, but praises what he excels in, thinking that in doing so he is praising himself. The best thing, in my opinion, is to partake of both. It is good to partake of philosophy by way of education, and it is not ungraceful in a young man to philosophize. But, if he continues to do so when he grows older, he becomes ridiculous, and I feel towards him as I should towards a grown person who lisped and played at childish plays. When I see an old man still continuing to philosophize, I think he deserves to be flogged. However great his natural talents, he is under the necessity of avoiding the assembly and public places, where, as the poet says, men become eminent, and to hide himself, and to pass his life whispering to two or three striplings in a corner, but never speaking out any thing great, and bold, and liberal."

That Protagoras, no less than Prodicus,* was a teacher of ex-

---

* Prodicus is especially excepted by Aristophanes in his sweeping condemnation of the Sophists; and, indeed, the author of the well-known parable, *The Choice of Hercules*, must command the respect even of antagonists.

cellent morality, if not of the highest abstract views of the Good, is clearly made out, not only in Mr. Grote's work, but in that of Zeller, where the Sophists are unfavorably treated on the whole,[*] and is indeed supported by the testimony of Plato and Xenophon. The ethics of the Sophists may not have been of a very lofty kind, but they were considered, even by enemies, to be adapted to the exigencies of the day. They doubted the possibility of Philosophy; they were assured only of the advantage of Oratory. In their visits to various cities, they could not fail to remark the variety of laws and ordinances in the different States. This variety impressed them with a conviction that there were no such things as Right and Wrong by nature, but only by convention. This, therefore, became a fundamental precept with them. It was but a corollary of their dogma respecting Truth. For man there was no Eternal Right, because there was no Eternal Truth; τὸ δίκαιον καὶ τὸ αἰσχρὸν οὐ φύσει ἀλλὰ νόμῳ: law was but the law of each city. "That which appears just and honorable to each city, is so *for that city*, as long as the opinion is entertained," says Protagoras in the *Theætetus* (p. 229). This denial of abstract Truth and abstract Justice is easily pushed to absurd and immoral consequences; but we have no evidence that such consequences were maintained by the Sophists. Plato often judges them by such consequences; but independently of the want of any confidence in his representations as faithful, we can often detect in Plato himself evidences of the exaggeration of his general statements. Thus, he on various occasions makes the Sophists maintain that Might is Right. Moderns, who always accept him as positive testimony, have therefore unanimously repeated this statement. Yet, it is obvious that they could not have held this opinion except in a very qualified form. And, in

---

[*] See *Philos. der Griechen*, i. 775. In one of his notes, Zeller alludes to Steinhart's doubt respecting the authorship of the Myth, attributed by Plato to Protagoras, as being "quite worthy of Plato himself." This is very characteristic of the ordinary tone of commentators, and we may well ask with Zeller, "Aber warum soll er fur Protagoras zu gut seyn?"

the first Book of the *Republic*, Thrasymachus the Sophist is made to explain his meaning; namely, that Justice is the law ordained by the party which is strongest in the State. Thus, in a democracy the enactments of the people are the laws: these laws are for their advantage; therefore just. Now, in this admission, by Plato, of a qualification of the abstract formula, " Might is Right," we see evidence of that formula never having been promulgated by the Sophists; it was only an interpretation by Plato. What they meant was this: All law is but convention: the convention of each State is therefore just *for it*; and, inasmuch as any such convention must necessarily be ordained by the strongest party, *i. e.* must be the will of the many, so we may see that justice is but the advantage of the strongest.

The foregoing will, we trust, suffice to show that the tenets attributed to them by Plato, are often caricatures, and admit of very different explanation. Well might Gorgias exclaim, on reading the Dialogue which bears his name, " I did not recognize myself. The young man, however, has great talent for satire."

The Sophists were the natural production of the opinions of the epoch. In them we see the first energetic protest against the possibility of metaphysical science. This protest, however, must not be confounded with the protest of Bacon—must not be mistaken for the germ of positive philosophy. It was the protest of baffled minds. The Philosophy of the day led to skepticism; but with Skepticism no energetic man could remain contented. Philosophy was therefore denounced, not because a surer, safer path of inquiry had been discovered, but because Philosophy was found to lead nowhither. The skepticism of the Sophists was a skepticism with which no great speculative intellect could be contented. Accordingly with Socrates Philosophy again reasserted her empire.

FOURTH EPOCH.

A NEW ERA OPENED BY THE INVENTION OF A NEW METHOD.

CHAPTER I.

SOCRATES.

§ I. The Life of Socrates.

WHILST the brilliant Sophists were reaping money and renown by protesting against Philosophy, and teaching the word-jugglery which they called Disputation and Oratory, there suddenly appeared amongst them a strange antagonist. He was a perfect contrast to them. They had slighted Truth; they had denied her. He had made her his soul's mistress; and, with patient labor, with untiring energy, did his large wise soul toil after perfect communion with her. They had deserted Truth for Money and Renown. He had remained constant to her in poverty. They professed to teach every thing. He only knew that he knew nothing; and denied that any thing could be taught. Yet he believed he could be of service to his fellow-men; not by teaching, but by helping them to learn. His mission was to examine the thoughts of others. This he humorously explained by reference to his mother's profession, namely that of a midwife. What she did for women in labor he could do for men pregnant with ideas. He was an accoucheur of ideas. He assisted ideas in their birth, and, having brought them into light, he examined them, to see if they were fit to live: if true, they were welcomed·

if false, destroyed. And for this assistance he demanded no pecuniary recompense, but steadfastly refused every bribe of the kind.

He was the declared questioner of all men who were renowned for wisdom, or any intellectual eminence; and they were somewhat puzzled with their new antagonist. Who is he?—Socrates, the son of Sophroniscus. What does he?—Converse. For what purpose?—To expose error.

Some gorgeous Sophists, in their flowing robes, followed by crowds of eager listeners, treated the poor and humbly-clad Socrates with ineffable contempt. He was rude and ungainly in his movements; unlike all respectable citizens in his habits. Barefoot, he wandered about the streets of Athens absorbed in thought; sometimes he stood still for hours, fixed in meditation. Every day he strolled into the market-place, and disputed with all who were willing. In appearance he resembled a Silenus. His flattened nose, with wide and upturned nostrils, his projecting eyeballs, his thick and sensual lips, his squab figure and unwieldy belly, were all points upon which ridicule might fasten. Yet when this Silenus spoke there was a witchery in his tongue which fascinated those whom his appearance had disgusted; and Alcibiades declared that he was forced to stop his ears and flee away, that he might not sit down beside Socrates and "grow old in listening to his talk." Let us hear Alcibiades describe him.*

" I will begin the praise of Socrates by comparing him to a certain statue. Perhaps he will think that this statue is introduced for the sake of ridicule; but I assure you that it is necessary for the illustration of truth. I assert, then, that Socrates is exactly like those Silenuses that sit in the sculptor's shops, and which are carved holding flutes or pipes, but which, when divided in two, are found to contain withinside the images of the gods. I assert that Socrates is like the Satyr Marsyas; that your form and appearance are like these Satyrs, I think that even you will

---

* Plato, *Symposium*, Shelley's translation.

not venture to deny; and how like you are to them in all other things, now hear. Are you not scornful and petulant? If you deny this, I will bring witnesses. Are you not a piper, and far more wonderful a one than he? for Marsyas, and whoever now pipes the music that he taught, that music which is of heaven, and described as being taught by Marsyas, enchants men through the power of the mouth; for, if any musician, be he skilful or not, awakens this music, it alone enables him to retain the minds of men, and from the divinity of its nature makes evident those who are in want of the Gods and initiation. You differ only from Marsyas in this circumstance, that you effect without instruments, by mere words, all that he can do; for, when we hear Pericles, or any other accomplished orator, deliver a discourse, no one, as it were, cares any thing about it. But when any one hears you, or even your words related by another, though ever so rude and unskilful a speaker, be that person a woman, man, or child, we are struck and retained, as it were, by the discourse clinging to our minds.

"If I was not afraid that I am a great deal too drunk, I would confirm to you by an oath the strange effects which I assure you I have suffered from his words, and suffer still; for, when I hear him speak, my heart leaps up far more than the hearts of those who celebrate the Corybantic Mysteries; my tears are poured out as he talks—a thing I have seen happen to many others besides myself. I have heard Pericles and other excellent orators, and have been pleased with their discourses, but I suffered nothing of this kind; nor was my soul ever on those occasions disturbed and filled with self-reproach, as if it were slavishly laid prostrate. But this Marsyas here has often affected me in the way I describe, until the life which I lead seemed hardly worth living. Do not deny it, Socrates; for I well know that if even now I chose to listen to you, I could not resist, but should again suffer the same effects; for, my friends, he forces me to confess, that while I myself am still in want of many things, I neglect my own necessities, and attend to those of the Athenians. I stop my ears, therefore, as from the Sirens, and flee away as fast as possible, that I may not sit down beside him and grow old in listening to his talk; for this man has reduced me to feel the sentiment of shame, which I imagine no one would readily believe was in me; he alone inspires me with remorse and awe; for I feel in his presence my incapacity of refuting what he says, or of refusing to do that which he directs; but, when I depart from him, the glory which the multitude confers overwhelms me. I escape, therefore, and hide myself from him, and when I see him I am overwhelmed with humiliation, because I have neglected to do what I have confessed to him ought to be done; and often and often have I wished that he were no longer to be seen among men. But, if that were to happen, I well know that I should suffer far greater pain; so that where I can turn, or what I can do with this man, I know not. All this have I and many others suffered from the pipings of this Satyr.

"And observe how like he is to what I said, and what a wonderful power he possesses. I know that there is not one of you who is aware of the real nature of Socrates; but since I have begun, I will make him plain to you. You observe how passionately Socrates affects the intimacy of those who are beautiful, and how ignorant he professes himself to be; appearances in themselves excessively Silenic. This, my friends, is the external form with which, like one of the sculptured Sileni, he has clothed himself; for, if you open him, you will find within admirable temperance and wisdom: for he cares not for mere beauty, but despises more than any one can imagine all external possessions, whether it be beauty, or wealth, or glory, or any other thing for which the multitude felicitates the possessor. He esteems these things, and us who honor them, as nothing, and lives among men, making all the objects of their admiration the playthings of his irony. But I know not if any one of you have ever seen the divine images which are within, when he has been opened and is serious. I have seen them, and they are so supremely beautiful, so golden, so divine and wonderful, that every thing which

Socrates commands surely ought to be obeyed, even like the voice of a God.

"Many other and most wonderful qualities might well be praised in Socrates, but such as these might singly be attributed to others. But that which is unparalleled in Socrates is, that he is unlike, and above comparison with all other men, whether those who have lived in ancient times, or those who exist now; for, it may be conjectured, that Brasidas and many others are such as was Achilles. Pericles deserves comparison with Nestor and Antenor; and other excellent persons of various times may, with probability, be drawn into comparison with each other. But to such a singular man as this, both himself and his discourses are so uncommon, no one, should he seek, would find a parallel among the present or the past generations of mankind; unless they should say that he resembled those with whom I lately compared him; for, assuredly, he and his discourses are like nothing but the Sileni and the Satyrs. At first I forgot to make you observe how like his discourses are to those Satyrs when they are opened; for, if any one will listen to the talk of Socrates, it will appear to him at first extremely ridiculous; the phrases and expressions which he employs fold around his exterior the skin, as it were, of a rude and wanton Satyr. He is always talking about brass-founders, and leather-cutters, and skin-dressers; and this is his perpetual custom, so that any dull and unobservant person might easily laugh at his discourse. But, if any one should see it opened, as it were, and get within the sense of his words, he would then find that they alone of all that enters into the mind of man to utter, had a profound and persuasive meaning, and that they were most divine; and that they presented to the mind innumerable images of every excellence, and that they tended towards objects of the highest moment, or rather towards all that he who seeks the possession of what is supremely beautiful and good need regard as essential to the accomplishment of his ambition.

"These are the things, my friends, for which I praise Socrates."

This Silenus was the most formidable antagonist that the Sophists had encountered; but this is small praise for him who was hereafter to become one of the most reverenced names in the world's Pantheon—who was to give a new impulse to the human mind, and leave, as an inheritance to mankind, the grand example of an heroic life devoted to Truth and crowned with martyrdom.

Every thing about Socrates is remarkable—personal appearance, moral physiognomy, position, object, method, life and death. Fortunately, his character and his tendencies have been so clearly pictured in the works of Plato and Xenophon, that although the portrait may be flattered, we are sure of its resemblance.

He was born B. C. 469, the son of Sophroniscus, a sculptor,* and Phænarete, a midwife. His parents, though poor, managed, it is said, to give him the ordinary education. Besides which, he learned his father's art; whether he made any progress in it we are unable to say: probably not, as he relinquished it early. A group of Graces, which tradition attributed to the chisel of Socrates, was exhibited for centuries among the art treasures of the Acropolis; but we have of course no means of determining the authenticity of the relic. Diogenes Laertius tells us that Crito, a wealthy Athenian, charmed with the manners of Socrates, is said to have withdrawn him from the shop, and to have educated him. This Crito afterwards became a reverential disciple of the great genius he had discovered.

Considering that we have his own assertion as evidence of his having early studied Physics, for which he had an astonishing longing, and considering further that he so entirely relinquished that study, even declaring it to be impious,† it is of little importance to discuss, with German critics, whether he did or did not

---

* Dr. Wiggers says, that Timon the Sillograph calls Socrates, with a sneer, λιθοξόος, "a stone-scraper." He forgets that λιθοξόος was one of the names for a sculptor, as Lucian informs us in the account of his early life.

† In Xenophon, "madness."—*Memorab.*, lib. i. c. 1.

learn from Archelaus and Anaxagoras. That he learned oratory from Prodicus* is not discountenanced by the passage in Xenophon,† where he is made to say, "You despise me because you have squandered money upon Protagoras, Gorgias, Prodicus, and so many others, in return for their teaching; whereas I am forced to draw my philosophy from my own brain;" for certainly, if any one can claim originality, it is Socrates: his philosophy he learned from no one. He struck into a new path. Instead of trying to account for the existence of the universe, he was ever craving, as Mr. Maurice well says, for a light to show him his own path through it.‡

He did not commence teaching till about the middle of his career. We have but few records of the events which filled up the period between his first leaving his father and his first teaching. One of these was his marriage with Xanthippe, and the domestic squabbles which ensued. She bore him three children. The violence of her temper, and the equanimity with which he submitted to it, are proverbial. She has become a type; her name is synonymous with Shrew. He gave a playful explanation of his choice by remarking, that "those who wish to become skilled in horsemanship select the most spirited horses; after being able to bridle those, they believe they can bridle all others. Now, as it is my wish to live and converse with men, I married this woman, being firmly convinced that in case I should be able to endure her, I should be able to endure all others."§

Before he gave himself up to teaching, he performed military service in three battles, and distinguished himself in each. In the first, the prize of bravery was awarded to him. He relinquished his claim in favor of Alcibiades, whom it might encourage to deserve such honor. Various anecdotes are related of him during his campaigns. In spite of the severity of winter, when the ice and snow were thick upon the ground, he went barefoot

---

* Plato, *Meno*, p. 96. † *Convivium*, i. 5.
‡ Maurice, *Moral and Metaphysical Philosophy*, i. 118.
§ Xenophon, *Convivium*, ii.

and lightly clad. On one occasion he stood before the camp for four-and-twenty hours on the same spot, wrapt in meditation. Plato has given us a beautiful description of Socrates during the campaign, which we quote in the translation by Shelley:

"At one time we were fellow-soldiers, and had our mess together in the camp before Potidæa. Socrates there overcame not only me, but every one besides, in endurance of toils: when, as happens in a campaign, we were reduced to few provisions, there were none who could sustain hunger like Socrates: and, when we had plenty, he alone seemed to enjoy our military fare. He never drank much willingly; but, when he was compelled, he conquered all even in that to which he was least accustomed, and, what is most astonishing, no person ever saw Socrates drunk either then or at any other time. In the depth of winter (and the winters there are excessively rigid) he sustained calmly incredible hardships: and, amongst other things, whilst the frost was intolerably severe, and no one went out of their tents, or, if they went out, wrapt themselves up carefully and put fleeces under their feet, and bound their legs with hairy skins, Socrates went out only with the same cloak on that he usually wore, and walked barefoot upon the ice, more easily indeed than those who had sandalled themselves so delicately: so that the soldiers thought that he did it to mock their want of fortitude. It would indeed be worth while to commemorate all that this brave man did and endured in that expedition.

"In one instance he was seen early in the morning, standing in one place, wrapt in meditation, and, as he seemed not to be able to unravel the subject of his thoughts, he still continued to stand as inquiring and discussing within himself; and, when noon came, the soldiers observed him, and said to one another, 'Socrates has been standing there thinking, ever since the morning.' At last some Ionians came to the spot, and, having supped, as it was summer, bringing their blankets, they lay down to sleep in the cool: they observed that Socrates continued to stand there the whole night until morning, and that, when the sun rose, he saluted it with a prayer, and departed.

"I ought not to omit what Socrates is in battle; for, in that battle after which the Generals decreed to me the prize of courage, Socrates alone of all men was the savior of my life, standing by me when I had fallen and was wounded, and preserving both myself and my arms from the hands of the enemy. On that occasion I entreated the Generals to decree the prize, as it was most due, to him. And this, O Socrates, you cannot deny, that when the Generals, wishing to conciliate a person of my rank, desired to give me the prize, you were far more earnestly desirous than the Generals, that this glory should be attributed, not to yourself, but me.

"But to see Socrates when our army was defeated and scattered in flight at Delium, was a spectacle worthy to behold. On that occasion I was among the cavalry, and he on foot, heavily armed. After the total rout of our troops, he and Laches retreated together: I came up by chance, and, seeing them, bade them be of good cheer, for that I would not leave them. As I was on horseback, and therefore less occupied by a regard of my own situation, I could better observe, than at Potidæa, the beautiful spectacle exhibited by Socrates on this emergency. How superior was he to Laches in presence of mind and courage! Your representation of him on the stage, O Aristophanes, was not wholly unlike his real self on this occasion; for he walked and darted his regards around with a majestic composure, looking tranquilly both on his friends and enemies; so that it was evident to every one, even from afar, that whoever should venture to attack him would encounter a desperate resistance. He and his companion thus departed in safety; for those who are scattered in flight are pursued and killed, whilst men hesitate to touch those who exhibit such a countenance as that of Socrates, even in defeat."

We must cast a glance at his public career. His doctrine being Ethical, there is great importance in seeing how far it was practical. He proclaimed the supremacy of Virtue over all other rules of life; he exhorted men to a brave and unflinching adhesion to Justice, as the only real happiness; he declared that the unjust alone are unhappy. Was he himself virtuous? was he happy? The question is pertinent; fortunately it can be answered.

His bravery as a soldier was surpassed by his bravery as a Senator. He had that high moral courage which can brave not only death, but opinion. He presents an example, almost unique in history, of a man who could defy a tyrant, and also defy a tyrannical mob, an impetuous, imperious mob. The Thirty Tyrants on one occasion summoned him, together with four others, to the Tholus, the place in which the Prytanes took their meals. He was there commanded to bring Leon of Salamis to Athens. Leon had obtained the right of Athenian citizenship, but fearing the rapacity of the tyrants, had retired to Salamis. To bring back Leon, Socrates steadily refused. He says himself, that the "Government, although it was so powerful, did not frighten me into doing any thing unjust; but, when we came out of the Tholus, the four went to Salamis and took Leon, but I went away home. And perhaps I should have suffered death on account of this, if the Government had not soon been broken up."

On another occasion he braved the clamorous mob. He was then a Senator, the only State office he ever held. The Athenian Senate consisted of the Five Hundred who were elected from the ten tribes. During a period of thirty-five or thirty-six days the members of each tribe in turn had the presidency, and were called *Prytanes*. Of the fifty Prytanes, ten had the presidency every seven days; each day one of these ten enjoyed the highest dignity, with the name of *Espitates*. He laid every thing before the assembly of the people, put the question to the vote, examined the votes, and, in short, conducted the whole business of the assembly. He enjoyed this power, however, only for a single day; for that day he was intrusted with the keys of the citadel and the treasury of the republic.

Socrates was Epistates on the day when the unjust sentence was to be passed on the Admirals who had neglected to bury the dead after the battle of Arginusæ. To take care of the burial of the dead was a sacred duty.* The shades of the unburied were believed to wander restlessly for a hundred years on the banks of the Styx. After the battle of Arginusæ, a violent storm arose, which prevented the Admirals from obtaining the bodies of the slain. In order to remedy this, they left behind them some inferior officers (Taxiarchs) to attend to the office. But the violence of the storm rendered it impossible. The Admirals were tried. They produced the evidence of the pilots to show that the tempest had rendered the burial impracticable; besides which they had left the Taxiarchs behind, so that the blame, if any, ought to fall on the latter. This produced its natural effect on the people, who would instantly have given an acquittal if put to the vote. But the accusers managed to adjourn the assembly, pretending that it was too dark to count the show of hands. In the mean while the enemies of the Admirals did all they could to inflame the minds of the people. The lamentations and mournful appearance of the kinsmen of the slain, who had been hired for the tragic scene, had a powerful influence on the assembly. The votes were to be given on the general question, whether the Admirals had done wrong in not taking up the bodies of the dead; and, if they should be condemned by the majority (so the Senate ordained), they were to be put to death and their property confiscated. But to condemn all by one vote was contrary to law. The Prytanes, with Socrates at their head, refused to put the illegal question to the vote. The people became furious, and loudly demanded that those who resisted their pleasure, should themselves be brought to trial. The Prytanes wavered, yielded. Socrates alone remained firm, defying the threats of the mob. He stood there to administer justice. He would not administer injustice. In consequence of his refusal, the ques-

---

* The *Antigone* of Sophocles is founded on the sacredness of this duty.

tion could not be put to the vote, and the assembly was again adjourned. The next day a new Epistates and other presidents succeeded, and the Admirals were condemned.*

It was impossible for Socrates to enter the market-place without at once becoming an object of attention. His ungainly figure, his moral character, and his bewitching tongue, excited and enchained curiosity. He became known to every citizen. Who had not listened to him? Who had not enjoyed his inimitable irony? Who had not seen him demolish the arrogance and pretension of some reputed wise man? Socrates must have been a terrible antagonist to all people who believed that they were wise because they could discourse fluently; and these were not few. He always declared that he knew nothing. When a man professed knowledge on any point, especially if admiring crowds gave testimony to that profession, Socrates was sure to step up to him, and, professing ignorance, entreat to be taught. Charmed with so humble a listener, the teacher began. Interrogated, he unsuspectingly assented to some very evident proposition; a conclusion from that, almost as evident, next received his assent; from that moment he was lost. With great power of logic, with much ingenious subtlety, and sometimes with daring sophistication, a web was formed from which he could not extricate himself. His own admissions were proved to lead to monstrous conclusions; these conclusions he repugned, but could not see where the gist of his error lay. The laughter of all bystanders bespoke his defeat. Before him was his adversary, imperturbably calm, apparently innocent of all attempt at making him ridiculous. Confused, but not confuted, he left the spot indignant with himself, but more indignant with the subtlety of his adversary.

It was thus that Socrates became mistaken for a Sophist; but he was distinguished from the Sophists by his constant object. Whilst they denied the possibility of truth, he only sought to make truth evident, in the ironical, playful, and, sometimes, quib-

---

* Wiggers, pp. 51–55.

bling manner in which he destroyed the arguments of opponents. Truth was his object, even in his lightest moments.

This sort of disputation daily occurred in Athens; and by it, doubtless, Socrates acquired that notoriety which induced Aristophanes to select him as the Sophist hero of the comedy of *The Clouds*. No one will doubt that to his adversaries he must have been an exasperating opponent. No one was safe from his attack. No one who presumed to know any thing could escape him. In confirmation, let us quote the account Socrates gives of his procedure, as reported by Plato in the *Apology*. Socrates there describes his sensations on hearing that Apollo had declared him to be the wisest of men. He could not understand this. Knowing himself to be wise in nothing, yet not daring to think the words of the god could be false, he was puzzled. "I went to one of those who are esteemed to be wise, thinking that here, if anywhere, I should prove the oracle to be wrong, and to be able to say, 'Here is a man wiser than I.' After examining this man (I need not name him, but he was one of the politicians), and conversing with him, it was my opinion that this man *seemed* to many others, and especially to himself, to be wise, but *was* not so. Thereupon I tried to convince him that he thought himself wise, but was not. By this means I offended him and many of the bystanders. When I went away, I said to myself, 'I am wiser than this man; for neither of us, it would seem, knows any thing valuable: but he, not knowing, fancies he does know; I, as I really do not know, so I do not think I know. I seem, therefore, to be in one small matter wiser than he.' After this I went to another still wiser than he, and came to the same result; and by this I affronted him too, and many others. I went on in the same manner, perceiving with sorrow and fear that I was making enemies; but it seemed necessary to postpone all other considerations to the service of the god, and therefore to seek for the meaning of the oracle by going to all who appeared to know any thing. And, O Athenians, the impression made on me was this: The persons of most reputation seemed to me nearly the most deficient of all; other persons of much smaller account seemed much more rational.

"When I had done with the politicians, I went to the poets, tragic, dithyrambic, and others, thinking that I should surely find myself less knowing than they. Taking up those of their poems which appeared to me most labored, I asked them (that I might at the same time learn something from them) what these poems meant? I am ashamed, O Athenians, to say the truth, but I must say it; there was scarcely a person present who could not have spoken better concerning their poems than they. I soon found that what poets do, they accomplish not by wisdom, but by a kind of natural turn, and an enthusiasm like that of prophets and those who utter oracles; for these, too, speak many fine things, but do not know one particle of what they speak.

"Lastly, I resorted to artificers; for I was conscious that I myself knew, in a manner, nothing at all, but should find them knowing many valuable things. And in this I was not mistaken; they knew things which I knew not, and were, so far, wiser than I. But they appeared to me to fall into the same error as the poets; each, because he was skilled in his own art, insisted upon being the wisest man in other and greater things; and this mistake of theirs overshadowed what they possessed of wisdom. From this search, O Athenians, the consequences to me have been, on the one hand, many enmities, and of the most formidable kind, which have brought upon me many false imputations; but, on the other hand, the name and general repute of a wise man."

Socrates, like Dr. Johnson, did not care for the country. "Sir," said the Doctor, "when you have seen one green field, you have seen all green fields: Sir, I like to look upon men. Let us walk down Cheapside." In words of the same import does Socrates address Phædrus, who accused him of being unacquainted even with the neighborhood of Athens. "I am very anxious to learn; and from fields and trees I can learn nothing. I can only learn from men in the city." And he was always to be found where men were assembled.* Ready to argue with every one, he demanded money from none. He gave no lectures: he only talked. He wrote no books: he argued.† He cannot properly be said to have had a school, since he did not even give a systematic exposition of his doctrine. What has been called his school, must be understood to refer to the many delighted admirers whose custom it was to surround him whenever he appeared, to talk with him as often as possible, and to accept his leading opinions.

"At what time Socrates relinquished his profession as a statuary we do not know; but it is certain that all the middle and later part of his life, at least, was devoted exclusively to the self-imposed task of teaching; excluding all other business, public or private, and to the neglect of all means of fortune. We can hardly avoid speaking of him as a teacher, though he himself disclaimed the appellation; his practice was to talk or converse. Early in the morning he frequented the public walks, the gymnasia for bodily training, and the schools where youths were receiving instruction; he was to be seen in the market-place at the hour when it was most crowded, among the booths and tables where goods were exposed for sale; his whole day was usually spent in this public manner. He talked with any one, young or old, rich or poor, who sought to address him, and in the hearing of all who stood by; not only he never either asked or received any reward, but he made no distinction of persons, never withheld his conversation from any one, and talked on the same general subjects with all. . . . As it was engaging, curious, and instructive to hear, certain persons made it their habit to attend him in public, as companions and listeners. These men, a fluctuating body, were commonly known as his disciples and scholars; though neither he nor his personal friends ever employed the

---

* Xenophon, *Memorab.* i. 1. Καὶ ἔλεγε μὲν ὡς τὸ πολὺ, τοῖς δὲ βουλομένοις ἐξῆν ἀκούειν.

† We are, therefore, disposed to accept as historical, the language Plato puts into his mouth respecting the inefficiency of books. Books cannot be interrogated, cannot answer; therefore, cannot teach: we can only learn from them that which we knew before.—*Phædrus*, p. 96.

terms *teacher* and *disciple* to describe the relation between them Now no other person in Athens, nor in any other Grecian city, appears ever to have manifested himself in this perpetual and indiscriminate manner, as a public talker for instruction. By the peculiar mode of life which Socrates pursued, not only his conversation reached the minds of a much wider circle, but he became more abundantly known as a person. While acquiring a few friends and admirers, and raising a certain intellectual interest in others, he at the same time provoked a large number of personal enemies. This was probably the reason why he was selected by Aristophanes and the other comic writers to be attacked as a general representative of philosophical and rhetorical teaching."*

Although Socrates was a knight-errant of philosophy, ever on the alert to rescue some forlorn truth from the dungeons of prejudice, and therefore was not scrupulous as to who or what his adversary might be, yet his especial enemies were the Sophists. He never neglected an opportunity of refuting them. He combated them with their own weapons, and on their own ground. He knew all their tactics. He knew their strength and their weakness. Like them he had studied Physics, in the speculations of the early thinkers; and like them had seen that these speculations led to no certainty. But he had not, like them, made skepticism a refuge; he had not proclaimed Truth to be a Phantom, because he could not embrace her. No: defeated in his endeavor to penetrate the mysteries of the world *without*, he turned his attention to the world *within*. For Physics he substituted Morals. The certitude which he failed to gain respecting the operations of nature, had not shaken his conviction of the certitude of the moral truths which his conscience irresistibly impressed upon his attention. The world of sense might be fleeting and deceptive. The voice of conscience could not deceive. Turning his attention inwards, he discovered certain

---

* Grote, viii. 555.

truths which admitted of no question. They were eternal, immutable, evident. These he opposed to the skepticism of the Sophists. Moral certitude was the rock upon which his shipwrecked soul was cast. There he could repose in safety. From its heights he could survey the world, and his relation to it.

Thus was his life spent. In his old age he had to appear before his judges to answer the accusations of Impiety and Immorality. He appeared, and was condemned.

When we think upon the character of this great man, whose virtues, luminous in the distance, and surrounded with the halo of imperishable glory, so impose on our imaginations, that they seem as evident as they were exalted, we cannot hear of his trial and condemnation without indignant disgust at the Athenians. But, for the sake of humanity, let us be cautious ere we decide. The Athenians were volatile, credulous, and cruel: all masses of men are; and they, perhaps, were eminently so. But it is too much to suppose that they, or any people, would have condemned Socrates had he appeared to them what he appears to us. Had a tyrant committed such a deed, the people would have avenged it. But Socrates was not to them what he appears to us. He was offensive to them, and paid the penalty.

A great man cannot be understood by his contemporaries. He can only be understood by his peers; and his peers are few. Posterity exalts a great man's fame by producing a number of great men to appreciate him. The great man is also necessarily a reformer in some shape or other. Every reformer has to combat with existing prejudices and deep-rooted passions. To cut his own path, he must displace the rubbish which encumbers it. He is therefore in opposition to his fellow-men, and attacks their interests. Blinded by prejudice, by passion, and by interest, men cannot see the excellence of him they oppose; and hence it is that, as Heine so admirably says, " wherever a great soul gives utterance to his thoughts, there also is Golgotha."

Reformers are martyrs; and Socrates was a reformer. Although, therefore, his condemnation appears to us very unjust and very frightful, to the Athenians it was no more than the banishment of Empedocles, or the condemnation of Protagoras. Pure as were his intentions, his actions and opinions were offensive. He incurred the hatred of party-spirit; and by that hatred fell. *We* recognize the purity of his intentions; he does not oppose *us*. We can pardon what we believe to be his errors, because those errors wage no war with our interests. Very differently were the Athenians situated. To them he was offensive. He hated injustice and folly of all kinds, and never lost an occasion of exposing them. A man who undertakes to be the critic of his age cannot escape the critic's penalty. Socrates censured freely, openly.*

But, perhaps, the most exasperating part of his behavior was the undisguised contempt which he uniformly expressed for the readiness with which men assumed they had a capacity for government. Only the wise, he said, were fit to govern, and they were few. Government is a science, and a difficult science. It is infinitely more difficult to govern a State than to govern the helm of a ship. Yet, the same people who would not trust themselves in a ship without an experienced pilot, not only trust themselves in a State with an inexperienced ruler, but also endeavor to become rulers themselves. This contempt was sufficient to cause his condemnation; but a better pretext was wanted, and it was found in his impiety. His defenders, ancient and modern, have declared that he was not guilty of impiety; and Xenophon "wonders" that the charge could have been credited for an instant. But we believe that the charge was as much merited as in the case of the other philosophers against whom it was made.†
He gave new interpretations to the reigning dogmas; and op-

---

* The masterly account of the trial of Socrates, given by Mr. Grote, should be read and re-read by all interested in this subject.

† Sextus Empiricus, speaking of the Socratic heresy, calls it ὡς ἰκρανλί-λουσαν τὸ θεῖον.—*Adv. Math.* ii. p. 69.—Plato's dialogues of *The Second Alcibiades* and the *Euthyphro* are evidence enough of Socrates' opposition to the Mythology of his day.

posing the mythological interpretations, he was chargeable with impiety.

It has been remarked by an anonymous writer, that, in complying with the rites of his country, Socrates avoided her superstitions. The rite of sacrifice, so simple and natural that it harmonizes with all and any religious truth, required to be guarded against a great abuse, and against this he warned his countrymen.

"When," says Xenophon, ' he sacrificed, he feared not his offering would fail of acceptance in that he was poor; but, giving according to his ability, he doubted not but, in he sight of the Gods, he equalled those men whose gifts and sacrifices overspread the whole altar; for Socrates always reckoned upon it as a most indubitable truth, that the service paid the Deity by the pure and pious soul was the most grateful service.

"When he prayed, his petition was only this,—that the Gods would give to him those things that were good. And this he did, forasmuch as they alone knew what was good for man. But he who should ask for gold or silver, or increase of dominion, acted not, in his opinion, more wisely than one who should pray for the opportunity to fight, or game, or any thing of the like nature; the consequence whereof being altogether doubtful, might turn, for aught he knew, not a little to his disadvantage."*

It was more difficult for the philosopher either innocently to comply with, or safely to oppose, that part of the popular religion which related to oracles and omens. Socrates appears to have done what was possible, and what therefore was best ultimately, towards correcting this great evil.

"He likewise asserted, that the science of divination was necessary for all such as would govern successfully, either cities or private families; for, although he thought every one might choose his own way of life, and afterwards, by his industry, excel there in (whether architecture, mechanics, agriculture, superintending the laborer, managing the finances, or practising the art of war),

* *Memorabilia*, i. 8.

yet even here, the Gods, he would say, thought proper to reserve to themselves, in all these things, the knowledge of that part of of them which was of the most importance, since he who was the most careful to cultivate his field, could not know of a certainty who should reap the fruit of it.

"Socrates therefore esteemed all those as no other than madmen who, excluding the Deity, referred the success of their designs to nothing higher than human prudence. He likewise thought those not much better who had recourse to divination on every occasion, as if a man was to consult the oracle whether he should give the reins of his chariot into the hands of one ignorant or well-versed in the art of driving, or place at the helm of his ship a skilful or unskilful pilot.

"He also thought it a kind of impiety to importune the Gods with our inquiries concerning things of which we may gain the knowledge by number, weight, or measure; it being, as it seemed to him, incumbent on man to make himself acquainted with whatever the Gods had placed within his power: as for such things as were beyond his comprehension, for these he ought always to apply to the oracle; the Gods being ever ready to communicate knowledge to those whose care had been to render them propitious."*

The trial of Socrates belongs rather to the history of Greece than to the history of Philosophy. It was a political trial. His bearing during the whole period was worthy of him: calm, grave, and touching; somewhat haughty perhaps, but with the haughtiness of a brave soul fighting for the truth. It increased the admiration of his admirers, and exasperated his adversaries.

Plato, then a young man, was present at the trial, and has preserved an admirable picture of it in his *Apology*. The closing speech, made by Socrates, after sentence of death had been pronounced, is supposed to be given with substantial accuracy by Plato. We extract it:—

---

* *Memorabilia*, i. 1.

"It is for the sake of but a short span, O Athenians, that you have incurred the imputation from those who wish to speak evil of the city, of having put to death Socrates, a wise man (for those who are inclined to reproach you will say that I am wise, even if I am not). Had you waited a short time the thing would have happened without your agency; for you see my years; I am far advanced in life, and near to death. I address this not to all of you, but to those who have voted for the capital sentence, and this, too, I say to the same persons,—Perhaps you think that I have been condemned for want of skill in such modes of working upon your minds, as I might have employed with success, if I had thought it right to employ all means in order to escape from condemnation. Far from it: I have been condemned, and not from want of things to say, but from want of daring and shamelessness; because I did not choose to say to you the things which would have been pleasantest for you to hear, weeping, and lamenting, and saying and doing other things which I affirm to be unworthy of me; as you are accustomed to see others do. But neither did I then think fit to do or say any thing unworthy of a freeman; nor do I now repent of having thus defended myself. I would far rather have made the one defence and die, than have made the other and live. Neither in a court of justice, nor in war, ought we to make it our object that, whatever happen, we may escape death. In battle it is often evident that a man may save his life by throwing away his arms and imploring mercy of his pursuers; and in all other dangers there are many contrivances by which a person may get off with life if he dare do or say every thing. The difficulty, O Athenians, is not to escape from death, but from guilt; for guilt is swifter than death, and runs faster. And now I, being old and slow of foot, have been overtaken by Death, the slower of the two; but my accusers, who are brisk and vehement, by wickedness, the swifter. We quit this place: I have been sentenced by you to death; but they, having sentence passed upon them, by Truth, of guilt and injustice. I submit to my punishment, and they to theirs.

"But I wish, O men who have condemned me, to prophesy to you what next is to come. I say, then, that, immediately after my death, there will come upon you a far severer punishment than that which you have inflicted upon me; for you have done this, thinking by it to escape from being called to account for your lives. But I affirm that the very reverse will happen to you. There will be many to call you to account whom I have hitherto restrained, and whom you saw not; and, being younger, they will give you more annoyance, and you will be still more provoked; for, if you think by putting men to death to deter others from reproaching you with living amiss, you think ill. That mode of protecting yourselves is neither very possible nor very noble: the noblest and the easiest too is not to cut off other people, but so to order yourselves as to attain the greatest excellence.

"Thus much I beg of you: When my sons grow up, punish them, O Athenians, by tormenting them as I tormented you, if they shall seem to study riches, or any other ends, in preference to virtue. And, if they are thought to be something, being really nothing, reproach them, as I have reproached you, for not attending to what they ought, and fancying themselves something when they are good for nothing. And, if you do this, both I and my sons shall have received what is just at your hands.

"*It is now time that we depart, I to die, you to live; but which has the better destiny is unknown to all except the God.*"

This is very grand and impressive, and paints the character of the man. *Magno animo et vultu carcerem intravit*, says Seneca. He consoled his weeping friends, and gently upbraided them for their complaints at the injustice of the sentence. No man ever faced death with greater calmness; for no man ever welcomed it with greater faith as a new birth to a higher state of being.

He would have been executed the next day, but it happened that the next day was the first of the festival of the Delian Theoria, during which no criminal could be put to death. This festival lasted thirty days. Socrates, though in chains and awaiting his end, spent the interval in cheerful conversation with his friends, and in composing verses. "During this time," says Xenophon, "he lived before the eyes of all his friends in the same manner as in former days; but now his past life was most admired on account of his present calmness and cheerfulness of mind." On the .ast day he held a conversation with his friends on the immortality of the soul. This forms the subject of Plato's *Phædo*. The arguments in that dialogue are most probably Plato's own; and it is supposed that the dying speech of Cyrus, in Xenophon's *Cyropædia*, is a closer copy of the opinions of Socrates.

Phædo, describing the impression produced on him by the sight of Socrates on this final day, says:—" I did not feel the pity which it was natural I should feel at the death of a friend: on the contrary, he seemed to me perfectly happy as I gazed on him and listened to him: so calm and dignified was his bearing. And I thought that he only left this world under the protection of the Gods, who destined him to a more than mortal felicity in the next." He then details the conversation on the immortality of the soul; after which, he narrates the close of that glorious life in language worthy of it. Even in the English version of Taylor the beauty of the narrative stands manifestly out.

"When he had thus spoke, he rose, and went into a room, that he might wash himself, and Crito followed him: but he ordered us to wait for him. We waited, therefore, accordingly, discoursing over, and reviewing among ourselves, what had been said, and sometimes speaking about his death, how great a calamity it would be to us; and sincerely thinking that we, like those who are deprived of their father, should pass the rest of our life in the condition of orphans. But, when he had washed himself, his sons were brought to him (for he had two little ones, and one considerably advanced in age), and the women belonging to his family likewise came in to him: but when he had spoken to them before Crito, and had left them such injunctions as he thought proper, he ordered the boys and women to depart; and he himself returned to us. And it was now near the setting of the sun: for he had been absent for a long time in the bathing-room. But, when he came in from washing, he sat down, and did not speak much afterwards; for, then, the servant of the eleven magistrates came in, and, standing near him, I do not perceive that in you, Socrates (says he), which I have taken notice of in others; I mean that they are angry with me, and curse me, when, being compelled by the magistrates, I announce to them that they must drink the poison. But, on the contrary, I have found you at the present time to be the most generous, mild, and best of all the men who ever came into this place: and, therefore, I am now well convinced that you are not angry with me, but with the authors of your present condition. You know those whom I allude to. Now, therefore (for you know what I came to tell you), farewell! and endeavor to bear this necessity as easily as possible. And at the same time, bursting into tears, and turning himself away, he departed.

"Then Crito gave the sign to the boy that stood near him. And the boy departing, and, having staid for some time, came, bringing with him the person that was to administer the poison, and who brought it properly prepared in a cup. But, Socrates, beholding the man,—It's well, my friend (says he); but what is proper to do with it? for you are knowing in these affairs. You have nothing else to do (says he) but when you have drunk it to walk about, till a heaviness takes place in your legs, and afterwards lie down: this is the manner in which you should act. And, at the same time, he extended the cup to Socrates. But Socrates received it from him, and, indeed, with great cheerfulness; neither trembling nor suffering any alteration for the worse in his color or countenance, but, as he was accustomed to do, beholding the man with a bull-like aspect. What say you (says he) respecting this potion? Is it lawful to make a libation of it, or not? We only bruise (says he), Socrates, as much as we think sufficient for the purpose. I understand you (says he); but it is certainly both lawful and proper to pray to the Gods, that my departure from hence thither may be attended with prosperous fortune; which I entreat them to grant may be the case. And, at the same time ending his discourse, he drank the poison with exceeding facility and alacrity. And thus far, indeed, the greater part of us were tolerably well able to refrain from weeping; but, when we saw him drinking, and that he had drunk it, we could no longer restrain our tears. But from me, indeed, notwithstanding the violence which I employed in checking them, they flowed abundantly; so that, covering myself with my mantle, I deplored my misfortune. I did not, indeed, weep for him, but for my own fortune, considering what an associate I should be deprived of. But, Crito, who was not able to restrain his tears, was compelled to rise before me. And Apollodorus, who, during the whole time prior to this, had not ceased from weeping, then wept aloud, and with great bitterness; so that he infected all who were present except Socrates. But Socrates, upon seeing this, exclaimed: What are you doing, excellent men? For, indeed, I principally sent away the women, lest they should produce a disturbance of this kind. For I have heard it is proper to die attended with propitious omens. Be quiet, therefore, and summon fortitude to your assistance. But when we heard this we blushed, and restrained our tears. But he, when he found, during his walking, that his legs felt heavy, and had told us so, laid himself down in a supine position. For the man had ordered him to do so. And, at the same time, he who gave him the poison, touching him at intervals, considered his feet and legs. And, after he had vehemently pressed his foot, he asked him if he felt it. But Socrates answered he did not. And, after this, he again pressed his thighs: and, thus ascending with his hand, he showed us that he was cold and stiff. And Socrates also touched himself, and said that when the poison reached his heart he should then leave us. But now his lower belly was almost cold; when, uncovering himself (for he was covered) he said (which were his last words), Crito, we owe a cock to Æsculapius. Discharge this debt, therefore, for me, and don't neglect it. It shall be done (says Crito); but consider whether you have any other commands. To this inquiry of Crito he made no reply; but shortly after moved himself, and the man covered him. And Socrates fixed his eyes. Which, when Crito perceived, he closed his mouth and eyes. This was the end of our associate; a man, as it appears to me, the best of those whom we were acquainted with at that time; and, besides this, the most prudent and just."

Thus perished this great and good man, a martyr to Philosophy. His character we have endeavored to represent fairly, though briefly. Let us now add the summing-up of Xenophon, who loved him tenderly, and expressed his love gracefully:

"As to myself, knowing him of a truth to be such a man as I have described; so pious towards the Gods, as never to undertake any thing without first consulting them; so just towards men, as never to do any injury, even the very slightest, to any one, whilst many and great were the benefits he conferred on all with whom he had any dealings; so temperate and chaste, as not to indulge any appetite or inclination at the expense of whatever was modest and becoming; so prudent, as never to err in judging of good and evil, nor wanting the assistance of others to discriminate rightly concerning them; so able to discourse upon, and define with the greatest accuracy, not only those points of which we have been speaking, but likewise every other, and looking as it were into the minds of men, discover the very moment for reprehending vice, or stimulating to the love of virtue: experiencing, as I have done, all these excellencies in Socrates, I can never cease considering him as the most virtuous and the most happy of all mankind. But, if there is any one who is disposed to think otherwise, let him go and compare Socrates with any other, and afterwards let him determine."*

After ages have cherished the memory of his virtues and his

---

* *Memorabilia*, iv. 7

fate; but without profiting much by his example, and without learning tolerance from his story.

§ II. Philosophy of Socrates.

Opinions vary so considerably respecting the philosophy of Socrates, and materials whereby they can be tested are so scanty, that any attempt at exposition must be made with diffidence. The historian has to rely solely on his critical skill; and on such grounds, he will not, if prudent, be very confident.

Amongst the scattered materials from which an opinion may be formed are, 1st. The very general tradition of Socrates having produced a revolution in thought; in consequence of which he is by all regarded as the initiator of a new epoch; and by some as the founder of Greek Philosophy, properly so called. 2dly. The express testimony of Aristotle, that he first made use of *definitions* and proceeded by *induction*.* These two positions involve each other. If Socrates produced a revolution in philosophy, he could only have done so by a new Method. That Method we see exhibited in the phrase of Aristotle, but it is there only exhibited in a brief concentrated manner, and requires to be elucidated.

Assuredly we may echo Mr. Grote's statement, that it requires at the present day some mental effort to see any thing important in the invention of notions so familiar as those of Genus—Definition—Individual things as comprehended in a genus—what each thing is, and to what genus it belongs, etc. Nevertheless four centuries before Christ these terms denoted mental processes which few, if any but Socrates, had a distinct recognition of, in the form of analytical consciousness. "The ideas of men—

---

* "There are two things of which Socrates must justly be regarded as the author, the *Inductive Reasoning* and *Abstract Definitions*,"—τοὺς τ' ἐπακτικοὺς λόγους καὶ τὸ ὁρίζεσθαι καθόλου. (Arist. *Metaph.* xiii. 4.) Xenophon has several indications of the inductive method: he also says that Socrates always proceeded from propositions best known to those less known, which is a definition of Induction.

speakers as well as hearers, the productive minds as well as the recipient multitude—were associated together in groups, favorable rather to emotional results, or to poetical, rhetorical narrative, and descriptive effect, than to methodical generalization, to scientific conception, or to proof either inductive or deductive. That reflex act of attention which enables men to understand, compare, and rectify their own mental process was only just beginning. It was a recent novelty on the part of the rhetorical teachers to analyze the component parts of a public harangue, and to propound some precepts for making men tolerable speakers. It may be doubted whether any one before Socrates ever used the words Genus and Species (originally meaning Family and Form), in the philosophical sense now exclusively appropriated to them. Not one of those many names (called by logicians *names of the second intention*) which imply distinct attention to various parts of the logical process, and enable us to criticize it in detail, then existed. All of them grew out of the schools of Plato, Aristotle, and the subsequent philosophers, so that we can thus trace them in their beginning to the common root and father, Socrates."* The novelty was very distasteful to all who were not seduced by it. Men resent being forced to rigor of speech and thought; they call you "pedantic" if you insist on their using terms with definite meanings; they prefer the loose flowing language of indefinite association which picks up in its course a variety of heterogeneous meanings; and are irritated at any speaker who points out to them the inaccuracy of their phrases. Aristotle says it was thought bad taste in his day—ἡ ἀκριβολογία μικροπρεπές: and Timon the Sillograph sarcastically calls Socrates one of the ἀκριβόλογοι, as if precision of language were a vice.

"The notions of Genus, subordinate genera, and individuals as comprehended under them, were at that time newly brought into clear consciousness in the human mind. The profusion of

---

* Grote, viii. 578.

logical distribution employed in some of the dialogues of Plato seems partly traceable to his wish to familiarize his hearers with that which was then a novelty, as well as to enlarge its development and diversify its mode of application." "We must always consider the Method of Socrates in conjunction with the subjects to which he applied it. . . . On such questions as these—What is justice?—What is piety?—What is democracy?—What is law?—every man fancied that he could give a confident opinion, and even wondered that any other person should feel a difficulty. When Socrates, professing ignorance, put any such question, he found no difficulty in obtaining an answer, given offhand and with very little reflection. The answer purported to be the explanation or definition of a term, familiar indeed, but of wide and comprehensive import,—given by one who had never before tried to render to himself an account of what it meant. Having got this answer, Socrates put fresh questions, applying it to specific cases, to which the respondent was compelled to give answers inconsistent with the first; showing that the definition was either too narrow or too wide, or defective in some essential condition. The respondent then amended his answer; but this was a prelude to other questions, which could only be answered in ways inconsistent with the amendment; and the respondent, after many attempts to disentangle himself, was obliged to plead guilty to the inconsistencies, with an admission that he could make no satisfactory answer to the original query which at first had appeared so easy and familiar. . . The discussion first raised by Socrates turns upon the meaning of some large generic term. The queries whereby he follows it up bring the answer given into collision with various particulars which it ought not to comprehend, or with others which it ought to comprehend, but does not. The inconsistencies into which the hearer is betrayed in his various answers proclaim to him the fact that he has not yet acquired any thing like a clear and full conception of the common attribute which binds together the various particulars embraced under some term which is ever upon his lips. He is thus put upon the train of thought which leads to a correction of the generalization, and lights him on to that which Plato calls seeing the One in the Many, and the Many in the One."*

Because Socrates employed Induction, it is frequently stated that he anticipated Bacon's Inductive Method. Passages can certainly be quoted in which Socrates and Bacon hold very similar language; and in some respects their reform was analogous; but the differences are more profound than the resemblances. The aim and purpose of Socrates was confessedly to withdraw the mind from contemplating the phenomena of nature, and to fix it on its own phenomena: truth was to be sought by looking inwards, not by looking outwards. The aim and purpose of Bacon's philosophy was the reverse of this; he exhorted men to the observation and interpretation of nature, and energetically denounced all attempts to discover the operations of mind. If Socrates pushed too far this contempt of physics, Bacon pushed too far his contempt of psychology: the exaggeration was, in each case, produced by the absurdities of contemporaries.

Not more decided is the contrast between their conceptions of Induction. With Socrates it was little more than *Inductio per enumerationem simplicem*, or "reasoning by analogy,"—the mere collection of particular facts,—a process which it was Bacon's peculiar merit to have utterly destroyed. The whole force of the *Novum Organum* may be said to be directed against this erroneous method. The triviality of the method may indeed be seen in the quibbles to which it furnishes support in Plato; it may be seen also in the argument used by Aristippus to justify his living with Laïs the courtesan. "Do you think, Diogenes, that there is any thing odd in inhabiting a house that others have inhabited before you?—No. Or sailing in a ship in which many men have sailed before you?—No. By parity of reasoning, then, there is nothing odd in living with a woman

---

* Grote, viii. 583-3.

whom many men have lived with before." This quibble is a legitimate Socratic induction; and it was made by a pupil of Socrates. It is only a parody of the arguments by which it was proved that to inflict injustice is more painful than to suffer it; one of the many startling dogmas attributed to Socrates. Whoever supposes this Induction to be the Baconian Induction (which is an *interrogation* of nature), has missed the sense of the *Novum Organum*. Indeed, to suppose that such a conception as Bacon's could have been originated so early in the history of science, is radically to mistake the course of human development.

Mr. Grote has quoted several striking passages from Bacon,[*] to show the parallel between the spirit and purpose of the Baconian and Socratic Methods; and probably most readers will agree with him when he says that Socrates "sought to test the fundamental notions and generalizations respecting man and society in the same spirit in which Bacon approached those of Physics: he suspected the unconscious process of the growing intellect, and desired to revise it, by comparison with particulars, and from particulars, too, the most clear and certain, but which, from being of vulgar occurrence, were least attended to. And that which Socrates described in his language as the 'conceit of knowledge without the reality' is identical with what Bacon designates as the *primary notions*—the *puerile observations*—the *aberrations* of the intellect left to itself." But in spite of this resemblance the difference is profound, and it rises into unmistakable distinctness when we consider the results in the philosophies of the two; the Socratic Method is seen developed in Plato and Aristotle, the Baconian in Newton and Faraday; and if, as was stated in our Introduction, the adoption of the Method of graduated Verification was not owing to a previous circumscription of the aims of Philosophy, but, on the contrary, if this Method necessarily led to the circumscription, it follows that systems so metaphysical as those which came out of the Socratic teaching

---

[*] Vol. viii. p. 612.

must have been the produce of a very different Method from that which led to modern science.

Conceit of knowledge, without the reality, was by Socrates perpetually stigmatized as the most disgraceful of mental defects,[*] and the whole effort of his terrible questioning—the "cross-examining Elenchus"—was to make men aware of this conceit, to prove to them that their knowledge was a *sham*, as Carlyle would call it. Instead of the loose, heterogeneous conceptions with which men deceived themselves and others into the belief of knowledge, he insisted on the substitution of rigorous and distinct conceptions.

How could this be done but by definitions? To know the essence of a thing you must consider it as distinct from every thing else, you must *define* it; by defining it you demarcate it from what it is *not*, and so present the thing before you in its essence.

It was a fundamental conviction with him that it is impossible to start from one true thought, and be entangled in any contradiction with another true thought; knowledge derived from any one point, and obtained by correct combination, cannot contradict that which has been obtained from any other point. He believed that Reason was pregnant with Truths, and only needed an accoucheur. An accoucheur he announced himself; his main instruments were Definitions. By Definition he enabled the thinker to separate the particular thought he wished to express, from the myriad of other thoughts which clouded it. By Definition he enabled a man to contemplate the essence of a thing, because he admitted nothing which was not essential into the definition.

The radical mistake here is the confusion between Definitions of Names and Definitions of Things. In the Definition of a Name nothing more is applied than the meaning *intended* to be affixed·

---

[*] Plato, *Apologia*, p. 29 (p. 114, ed. Bekker): καὶ τοῦτο πῶς οὐκ ἀμαθία ἐστὶν αὕτη ἡ ἐπονείδιστος, ἡ τοῦ οἴεσθαι εἰδέναι ἃ οὐκ οἶδεν;

in the definition of a Thing there is, over and above this intended meaning, the assertion of a corresponding fact which the definition describes.

We have more than once commented on the natural tendency of the early thinkers to mistake distinctions in words for distinctions in things. We have now to signalize, in the history of speculation, the reduction of this tendency to a systematic formula. Names henceforth have the force of things.* A correct Definition is held to be a true description of the Thing *per se:* the *explanation of terms* as equivalent to the *explanation of things*, and the *exhibition of the nature of any thing in a definition* as equivalent to our *actual analysis of it in a laboratory*—are the central errors of the Platonic and Aristotelian philosophy. These errors continue to flourish in all the metaphysical systems of the present day.

When stated in a naked manner, the absurdity of this Method is apparent; but it may be so disguised as to look profoundly philosophic. Hence the frequent use of such locutions as that certain properties are "involved in the idea" of certain things; as if being involved in the idea, *i. e.* being included in the definition, necessarily implied a correspondent *objective* existence; as if human conceptions were the faithful copies of external things. The conceptions of men widely differ; consequently different properties are "involved" in these different conceptions; but all cannot be true, and the question arises, Which conception is true? To answer this question by any thing like a definition, is to argue in a circle. A principle of certitude must be sought. That principle, however, is still to seek.

The influence of the theory of definitions will be more distinctly discernible as we proceed. It is the one grand characteristic of the Method Socrates originated. In it must be sought the explanation of his views of Philosophy.

He has been almost taunted with never having promulgated

---

* See Plato's *Cratylus, passim.*

any system of his own. His rank in the history of philosophy has been questioned, and has been supposed to be only that of a moralist. A passage of Aristotle has been quoted as decisive on this point: "The speculations of Socrates were only concerning Ethics, and not at all concerning Nature in general" (τῆς ὅλης φύσεως). But this is not *all* the passage: it continues thus: "In these speculations he sought the Abstract (τὸ καθόλου), and was the first who thought of giving definitions." Now in this latter portion we believe there is contained a hint of something more than the mere moralist—a hint of the metaphysician. On turning to another part of Aristotle's treatise* we accordingly find this hint more clearly brought out; we find an express indication of the metaphysician. The passage is as follows: "Socrates concerned himself with ethical virtues, and he first sought the abstract definitions of these. Before him Democritus had only concerned himself with a part of Physics, and defined but the Hot and the Cold. But Socrates, reasonably (εὐλόγως), sought the Essence of Things, *i. e.* sought *what exists.*"

Moveover, in another passage (lib. iii. c. 2) Aristotle reproaches Aristippus for having rejected science, and concerned himself solely with morals. This is surely negative evidence that Socrates was not to be blamed for the same opinion; otherwise he would have been also mentioned.

It was a natural mistake to suppose that Socrates was only a Moralist, seeing that his principal topics were always Man and Society, and never Physical speculations, which he deemed beyond the reach of human intellect. If, however, Socrates had been merely a Moralist, his place in the history of Philosophy would not have been what it is; no Plato, no Aristotle would have called him master. He made a new epoch. The previous philosophers had directed their attention to external Nature, endeavoring to explain its phenomena; he gave up all such speculations, and directed his attention solely to the nature of Knowledge.

---

* *Metaph.* xiii. 4.

Men speculated at random. They sought truth, but they only built hypotheses, because they had not previously ascertained the *limits and conditions of inquiry.* They attempted to *form sciences* before having settled the *conditions of Science.* It was the peculiar merit of Socrates to have proposed, as the grand question of philosophy, the nature and conditions of Science.

The reader may now begin to appreciate the importance of Definitions in the Socratic Method, and may understand why Socrates did not himself invent systems, but only a Method. He likened himself to a Midwife, who, though unable to bring forth children herself, assisted women in their labors. He believed that in each man lay the germs of wisdom. He believed that no science could be *taught;* only *drawn out.* To borrow the ideas of another was not to learn; to guide one's self by the judgment of another was blindness. The philosophers, who pretended to teach every thing, could teach nothing; and their ignorance was manifest in the very pretension. Each man must conquer truth for himself, by rigid struggle with himself. He, Socrates, was willing to assist any man when in the pains of labor: he could do no more.

Such being the Method, we cannot wonder at his having attached himself to Ethical rather than to Physical speculations. His philosophy was a realization of the inscription at Delphos— *Know Thyself.* It was in himself that he found the ground of certitude which was to protect him against skepticism. It was therefore moral science which he prized above all others. Indeed, we have great reason to believe that his energetic denouncement of Physical speculations, as reported by Xenophon was the natural, though exaggerated, conclusion to which he had been hurried by a consideration of the manifold absurdities into which they drew the mind, and the skepticism which they induced. There could be nothing but uncertainty on such subjects.

"I have not leisure for such things," he is made to say by Plato, "and I will tell you the reason: I am not yet able, according to the Delphic Inscription, to *Know myself;* and it appears to me very ridiculous, while ignorant of myself, to inquire into what I am not concerned in."* That he did, however, at one period occupy himself with them is clear from other sources, and is a point in the comedy of the *Clouds*, where he is represented "air-treading and speculating about the sun,"—ἀεροβατῶ καὶ περιφρονῶ τὸν ἥλιον,—and his disciples seeking things hidden underground —τὰ κατὰ γῆς. This has led many to suppose that Aristophanes knew nothing whatever of Socrates, but only took him as an available comic type of the Sophists,—a supposition to which there are several objections. Firstly, it is not usual in satirists to select for their butt a person of whom they know nothing. Secondly, Socrates, of all Athenians, was the most notorious, and most easily to be acquainted with in a general way. Thirdly, he could not be a type of the Sophists, in as far as related to physical speculations, since we well know the Sophists scouted physics. Fourthly, he did occupy himself with Physics early in his career; and probably did so when Aristophanes satirized him, although in after-life he regarded such speculations as trivial.

It was quite possible that Aristophanes should have made no such nice discrimination between the dialectical quibbling of Socrates and that of the Sophists, as would prevent him from representing Socrates teaching "the art to make the worse appear the better reason;"† but it is scarcely credible that he should have made so flagrant a mistake as to accuse Socrates of busying himself with Physics, when every one of the audience could answer that Socrates never troubled himself at all about it. In our day Proudhon and Louis Blanc are often classed together as teachers of the same Socialist doctrines; or Strauss and Feuerbach as teachers of the same theological doctrines; but no satirist would laugh at Louis Blanc for his astronomical speculations, or at Strauss for his devotion to the Microscope. The Aristophanic evidence, therefore, seems perfectly admissible as respects the physical speculations of Socrates at or about the time when the *Clouds* was pro-

---

* *Phædrus*, p. 8. † *Nubes*, v. 112–15.

duced. If they were afterwards relinquished, it was because they led to no certainty.

That Philosophy, and not Morals, was really the aim of Socrates, is clear from his subordination of all morals to science. He considers Virtue to be identical with Knowledge.* Only the wise man, said he, can be brave, just, or temperate. Vice of every kind is Ignorance; and involuntary, because ignorant. If a man is cowardly, it is because he does not rightly appreciate the importance of life and death. He thinks death an evil, and flees it. If he were wise, he would know that death is a good thing, or, at the worst, an indifferent one, and therefore would not shun it. If a man is intemperate, it is because he is unable to estimate the relative value of present pleasure and future pain. Ignorance misleads him. It is the nature of man to seek good and shun evil: he would never seek evil, knowing it to be such; if he seeks it, he mistakes it for good: if he is intemperate, it is because he is unwise.

Method was his all-in-all. Nor is it impossible to trace the origin of this conception in his mind. The Pythian oracle had declared him to be the wisest of men. The assertion greatly puzzled him, for he found on deep introspection that he knew nothing; all his fancied knowledge was that conceit of knowledge without the reality, which he saw puffing up other men; and his sole distinction was that *he* knew the depth of his own

---

* Φρονήσεις ᾤετο ἵλαι πάσας τὰς ἀρετάς.—Aristot. *Ethic. Nicomach.* vi. 13. Plato, in the *Meno*, makes him maintain that Virtue cannot be Science, cannot be taught. But this is not Socratic. "Whether Virtue can be taught was a question much agitated in the time of Socrates, who appears to give contradictory decisions on different occasions. Comp. Plat. *Meno*, pp. 96, 98, with *Protagoras*, p. 361, in the latter of which passages he censures his own inconsistency, in first denying that Virtue can be taught, and then maintaining that Virtue is Science. Ascending to Xenophon, *Mem.* i. 2, 19, Socrates seems to have adopted the common-sense view that Virtue is partly matter of teaching, partly of practice (ἀσκητόν), and partly of natural disposition. But Xenophon was unconscious of the logical difficulty of reconciling this with that identification of Virtue with Science or Wisdom which he elsewhere distinctly attributes to his master."—Thompson's Note to *Butler's History of Philosophy*, i. 374.

ignorance, while *they* believed themselves to be knowing; and it was because he knew this that he understood the meaning of the oracle. Thus much we have on his explicit authority. If we now consider that his title of the "wisest" was owing to the profound consciousness of the unreality of all which hitherto had passed for wisdom (the proof of which was exposed by means of his cross-examining Elenchus), we shall be able to understand how it was he came to make his Method in and for itself the great aim of Philosophy, and how instead of desiring to make converts to any system, or to gain acceptance for any special theories on physics or ethics, he always and everywhere desired to awaken the cross-examining spirit in the minds of his hearers, so that each in his own turn might awaken it in others, because in this, and this alone, consisted real Wisdom. Previous philosophies had shown the futility of speculation; certitude was nowhere to be had; all such theories were but the conceit of knowledge. The Method which he taught was that by which alone man could become wiser and better.

It is clear that the novelty of the Method so completely fascinated him, as to prevent his detecting the confusion he made between end and means. And the reader may understand how such a confusion might very naturally have maintained itself, if he reflects how very analogous is the pursuit of purely mathematical science by hundreds who care nothing for the applications of mathematics. Lying at the base of all physical science is a great and complex science of Quantity,—the one indispensable Instrument by means of which Knowledge becomes Science (for Science is only quantitative knowledge); but so vast and so complex is this Instrument, that numerous intellects are constantly engaged in studying and perfecting it, never once withdrawn from it by any attempt at application. In a similar way Socrates, and for the most part Plato likewise, cared exclusively for Method; perfecting the Instrument of search, rather than seeking.

Although Socrates was not the first to teach the doctrine of the immortality of the soul, he was the first to give it a philosophical basis. Nor can we read without admiration the arguments by which he anticipated writers on Natural Theology, by pointing out the evidences of a beneficent Providence. Listen to Xenophon:

"I will now relate the manner in which I once heard Socrates discoursing with Aristodemus, surnamed *the Little*, concerning the Deity; for observing that he neither prayed nor sacrificed to the Gods, but, on the contrary, ridiculed and laughed at those who did, he said to him:

"Tell me, Aristodemus, is there any man whom you admire on account of his merit? Aristodemus having answered 'Many,' —Name some of them, I pray you. I admire, said Aristodemus, Homer for his Epic poetry, Melanippides for his dithyrambics, Sophocles for tragedy, Polycletus for statuary, and Zeuxis for painting.

"But which seems to you most worthy of admiration, Aristodemus?—the artist who forms images void of motion and intelligence, or one who hath the skill to produce animals that are endued not only with activity, but understanding?—The latter, there can be no doubt, replied Aristodemus, provided the production was not the effect of chance, but of wisdom and contrivance.—But since there are many things, some of which we can easily see the use of, while we cannot say of others to what purpose they were produced, which of these, Aristodemus, do you suppose the work of wisdom?—It should seem the most reasonable to affirm it of those whose fitness and utility are so evidently apparent.

"But it is evidently apparent that He who at the beginning made man, endued him with senses because they were good for him; eyes, wherewith to behold whatever was visible; and ears, to hear whatever was to be heard; for say, Aristodemus, to what purpose should odors be prepared, if the sense of smelling had been denied? or why the distinctions of bitter and sweet, of savory and unsavory, unless a palate had been likewise given, conveniently placed, to arbitrate between them and declare the difference!

Is not that Providence, Aristodemus, in a most eminent manner conspicuous, which, because the eye of man is so delicate in its contexture, hath therefore prepared eyelids like doors, whereby to secure it, which extend of themselves whenever it is needful, and again close when sleep approaches? Are not these eyelids provided as it were with a fence on the edge of them, to keep off the wind and guard the eye? Even the eyebrow itself is not without its office, but, as a penthouse, is prepared to turn off the sweat, which, falling from the forehead, might enter and annoy that no less tender than astonishing part of us. Is it not to be admired that the ears should take in sounds of every sort, and yet are not too much filled by them? That the fore-teeth of the animal should be formed in such a manner as is evidently best suited for the cutting of its food, as those on the side for grinding it to pieces? That the mouth, through which this food is conveyed, should be placed so near the nose and eyes as to prevent the passing unnoticed whatever is unfit for nourishment; while Nature, on the contrary, hath set at a distance and concealed from the senses all that might disgust or any way offend them? And canst thou still doubt, Aristodemus, whether a disposition of parts like this should be the work of chance, or of wisdom and contrivance?—I have no longer any doubt, replied Aristodemus; and, indeed, the more I consider it, the more evident it appears to me that man must be the masterpiece of some great artificer; carrying along with it infinite marks of the love and favor of Him who hath thus formed it.

"And what thinkest thou, Aristodemus, of that desire in the individual which leads to the continuance of the species? Of that tenderness and affection in the female towards her young, so necessary for its preservation? Of that unremitted love of life, and dread of dissolution, which take such strong possession of us from the moment we begin to be? I think of them, answered Aristodemus, as so many regular operations of the same great and wise Artist, deliberately determining to preserve what he hath made.

"But, farther (unless thou desirest to ask me questions), seeing, Aristodemus, thou thyself art conscious of reason and intelligence, supposest thou there is no intelligence elsewhere? Thou knowest thy body to be a small part of that wide extended earth which thou everywhere beholdest: the moisture contained in it, thou also knowest to be a small portion of that mighty mass of waters, whereof seas themselves are but a part, while the rest of the elements contribute out of their abundance to thy formation. It is the soul then alone, that intellectual part of us, which is come to thee by some lucky chance, from I know not where. If so be there is indeed no intelligence elsewhere: and we must be forced to confess, that this stupendous universe, with all the various bodies contained therein,—equally amazing, whether we consider their magnitude or number, whatever their use, whatever their order,—all have been produced, not by intelligence, but by chance!—It is with difficulty that I can suppose otherwise, returned Aristodemus; for I behold none of those Gods whom you speak of as making and governing all things; whereas I see the artists when at their work here among us.—Neither yet seest thou thy soul, Aristodemus, which, however most assuredly governs thy body; although it may well seem, by thy manner of talking, that it is chance, and not reason, which governs thee.

"I do not despise the Gods, said Aristodemus: on the contrary, I conceive so highly of their excellence, as to suppose they stand in no need either of me or of my services.—Thou mistakest the matter, Aristodemus; the greater magnificence they have shown in their care of thee, so much the more honor and service thou owest them.—Be assured, said Aristodemus, if I once could be persuaded the Gods take care of man, I should want no monitor to remind me of my duty.—And canst thou doubt, Aristodemus, if the Gods take care of man? Hath not the glorious privilege of walking upright been alone bestowed on him, whereby he may with the better advantage survey what is around him, contemplate with more ease those splendid objects which are above, and avoid the numerous ills and inconveniences which would otherwise befall him? Other animals indeed they have provided with feet, by which they may remove from one place to another; but to man they have also given hands, with which he can form many things for his use, and make himself happier than creatures of any other kind. A tongue hath been bestowed on every other animal; but what animal, except man, hath the power of forming words with it, whereby to explain his thoughts, and make them intelligible to others?

"But it is not with respect to the body alone that the Gods have shown themselves thus bountiful to man. Their most excellent gift is that soul they have infused into him, which so far surpasses what is elsewhere to be found; for by what animal, except man, is even the existence of those Gods discovered, who have produced and still uphold, in such regular order, this beautiful and stupendous frame of the universe? What other species of creature is to be found that can serve, that can adore them? What other animal is able, like man, to provide against the assaults of heat and cold, of thirst and hunger? that can lay up remedies for the time of sickness, and improve the strength nature has given by a well-proportioned exercise? that can receive like him information or instruction; or so happily keep in memory what he hath seen, and heard, and learnt? These things being so, who seeth not that man is, as it were, a God in the midst of this visible creation? so far doth he surpass, whether in the endowments of soul or body, all animals whatsoever that have been produced therein; for if the body of the ox had been joined to the mind of man, the acuteness of the latter would have stood him in small stead, while unable to execute the well-designed plan; nor would the human form have been of more use to the brute, so long as it remained destitute of understanding! But in thee, Aristodemus, hath been joined to a wonderful soul a body no less wonderful; and sayest thou, after this, the Gods take no thought for me? What wouldst thou then more to convince thee of their care?

"I would they should send and inform me, said Aristodemus, what things I ought or ought not to do, in like manner as thou sayest they frequently do to thee.—And what then, Aristodemus? supposest thou, that when the Gods give out some oracle to all the Athenians they mean it not for thee? If by their prodigies they declare aloud to all Greece, to all mankind, the things which shall befall them, are they dumb to thee alone? And art thou the only person whom they have placed beyond their care? Believest thou they would have wrought into the mind of man a persuasion of their being able to make him happy or miserable, if so be they had no such power? or would not even man himself, long ere this, have seen through the gross delusion? How is it, Aristodemus, thou rememberest or remarkest not, that the kingdoms and commonwealths most renowned as well for their wisdom as antiquity, are those whose piety and devotion hath been the most observable? and that even man himself is never so well disposed to serve the Deity as in that part of life when reason bears the greatest sway, and his judgment is supposed in its full strength and maturity? Consider, my Aristodemus, that the soul which resides in thy body can govern it at pleasure; why then may not the soul of the universe, which pervades and animates every part of it, govern it in like manner? If thine eye hath the power to take in many objects, and these placed at no small distance from it, marvel not if the eye of the Deity can at one glance comprehend the whole. And as thou perceivest it not beyond thy ability to extend thy care, at the same time, to the concerns of Athens, Egypt, Sicily, why thinkest thou, my Aristodemus, that the Providence of God may not easily extend itself through the whole universe?

"As therefore, among men, we make best trial of the affection and gratitude of our neighbor by showing him kindness, and discover his wisdom by consulting him in his distress, do thou in like manner behave towards the Gods; and if thou wouldst experience what their wisdom and what their love, render thyself deserving the communication of some of those divine secrets which may not be penetrated by man, and are imparted to those alone who consult, who adore, who obey the Deity. Then shalt thou, my Aristodemus, understand there is a Being whose eye pierceth throughout all nature, and whose ear is open to every sound; extended to all places, extending through all time; and whose bounty and care can know no other bound than those fixed by his own creation.

"By this discourse, and others of the like nature, Socrates taught his friends that they were not only to forbear whatever was impious, unjust, or unbecoming before man; but even when alone they ought to have a regard to all their actions, since the Gods have their eyes continually upon us, and none of our designs can be concealed from them."*

To this passage we must add another equally deserving of attention:

"Even among all those deities who so liberally bestow on us good things, not one of them maketh himself an object of our sight. And He who raised this whole universe, and still upholds the mighty frame, who perfected every part of it in beauty and in goodness, suffering none of these parts to decay through age, but renewing them daily with unfading vigor, whereby they are able to execute whatever he ordains with that readiness and precision which surpass man's imagination; even He, the supreme God, who performeth all these wonders, still holds himself invisible, and it is only in his works that we are capable of admiring him. For consider, my Euthydemus, the sun, which seemeth as it were set forth to the view of all men, yet suffereth not itself to be too curiously examined; punishing those with blindness who too rashly venture so to do; and those ministers of the Gods, whom they employ to execute their bidding, remain to us invisible; for though the thunderbolt is shot from on high, and breaketh in pieces whatever it findeth in its way, yet no one seeth it when it falls, when it strikes, or when it retires; neither are the

---

* *Memorabilia*, i. 4.

winds discoverable to our sight, though we plainly behold the ravages they everywhere make, and with ease perceive what time they are rising. And if there be any thing in man, my Euthydemus, partaking of the divine nature, it must surely be the soul which governs and directs him; yet no one considers this as an object of his sight. Learn, therefore, not to despise those things which you cannot see; judge of the greatness of the power by the effects which are produced, and reverence the Deity."*

In conclusion, we must notice the vexed question of the Demon of Socrates. The notion most generally current is that he believed himself accompanied by a Dæmon, or Good Angel, who whispered counsels in his ear, and forewarned him on critical occasions. This has been adduced as evidence of his "superstition;" and one writer—to be sure he is a Frenchman—makes it a text to prove that Socrates was mad.† Olympiodorus said that the Dæmon only meant Conscience, an explanation which, while it effaces the peculiar characteristics of the conception, is at the same time totally inapplicable to those cases when the "Dæmonic voice" spoke to Socrates concerning the affairs of his friends, as we read in Plato's *Theages*. By other writers the Dæmon has been considered as purely allegorical.

The first point necessary to be distinctly understood is, that Socrates believed in no special Dæmon at all; and to translate Plutarch's treatise into *De Genio Socratis*, and hence to speak of *le démon de Socrate*, is gross misconception. Nowhere does Socrates, in Plato or Xenophon, speak of *a* genius or demon, but always of a *dæmonic something* (τὸ δαιμόνιον, δαιμόνιον τι), or of a *sign*, a *voice*, a *divine sign*, a *divine voice*.‡ The second point

---

* *Memorabilia*, iv. 3.

† Lélut, *Du Démon de Socrate*, 1836. A new edition of this work appeared in 1856, and excited a "sensation."

‡ See passages cited in Zeller, ii. 28 (1846). Mr. Thompson in his note to Butler, i. 375, says:—"Clemens Alexandrinus in one passage *conjectures* that the δαιμόνιον of Socrates may have been a familiar genius. *Strom.* v. p. 592. This conjecture becomes an assertion in Lactantius (*Inst. D.* ii. 14) who con-

necessary to be remembered is, that this "divine voice" was only an *occasional* manifestation, and exercised only a *restraining* influence. On the great critical occasions of his life, if the voice warned him against any step he was about to take, he unhesitatingly obeyed it; if the voice was unheard, he concluded that his proposed step was agreeable to the Gods. Thus, when on his trial, he refused to prepare any defence, because when he was about to begin it the voice restrained him, whereupon he resigned himself to the trial, convinced that if it were the pleasure of the Gods that he should die, he ought in no wise to struggle—if it were their pleasure that he should be set free, defence on his part was needless.

This is his own explicit statement; and surely in a Christian country abounding in examples of persons believing in direct intimations from above, there can be little difficulty in crediting such a statement. Socrates was a profoundly religious man; he was moreover, as we learn from Aristotle, a man of that bilious melancholic temperament* which has in all times been observed in persons of unusual religious fervor, such as is implied in those momentary exaltations of the mind which are mistaken for divine visits; and when the rush of thought came upon him with strange warning voices, he believed it was the Gods who spoke directly to him. Unless we conceive Socrates as a profoundly religious man, we shall misconceive the whole spirit of his life and teaching. In many respects he was a fanatic, but only in the noble sense of the word: a man, like Carlyle, intolerant, vehement, "possessed" by his ideas, but, like Carlyle, preserved from all the worst consequences of such intolerance and possession by an immense humor and a tender heart. His

---

verts the *dæmonium* into *dæmon*. Apuleius, it is true, had already led the way to this error in his treatise *De Deo Socratis*. It is adopted without scruple by Augustine and other Christian writers; and, as might have been expected, by Ficinus and the earlier moderns, as Stanley and Dacier, in whose writings the *dæmonium* appears full-fledged as "an attendant spirit" or "good angel."

* φύσιν μελαγχολικήν, Aristotle, *Problem*. 30.

Saturnine melancholy was relieved by laughter, which softened and humanized a spirit otherwise not less vehement than that of a Dominic or a Calvin. Thus strengthened and thus softened, Socrates stands out as the grandest figure in the world's Pantheon: the bravest, truest, simplest, wisest of mankind.

FIFTH EPOCH.

PARTIAL ADOPTION OF THE SOCRATIC METHOD.

§ I. THE MEGARIC SCHOOL.—EUCLID.

"SEVERAL philosophers," says Cicero, "drew from the conversations of Socrates very different results; and, according as each adopted views which harmonized with his own, they in their turn became heads of philosophical schools all differing amongst each other." It is one of the peculiarities of a *philosophical* Method, to adapt itself indiscriminately to all sorts of systems. A *scientific* Method is confined to one: if various and opposing systems spring from it, they spring from an erroneous or imperfect application of it.

We must not be surprised therefore to find many contradictory systems claiming the parentage of Socrates. But we must be on our guard against supposing that this adaptation to various systems is a proof of the excellence of the Socratic Method. It is only a proof of its vagueness. It may be accepted as a sign of the great influence exercised upon succeeding philosophers: it is no sign that the influence was in the right direction.

As we said, Socrates had no school; he taught no system. He exhibited a Method; and this Method his hearers severally applied. Around him were men of various ages, various temperaments, and various opinions. He discoursed with each upon his own subject: with Xenophon on politics; with Theages or Theætetus on science; with Antisthenes on morals; with Ion on poetry. Some were *convinced* by him; others were merely *refuted*. The difference between the two is great. Of those who were convinced, the so-called Socratic Schools were formed; those who were only refuted became his enemies. But, of the former, some were naturally only more or less convinced; that is, were willing to adopt his opinions on some subjects, but remained stubborn on others. These are the imperfect Socratists. Amongst the latter was Euclid of Megara.

Euclid, who must not be confounded with the great Mathematician, was born at Megara; date probably between 450 and 440 B. C. He had early imbibed a great love of philosophy, and had diligently studied the writings of Parmenides and the other Eleatics. From Zeno he acquired great facility in dialectics; and this continued to be his chief excellence even, after his acquaintance with Socrates, who reproved him for it as sophistical.

His delight in listening to Socrates was so great that he frequently exposed his life to do so. A decree was passed, in consequence of the enmity existing between Athens and Megara, that any inhabitant of Megara found in Athens should forfeit his life; Euclid, however, braved the penalty. He frequently came to Athens at night, disguised as a female. The distance was twenty miles. At the end of his journey he was recompensed by the fascinating conversation of Socrates; and he returned to meditate on the results of their arguments.

Brucker's supposition that a rupture was caused between them in consequence of Socrates having reproved Euclid's disputatious tendency, is wholly without foundation, and seems contradicted by the notorious fact that when, on the death of Socrates, Plato and the majority of the disciples retired to Megara, in fear of some popular outbreak of the Athenians, who were in a state of rage against all the philosopher's friends, Euclid received them well. Bound by the same ties of friendship towards the illustrious martyr, and sharing some of his opinions, the Socratists made some stay in Megara. Differences however arose, as they will amongst all communities of the kind. Plato and some others returned to Athens, as soon as the state of the public mind admitted their doing so with safety. The rest remained with Euclid

"The character of the Megaric doctrine," says Ritter, "so far as it is possible to fix it in the defective state of our information, may be briefly given as the Eleatic view enlarged by the Socratic conviction of the *moral obligation, and the laws of scientific thought.*"

We confess our inability to comprehend this. In Euclid we have no hint of "moral obligation;" in Socrates we fail to detect the "laws of scientific thought." If by the former Ritter means, that Euclid gave an Ethical and Socratic meaning to the Eleatic doctrine, he is correct; if by the latter he means, that Euclid adopted the Socratic Method of Induction and Definitions, he is hopelessly wrong; and, if this is not what he means by "laws of scientific thought," we are at a loss to understand him.

Euclid agreed with the Eleatics in maintaining that there was but One unalterable Being, to be known by Reason only. This One Being was not simply *The One;* neither was it simply Intelligence; it was *The Good.* This One Being received various names according to its various aspects: thus it was sometimes Wisdom (φρόνησις); sometimes God (θεός); at others Reason (νοῦς); and so forth. This One Good (ἕν τὸ ἀγαθόν) is the only Being that really *exists;* every thing opposed to it has nothing but a phenomenal, transitory existence.

Such is the outline of his doctrine, as presented by Diogenes Laertius. In it the reader will have no difficulty in detecting both the Eleatic and Socratic elements. The conception of God as τὸ ἀγαθόν—the Good—is purely Socratic; and the denial of any existence to things opposed to the Good is an explanation of that passage in Plato's *Republic,* where Socrates declares God not to be the author of all things, but only of such as are good.*

The Megaric doctrine is therefore the Eleatic doctrine, with an Ethical tendency borrowed from Socrates, who taught that virtue was not any partial cultivation of the human mind, but constitutes the true and entire essence of the rational man, and

---

* Μὴ πάντων αἴτιον τὸν θεὸν, ἀλλὰ τῶν ἀγαθῶν.—ii. 100.

indeed of the whole universe. The identification of Virtue with Wisdom is also Socratic.

With respect to Euclid's dialectics there is one point, often alluded to, variously interpreted, and which is in direct opposition to the Method of Socrates. In refuting his adversaries he did not attack the premises, but the conclusion.* This is certainly not the manner of Socrates, who always managed to draw new conclusions from old premises, and who, as Xenophon says, proceeded from the generally known to the less known. As if to mark this distinction more completely, we are told that Euclid rejected the *analogical* mode of reasoning (τὸν διὰ παραβολῆς λόγον). If, said he, the things compared are alike, it is better to confine the attention to that originally in question; if the things compared are unlike, there must be error in the conclusion. This precept strikes into the weakness of Socrates' method of induction; which was a species of analogical reasoning not of the highest order.

In dialectics therefore we see Euclid following out the Eleatic tendency, and carrying forward the speculations of Zeno. It was this portion of his doctrine that his immediate followers, Eubulides, Diodorus, and Alexinus, undertook to carry out. The Socratic element was further developed by Stilpo.

"The majority of the later members of the Megaric School," says Ritter, "are famous either for the refutation of opposite doctrines, or for the invention and application of certain fallacies; on which account they were occasionally called Eristici and Dialectici. Still it may be presumed that they did not employ these fallacies for the purposes of delusion, but of instructing rash and hasty thinkers, and exemplifying the superficial vanity of common opinion. At all events, it is certain that they were mainly occupied with the forms of thought, more perhaps with a

---

* *Diog. Laert.* ii. 107. This is paraphrased by Enfield into the following contradictory statement:—"He judged that legitimate argumentation consists in deducing fair conclusions from acknowledged premises."—*Hist. of Phil.* i. 199.

view to the discovery of particular rules, than to the foundation of a scientific system or method."

§ II. The Cyrenaic School.—Aristippus.

Among the "imperfect Socratists" we must rank Aristippus, the founder of the Cyrenaic School, which borrowed its name from the birthplace of its founder—Cyrene, in Africa.

Aristippus was descended from wealthy and distinguished parents, and was consequently thrown into the vortex of luxurious debauchery which then characterized the colony of Minyæ. He came over to Greece to attend the Olympic games: there he heard so much of the wisdom of Socrates that he determined on listening to his enchanting discourse. He made Socrates an offer of a large sum of money, which, as usual, was declined. The great Talker did not accept money; but he willingly admitted Aristippus among the number of his disciples. It is commonly asserted that the pupil did not agree well with his master, and that his fondness for pleasure was offensive to Socrates. There is no good authority for such an assertion. He remained with Socrates until the execution of the latter; and there was no bond on either side to have prevented their separation as soon as they disagreed. The impression seems to have originated in the discussion reported by Xenophon,* wherein Aristippus expresses his political indifference, and Socrates, by an exaggerated extension of logic, endeavors to prove his views to be absurd. But this is simply a divergence of opinion, such as must have existed between Socrates and many of his followers. It merely shows that Aristippus thought for himself. Socrates with such men as Aristippus and Alcibiades reminds one of Dr. Johnson with the "young bloods" Topham Beauclerk and Bennet Langton: he was wise enough and tolerant enough not to allow his virtue to be scandalized by their love of pleasure.

From Athens he went to Ægina, where he met with Laïs, the

---

* *Memorabilia*, ii. 1.

world-renowned courtesan, whom he accompanied to Corinth. On his way from Corinth to Asia he was shipwrecked on the island of Rhodes. On the sea-coast he discovered a geometrical diagram, and exclaimed, "Take courage; I see here the footsteps of men." On arriving at the principal town, he managed to procure for himself and friends a hospitable reception. He used to say, "Send two men amongst strangers, and you will see the advantage of the philosopher."

Aristippus was one of those

"Children of the Sun, whose blood is fire;"

but to strong sensual passions he united a calm regulative intellect. Prone to luxury, he avoided excess. Easy and careless in ordinary affairs, he had great dominion over his desires. Pleasure was his grand object in life; but he knew how to temper enjoyment with moderation. In disposition he was easy and yielding, a "fellow of infinite mirth," a philosopher whose brow was never "sicklied o'er with the pale cast of thought." He had none of that dignity which mistakes a stiff neck for healthy virtue. He had no sternness. Gay, brilliant, careless, and enjoying, he became the ornament and delight of the Court of Dionysius; that Court already illustrious by the splendid genius of Plato and the rigid abstinence of Diogenes. The grave deportment of Plato and the savage virtue of Diogenes had less charm for the Tyrant than the easy gayety of Aristippus, whose very vices were elegant. His ready wit was often put to the test. On one occasion three *hetæræ* were presented for him to make a choice: he took them all three, observing that it had been fatal even to Paris to make a choice. On another occasion, in a dispute with Æschines, who was becoming violent, he said: "Let us give over. We have quarrelled, it is true; but I, as your senior, have a right to claim the *precedency in the reconciliation.*"* In his old-age he appears to have returned to Cyrene, and there opened his school.

---

* Several of his repartees are recorded by Laertius. We add the best of

His philosophy, as Hegel remarks, takes its color from his personality. So individual is it, that we should have passed it over entirely, had it not been a precursor of Epicureanism. Its relation to Socrates is also important.

In the only passage in which, as far as we know, Aristotle* mentions Aristippus, he speaks of him as a Sophist. What does this mean? Was he one of the professed Sophists? No. It means, we believe, that he shared the opinion of the Sophists respecting the uncertainty of Science. That he did share this opinion is evident from Sextus Empiricus,† who details his reasons: such as, that external objects make different impressions on different senses; the names which we impose on these objects express our sensations, but do not express the things; there is no *criterium* of truth; each judges according to his impressions; none judge correctly.

In so far he was a Sophist; but, as the disciple of Socrates, he learned that the *criterium* of truth must be sought within. He dismissed with contempt all physical speculations, as subjects beyond human comprehension, and concentrated his researches upon the moral constitution of man.

In so far he was a Socratist. But, although he took his main direction from Socrates, yet his own individuality quickly turned him into by-paths which his master would have shunned. His was not a scientific intellect. Logical deduction, which was the rigorous process of his master, suited neither his views nor his disposition. He was averse from abstract speculations. His

---

them:—Scinus, the treasurer of Dionysius, a man of low character but immense wealth, once showed Aristippus over his house. While he was expatiating on the splendor of every part, even to the floors, the philosopher spat in his face. Scinus was furious. "Pardon me," exclaimed Aristippus, "there was no other place where I could have spat with decency." One day, in interceding with the Tyrant for a friend, he threw himself on his knees. Being reproached for such want of dignity, he answered, "Is it my fault if Dionysius has his ears in his feet?" One day he asked the Tyrant for some money. Dionysius made him own that a philosopher had no need of money. "Give, give," replied Aristippus, "and we will settle the question at once." Dionysius gave. "*Now*," said the philosopher, "I have no need of money." * *Metaph*. iii. 2. † *Adv. Math*. vii. 178.

tendency was directly towards the concrete. Hence, while Socrates was preaching about The Good, Aristippus wished to specify what it was; and resolved it into Pleasure. It was the pith and kernel of Socrates' Ethical system, that Happiness was the aim and desire of all men—the motor of all action; men only erred because of erroneous notions of what constituted Happiness. Thus the wise man alone knew that to endure an injury was better than to inflict it; he alone knew that immoderate gratification of the senses, being followed by misery, did not constitute Happiness, but the contrary. Aristippus thought this too vague. He not only reduced this general idea to a more specific one, namely, Pleasure; he endeavored to show how truth had its only *criterium* in the sensation of pleasure or of pain. Of that which is without us we can know nothing truly; we only know through our senses, and our senses deceive us with respect to objects. But our senses do not deceive us with respect to our sensations. We may not perceive things truly; but it is true that we perceive. We may doubt respecting external objects; we cannot doubt respecting our sensations. Amongst those sensations we naturally seek the repetition of such as are pleasurable, and shun those that are painful.

Pleasure, then, as the only positive good, and as the only positive test of what was good, he declared to be the end of life; but, inasmuch as for constant pleasure the soul must preserve its dominion over desires, this pleasure was only another form of the Socratic temperance. It is distinguished from the Socratic conception of Pleasure, however, in being positive, and not merely the gratification of a want. In the *Phædo*, Socrates, on being released from his chains, reflects upon the intimate connection of pleasure and pain; and calls the absence of pain, pleasure Aristippus, on the contrary, taught that pleasure is not the mere removal of pain: they are both positive emotions; non-pleasure and non-pain are not emotions, but as it were the sleep of the soul.*

---

* Diog. Laert. ii. 89.

In the application of this doctrine to ethics, Aristippus betrays both his Sophistic and Socratic education. With the Sophists he regarded pleasure and pain as the proper *criteria* of actions; no action being in itself either good or bad, but only such according to convention. With Socrates, however, he regarded the advantages acquired by injustice to be trifling; whereas the evils and apprehensions of punishment are considerable; and pleasure was the result, not of individual prosperity alone, but of the welfare of the whole State.

In reviewing the philosophy, such as it was, of Aristippus, we cannot fail to be struck with the manifest influence of Socrates; although his method was not followed, we see the ethical tendency predominating. In the Megaric School the abstract idea of The Good (τὸ ἀγαθόν) of Socrates, was grounded on the Eleatic conception of The One. In the Cyrenaic, the abstract conception was reduced to the concrete, Pleasure; and this became the only ground of certitude, and morals the only science. In the Cynic School we shall see a still further development in this direction.

§ III. THE CYNICS.—ANTISTHENES AND DIOGENES.

Cynicism is an imposing blasphemy. It imposed on antiquity; it has imposed on many modern imaginations by the energy of its self-denials; but it is a "blasphemy against the divine beauty of life," blasphemy against the divinity of man. To lead the life of a Dog is *not* the vocation of Man.

Nevertheless there were some points both in the characters and doctrines of the founders of this School which may justly claim the admiration of mankind. Their contemporaries regarded them with feelings mingled with awe. We at least may pay a tribute to their energy.

Antisthenes was born at Athens, of a Phrygian mother. In early life he distinguished himself at the battle of Tanagra. After this he studied under Gorgias, the Sophist, and established a school for himself; but, captivated by the practical wisdom of

Socrates, he ceased to teach, and became once more a pupil nay more, he persuaded all his pupils to come with him to Socrates, and there learn true wisdom. This is genuine modesty, such as philosophers have rarely exhibited. He was then somewhat advanced in life; his opinions on many points were too deeply rooted to be exchanged for others; but the tendency of the Socratic philosophy towards Ethics, and the character of that system as leading to the moral perfection of man, seemed entirely to captivate him. It will be remembered that Socrates did not teach positive doctrines; he enabled each earnest thinker to evolve a doctrine for himself. All Socrates did, was to give an impulsion in a certain direction, and to furnish a certain Method. His real disciples accepted the Method; his imperfect disciples only accepted the impulsion. Antisthenes was of the latter. Accordingly his system was essentially personal. He was stern, and his doctrine was rigid; he was proud, and his doctrine was haughty; he was cold, and his doctrine was unsympathizing and self-isolating; he was brave, and his doctrine was a battle. The effeminacy of the luxurious he despised; the baseness of courtiers and flatterers he hated. He worshipped Virtue; but it was Virtue sometimes ferocious and unbending.

Even whilst with Socrates he displayed his contempt of ordinary usages, and his pride in differing from other men. He used to appear in a threadbare cloak, with ostentatious poverty. Socrates saw through it all, and exclaimed, "I see your vanity, Antisthenes, peering through holes in your cloak!" How different was this from Socrates! He, too, had inured himself to poverty, to heat, and to cold, in order that he might bear the chances of fortune; but he made no virtue of being ragged, hungry, and cold. Antisthenes thought he could only preserve his virtue by becoming a savage. He wore no garment except a coarse cloak; allowed his beard to grow; carried a wallet and a staff; and renounced all diet but the simplest. His manners corresponded to his appearance. Stern, reproachful, and bitter in his language; careless and indecent in his gestures. His con tempt of all sensual enjoyment was expressed in his saying, "I would rather be mad than sensual!"*

On the death of Socrates he formed a school, and chose for his place of meeting a public place in that quarter of Athens called the Cynosarges, from which some say the sect of Cynics derives its name; others derive it from the snarling propensities of the founder, who was frequently called "The Dog." As he grew old, his gloomy temper became morose: he became so insupportable that all his scholars left him, except Diogenes of Sinope, who was with him at his death. In his last agony, Diogenes asked him whether he needed a friend. "Will a friend release me from this pain?" he replied. Diogenes gave him a dagger, saying, "This will." "I wish to be freed from pain, not from life," was the reply.

The contempt he uniformly expressed for mankind may be read in two of his sayings. Being asked, what was the peculiar advantage to be derived from philosophy, he answered, "It enables me to keep company with myself." Being told that he was greatly praised by many, "Have I done any thing *wrong*, then, that I am praised?" he asked.†

DIOGENES of Sinope is generally remembered as the representative of Cynicism; probably because more anecdotes of his life have descended to us. He was the son of a banker at Sinope, who was convicted of debasing the coin; an affair in which the son was also supposed to have been implicated. Diogenes fled to Athens. From the heights of splendor and extravagance, he found himself reduced to squalid poverty. The magnificence of poverty, which Antisthenes proclaimed,‡ attracted him. Poor,

---

* It is thus we would interpret Diog. Laert. vi. 3:—Μανείην μᾶλλον ἢ ἡσθείην. Ritter gives this version:—"I had rather go mad than experience pleasure;" which is an outrageous sentiment.

† Dr. Enfield, who generally manages to introduce some blunder into every page, has spoiled this repartee, by giving it as a reply to the praise of a *bad* man. Yet the language of Diogenes Laertius is very explicit:—Πολλοὶ σε ἐπαινοῦσι (vi. 8).

‡ See the *Banquet* of Xenophon.

he was ready to embrace the philosophy of poverty; an outcast, he was ready to isolate himself from society; branded with disgrace, he was ready to shelter himself under a philosophy which branded all society. Having in his own person experienced how little wealth and luxury can do for the happiness of man, he was the more inclined to try the converse; having experienced how wealth prompts to vice, and how desires generate desires, he was willing to try the efficacy of poverty and virtue. He went to Antisthenes; was refused. He continued to offer himself to the Cynic as a scholar; the Cynic raised his knotty staff, and threatened to strike him if he did not depart. "Strike!" replied Diogenes; "you will not find a stick hard enough to conquer my perseverance." Antisthenes, overcome, accepted him as a pupil.

To live a life of virtue was henceforward his sole aim. That virtue was Cynicism. It consisted in the complete renunciation of all luxury—the subjugation of all sensual desires. It was a war carried on by the Mind against the Body. As with the Ascetics of a later day, the basis of a pure life was thought to be the annihilation of the Body; the nearer any one approached to such a suicide, the nearer he was to the ideal of virtue. The Body was vile, filthy, degraded, and degrading; it was the curse of man; it was the clog upon the free development of Mind; it was wrestled with, hated, and despised. This beautiful Body, so richly endowed for enjoyment, was regarded as the "sink of all iniquity."

Accordingly, Diogenes limited his desires to necessities. He ate little; and what he ate was of the coarsest. He tried to live upon raw meat and unboiled vegetables, but failed. His dress consisted solely of a cloak: when he asked Antisthenes for a shirt, he was told to fold his cloak in two; he did so. A wallet and a huge stick completed his accoutrements. Seeing a little boy drinking water out of his scooped hand, he threw away his cup, declaring it superfluous. He slept under the marble porticoes of the buildings, or in his celebrated Tub, which was his place of residence. He took his meals in public. In public he performed all those actions which decency has condemned to privacy. Decency of every kind he studiously outraged. It was a part of his system to do so. Every thing, not in itself improper, ought, he said, to be performed publicly. Besides, he was wont to annoy people with indecent gestures; had he a philosophical reason for that also?

Doubts have been expressed respecting his Tub, which, it is thought, was only an occasional residence, and used by him as expressive of his contempt for luxury. We incline, however, to the tradition. It is in keeping with all we know of the man; and that a Tub could suffice for a domicile we may guess from Aristophanes.*

It is not difficult to imagine the effect created by the Cynics in the gay, luxurious city of Athens. There the climate, no less than the prevailing manners, incited every one to enjoyment. The Cynics told them that enjoyment was unworthy of men; that there were higher and purer things for man to seek. To the polished elegance of Athenian manners the Cynics opposed the most brutal coarseness they could assume. To the friendly flatteries of conversation they opposed the bitterest pungencies of malevolent frankness. They despised all men; and told them so.

Now, although we cannot but regard Cynicism as a very preposterous doctrine—as a feeble solution of the great problem of morals, and not a very amiable feebleness—we admit that it required some great qualities in its upholders. It required a great rude energy; a fanatical logicality of mind; a power over self,—narrow it may be, but still a power. These qualities are not common qualities, and therefore they command respect. Any deviation from the beaten path implies a certain resolution; a steady and consistent deviation implies force. All men respect

---

* *Knights*, 793: the people are there spoken of as having been forced to live, during the war, in "pigeon-holes and corners of turrets:" γυπαρίοις καὶ πυργιδίοις; unless, indeed, this is purely a metaphorical expression.

force. The power of subjugating ordinary desires to one remote but calculated end, always impresses men with a sense of unusua power. Few are aware that to *regulate* desires is more difficult than to *subjugate* them—requires greater power of mind, greater will, greater constancy. Yet every one knows that abstinence is easier than temperance: on the same principle, it is easier to be a Cynic than a wise and virtuous Epicurean.

That which prevents our feeling the respect for the Cynics which the ancients seem to have felt, and which, indeed, some portions of the Cynical doctrine would otherwise induce us to feel, is the studious and uncalled-for outrages on common decency and humanity which Diogenes, especially, perpetrated. All the anecdotes that have come down to us seem to reveal a snarling and malevolent spirit, worshipping Virtue only because it was opposed to the vices of contemporaries; taking a pride in poverty and simplicity only because others sought wealth and luxury. It may be well to raise an earnest protest against the vices of one's age; but it is not well to bring virtue into discredit by the manner of the protest. Doubtless the Athenians needed reproof and reformation, and some exaggeration on the opposite side might have been allowed to the reformers. But Diogenes was so feeble in doctrine, so brutal in manner, that we doubt whether the debauchery of the first profligate in that profligate city were more reprehensible than the debauchery of pride which disgraced the Cynic. The whole character of the man is exhibited in one anecdote. Plato had given a splendid entertainment to some friends. Diogenes entered, unbidden, and stamping on the rich carpets, said, "Thus I trample on the pride of Plato;" whereupon Plato admirably replied, "With greater pride, O Diogenes."

Diogenes, doubtless, practised great abstinence. He made a virtue of his necessity; and, being poor, resolved to be ostentatiously poor. The ostentation being novel, was mistaken for something greater than it was; being in contradiction to the universal tendency of his contemporaries, it was supposed to spring from higher motives. There are men who bear poverty meekly; there are men who look upon wealth without envy, certain that wealth does not give happiness; there are men whose souls are so fixed on higher things as utterly to disregard the pomps and shows of the world; but none of these *despise* wealth, they *disregard* it; none of these *display* their feelings, they are content to act upon them. The virtue which is loud, noisy, ostentatious, and self-affirmative, looks very like an obtrusive egoism. And this was the virtue of the Cynics. Pretending to reform mankind, it began by blaspheming humanity; pretending to correct the effeminacies of the age, it studiously outraged all the decencies of life. Eluding the real difficulty of the problem, it pretended to solve it by unabashed insolence.

In his old age Diogenes was taken captive by pirates, who carried him to Crete, and exposed him for sale as a slave. On being asked what he could do, he replied, "Govern men: sell me, therefore, to one who wants a master." Xeniades, a wealthy Corinthian, struck with this reply, purchased him, and, on returning to Corinth, gave him his liberty and consigned his children to his education. The children were taught to be Cynics, much to their own satisfaction. It was during this period that his world-renowned interview with Alexander took place. The prince, surprised at not seeing Diogenes joining the crowd of his flatterers, went to see him. He found the Cynic sitting in his tub, basking in the sun. "I am Alexander the Great," said he. "I am Diogenes the Cynic," was the reply. Alexander then asked him if there was any thing he could do for him. "Yes, stand aside from between me and the sun." Surprised at such indifference to princely favor—an indifference so strikingly contrasted with every thing he could hitherto have witnessed—he exclaimed, "Were I not Alexander, I would be Diogenes!" One day, being brought before the King, and being asked who he was, Diogenes replied, "A spy on your cupidity;" language, the boldness of which must have gained him universal admiration, because implying great singularity as well as force of character.

Singularity and Insolence may be regarded as his grand characteristics. Both of these are exemplified in the anecdote of his lighting a lamp in the daytime, and peering about the streets as if earnestly seeking something: being asked what he sought, he replied, "A Man." The point of this story is lost in the usual version, which makes him seek "an honest man." The words in Laertius are simply, ἄνθρωπον ζητῶ—"I seek a man." Diogenes did not seek honesty; he wanted to find a Man, in whom honesty would be included with many other qualities. It was his constant reproach to his contemporaries, that they had no manhood. He said he had never seen men; at Sparta he had seen children; at Athens, women. One day he called out, "Approach, all men!" When some approached, he beat them back with his club, saying, "I called for men; ye are excrements."

Thus he lived till his ninetieth year, bitter, brutal, ostentatious, and abstemious; disgracing the title of "The Dog" (for a dog has affection, gratitude, sympathy, and caressing manners), yet growling over his unenvied virtue as a cur growls over his meatless bone, forever snarling and snapping without occasion; an object of universal attention, and from many quarters, of unfeigned admiration. One day his friends went to see him. On arriving at the portico under which he was wont to sleep, they found him still lying on the ground wrapped in his cloak. He seemed to sleep. They pushed aside the folds of his cloak: he was dead.*

The Doctrine of the Cynics may be briefly expounded. Antisthenes, as the disciple of Gorgias, was imbued with the sophistical principles respecting Science; principles which his acquaintance with Socrates did not alter. He maintained that Science was impossible. He utterly rejected the Socratic notion of Defini-

---

* It was thought that he had committed suicide by holding his breath,—a physical impossibility. Other versions of the cause of his death were current in antiquity; one of them seems consistent with his character; it makes him die in consequence of devouring a neat's foot raw.

tions. He said that a Definition was nothing but a *series of words* (λόγον μακρόν, "a long discourse"); for which Aristotle calls him an ignoramus.* To the Socratic notion of a Definition, as including the essence of a thing, he opposed the Sophistic notion of a Definition, as expressing a purely subjective relation. You can only express qualities, not essences; you can call a thing silver, but you cannot say in what it consists. Your definition is only verbal: hence the first step in education should be the study of words.†

What was the consequence of this skepticism? The consequence was, that the Cynics answered arguments by facts. When some one was arguing in support of Zeno of Elea's notion respecting the impossibility of movement, Diogenes rose and walked. Definitions might prove that there was no motion; but definitions were only verbal, and could be answered by facts.

This refuge found in common-sense against the assaults of logic, enabled the Cynics to shape a doctrine of morals which had some certain basis. As they answered arguments by facts, so they made actions take the place of precepts. Instead of speculating about virtue, they endeavored to be virtuous. Socrates had brought philosophy from the clouds; the Cynics endeavored to bring it into daily practice. Their personal dispositions gave the peculiar coloring to their doctrine, as that of Aristippus had done to the Cyrenaic.

---

* Ἀπαίδευτος.—*Metaph.* viii. 3.
† Arrian, *Epictet.*, Diss. i. 17, quoted in Ritter and Preller, *Hist. Philos Græco-Romanæ ex fontium locis contexta* (Hamburg, 1838), p. 174.

SIXTH EPOCH.

COMPLETE ADOPTION AND APPLICATION OF THE SOCRATIC METHOD.—PLATO.

§ I. Life of Plato.

PERHAPS of all ancient writers, Plato's name is the best known. Homer himself is unknown to many who have some dim notion of Plato as the originator of the so-called Platonic love. There is a great and wide-spread interest about the Grecian sage. The young and romantic have strange, romantic ideas of him. "The general reader," especially if a dabbler in fashionable philosophy, or rather in the philosophy current in fashionable novels, has a very exalted notion of him as the "great Idealist." The theological reader regards him with affection, as the stout and eloquent upholder of the doctrine of the immateriality and immortality of the soul. The literary critic often regards him as the type of metaphysical eloquence, and classes with him every vapory, mystical, metaphorical writer of "poetical philosophy."

Now, except that of the theologian, these notions, derived at second-hand, are all false. It would be idle to inquire how such extravagant opinions came into circulation. Enough for us that they are false. Plato was any thing but "dreamy;" any thing but "an Idealist," as that phrase is usually understood. He was an inveterate dialectician, a severe and abstract thinker, and a great quibbler. His metaphysics are of a nature to frighten away all but the most determined students, so abstract and so subtle are they. His morals and politics, so far from having any romantic tinge, are the *ne plus ultra* of logical severity; hard, uncompromising, and above humanity. In a word, Plato the man was almost completely absorbed in Plato the Dialectician: he had learned to look upon human passion as a disease, and human pleasure as a frivolity. The only thing worth living for was truth. Dialectics was the noblest exercise of humanity.

Even the notions respecting his style are erroneous. It is not the "poetical" metaphorical style usually asserted. It has unmistakable beauties, but not the beauties popularly attributed to it. Its immense power is dramatic power. The best dialogues are inimitable scenes of comedy. Character, banter, irony, and animation are there, but scarcely any imagery, and that seldom beautiful.* His object was to refute or to convince; his illustrations are therefore homely. When fit occasion arrives he can be eloquent and familiar. He clothes some myths in language of splendid beauty; and there are many felicitous passages scattered through the dreary waste of dialectical quibbling and obscurity. These passages have been quoted by various writers; hence readers have supposed that Plato always wrote in such strains. But very fine passages are also to be found in Aristotle, who is nevertheless a repulsive writer on the whole.

In truth, Plato is a very difficult, and, as far as regards matter, somewhat tedious writer; this is the reason of his being so little read: for we must not be deceived by the many editions. He is often mentioned and often quoted at second-hand; but he is rarely read, except by professed scholars and critics. Men of culture usually attack a dialogue or two out of curiosity. Their curiosity seldom inspirits them to further progress. The difficul-

---

* "Even upon abstract subjects, whether moral, metaphysical, or mathematical, the language of Plato is clear as the running stream; and in simplicity and sweetness vies with the humble violet which perfumes the vale." —*Dr. Enfield, Hist. of Phil.* ii. 221. Whenever you meet with such trash as this, be dubious that the writer of it ever read Plato. Aristotle capitally describes Plato's style as "a middle species of diction between verse and prose." It has rhythm rather than imagery.

ty of mastering the ideas, and their unsatisfactory nature when mastered, are barriers to any general acquaintance with Plato. But those who persevere believe themselves repaid; the journey has been difficult, but it was worth performing.

Aristocles, surnamed Plato (the broad-browed),* the son of Ariston and Perictione, was born at Athens or Ægina, Ol. 87.3, on the 7th Thargelion (about the middle of May, B. C. 430). His childhood and youth consequently synchronize with the Peloponnesian war, the most active and brilliant period of Grecian thought and action. His lineage was illustrious: on the maternal side he was connected with Solon.

So great a name could not escape becoming the nucleus of many fables, and we find the later historians gravely repeating various miraculous events connected with him. He was said to be the child of Apollo, his mother a virgin. Ariston, though betrothed to Perictione, delayed his marriage because Apollo had appeared to him in a dream, and told him that she was with child.

Plato's education was excellent; and in gymnastics he was sufficiently skilled to contend at the Pythian and Isthmian games. Like a true Greek, he attached extreme importance to gymnastics, as doing for the body what dialectics did for the mind; and, like a true Greek, he did not suffer these corporeal exercises to absorb all his time and attention: poetry, music, and rhetoric were assiduously cultivated, and with some success. He wrote an epic poem, besides some tragedies, dithyrambics, lyrics, and epigrams. The epic he is said to have burned in a fit of despair on comparing it with Homer. The tragedies he burned on be-

---

* Some writers incline to the opinion that "Plato" was the epithet of broad-browed; others of broad-shouldered; others, again, that it was expressive of the breadth of his style. This last is absurd. The author of the article *Plato* in the *Penny Cyclopædia* pronounces all the above explanations to be "idle, as the name of Plato was of common occurrence among the Athenians of that time." But surely Aristocles was not endowed with this surname of Plato without cause? Unless he derived the name from a relation, he must have derived it from one of the above causes.

coming acquainted with Socrates. The epigrams have been partially preserved. One of them is very beautiful:

'Αστέρας εἰσαθρεῖς, ἀστὴρ ἐμός· εἴθε γενοίμην
Οὐρανός, ὡς πολλοῖς ὄμμασιν εἰς σὲ βλέπω.

"Thou gazest on the stars, my Life! Ah! gladly would I be
Yon starry skies, with thousand eyes, that I might gaze on thee!"

His studies of poetry were mingled with those of philosophy, which he must have cultivated early; for we know that he was only twenty when he first went to Socrates, and we also know that he had been taught by Cratylus before he knew Socrates. Early he must have felt

" A presence that disturbed him with the joy
Of elevated thoughts; a sense sublime
Of something far more deeply interfused,
Whose dwelling is the light of setting suns,
And the round ocean, and the living air,
And the blue sky, and in the mind of man:
A motion and a spirit that impels
All thinking things, all objects of all thought,
And rolls through all things."

A deep and meditative spirit led him to question Nature in her secret haunts. The sombre philosophy of Heraclitus suited well with his melancholy youth. Skepticism, which was the fever of that age, had seized on Plato as on all the rest. This skepticism, together with an imperious craving for belief which struggled with the skepticism, found breathing-room in the doctrines of Socrates; and the young scholar learned that without impugning the justice of his doubts, he could escape them by seeking Truth elsewhere.

He remained with Socrates ten years, and was separated from him only by death. He attended his beloved master during the trial; undertook to plead his cause; indeed, began a speech which the violence of the judges would not allow him to continue; and pressed his master to accept a sum of money sufficient to purchase his life.

On the death of Socrates he went to Megara to visit Euclid, as we mentioned before. From thence he proceeded to Cyrene.

where he was instructed in mathematics by Theodorus, whom he had known in Athens, if we may credit the *Theætetus*, where Theodorus is represented discoursing with Socrates. From Cyrene he went to Egypt, in company, it is said, with Euripides. There is very little authority for this visit, and that Euripides was his companion is not very probable, because Euripides had been dead some years. (The influence of Egypt on Plato has certainly been exaggerated.) There is no trace, in his works, of Egyptian research. "All he tells us of Egypt indicates at most a very scanty acquaintance with the subject; and although he praises the industry of the priests, his estimate of their scientific attainments is far from favorable."*

In these travels the broad-browed meditative man greatly enlarged the Socratic doctrine, and indeed introduced antagonistic elements. But he strictly preserved the Socratic Method. "Whilst studious youth," says Valerius Maximus, "were crowding to Athens from every quarter in search of Plato for their master, that philosopher was wandering along the winding banks of the Nile, or the vast plains of a barbarous country, himself a disciple to the old men of Egypt."

He returned at last, and eager scholars flocked around him. With a mind richly stored by foreign travel and constant meditation, he began to emulate his beloved master, and devote himself to teaching. Like Socrates, he taught gratuitously. The Academia, a public garden in the neighborhood of Athens, was the favorite resort of Plato, and gave its name to the school which he founded. This garden was planted with lofty plane trees, and adorned with temples and statues; a gentle stream rolled through it, with

> "A sound as of a hidden brook
> In the leafy month of June,
> Which to the sleeping woods all night
> Singeth a quiet tune."

It was a delicious retreat, "for contemplation framed." The

---

* Ritter, ii. 147.

nging thoughts of posterity have often hovered round it as the centre of myriad associations. Poets have sung of it. Philosophers have sighed for it.

> "See there the olive grove of Academe,
> Plato's retirement, where the Attic bird
> Thrills her thick-warbled notes the summer long."

In such a spot, where the sound

> "Of bees' industrious murmur oft invites
> To studious musing,"

one would imagine none but the Graces could enter; and coupling this with the poetical beauties of Plato's *Dialogues*, people have supposed that the lessons in the Academy were magnificent outbursts of eloquence and imagery upon philosophical subjects.

Nothing can be further from the truth. The lectures were hard exercises of the thinking faculty, and demanded great power of continued abstraction. Whatever graces might have adorned Plato's compositions, his lectures were not literary, but dialectical exercises.

Ritter thinks differently. "His school was less a school of hardy deeds for all, than of polished culture for the higher classes, who had no other object than to enhance the enjoyment of their privileges and wealth." Does this mean that Plato did not teach Stoicism? If so, it is a truism; if not, a falsism; since what has Dialectics to do with "hardy deeds?" We are then informed that it was "a school of polished culture for the higher classes:" a mere assertion, and a questionable one. The "higher classes" principally frequented the Sophists; besides, Plato's lectures were gratuitous, and every free citizen might attend them, on certain conditions. There were no aristocratical exclusives in Athens; there were no "polished circles," with a culture differing from that of the other free citizens. When Ritter says that their object was "to enhance the enjoyment of their privileges and wealth," we are at a loss to conceive his meaning, because we do not see how they were to do this by listening to speculations on essences and archetypal Ideas; the more so as Ritter himself tells us Plato's views of justice and honor were "wholly impracticable in the corrupt state of the Athenian constitution; and all empirical knowledge, such as is indispensable to a politician, was in his view contemptible."*

Whatever their purpose, the Lectures were severe trials to the capacities of students; and their purely argumentative nature may have originated the story respecting the inscription over the door of his Academy, "*Let none but Geometricians enter here;*" a story which is very widely circulated, although wholly without good evidence.† The story is in direct contradiction to Plato's views of Geometry, which he excludes from Philosophy, because it assumes its axioms without proof, and because it occupies a middle position between Opinion and Philosophy, more accurate than the one, but less certain than the other.‡

In his fortieth year Plato made his first visit to Sicily. It was then he became acquainted with Dionysius I., the Tyrant of Syracuse, Dion, his brother-in-law, and Dionysius II. With Dionysius I. he soon came to a rupture, owing to his political opinions; and he so offended the Tyrant, that his life was threatened. Dion, however, interceded for him; and the Tyrant

---

* Some countenance seems given to the ordinary notion of Plato's Lectures by the tradition that even some women attended them. We confess this statement is to us suspicious, especially as it is also said that one woman disguised herself in man's clothes. Disguise, then, was necessary. The fact, however, if correct, would only show the high cultivation of the *hetæræ* (for such the women must have been); and when we think of such women as Aspasia, we see no reason for supposing they could not follow the abstrusest lectures.

† Mr. Thompson says the only authorities for the inscription are Philoponus, in his Commentary on Aristotle, *De Animâ*, and a verse in the *Chiliads* of Tzetzes. See Notes to *Butler's Lectures*, ii. 79.

‡ I have been unable to recover a passage in the *Republic* where Plato expresses himself as in the text, but I found this, which approximates to it, although not the passage I had in my mind. See *Repub.* vi. towards the end, beginning, Μανθάνω, ἔφη, κ.τ.λ. . . . and ending, διάνοιαν δὲ καλεῖν μοι δοκεῖς τὴν τῶν γεωμετρικῶν τε καὶ τὴν τῶν τοιούτων ἕξιν, ἀλλ' οὐ νοῦν, ὡς μεταξύ τι δόξης τε καὶ νοῦ τὴν διάνοιαν ⸱ῦσαν.

spared his life, but commissioned Pollis, the Spartan Ambassador, in whose ship Plato was to return, to sell him as a slave He was sold accordingly. Anniceris of Cyrene bought him, and immediately set him free. On his return to Athens, Dionysius wrote, hoping that he would not speak ill of him. Plato contemptuously replied, that he had not "leisure to think of Dionysius."

Plato's second visit to Syracuse was after the death of Dionysius I., and with the hope of obtaining from Dionysius II. the establishment of a colony according to laws framed by himself. The colony was promised; but never granted. Plato incurred the Tyrant's suspicions of having been concerned in Dion's conspiracy; but he was allowed to return home in peace.

He paid a third visit; and this time solely to endeavor to reconcile Dionysius with his uncle Dion. Finding his efforts fruitless, and perhaps dangerous, he returned.

In the calm retirement of the Academy, Plato passed the remainder of his days. Lecturing and writing were his chief occupations. The composition of those dialogues which have been the admiration of posterity, was the cheering solace of his life, especially of his declining years. He died at the advanced age of eighty-three.

Plato was intensely melancholy. That great broad brow, which gave him his surname, was wrinkled and sombre. Those brawny shoulders were bent with thought, as only those of thinkers are bent. A smile was the utmost that ever played over his lips; he never laughed. "As sad as Plato," became a phrase with the comic dramatists. He had many admirers; scarcely any friends.

In Plato, the thinker predominated over the man. That great expansive intellect had so fixed itself upon the absorbing questions of philosophy, that it had scarcely any sympathy left for other matters. Hence his constant reprobation of Poets. Many suppose that the banishment of poets from his *Republic* was but an insincere extension of his logical principles, and that he really loved poetry too well to condemn it. Plato's opposition to poets was however both deep and constant. He had a feeling not unallied to contempt for them, because he saw in them some resemblance to the Sophists, in their indifference to truth, and preference for the arts of expression. The only poetry Plato ever praises is *moral* poetry, which is versified philosophy. His soul panted for Truth. Poets, at the best, he held to be inspired madmen, unconscious of what fell from their lips. Let the reader open the *Ion* (it has been translated by Shelley); he will then perceive the cause of poets being banished from the *Republic*. Plato had a repugnance to poetry, partly because it was the dangerous rival of philosophy, partly because he had a contempt for pleasure.* It is true that he frequently quotes Homer, and, towards the close of the *Republic*, some misgivings of having harshly treated the favorite of his youth, escape him; but he quickly withdraws them, and owns that Truth alone should be man's object.

There is something unpleasant in Plato's character, which finds its echo in his works. He was a great, but not an amiable man; his works are great, but lamentably deficient. His ethics are the ethics of a logician, not of a large-souled man, familiar with and sympathizing with the complexities of life; they are suited only to an impossible state of humanity.

In bringing forward this view of Plato's character, we shall doubtless shock many preconceptions. The Plato we have drawn, if not so romantic as that usually drawn, is the only one which seem to us consonant with what the ancient writers transmit. Let no one object to our assertion of his constant melancholy, on the ground of the comic talent displayed in his *Dialogues*. The comic writers are not the gayest men; even Molière, whose humor is so genial, overflowing, and apparently spontaneous, was one of the austerest. Comedy often springs from the deepest melancholy, as if in sudden rebound. Moreover, in Plato's

---

* Comp. *Philebus*, p. 181.

comedy there is almost always some under-current of bitterness:
it is Irony, not Joyousness.

§ II. Plato's Writings: their Character, Object, and Authenticity.

Before attempting an exposition of Plato's doctrines, it may be useful to say something respecting the character and authenticity of his *Dialogues*. Modern criticism, which spares nothing, has not left them untouched. Dialogues, the authenticity of which had never been questioned in antiquity, have been rejected by modern critics upon arbitrary grounds.

We cannot enter here into the details; we have no space; and, had we space, we might be excused from combating the individual positions, when we refuse to accept as valid the fundamental assumptions on which they repose. Internal evidence is generally deceptive; but the sort of internal evidence supposed to be afforded by comparative inferiority in artistic execution, is never free from great suspicion. Some of Plato's dialogues not being found equal to the exalted idea which his great works have led men to entertain, are forthwith declared to be spurious. But what writer is at all times equal to the highest of his own flights? What author has produced nothing but *chefs-d'œuvre?* Are there not times when the most brilliant men are dull, when the richest style is meagre, when the compactest style is loose? The same subjects will not always call forth the same excellence; how unlikely then that various subjects should be treated with uniform power! The *Theages* could hardly equal the *Theætetus;* the *Euthydemus* must be inferior to the *Gorgias.* No one thinks of disputing Shakspeare's claim to the *Merry Wives of Windsor*, because it is immeasurably inferior to *Twelfth Night*, which, in its turn, is inferior to *Othello.*

Besides the dialogues rejected on account of inferior art, there are others rejected on account of immature or contradictory opinions. But this ground is as untenable as the former. No one has yet been able to settle definitively *what* was Plato's philosophy; yet opinions are said to be unworthy of that unsettled philosophy! A preconceived notion of Plato's having been a pure Socratist, has led to the rejection of whatever seemed contradictory to Socratic views. But there is abundant evidence to show that Plato was not a mere exponent of Socratic opinions. Moreover, in a long life a man's opinions undergo many modifications; and Plato was no exception to the rule. He contradicts himself constantly. He does so in works the authenticity of which no one has questioned; and we are not to be surprised if we find him doing so in others.

It is somewhat amusing to observe the confidence of modern criticism on this point.* An Ast, or a Socher, or a Schleiermacher, rejects, on the most fallacious assumptions, the authenticity of dialogues quoted by Aristotle as the works of his master, Plato. Now really, to suppose that Aristotle could be mistaken on such a matter is a great extension of the conjectural privilege; but to make this supposition on no better ground than that of internal evidence, derived from inferiority of execution, or variation in opinion in the works themselves, seems truly preposterous.

The ancients themselves admitted the *Epinomis*, the *Eryxias*, the *Axiochus*, and the *Second Alcibiades*, to be spurious. The *Epistles* are also now generally regarded as forgeries. With these exceptions, we really see no reason for rejecting any of the dialogues. The *Theages* and the *Hippias Major* are certainly as much in Plato's manner as *Measure for Measure* is in Shakspeare's; indeed, the *Hippias* seems to us a remarkably happy specimen of his dramatic talent.

But whether all the Dialogues were the production of Plato or not, they equally serve the purpose of this history, since no one

---

* "According as the deification has directed itself to this or that aspect of his character, the opinions raised as to the genuineness or falsity of his works have fluctuated; so that we might safely say, the more his writings have been examined, the more has the decision of their authenticity become complicated."—*Ritter.*

denies them to be *Platonic*. We may therefore leave this question, and proceed to others.

Do the Dialogues contain the real opinions of Plato? This question has three motives. 1st. Plato himself never speaks *in propriâ personâ*, unless indeed the Athenian in the *Laws* be accepted as representing him; a supposition in which we are inclined to concur. 2dly. From certain passages in the *Phædrus* and the *Epistles*, it would appear that Plato had a contempt for written opinions, as inefficient for instruction. 3dly. On the testimony of a phrase in Aristotle, it is supposed that Plato, like Pythagoras, had exoteric and esoteric opinions; the former being, of course, those set forth in his Dialogues.

We will endeavor to answer these doubts. The first is of very little importance; the second of greater; the last of very great importance. That Plato adopts the dramatic form, and preserves it, is true; but this form, which quite baffles us with Shakspeare, baffles us with no one else. It is easy to divine the opinions of Aristophanes, Molière, or Schiller. It is still more easy to divine the opinions of Plato, because, unlike the dramatists, he selects his dialogues solely with a view to the illustration of his opinions. Besides, it is reasonable to suppose that "Socrates," in the Dialogues, represents Platonic opinions seen through the *manner* of Socrates. And, whatever the variations may be with respect to subordinate points, we find but one Method in all the Dialogues, but one conception of science; in a word, we find an unmistakable *tendency*, which we pronounce to be Platonic.

Respecting his opinion on the insufficiency of books to convey instruction, we may first quote what "Socrates" says on the subject in the *Phædrus*:

"Writing is something like painting; the creatures of the latter art *look* very like living beings; but, if you ask them a question, they preserve a solemn silence. Written discourses do the same: you would fancy, by what they say, that they had some sense in them; but, if you wish to learn, and therefore interrogate them, they have only their first answer to return to all questions. And when the discourse is once written, it passes from hand to hand, among all sorts of persons, those who can understand it, and those who cannot. It is not able to tell its story to those only to whom it is suitable; and, when it is unjustly criticised, it always needs its author to assist it, for it cannot defend itself. There is another sort of discourse, which is far better and more potent than this.—What is it? That which is written scientifically in the learner's mind. This is capable of defending itself, and it can speak itself, or be silent, as it sees fit.—You mean the real and living discourse of the person who understands the subject; of which discourse the written one may be called the picture? Precisely.—Now, think you that a sensible husbandman would take seed which he valued, and wishing to produce a harvest, would seriously, after the summer had begun, scatter it in the gardens of Adonis,* for the pleasure of seeing it spring up and look green in a week? Or do you not rather think that he might indeed do this for sport and amusement; but, when his purpose was serious, would employ the art of agriculture, and, sowing the seed at the proper time, be content to gather in his harvest in the eighth month? The last, undoubtedly.—And do you think that he who possesses the knowledge of what is just, and noble, and good, will deal less prudently with *his* seeds than the husbandman with his? Certainly not.—He will not, then, set about sowing them with a pen and a black liquid; or (to drop the metaphor) scattering these truths by means of discourses, which cannot defend themselves against attack, and which are incapable of adequately expounding the truth. No doubt he will, *for the sake of sport*, occasionally scatter some of the seeds in this manner, and will thus *treasure up memoranda for himself*, in case he should fall into the forgetfulness of old age, and for all others who follow in the same track; and he will be pleased when he sees the blade growing up green."†

Now, this remarkable passage is clearly biographical. It is the

---

* "The gardens of Adonis," a periphrasis for mignonette-boxes.
† *Phædrus*, p. 98.

justification of Socrates' philosophical career. But it must not be too rigorously applied to Plato, whose voluminous writings contradict it; nor must we suppose that those writings were designed only for amusement, or as memoranda for his pupils. The main idea of this passage is one which few persons would feel disposed to question. We are all aware that books labor under very serious deficiencies; they cannot replace oral instruction The frequent misapprehensions of an author's meaning would in a great measure be obviated if we had him by our side to interrogate him. And oral instruction has the further advantage of not allowing the reader's mind to be so *passive* as it is with a book: the teacher by his questions excites the activity of the pupil. All this may reasonably be conceded as Plato's opinion, without at all affecting the serious purpose of his writings. Plato thought that conversation was more instructive than reading; but he knew that reading was also instructive, and he wrote: to obviate as much as possible the necessary inconveniences of written discourse, he threw all his works into the form of dialogue. Hence the endless repetitions, divisions, and illustrations of positions almost self-evident. The reader is fatigued by them; but, like Addison's tediousness, they have a "design" in them: that design is, by imitating conversation, to leave no position unexplained. As a book cannot be interrogated, Plato makes the book anticipate interrogations. The very pains he takes to be tedious, the very minuteness of his details, is sufficient to rescue his works from the imputation of being mere amusements. He was too great an artist to have sacrificed his art to any thing but his convictions. That he did sacrifice the general effect to his scrupulous dialectics, no one can doubt; and we believe that he did so for the sake of deeply impressing on the reader's mind the real force of his Method. Had the critics recognized Plato's real drift, we believe they would have spared much of their censure, and hesitated before pronouncing against the genuineness of certain dialogues.

Connected with Plato's expressions respecting the imperfection of written works, there is the passage in Aristotle, referring to the ἄγραφα δόγματα, or "unwritten opinions," which is supposed to indicate an esoteric doctrine. If Aristotle's words do bear that meaning, then is the opinion consistent and valid, which regards the exoteric works—the Dialogues—as mere divertisements. Let us examine it.

Aristotle says that Plato, in the *Timæus*, maintained space and matter to be the same, but that, in what are called the unwritten opinions (ἐν τοῖς λεγομένοις ἀγράφοις δόγμασι), he considered space and place (τὸν τόπον καὶ τὴν χώραν) to be the same.* From such a passage it is surely somewhat gratuitous to conclude that Plato had an esoteric doctrine. The ἄγραφα δόγματα probably meant his lectures, or, as Ritter suggests, notes taken from the lectures by his scholars. At any rate, there is no ground for supposing them to have been esoterical opinions; the more so as Aristotle, his most illustrious pupil, never speaks of any such distinct doctrine, but draws his statements of Plato's views from published works.

We are convinced that the Dialogues contain the real opinions of Plato, in as far as Plato ventured to express them. We make this reservation because it is pretty generally known that in the Socratic philosophy individual opinions were not of so much importance as Method. It would perhaps be better to say, therefore, that the Dialogues exhibit Plato's real Method and tendencies. Certain it is that the Method and tendencies can only rightly be appreciated after a survey of all the Dialogues. The ancients, we are told by Sextus Empiricus,† were divided amongst them-

---

* *Phys.* iv. c. 2, p. 53. Ritter, who refers to but does not cite the passage, gives us to understand that, in these unwritten opinions, "much was explained differently, or, at least, more definitely than in the Dialogues." But no such conclusion can be drawn from Aristotle. There is no greater difference alluded to in the passage than may frequently be found between one dialogue and another. If the written (published) opinions differ, surely those unwritten may be allowed also to differ from the written? If the *Republic* differs from the *Timæus*, surely the "unwritten opinion" may differ from the *Timæus*.

† *Pyrrhon. Hypot.* i. p. 44.

selves as to whether Plato was a skeptic or a dogmatist. Nor was the dispute irrational: for, as some of the Dialogues are expository and dogmatical, and others are mere exercises of the dialectical method—mere contests in which nothing is definitively settled—any one having studied only one class of these Dialogues would think Plato either a skeptic or a dogmatist, according to the nature of those which he had read. Thus Cicero, an ardent admirer, says, "Plato affirms nothing; but, after producing many arguments, and examining a question on every side, leaves it undetermined." This is true of such dialogues as the *Theætetus*, or the *Hippias Major*; but untrue of the *Phædo, Timæus, Laws*, etc.

This leads us to a consideration of the various attempts at classifying the Dialogues. That some sort of classification should be adopted is admitted by all; but no two persons seem to agree as to the precise arrangement. Any attempt at chronological arrangement must inevitably fail. Certain dialogues can be satisfactorily shown to have been written subsequently to some others; but any regular succession is beyond our ingenuity. We may be pretty sure that the *Phædrus* was the earliest,[*] or one of the earliest, and the *Laws* the latest. We may be sure that the *Republic* was earlier than the *Laws*, because the latter is a maturer view of politics. But *when* the *Republic* was written baffles conjecture. It is usually placed with the *Timæus* and the *Laws*; that is to say, with the last products of its author. But we demur to this on several accounts. The differences of style and of ideas observable in the *Republic* and the *Laws*, imply considerable distance between the periods of composition. Besides, a man not writing for his bread does not so soon resume a subject which he has already treated with great fulness. Plato had uttered his opinions in the *Republic*. He must have waited till new ideas were developed, before he could be tempted again to write; for

---

[*] See on this point Mr. Thompson's note to *Butler's Lectures on Hist. of Ancient Phil.* ii. p. 44.

observe, both these dialogues are expository and dogmatical: they express Plato's opinions; they are not merely dialectical exercises.

It strikes us also that there is but one safe principle to be applied to the testing of such points. Whenever two works exhibit variations of opinion, we should examine the nature of the variations and ask, which of the two opinions is the later in development—which must have been the earlier?

Let us take an example. In the *Republic* (iii. p. 123) he attempts to prove that no one can excel in two arts; that the comic poet cannot be the same as the tragic, the same actor cannot act in tragedy and comedy with success. In the *Amatores* (p. 289) he has the same idea, though there only mentioned briefly.* In the *Symposium*, however, Plato's opinion is directly the reverse; for, in a celebrated passage, he makes Socrates convince Agathon that the tragic and comic poet are the same person. Now, it is not difficult to decide which is the earlier opinion: in the *Republic* it is the logical consequence of his premises; but in the *Symposium* that opinion is corrected by experience, for in the poets of his own day Plato found both tragedy and comedy united; and as Socrates is made to convince Agathon, we may conclude that the former opinion was not uncommon, and that Plato here makes a retractation. No one will deny that the former opinion is superficial. The distinction between tragedy and comedy is such that it *seems* to imply a distinct nature to attain excellence in each. But Euripides, Shakspeare, Racine, Cervantes, Calderon, and many others, confute this seeming by their dramas.

Perhaps a still more conclusive example is that of the "crea-

---

* According to Ritter's principle, this would prove the *Republic* to be later than the *Amatores*. He maintains, and with plausibility, that, when a subject which has been developed in one dialogue is briefly assumed in another, the latter is subsequent in composition. (Ritter, vol. ii. p. 183.) Yet, on this principle the *Phædo* is earlier than the *Phædrus*, inasmuch as the doctrine of reminiscence is developed in the former and alluded to in the latter.

tion of Ideas," so expressly stated in the *Republic*, and the "eternity and uncreated nature of Ideas," as expressly stated in the *Timæus*. So radical a difference in the most important position of his philosophy, would at once separate the epochs at which the two dialogues were composed. And to this may be added the difference in artistic treatment between the *Republic* and the *Timæus*. The former, although expository, has much of the vivacity and dramatic vigor of the early dialogues. The *Timæus* and the *Laws* have scarcely a trace of art.

Ritter has well observed that "the excellence of the Platonic dialogues, as pieces of art, is twofold:—the rare imitative powers exhibited in the dialogue, and the acuteness with which philosophical matters are dialectically treated. No one will deny that these two qualities have only an outward connection, and consequently that they cannot advance equally. With the philosopher the latter is manifestly the more important, whereas the former is of secondary importance. The degree of perfection therefore in any dialogue, as such, affords at most a very uncertain means for the determination of its date; whereas the greatest weight ought to be laid on the dialectical skill." In proportion as the dialectical skill became mature, it is natural to suppose that the dramatic imitation was less cared for. In proportion as Plato became settled in his convictions he became anxious solely for their clear exposition. He began life with a love of poetry; but this he soon abandoned for philosophy.

The whole inquiry may seem idle; but until something like a positive arrangement of his works can be made, there will be no end to the misconceptions of his opinions; for it is preposterous to cite passages in support of a doctrine, before having ascertained the date of the work whence the passages are drawn. Yet this is the way critics and historians draw up an imaginary outline of Plato's philosophy, and squabble amongst each other as to who is right. When it is said that Plato held such or such an opinion, it should be distinctly understood at what period of his career he held it; because, in so long a career, and with so many changes of opinion, it is necessary to be precise. For our own part we can scarcely name a single opinion held by him *throughout* his works. Even the Socratic idea of Virtue being identical with Knowledge, consequently of Vice being Ignorance, and therefore involuntary—even this idea he learned in his old-age to repudiate, as we see in the *Laws* (book v. p. 385), where he calls *incontinence*, no less than ignorance (ἢ δι' ἀμαθίαν ἢ δι' ἀκράτειαν), the causes of vice. In the same sense (book iv. p. 138), after speaking of anger and pleasure as causes of error, he says, "There is a third cause of our faults, and that is ignorance" (τρίτον ἄγνοιαν τῶν ἁμαρτημάτων αἰτίαν). So that here he places ignorance only as a third cause; and by so doing destroys the whole Socratic argument respecting the identity of Virtue and knowledge.*

This being the case, it will readily be acknowledged, that to make up a doctrine from passages culled here and there, must inevitably lead into error. A *consistent doctrine* cannot be made out. Indeed it is questionable whether Plato ever elaborated one. Like Socrates, he occupied himself with Method rather than with results; like Socrates, he had doubts respecting the certainty of knowledge on the higher subjects of thought; like Socrates, he sought Truth, without professing to have found her.

As a chronological arrangement has been impossible, a philosophical arrangement has frequently been attempted. The most celebrated is that of Schleiermacher, who divides the Dialogues into three classes:—" 1st. *Elementary dialogues,* or those which contain the germs of all that follows,—of logic as the instrument of philosophy, and of ideas as its proper object; consequently, of the possibility of the conditions of knowledge: these are the *Phædrus, Lysis, Protagoras, Laches, Charmides, Euthyphro,*

---

* The *Meno* is a further confirmation. In it virtue is shown to be unsusceptible of being taught; *ergo,* it is not Knowledge. This would make the *Meno* one of the latest works. Neither of these contradictions has, to our knowledge, been noticed before. It was our intention to insert a Chapter on the self-contradictions of Plato, but the space such a Chapter must have occupied, would have been utterly beyond our limits.

and *Parmenides;* to which he subjoins, as an appendix, the *Apologia, Crito, Ion, Hippias Minor, Hipparchus, Minos,* and *Alcibiades II.* 2d. *Progressive dialogues,* which treat of the distinction between philosophical and common knowledge in their united application to the two proposed and real sciences, Ethics and Physics: these are the *Gorgias, Theætetus, Meno, Euthydemus, Cratylus, Sophistes, Politicus, Symposium, Phædo,* and *Philebus;* with an appendix containing the *Theages, Amatores, Alcibiades I., Menexemus, Hippias Major,* and *Clitophon.* 3d. *Constructive dialogues,* in which the practical is completely united with the speculative; these are the *Republic, Timæus, Critias,* with an appendix containing the *Laws* and the *Epistles.*"* There is considerable ingenuity in this; and it has been adopted by Bekker in his edition. It has however been much criticised, as every such attempt must necessarily be. Van Heusde, in his charming work,† has suggested another. He proposes three classes: 1, those wherein the subject-matter relates to the Beautiful; 2, those wherein it relates to the True; 3, those wherein it relates to the Practical. Of the first are those concerning Love, Beauty, and the Soul. Of the second, those concerning Dialectics, Ideas, Method; in which Truth and the means of attaining it are sought. Of the third, those concerning justice; *i. e.* morals and politics. These three classes represent the three phases of the philosophical mind: the desire for Truth, the appreciation of Truth, and the realization of it, in an application to human life.

There is one great objection to this classification, namely, the impossibility of properly arranging the Dialogues under the separate heads. The *Phædrus,* which Van Heusde believes devoted to Love and Beauty, Schleiermacher has clearly shown to be devoted to Dialectics. So of the rest: Plato mixes up in one dia.ogue very opposite subjects. Van Heusde is also under the er

---

* *Penny Cyclopædia,* Art. *Plato,* p. 236.
† *Initia Philosophiæ Platonicæ,* i. p. 72.

roneous conviction of Plato's having been only a Socratist till he went to Megara, where he became imbued with the Eleatic doctrines; and that it was in his maturer age that he became acquainted with the Pythagorean philosophy.

It may be presumptuous to suggest a new classification, yet it is difficult to resist the temptation. It seems to us that the Dialogues may reasonably be divided into the two classes named by Sextus Empiricus:—Dogmatic and Agonistic, or Expository and Polemical. The advantage of this division is its clearness and practicability. There will always be something arbitrary in the endeavor to classify the dialogues according to their subject-matter, because they are almost all occupied with more than one subject. Thus the *Republic* would certainly be classed under the head of Ethics; yet it contains very important discussions on the nature of human knowledge, and on the theory of Ideas; and these discussions ought properly to be classed under the head of Metaphysics. Again, the *Phædrus* is more than half occupied with discourses about Love; but the real subject of the work is Dialectics.

In the division we propose, such inconveniences are avoided. It is easy to see which dialogues are polemical and which are expository. The *Hippias Major* and the *Timæus* may stand as representatives of each class. In the former no attempt is made to settle the question raised. Socrates contents himself with refuting every position of his antagonist. In the *Timæus* there is no polemic of any sort: all is calmly expository.

A further subdivision might also be made of the agonistic dialogues, into such as are purely polemical and such as by means of polemics enforce ideas. Sometimes Plato only destroys; at other times the destruction is a clearance of the ground, which opens to us a vista of the truth: of this kind is the *Theætetus*.

We are however firmly persuaded that one distinct purpose runs through all the Dialogues, whatever may be their varieties of form or of opinion; one great and fruitful purpose which may rightly be called the philosophy of Plato, and which we will now attempt to exhibit.

§ III. Plato's Method.

By some, Plato is regarded as the mere literary exponent of the Socratic doctrines; by others, as the real founder of a new epoch and of a new philosophy. Both of these views appear to us questionable; but on the subject of Plato, errors are so numerous, and we had almost said so inevitable, that no one who rightly appreciates the difficulty of ascertaining the truth, will be disposed to dogmatize. Although we claim the right of enforcing our opinions—a right purchased with no contemptible amount of labor in the inquiry—we would be distinctly understood to place no very great confidence in their validity. After this preface, we trust, we may speak openly without incurring the charge of dogmatism, when simply recording the results of study.*

Plato we hold to be neither a simple Socratist, nor the creator of a new philosophy. He was the inheritor of all the wisdom of his age. he fully seized the importance of the Socratic Method; he adopted it, enlarged it. But he also saw the importance of those ideas which his predecessors had so laboriously excogitated: he adopted and enlarged the leading features of the Pythagoreans and the Eleatics, of Anaxagoras and Heraclitus. With vast learning and a puissant Method, he created an influence which is not yet totally extinct. But his philosophy was critical, not dogmatical. He enlarged, ameliorated the views of others, introducing little that was new into the philosophy of his age. He was the culminating point of Greek philosophy. In his works

---

* It has been a principle with us throughout, to abstain from all unnecessary references. The absence of such references renders it the more needful for us to state that, previous to writing this Section, we renewed our acquaintance with Plato by carefully reading *all his works*, with the exception of two of the minor ones. (Since the first edition of this work a complete translation of Plato has appeared, so that the English reader has now the means of testing the validity of our conclusions.)

all the various and conflicting tendencies of preceding eras were collected under one Method.

That Method was doubtless the Method of Socrates, with some modifications, or rather with some enlargement. Schleiermacher, in a profound and luminous essay on the *Worth of Socrates as a Philosopher*,* looks upon the service rendered to Philosophy by Socrates as consisting less in the truths *arrived at*, than in the mode in which truth should be *sought*. Alluding to this view, John Mill has said, "This appears to us to be, with some modifications, applicable likewise to Plato. No doubt the disciple pushed his mere *inquiries* and *speculations* over a more extended surface, and to a much greater depth below the surface, than there is any reason to believe the master did. But, though he continually starts most original and valuable ideas, it is seldom that these, when they relate to the *results* of inquiry, are stated with an air of conviction, as if they amounted to fixed opinions. But, when the topic under consideration is the proper *mode* of philosophizing—either the moral spirit in which truth should be sought, or the intellectual processes and methods by which it is to be attained; or when the subject-matter is not any particular scientific principle, but knowledge in the abstract, the differences between knowledge and ignorance, and between knowledge and mere opinion—*then* the views inculcated are definite and consistent, are always the same, and are put forth with the appearance of earnest and matured belief. Even in treating of other subjects, and even when the opinions advanced have the least semblance of being seriously entertained, the discourse itself has generally a very strong tendency to illustrate the conception, which *does* seem to be really entertained, of the nature of some part or other of the process of philosophizing. The inference we would draw is, that on the science of the Investigation of Science, the theory of the pursuit of truth, Plato had not only satisfied himself that

---

* Translated by Bishop Thirlwall, in the *Philological Museum*, and reprinted in the English version of Dr. Wigger's *Life of Socrates*.

his predecessors were in error, and *how*, but had also adopted definite views of his own; while on all or most other subjects he contented himself with confuting the absurdities of others, pointing out the proper course for inquiry, and the spirit in which it should be conducted, and throwing out a variety of ideas of his own, of the value of which he was not quite certain, and which he left to the appreciation of any subsequent inquirer competent to sit in judgment upon them."

We have here to examine what that Method was which Plato constantly pursued. Socrates, as we have shown, relied upon the Inductive or Analogical Reasoning, and on Definitions, as the two principles of investigation. The incompleteness of these principles we have already pointed out; and Plato himself found it necessary to enlarge them.

Definitions form the basis of all Philosophy. To know a thing you must also know what it is *not*. In ascertaining the real Definition, Socrates employed his *accoucheur's* art (τέχνη μαιευτική), and proceeded inductively. Plato also used these arts; but he added to them the more efficient processes of Analysis and Synthesis, of generalization and classification.*

Analysis, which was first insisted on by Plato as a philosophic process, is the decomposition of the whole into its separate parts; whereby, after examining those parts attentively, the idea of the whole is correctly ascertained. To use Platonic language, Analysis is seeing the One in the Many. Thus, if the subject be Virtue, the general term Virtue must first be decomposed into all its parts, *i. e.* into all the Virtues; and from a thorough examination of the Virtues a clear idea of Virtue may be attained.†

Definitions were to Plato what general or abstract ideas were to later metaphysicians. The individual thing was held to be transitory and phenomenal, the abstract idea was eternal. Only

---

* Consult Van Heusde, *Initia Philosoph. Platonicæ*, ii. parts ii. 97, 98.

† A good example of his mode of conducting an inquiry may be seen in the *Gorgias*.

concerning the latter could philosophy occupy itself. But Socrates, although insisting on proper Definitions, had no conception of the classification of those Definitions which must constitute philosophy. Plato, therefore, by the introduction of this process, shifted philosophy from the ground of inquiries into man and society to that of Dialectics. What was Dialectics? It was the art of *discoursing*, *i. e.* the art of thinking, *i. e.* logic. Plato uses the word Dialectics, because with him Thinking was a silent discourse of the soul, and differed from speech only in being silent. In this conception of Philosophy as Dialectics, Plato absorbed the conversational method of Socrates, but gave it a new direction.

How erroneous the notion is which supposes that Plato's merit was exclusively literary, may be gathered from the above brief outline of his Method. He was pre-eminently a severe Dialectician. This is his leading peculiarity; but he has clothed his method in such attractive forms that the means have been mistaken for the end. His great dogma, like that of his master, Socrates, was the necessity of an untiring investigation into general terms (or abstract ideas). He did not look on life with the temporary interest of a passing inhabitant of the world. He looked on it as an immortal soul longing to be released from its earthly prison, and striving to catch by anticipation some faint glimpses of that region of eternal Truth where it would some day rest. The fleeting phenomena of this world he knew were nothing more; but he was too wise to overlook them. Fleeting and imperfect as they were, they were the indications of that eternal Truth for which he longed, footmarks on the perilous journey, and guides unto the wished-for goal. Long before him wise and meditative men perceived that sense-knowledge would only be knowledge of phenomena; that every thing men call Existence was but a perpetual flux—a something which, always *becoming*, never *was;* that the reports which our senses made of these things partook of the same fleeting and uncertain character. He could not, therefore, put his trust in them; he could not believe that Time was any thing more than the wavering image of Eternity.

But he was not a Skeptic. These transitory phenomena were not true existences; but they were *images* of true existences. Interrogate them; classify them; discover what qualities they have in common; discover that which is invariable, necessary, amidst all that is variable, contingent; discover The One in The Many, and you have penetrated the secret of Existence.*

Now in reducing this Platonic language to a modern formula, what is the thought? The thought is simply this: Things exist as classes and as individuals. These classes are but species of higher classes; *e. g.* men are individuals of the class Man, and Man is a species of the class Animal. But Philosophy, which is deductive, has nothing to do with individuals; it is occupied solely with classes. General Terms, or abstract ideas, are therefore the materials with which Philosophy works.

These General Terms, Plato said, stood for the only real Existences, the only objects of Philosophy. And as far as expression is concerned, he would seem to be in perfect accordance with modern thinkers. But we must be cautious how we mistake these coincidences of expression for coincidences of doctrine. Plato's philosophy was an inarticulate utterance, curious to the historian, but valueless as a solution of the problem.

We are here led to the origin of the world-famous dispute of Realism and Nominalism, which may be summed up in a sentence. The Realists maintain, that every General Term (or Abstract idea), such as Man, Virtue, etc., has a real and independent existence, quite irrespective of any concrete individual determination, such as Smith, Benevolence, etc. The Nominalists, on the contrary, maintain, that all General Terms are but the crea-

---

* To refer the reader to particular passages wherein this doctrine is expressed, or implied, would be endless: it runs through all his works, and is the only constant doctrine to be found there. Perhaps the easiest passage where it may be read is *Philebus*, p. 233-6.

tions of the mind, designating no distinct entities, being merely used as *marks* of aggregate conceptions.

In Realism, Plato separated himself from his master Socrates. On this point we have the indubitable, but hitherto little noticed, testimony of Aristotle, who, after speaking of the Socratic Method of Induction and Definition, says:—" But Socrates gave neither to General Terms nor to Definitions a distinct existence."[*] This is plain enough. Aristotle, in continuation, obviously speaks of Plato:—" Those who succeeded him gave to these General Terms a separate existence, and called them *Ideas*."

Thus we are introduced to Plato's famous Ideal theory; which, although confused and contradictory enough in detail, as is the case with all his special opinions, is clear enough in its general tendency.

§ IV. Plato's Ideal Theory.

The word Idea has undergone more changes than almost any word in philosophy; and nothing can well be more opposed to the modern sense of the word than the sense affixed to it by Plato. If we were to say, that *Ideas* were tantamount to the *Substantial Forms* of the schoolmen, we should run the risk of endeavoring to enlighten an obscurity by an obscurity no less opaque. If we were to say, that the Ideas were tantamount to *Universals*, the same objection might be raised. If we were to say, that the Ideas were *General Terms* or *Abstract Ideas*, we should mislead every Nominalist into the belief that Plato was an " Idealist;" otherwise the last explanation would be pertinent.

It will be better, however, to describe first, and to define afterwards. Plato, according to Aristotle, gave to General Terms a distinct existence, and called them Ideas. He became a Realist;

---

[*] *Met.* xiii. 4, 'Αλλ' ὁ μὲν Σωκράτης τὰ καθόλου οὐ χωριστὰ ἐποίει, οὐδὲ τοὺς ὁρισμούς.—The wording of this may appear strange. Many have supposed universals to exist separately; but how a separate existence could be given to Definitions may puzzle the stoutest Realist. We believe the difficulty vanishes, if we remember that the Platonic Definitions and Universals were the same things; Aristotle's phrase is, however, ambiguous.

and asserted, that there was the *Abstract Man* no less than the *Concrete Men;* the latter were Men only in as far as they participated in the Ideal Man. No one will dispute that we have a conception of a genus—that we do conceive and reason about Man quite independently of Smith or Brown, Peter or Paul. If we have such a conception, whence did we derive it? Our experience has only been of the Smiths and Browns, the Peters and Pauls; we have only known *men.* Our senses tell us nothing of Man. Individual objects only give individual knowledge. A number of stones placed before us will afford us no knowledge, will not enable us to say, These are stones; unless we have previously learned what is the nature of Stone. So, also, we must know the nature of Man, before we can know that Jones and Brown are Men. We do know Man, and we know Men; but our knowledge of the former is distinct from that of the latter, and must have a distinct source; so, at least, thought the Realists. What is that source? Reflection, not sense.

The Realists finding The One in The Many,—in other words, finding certain characteristics common to all Men, and not only common to them but necessary to their being Men,—abstracted these *general* characteristics from the *particular* accidents of individual men, and out of these characteristics made what they called *Universals* (what we call *genera*). These Universals existed *per se.* They are not only conceptions of the mind; they are entities; and our perceptions of them are formed in the same manner as our perceptions of other things.

Greek Philosophy, no less than Greek Art, was eminently Objective. Now what is the objective tendency, but the tendency to transform our *conceptions* into *perceptions*—to project our ideas out of us, and then to look at them as images, or as entities? Let then the conception of genera be rendered objective, and the Realist doctrine is explained. Our *conceptions* were held by Realism to be *perceptions* of existing Things; these Plato called *Ideas,* which he maintained to be the only real existences; they were the *noumena* of which all individual things were the *phenomena.* If then we define the Platonic "Idea," to be a "Noumenon," or "Substantial Form," we shall not be far wrong: and most of the disputes respecting the real meaning of the term will be set aside; for example, Ritter's wavering account of the word—in which he is at a loss to say whether *Idea* means the *universal,* or whether it does not also mean the *individual.* That Plato usually designates a General Term by the word Idea, there can be no doubt; there can be no doubt also that he sometimes designates the essence of some individual thing an Idea, as in the *Republic,* where he speaks of the Idea of a Table from which all other Tables were formed. There is no contradiction in this:—a general form is as necessary for Tables as for Men: this Idea, therefore, equally partakes of generality, even where exemplified by particular things.

We must now endeavor to indicate the position occupied by Ideas in the Platonic cosmology. To Socrates Plato was indebted for his Method; yet not wholly indebted, seeing that he enlarged the conception transmitted to him. To Pythagoras he was indebted for his theory of Ideas; yet not wholly indebted, seeing that he modified it and rendered it more plausible. What he did for Method we have seen: let us now see how he transformed the Pythagorean doctrine.

Aristotle, in a memorable passage, says.—"Plato followed Socrates respecting definitions, but, accustomed as he was to inquiries into universals (διὰ τὸ ζητῆσαι περὶ τῶν καθόλου), he supposed that definitions should be those of *intelligibles* (*i. e.* noumena), rather than of *sensibles* (*i. e.* phenomena): for it is impossible to give a general definition to *sensible objects,* which are always changing. Those *Intelligible Essences* he called *Ideas;* adding that *sensible objects* were different from Ideas, and received from them their names; for it is in consequence of their *participation* (κατὰ μέθεξιν) in Ideas, that all objects of the same genus receive the same name as the Ideas. He introduced the word *participation.* The Pythagoreans say, that 'Things are the *copies* of Numbers.' Plato says, 'the *participation;*' he only changes the name."*

With due submission, we venture to question the assertion of Aristotle in the last sentence. Plato did more than change a name. The conception alone of Ideas, as generical types, is a great advance on the conception of Numbers. But Plato did not stop here. He ventured on an explanation of the nature and the degree of that participation of sensible objects in Ideas. And Aristotle himself, in another place, points out a fundamental distinction. "Plato thought that sensible Things no less than their causes were Numbers; *but the causes are Intelligibles* (*i. e.* Ideas), *and other things Sensibles.*"† Surely this is something more than the invention of a name! It gives a new character to the theory; it renders it at once more clear, and more applicable.

The greatest difficulty felt in the Ideal theory is that of *participation*. How, and in how far, does this participation take place? A question which Plato did not, and could not, solve. All that he could answer was, that human knowledge is necessarily imperfect, that sensation troubles the intellectual eye, and only when the soul is free from the hindrances of the body shall we be able to discern things in all the ineffable splendor of truth. But, although our knowledge is imperfect, it is not false. Reason enables us to catch some glimpses of the truth, and we must endeavor to gain more. Whatever is the object of the soul's thought, purely as such, is real and true. The problem is to separate these glimpses of the truth from the prejudices and errors of mere opinion.

In this doctrine, opinion is concerned only with Appearances (phenomena); philosophy, with Existence. Our sensation, judgments, opinions, have only reference to τὰ γιγνόμενα; our philosophic conceptions have reference to τὰ ὄντα. The whole matter

---

* *Metaph.* i. 6. † Ib. i. 7, 'Ἀλλὰ τοὺς μὲν νοητοὺς αἰτίους, τούτους δὲ αἰσθητοῖς.

is comprised in Plato's answer to Diogenes, who thought he demolished the theory of Ideas by exclaiming, "I see indeed a table; but I see no Idea of a table." Plato replied, "Because you see with your eyes, and not with your reason." Hence at the close of the 5th Book of his *Republic*, he says that those only are to be called Philosophers who devote themselves to the contemplation of τὸ ὄν, *i. e.* Existence.

The phenomena which constitute what we perceive of the world (*i. e.* the world of sense) are but the resemblances of matter to Ideas. In other words, Ideas are the Forms of which material Things are copies; the *noumena*, of which all that we perceive are the Appearances (phenomena). But we must not suppose these copies to be exact; they do not at all participate in the nature of their models; they do not even represent them, otherwise than in a superficial manner. Or perhaps it would be more correct to say, that Ideas do not resemble Things; the man does not resemble his portrait, although the portrait may be a tolerable resemblance of him; a resemblance of his aspect, not of his nature. If, then, the Ideas as they exist realized in Nature, do not accurately resemble the Ideas as they exist *per se*—*i. e.* if the phenomena are not exact copies of the noumena—how are we ever to attain a knowledge of Ideas and of Truth? This question plunges us into the midst of his psychology, which we must first explain before the whole conception of the Ideal theory can be made consistent.

§ V. Plato's Psychology.

After the dreary dialectics of the two preceding Sections, it is some refreshment to be able to open this Section with a myth, and that perhaps the most fascinating of all Plato's myths.

In the *Phædrus* Socrates very justly declares his inability to explain the real nature of the soul. But though he cannot exhibit it, he can show what it resembles. Unable to give a demonstration, he can paint a picture; and that picture he paints as follows:

"We may compare it to a chariot, with a pair of winged horses and a driver. In the souls of the Gods, the horses and the drivers are entirely good: in other souls only partially so, one of the horses excellent, the other vicious. The business, therefore, of the driver is extremely difficult and troublesome.

"Let us now attempt to show how some living beings came to be spoken of as mortal, and others as immortal. All souls are employed in taking care of the things which are inanimate; and travel about the whole of heaven in various forms. Now, when the soul is perfect, and has wings, it is carried aloft, and helps to administer the entire universe; but the soul which loses its wings, drops down till it catches hold of something solid, in which it takes up its residence; and, having a dwelling of clay, which seems to be self-moving on account of the soul which is in it, the two together are called an animal, and mortal. The phrase 'immortal animal' arises not from any correct understanding, but from a fiction: never having seen, nor being able to comprehend, a deity, men conceived an immortal being, having a body as well as a soul, united together for all eternity. Let these things, then, be as it pleases God; but let us next state from what cause a soul becomes unfledged.

"It is the nature of wings to lift up heavy bodies towards the habitation of the Gods; and, of all things which belong to the body, wings are that which most partakes of the divine. The divine includes the beautiful, the wise, the good, and every thing of that nature. By these the wings of the soul are nourished and increased; by the contraries of these, they are destroyed.

"Jupiter, and the other Gods, divided into certain bands, travel about in their winged chariots, ordering and attending to all things, each according to his appointed function; and all who will, and who can, follow them. When they go to take their repasts, they journey towards the summit of the vault of heaven. The chariots of the Gods, being in exact equilibrium, and therefore easily guided, perform this journey easily, but all others with difficulty; for one of the two horses, being of inferior nature, when he has not been exceedingly well trained by the driver, weighs down the vehicle, and impels it towards the earth.

"The souls which are *called* immortal (viz. the Gods), when they reach the summit, go through, and, standing upon the convex outside of heaven, are carried round and round by its revolution, and see the things which lie beyond the heavens. No poet has ever celebrated these supercelestial things, nor ever will celebrate them, as they deserve. This region is the seat of *Existence* itself: Real Existence, colorless, figureless, and intangible Existence, which is visible only to Mind, the charioteer of the soul, and which forms the subject of Real Knowledge. The minds of the Gods, which are fed by pure knowledge, and all other thoroughly well-ordered minds, contemplate for a time this universe of 'Being' *per se*, and are delighted and nourished by the contemplation, until the revolution of the heavens brings them back again to the same point. In this circumvolution, they contemplate Justice itself, Temperance itself, and Knowledge; not that knowledge which has a generation or a beginning, not that which exists in a subject which is any of what we term beings, but that Knowledge which exists in Being in general; in that which really Is. After thus contemplating all real existences, and being nourished thereby, these souls again sink into the interior of the heavens, and repose.

"Such is the life of the Gods. Of other souls, those which best follow the Gods, and most resemble them, barely succeed in lifting the head of the charioteer into the parts beyond the heavens, and, being carried round by the circumvolution, are enabled with difficulty to contemplate this universe of Self-Existence. Others, being encumbered by the horses, sometimes rising and sometimes sinking, are enabled to see some Existences only. The remainder only struggle to elevate themselves, and, by the unskilfulness of their drivers, coming continually into collision, are lamed, or break their wings, and, after much labor, go away without accomplishing their purpose, and return to feed upon mere **opinion.**

"The motive of this great anxiety to view the supercelestial plain of Truth is that the proper food of the soul is derived from thence, and, in particular, the wings, by which the soul is made light and carried aloft, are nourished upon it. Now it is an inviolable law that any soul which, placing itself in the train of the Gods, and journeying along with them, obtains a sight of any of these self-existent Realities, remains exempt from all harm until the next circumvolution, and, if it can contrive to effect this every time, is forever safe and uninjured. But if, being unable to elevate itself to the necessary height, it altogether fails of seeing these realities, and, being weighed down by vice and oblivion, loses its wings and falls to the earth, it enters into and animates some Body. It never enters, at the first generation, into the body of a brute animal; but that which has seen most enters into the body of a person who will become a lover of wisdom, or a lover of beauty, or a person addicted to music, or to love; the next in rank, into that of a monarch who reigns according to law, or a warrior, or a man of talents for command; the third, into a person qualified to administer the State, and manage his family affairs, or carry on a gainful occupation; the fourth into a person fond of hard labor and bodily exercises, or skilled in the prevention and curing of bodily diseases; the fifth, into a prophet, or a teacher of religious ceremonies; the sixth, into a poet, or a person addicted to any other of the imitative arts; the seventh, into a husbandman or an artificer; the eighth, into a sophist, or a courtier of the people; the ninth, into a despot and usurper. And, in all these different fortunes, they who conduct themselves justly will obtain next time a more eligible lot; they who conduct themselves unjustly a worse. The soul never returns to its pristine state in less than ten thousand years, for its wings do not grow in a shorter time; except only the soul of one who philosophizes with sincerity or who loves with philosophy. Such souls, after three periods of one thousand years, if they choose thrice in succession this kind of life, recover their wings in the three thousandth year, and depart. The other souls, at the termination of their first life, are judged, and, having received their sentence, are either sent for punishment into the places of execution under the earth, or are elevated to a place in heaven, in which they are rewarded according to the life which they led while here. In either case they are called back on the thousandth year, to choose or draw lots for a new life. Then a human soul often passes into the body of a beast, and that of a beast, if it has ever been human, passes again into the body of a man; for a soul which has never seen the Truth at all cannot enter into the human form, it being necessary that man should be able to apprehend many things according to *kinds*, which kinds are composed of many perceptions combined by reason into *one*. Now, this mode of apprehending is neither more nor less than the *recollecting* of those things which the soul formerly saw when it journeyed along with the Gods, and, disregarding what we now call beings, applied itself to the apprehension of Real Being. It is for this reason that the soul of the philosopher is refledged in a shorter period than others; for, it constantly, to the best of its power, occupies itself in trying to recollect those things which the Gods contemplated, and by the contemplation of which they are Gods; by which means being lifted out of, and above, human cares and interests, he is, by the vulgar, considered as mad, while in reality he is inspired."

This is unquestionably the poetry of philosophy, and it is from such passages that the popular opinion respecting Plato has been formed; but they represent only a small portion of the real thinker. Towards the close the reader will have remarked that the famous doctrine of *reminiscence* is implied. This doctrine may be seen fully developed in the *Phædo;* it seems to have been a fundamental one. The difficulties of conceiving the possibility of any knowledge other than the sense-knowledge, which the Sophists had successfully proved to lead to skepticism, must early have troubled Plato's mind. If we know nothing but what our senses teach us, then is all knowledge trivial. Those who admit the imperfection of the senses and fall back upon Reason, beg the question. How do we know that Reason is correct? How can we be assured that Reason is not subject to some such inevitable imperfection as that to which sense is subject?

Here the ever-recurring problem of human knowledge presents itself. Plato was taught by Socrates that beyond the world of Sense, there was the world of eternal Truth; that men who differed greatly respecting individual things did not differ respecting universals; that there was a common fund of Truth, from which all human souls drew their share. Agreeing with his master that there were certain principles about which there could be no dispute, he wished to know how he came by those principles.

All who have examined the nature of our knowledge, are aware that it is partly made up of direct impressions received by the senses, and partly of ideas which never were, at least in their ideal state, perceived by the senses. It is this latter part which has agitated the schools. On the one side, men have declared it to be wholly independent of the senses—to be the pure action of the soul. In its simplest form, this doctrine may be called the doctrine of Innate Ideas. On the other side, men have as vigorously argued that, although all our ideas were not absolutely derived from the senses in a direct manner, yet they were all so derived in an indirect manner: thus, we have never *seen* a mermaid; but we have seen both a fish and a woman, and to combine these two impressions is all that the mind does in conceiving a mermaid. This doctrine is pushed to its limits in the eighteenth-century philosophy, which says, *Penser, c'est sentir:* thought is a transformed sensation.

Plato, in adopting the former view, rendered it more cogent than most of his successors; for is it not somewhat gratuitous to say, we are born with such and such ideas? It is different from saying we are born with certain faculties: *that* would be admissible. But, to be driven into a corner, and on being asked, whence came those ideas? to answer, they are innate,—is a pure *petitio principii.* What proof have you that they are in nate? Merely the proof that you cannot otherwise account for them?

Plato was more consistent. He said The Soul is and ever was immortal. In its anterior states of existence it had accurate conceptions of the eternal Truth. It was face to face with Existence. Now, having descended upon earth, having passed into a body, and, being subject to the hindrances of that bodily imprisonment, it is no longer face to face with Existence: it can see Existence only through the ever-changing flux of material phenomena. The world is only *becoming*, never *is*. The Soul would apprehend only the *becoming*, had it not some recollection of its anterior state—had it not in some sort the power of tracing the unvarying Idea under the varying phenomena. When, for example, we see a stone, all that our senses convey is the appearance of that stone: but, as the stone is large or small, the soul apprehends the Idea of Greatness; and this apprehension is a reminiscence of the world of Ideas, awakened by the sensation. So when we see or hear of a benevolent action, besides the fact, our Soul apprehends the Idea of Goodness. And all our recollection of Ideas is performed in the same way. It is as if in our youth we had listened to some mighty orator whose printed speech we are reading in old age. That printed page, how poor and faint a copy of that thrilling eloquence! how we miss the speaker's piercing, vibrating tones, his flashing eye, his flashing face! And yet that printed page in some dim way recalls those tones, recalls that face, and stirs us somewhat as we then were stirred. Long years and many avocations have somewhat effaced the impression he first made, but the printed words serve faintly to recall it. Thus it is with our immortal Souls. They have sojourned in that celestial region where the voice of Truth rings clearly, where the aspect of Truth is unveiled, undimmed. They are now sojourning in this fleeting, flowing river of life, stung with resistless longings for the skies, and solaced only by the reminiscences of that former state which these fleeting, broken, incoherent images of Ideas awaken in them.

It is a mistake to suppose this a mere poetical conception. Plato never sacrifices logic to poetry. If he sometimes calls poetry to his aid, it is only to express by it those ideas which logic cannot grasp, ideas which are beyond demonstration; but he never indulges in mere fancies. Instead therefore of saying that Reason was occupied with innate ideas, he consistently said that every thing which the senses did not furnish was a reminiscence of the world of Ideas.

We are now in a condition to answer the question with which the last Section was closed,—How to ascertain the Truth, if Phenomena are not exact copies of Noumena? The sensation awakens recollection, and the recollection is of Truth; the soul is confronted with the Many by means of Sense, and by means of Reason it detects the One in the Many; *i. e.* the particular things perceived by Sense awaken the recollection of Universals or Ideas. But this recollection of Truth is always more or less imperfect. Absolute Truth is for the Gods alone. No man is without some of the divine spark. Philosophers alone have any large share; and they might increase it by a proper method.

The philosophy of Plato has two distinct branches, somewhat resembling what we found in Parmenides. The universe is divided into two parts: the celestial region of Ideas, and the mundane region of material phenomena. These answer very well to the modern conception of Heaven and Earth. As the phenomena of matter are but copies of Ideas (not, as some suppose, their bodily *realization*), there arises a question: How do Ideas become Matter? In other words: How do Things participate in Ideas? We have mooted the question in the former Section, where we said that it admitted of no satisfactory solution; nor does it; and we must not be surprised to find Plato giving, at different times, two very different explanations. These two explanations are too curious to be overlooked. In the *Republic*, he says that God, instead of perpetually creating individual things, created a distinct type (Idea) for each thing. From this type all other things of the class are made. Thus, God made the Idea of a bed: according to this type, any carpenter may now fashion as many beds as he likes, in the same way as an artist may imitate in his paintings the types already created, but cannot himself create any thing new. The argument, as an illustration of Plato's Method, may be given here:

"Shall we proceed according to our usual Method? That Method, as you know, is the embracing under one general Idea the multiplicity of things which exist separately, but have the same name. You comprehend?

"Perfectly.

"Let us take any thing you like. For instance, there is a multiplicity of beds and tables?

"Certainly.

"But these two kinds are comprised, one under the Idea of a bed, and the other under the Idea of a table?

"Without doubt.

"And we say that the carpenter who makes one of these articles, makes the bed or the table according to the Idea he has of each. For he does not make the Idea itself. That is impossible?

"Truly, that is impossible.

"Well, now, what name shall we bestow on the workman whom I am now going to name?

"What workman?

"Him who makes what all the other workmen make separately.

"You speak of a powerful man!

"Patience; you will admire him still more. This workman has not only the talent of making all the works of art, but also all the works of nature; plants, animals, every thing else; in a word, himself.[*] He makes the Heaven, the Earth, the Gods; every thing in Heaven, Earth, or Hell.

---

[*] Τά τε ἄλλα καὶ ἑαυτόν. We are inclined to regard this passage as corrupt, the self-creation of God being certainly no Platonic notion; at least not countenanced by any other passage in any other work. The scholiast makes no comment on it.

"You speak of a wonderful workman, truly!

"You seem to doubt me? But, tell me, do you think there is no such workman; or, do you think that in one sense any one could do all this, but in another no one could? Could you not yourself succeed in a certain way?

"In what way?

"It is not difficult; it is often done, and in a short time. Take a mirror, and turn it round on all sides: in an instant you will have made the sun and stars, the earth, yourself, the animals and plants, works of art, and all we mentioned.

"Yes, the images, the appearances, but not the real things.

"Very well; you comprehend my opinion. The painter is a workman of this class, is he not?

"Certainly.

"You will tell me that he makes nothing real, although he makes a bed in a certain way?

"Yes; but it is only an appearance, an image.

"And the carpenter, did you not allow that the bed which he made was not the Idea which we call the essence of the bed, the real bed, but only a certain bed?

"I said so, indeed.

"If, then, he does not make the Idea of the bed, he makes nothing real, but only something which represents that which really exists. And, if any one maintain that the carpenter's work has a real existence he will be in error."*

In the *Timæus*, perhaps the most purely expository of all his works, and unquestionably one of the latest, Plato takes a totally different view of the creation of the world. God is there said, not to create types (Ideas); but these types having existed from all eternity, God in fashioning Chaos fashioned it *after the model of these Ideas*. In this view there is no participation in the *nature* of Ideas, but only a participation in their *form*.

Whichever hypothesis he adopted (and Plato did not much

---

* *Repub.* x. 467–8, ed. Bekker.

care for either), this conception of Heaven and Earth as two different regions, is completed by the conception of the double nature of the soul; or rather, of two souls: one Rational and the other Sensitive. These two souls are closely connected, as the two regions of Ideas and Phenomena are connected. Neither of them is superfluous; neither of them, in a human sense, sufficient: they complete each other. The Sensitive soul awakens the reminiscences of the Rational soul; and the Rational soul, by detecting the One in the Many, preserves Man from the skepticism inevitably resulting from mere sense-knowledge.

Thus did Plato resume in himself all the conflicting tendencies of his age; thus did he accept each portion of the truth supposed to be discovered by his predecessors, and reconcile these portions in one general tendency. In that vast system, all skepticism and all faith found acceptance: the skepticism was corrected, the faith was propped up by more solid arguments. He admitted, with the skeptics, the imperfection of all sense-knowledge; but, though imperfect, he declared it not worthless: it is no more like the Truth than phenomena are like Ideas; but, as phenomena are in some sort modelled after Ideas, and do, therefore, in some dim way, represent Ideas, so does sense-knowledge lead the patient thinker to something like the Truth: it awakens in him reminiscence of the Truth. As Ritter says, "He shows, in detail, that in the world of sense there is no perfect likeness, but that an object which at one time appears like, is at another thought to be unlike, and is, therefore, defective in completeness of resemblance, and has at most but a tendency thereto. The same is the case with the Beautiful, the Good, the Just, the Holy, and with all that really *is;* in the sensible world there is nothing exactly resembling them, neither similar nor dissimilar; all, however, that possesses any degree of correspondence with these true species of being is perceived by us through the senses, and thereby reminds us of what truly is. From this it is clear that he had previously seen it somewhere, or been conscious of it, and, as this could not have been in the present, it must have

been in some earlier state of existence. In this respect there is
a close connection between this doctrine and the view of sensible
objects, which represents them as mere copies or resemblances of
the super-sensible truth; for, even in perception, a feeling arises
upon the mind, that all we see or hear is very far from reaching
to a likeness to that which is the true being and the absolutely
like; but that, striving to attain, it falls short of perfect resem‐
blance; and consequently, the impressions of the sense are mere
tokens of the eternal ideas, whose similitude they bear, and of
which they are copies."

§ VI. Summary of Plato's Dialectics.

Having exhibited Plato's conceptions of Method, of Ideas, and
of the Soul, it will now be convenient to take a brief review of
them, to exhibit their position in the general doctrine.

Dialectics was the base of the Platonic doctrine. Indeed,
Plato believed in no other Science; Dialectics and Philosophy
were synonymous. For Dialectics (or Logic) to be synonymous
with Philosophy, the theory of Ideas was necessary. Dialectics
is the science of general propositions, of general terms, of univer‐
sals. To become *the* science it must necessarily be occupied with
more important things. Ideas are these important things; for
Ideas are at once the only real Existences, and General Terms.
Whoso discoursed about General Terms discoursed about Exist‐
ence; and deeper than that, no science could hope to penetrate.
Plato, whose opinions can scarcely ever be accepted as final, is
both explicit and constant in his conception of Dialectics as *the*
science. To determine the real nature of science, he devotes an
entire dialogue: the *Theætetus*. That remarkable work is pure‐
ly critical; it refutes the opinions of adversaries, in such a way
as to leave no doubt as to Plato's own opinion. All attempts to
constitute science either upon perception (αἴσθησις) or upon opin‐
ion (δόξα) he refutes in an irresistible manner. Perception can
only be of objects which have no stability, which have no real
Existence. Opinion, though it be correct, is unable to constitute

science; for there are two sorts of opinion,—false and true; and to distinguish the true from the false would require a science which knew the Truth. It follows, as a necessary consequence, that Ideas, which are the real immutable elements of science, must be known in themselves, and that science consists in seeking the order of development of these Ideas; that is to say, in Dialectics.

Owing to the Ideal theory, Dialectics was necessarily *the* science; that is, the science of Being. The distinction between his Dialectics and the Logic of his successors is very marked. While he spoke of Dialectics as the art of methodical classification of genera,—the art of speaking upon general notions,—he did not confine it to *subjective* truth; for he believed this subjective truth to be only a reflex of the objective reality: he believed that abstract ideas were images of real existences. Dialectics was therefore not only the "art of thinking," but the science of immutable being.

In the twofold aspect of Creation there was this division of knowledge:

Perception.

Matter, phenomena, τὰ γιγνόμενα = Sensation = Opinion.

Dialectics.

Existence, Ideas, τὰ ὄντα = Abstract Ideas = Science.

In the everchanging flux of Becoming, which was the object of Perception, there were traces of the immutable Being, which was the object of science. This distinction may be applied to Plato's own manifold works. We may say of them that the opinions on psychology, physics, ethics, and politics are constantly changing, uncertain; but amidst all these various opinions there reigns one constant Method. He never wavers as to Dialectics. We may therefore fully understand the importance bestowed on Dialectics; and we may also clearly see what is meant by identifying his Philosophy with Dialectics.

The basis of the Platonic doctrine therefore is *Dialectics;* the subject-matter of Dialectics consists of *Ideas;* and the Method consists of *Definitions, Analysis,* and *Induction.*

§ VII. Plato's Theology and Cosmology.

Hitherto we have been occupied solely with the general doctrine; we have now to descend to particulars. But, as so often remarked, particular doctrines have scarcely any stability in the Platonic writings; what is advanced to-day is refuted to-morrow; accordingly, critics and historians have squabbled about these wavering opinions, as if agreement were possible. One declares Plato held one opinion; and cites his passages in proof. Another thinks his predecessor a blockhead; and cites other passages wholly destructive of the opinion Plato is said to have maintained. A third comes, and, stringing passages from one dialogue to passages from another, interprets the whole in his own way. A consistent Theological doctrine will not therefore be expected from us: we can only reproduce some of the Platonic notions, those especially which have influenced later thinkers.

In the same way as Plato sought to detect the One amidst the Multiplicity of material phenomena, and, having detected it, declared it to be the real essence of matter, so also did he seek to detect the One amidst the Multiplicity of Ideas, and, having detected it, declared it to be God. What Ideas were to Phenomena, God was to Ideas: the last result of generalization. God was thus the One Being comprising within himself all other Beings, the ἓν καὶ πολλά, the Cause of all things, celestial and terrestrial. God was the supreme Idea. Whatever view we take of the Platonic cosmology—whether God created Ideas, or whether he only fashioned unformed matter after the model of Ideas—we are equally led to the conviction, that God represented the supreme Idea of all Existence; the great Intelligence, source of all other Intelligences; the Sun whose light illumined creation. God is perfect, ever the same, without envy, wishing nothing but good: for, although a clear knowledge of God is impossible to mortals, an approximation to that knowledge is possible: we cannot know what he is, we can only know what he is like. He must be good, because self-sufficing; and the world is good, because he made it. Why did he make it? God made the world because he was free from envy, and wished that all things should resemble him as much as possible; he therefore *persuaded* Necessity to become stable, harmonious, and fashioned according to Excellence. Yes, *persuaded* is Plato's word; for there were two eternal Principles, *Intelligence* and *Necessity*, and from the mixture of these the world was made; but Intelligence persuaded Necessity to be fashioned according to Excellence.* He arranged chaos into Beauty. But, as there is nothing beautiful but Intelligence, and as there is no Intelligence without a Soul, he placed a Soul into the body of the World, and made the World an animal.

Plato's proof of the world being an animal is too curious a specimen of his analogical reasoning to be passed over. There is warmth in the human being; there is warmth also in the world: the human being is composed of various elements, and is therefore called a body; the world is also composed of various elements, and is therefore a body; and, as our bodies have souls, the body of the world must have a soul; and that soul stands in the same relation to our souls, as the warmth of the world stands to our warmth.† Having thus *demonstrated* the world to be an animal, it was but natural he should conceive that animal as resembling its creator, and human beings as resembling the universal animal, τὸ πᾶν ζῶον. As soon as the World, that image of the eternal Gods, as soon as that vast Animal began to move, live, and think, God looked upon his work, and was glad.‡

But although God in his goodness would have made nothing

---

* Μεμιγμένη γὰρ οὖν ἡ τοῦδε τοῦ κόσμου γένεσις ἐξ ἀνάγκης τε καὶ νοῦ συστάσεως ἐγεννήθη, νοῦ δὲ ἀνάγκης ἀρχοντος τῷ πείθειν αὐτὴν τῶν γιγνομένων τὰ πλεῖστ᾽: ἐπ᾽ τὸ βέλτιστον ἄγειν.—*Timæus*, p. 56.

† *Philebus*, pp. 170-1.

‡ 'Ως δὲ κινηθὲν αὐτὸ καὶ ζῶν ἐνόησε τῶν ἀιδίων θεῶν γεγονὸς ἄγαλμα ὁ γεννήσας πατήρ, ἠγάσθη τε καὶ εὐφρανθεὶς ἔτι δὴ μᾶλλον ὅμοιον πρὸς τὸ παράδειγμα ἐπενόησεν ἀπεργάσασθαι.—*Timæus*, p. 36.

evil, he could not prevent the existence of it. Various disputes have been warmly carried on by scholars, respecting the nature of this Evil which Plato was forced to admit. Some have conceived it nothing less than the Manichæan doctrine. Thus much we may say: the notion of an antagonist principle is inseparable from every religious formula: as God can only be Good, and as Evil does certainly exist, it must exist independently of him; it must be eternal. Plato cut the matter very short by his logical principle,—that since there was a Good, there must necessarily be the *contrary* of Good, namely, Evil. If Evil exists, *how* does it exist, and *where?* It cannot find place in the celestial region of Ideas. It must therefore necessarily dwell in the terrestrial region of phenomena: its home is the world; it is banished from heaven. And is not this logical? What is the world of Phenomena but an imperfect copy of the world of Ideas, and how can the imperfect be the purely Good? When Ideas are "realized," as the Pantheists would say, when Ideas, pure immutable essences, are clothed in material forms, or when matter is fashioned after the model of those Ideas, what can result but imperfections? The Ideas *are* not in this world: they are only in a state of *becoming*, ὄντως ὄντα, not γιγνόμενα. Phenomena are in their very nature imperfect: they are perpetually striving to exist as realities. In their constitution there is *something* of the divine: an image of the Idea, and some participation in it; but more of the primeval chaos.

Those, therefore, who say that Plato thought that "Evil was inherent in matter," though expressing themselves loosely, express themselves on the whole correctly. Matter was the great Necessity which Intelligence fashioned. Because it was Necessity and unintelligent, it was Evil, for Intelligence alone can be good.*

---

* In the *Laws*, x. pp. 201-2, he curiously distinguished the νοῦς from the ψυχή in this manner. The ψυχή (vital principle) is the self-moving principle; but, inasmuch as it is sometimes moved to *bad* as well as to *good* (τῶν τε ἀγαθῶν αἰτίαν εἶναι ψυχὴν καὶ τῶν κακῶν), it was necessary to have some other

Now, as this world of phenomena is the region where Evil dwells, we must use our utmost endeavors to escape from it. And how escape? By suicide?—No. By leading the life of the Gods; and every Platonist knows that the life of the Gods consists in the eternal contemplation of Truth, of Ideas. Thus, as on every side, are we forced to encounter Dialectics as the sole salvation for man.

From the above explanation of the nature of Evil, it will be seen that there is no contradiction in Plato's saying, that the quantity of Evil in this life exceeded that of the Good; it exceeds it in the proportion that phenomena exceed noumena,—that matter exceeds Ideas.

But although Evil be a necessary part of the world, it is in constant struggle with Good. What is this but the struggle of *Becoming?* And man is endowed with Free Will and Intelligence: he may therefore choose between Good and Evil.* And according to his choice will his future life be regulated. Metempsychosis was a doctrine Plato borrowed from Pythagoras; and in that doctrine he could find arguments for the enforcement of a sage and virtuous life, which no other afforded at that epoch.

We have said nothing of the arguments whereby Plato proves the existence of God; for we have been forced to pass over many details: but we cannot close this chapter without alluding to an argument often used in modern times, and seldom suspected to have had so ancient an upholder,—God is proved to exist, by the very feeling of affinity to his nature which stirs within our souls.

Such opinions as those above set down were certainly expressed by Plato at different times: but we again warn the

---

principle which should determine its direction. He therefore makes νοῦς (intelligence) the principle which determines the soul (whether the soul of the world or of man, it is the same) to good; and ἄνοια (ignorance –want of *nous*) which determines it to evil

* *Laws,* x. p. 217.

reader against supposing them to have been his constant views. They are taken from works written at wide intervals, and bearing considerable difference of opinion; and in those very works there are occasional glimpses of an appalling doctrine, namely, that man is but the plaything of God, who alternately governs and forsakes the world. The first clause of this sentence seems derived from Heraclitus, who said, "that making worlds was the sport of Demiurgos." Plato's words are these: ἄνθρωπον δὲ θεοῦ τι παιγνίον εἶναι μεμηχανημένον: and this is said to be man's greatest excellence.* The second clause is formally expressed by Plato thus: "God," he says, "alternately governs and forsakes the world; when he governs it, things go on well: it is the age of gold; when he forsakes it, the world suddenly turns round in a contrary orbit,—a fearful crisis takes place, all things are disordered, mundane existence is totally disarranged, and only after some time do things settle down to a sort of order, though of a very imperfect kind."†

§ VIII. Plato's View of the Beautiful and the Good.

So much has been written and talked in modern times of τὸ καλόν, "the Beautiful," as conceived by Plato, and this by persons who never read a line of his works, that we must devote a few sentences to it.

The bond which unites the human to the divine is Love. And Love is the longing of the Soul for Beauty; the inextinguishable desire which like feels for like, which the divinity within us feels for the divinity revealed to us in Beauty. This is the celebrated Platonic Love, which, from having originally meant a communion of two souls, and that in a rigidly dialectical sense, has been degraded to the expression of maudlin sentiment between the sexes. Platonic love meant ideal sympathy; it now means the love of a sentimental young gentleman for a woman he cannot or will not marry.

---

* *Laws*, vii. p. 82.   † *Politicus*, p. 280.

But what is Beauty? Not the mere flattery of the senses. It does not consist in harmonious outlines and resplendent colors: these are but the *indications* of it. Beauty is Truth. It is the radiant image of that which was most splendid in the world of Ideas. Listen to Plato's description of it in the *Phædrus:*—
"For, as we have already said, every human soul has actually seen the Real Existences, or it would not have come into a human shape. But it is not easy for all of them to call to mind what they then saw; those, especially, which saw that region for a short time only, and those which, having fallen to the earth, were so unfortunate as to be turned to injustice, and consequent oblivion of the sacred things which were seen by them in their prior state. Few, therefore, remain who are adequate to the recollection of those things. These few, when they see here any image or resemblance of the things which are there, receive a shock like a thunderbolt, and are in a manner taken *out of themselves;* but, from deficiency of comprehension, they know not what it is which so affects them. Now, the likenesses which exist there of Justice and Temperance, and the other things which the soul honors, do not possess any splendor; and a few persons only, with great difficulty, by the aid of dull, blunt, material organs, perceive the terrestrial likenesses of those qualities, and recognize them. But Beauty was not only most splendid when it was seen by us forming part of the heavenly possession or choir, but here also the likeness of it comes to us through the most acute and clear of our senses, that of sight, and with a splendor which no other of the terrestrial images of supercelestial Existences possess. They, then, who are not fresh from heaven, or who have been corrupted, are not vehemently impelled towards that Beauty which is aloft when they see that upon earth which is called by its name; they do not, therefore, venerate and worship it, but give themselves up to physical pleasure after the manner of a quadruped. But they who are fresh from those divine objects of contemplation, and who have formerly contemplated them much, when they see a godlike

countenance or form, in which celestial beauty is imaged and well imitated, are first struck with a holy awe, and then, approaching, venerate this beautiful object as a god, and, if they were not afraid of the reputation of too raving a madness, would erect altars, and perform sacrifices to it.

"And the warmth and genial influence derived from the atmosphere which beauty generates around itself, entering through the eyes, softens and liquefies the inveterate induration, which coats and covers up the parts in the vicinity of the wings, and prevents them from growing. This being melted, the wings begin to germinate and increase, and this, like the growing of the teeth, produces an itching and irritation which disturbs the whole frame of the soul. When, therefore, by the contemplation of the beautiful object, the induration is softened and the wings begin to shoot, the soul is relieved from its pain and rejoices; but when that object is absent, the liquefied substance hardens again, and closes up the young shoots of the wings, which consequently boil up and throb, and throw the soul into a state of turbulence and rage, and will neither allow it to sleep nor remain at rest, until it can again see the beautiful object, and be relieved. For this reason it never willingly leaves that object, but for its sake deserts parents, and brothers, and friends, and neglects its patrimony, and despises all established usages on which it valued itself before. And this affection is Love."

The reader is doubtless by this time familiar enough with the Platonic philosophy to appreciate this passage. He will see the dialectical meaning of this poetical myth. He will comprehend, also, that the Platonic Love is naturally more appropriate between two men, master and pupil, than between the two sexes; because it is then purer, and less disturbed by other feelings.

Beauty is the most vivid image of Truth: it is divinity in its most perceptible form. But what is the Good? The Good, τὸ ἀγαθόν, is God, but God considered in the abstract. Truth, Beauty, Justice, are all aspects of the Deity; Goodness is his nature. The Good is therefore incapable of being perceived; it can only be known in reflection. In the same manner as the sun is the cause of sight, and also the cause of the objects of sight growing and being produced, so also the Good is the cause of science, and the cause of being to whatever is the object of science: and, as the sun itself is not sight, nor the object of sight, but presides over both; so also the Good is not science, nor the object of science, but is superior to both, for they are not the Good, but goodly.

§ IX. Plato's Ethics.

Plato was a Socratist. Hitherto, however, we have seen him following his master only in his Method. The speculations on ideas, Reminiscence, Metempsychosis, God, etc., were things he did not learn from Socrates, although the Socratic Method led him to these conceptions. We have before seen that Socrates occupied himself almost exclusively with Ethical topics; and it is in Ethics, therefore, that we may expect to find Plato resembling him.

Plato's ethical opinions are logical rather than ethical; that is to say, they are deductions from certain abstract logical premises, not from investigations into human nature. Thus, when "engaged with the discussion of particular sciences, he resolves them into the science of Good; when engaged with the particular virtues, he resolves them into the virtue of Science."* Everywhere the Good and the True are convertible terms, and Virtue is the same as Science. There is, moreover, considerable contradiction in his various works on this, as on other points. In one dialogue (*Timæus*) he advocates Free Will; in another (*Hippias Minor*), Fatalism. Sometimes vice is involuntary, at other times voluntary: sometimes, indeed generally, vice is nothing but ignorance; elsewhere, as we have shown, vice is said to be partly ignorance and partly incontinence. Virtue is said to be

---

* Archer Butler, *Lectures*, ii. 61.

Science; yet Knowledge alone does not constitute Happiness nor can Virtue be taught.

Although, therefore, many passages may be quoted in which morals are worthily spoken of, we cannot but regard as chimerical any attempt to deduce from them an ethical system. All that can safely be relied on is general views; such, for instance, as his subordination of Ethics to Dialectics. As M. De Gerando well observes, "he did not found his ethics on a principle of obligation, on the definition of duty, but on the tendency to perfection."

In Plato's Ethics the passions are entirely set aside; they are regarded as disturbances in the moral economy. Virtue is purely a matter of intelligence; and the intellect has therefore not only a regulative office, but the supreme direction of all action.* Now, as Chamfort admirably said, "the Philosopher who would set aside the passions, resembles a Chemist who would extinguish his fire." We are all aware that it is very common "to know the right, and yet the wrong pursue;" that the passions not only disturb the regulative action of Reason, but positively triumph over it; and that morals are our *mores*, our *habits*, as much as our beliefs.

The Ethics of Plato might suit the inhabitants of another world; they are useless to the inhabitants of this. His Politics are his Ethics applied to the State, and labor under the same errors. But his Utopian Government, the *Republic*, has had too much celebrity for us to neglect it.

The *Republic* is unquestionably one of the most interesting of his works; and so slow has been the progress of social science, compared with every other science, that many of the views Plato has there put forth are still entertained by very serious thinkers;

---

* We cannot interrupt our exposition with any examples; they are too numerous. But we may remind the student of that passage in the *Gorgias* respecting the misery of the unjust man, in which Plato endeavors to prove that he who does an injury suffers more than he who endures it.

whereas his views on morals seldom, his views on physics never find a defender.

The weakness of man is the cause why States are formed. As he cannot suffice to himself, he must live in society. This society should be an image of man himself. The faculties which belong to him must find a proper field of activity in society; and this vast union of intellects should form but one intelligence. Thus man's virtues are, 1. φρόνησις, wisdom; 2. ἀνδρεία, fortitude; 3. σωφροσύνη, temperance; 4. δικαιοσύνη, justice. The State, therefore must have its Rulers, the philosophers, who will represent wisdom; its Soldiers, who will represent fortitude; its Craftsmen and burghers, who will represent temperance. Justice is a quality which must be shared by all classes, as lying at the root of all virtuous action.

In wisdom and justice we have the alpha and omega of Plato's doctrine: justice is wisdom in act. The office of the Rulers is therefore to ordain such laws as will eventually prevent all injustice in the State. Their first care will be to instil into the minds of the citizens just notions respecting the Deity. All those who attribute to the Deity the passions and imperfections of men must be banished: hence the famous banishment of the poets, of which so much has been said. This law, pushed to its rigorous conclusions, is the law of fanaticism. Whatever the Rulers believed respecting Religion, was to be the Religion of the State. Strange that a pupil of Socrates should have advocated a law, the operation of which caused his master's condemnation! But there are other causes for the banishment of the poets besides their fictions respecting the Gods. They enervate the soul by pictures of immoderate desires; they give imitations of the vices and follies of men; they overstep the limits of that moderation which alone can balance the soul. Even the musicians are to be banished; those at least who are plaintive and harmonious. Only the Dorian and the Phrygian music can be admitted; the one impetuous and warlike, the other calm.

There is a germ of Stoicism in Plato, and that germ is here

seen developed. A measured equability of mind was his ideal of human happiness, and any thing which interfered with it was denounced. Poetry and music interfered with this equability, and so did conjugal love. As the State could not subsist without children, children must be begotten. But parents are foolishly fond; they are avaricious for their children; ambitious for them. Husbands are also foolishly fond. To prevent these disturbances of good order, Plato ordains community of wives, and interdicts parentage. Women are to be chosen for marriage as brood-mares are chosen. The violent women to be assorted to the mild men; the mild to be assorted to violent men. But the children belong to the State. They are, therefore, to be consigned to the State Nurses, who will superintend their early education. Because children manifest different capacities, Plato thought with St. Simon, that each citizen should be ranked according to his capacity, the State would undertake to decide to which class the young man should belong. But, if domestic life is thus at a blow sacrificed to the public good, do not imagine that women will lose their occupations. No: women must share with men the toils of war and agriculture. The female dog guards sheep as well as the male; why should not the women guard the State?* And, as some few women manifest a capacity for philosophy, those few will share with men the government. With community of wives and children, it is natural that community of property should be joined. Property is the great disturber of social life; it engenders crimes and luxuries which are scarcely better than crimes. Property, therefore, must be abolished. The State alone has riches.

In one word, the Family, no less than the individual, is sacrificed to the State; the State itself being an Abstraction. Like the Utopists of modern days, Plato has developed an *à priori* theory of what the State should be, and by this theory all human feelings are to be neglected; instead of developing a theory *à*

---

* This is Plato's own illustration.

posteriori, i. e. from an investigation into the nature of human wants and feelings.

By thus reducing the *Republic* to its theoretical formula, we are doubtless viewing it in its most unfavorable light. Its value, and its interest, do not consist in its political ideas, but in its collateral suggestions on education, religion, and morals. But these are beside our present purpose.*

Willingly would we discourse upon this remarkable book at greater length; but, although we have only touched on a few points connected with Plato, we have already exhausted the space we could afford, and must close here this imperfect account of one of the greatest minds of antiquity. If we have assigned him his due position in the history of human development—if we have in some sort presented the reader with a clue, whereby he may traverse the labyrinth of that celebrated but much misrepresented writer—if we have succeeded in conveying some impression of the man, more consonant with truth than that usually accredited, we have performed our task.

---

* In the *Laws*, many of the political and social notions are modified; but the general theory is the same.

SEVENTH EPOCH.

PHILOSOPHY AGAIN REDUCED TO A SYSTEM: CLOSE OF THE SOCRATIC MOVEMENT.—ARISTOTLE.

CHAPTER I.

ARISTOTLE.

§ I. LIFE OF ARISTOTLE.

WHEN Plato was leaving Athens for the journey into Sicily, of which we have spoken, and which occupied him three years or more, Aristotle appeared in that active city, a restless youth of seventeen; rich both in money and in knowledge, eager, impetuous, truth-loving, and insatiable in his thirst for philosophy. Tidings of the wondrous men who made that city illustrious, and whose fame still sheds a halo round its ruins, had reached him in his native land; tidings of the great thinkers and the crowded schools had lured him, though so young, to Athens.

Aristotle was born at Stagira, a colony in Thrace, Olympiad 99 (B. C. 384.) His father, Nicomachus, was an eminent physician, who had written several works on medicine and natural history; so that Aristotle's love of such subjects may be called hereditary. And this hereditary love so conspicuous in the marvellous results of the two treatises on the *History of Animals* and the *Parts of Animals*—works which modern science is daily enabling us to appreciate better—may have been fostered by the opportunities Stagira offered him in his boyhood. It was a town on the western side of the Strymonic Gulf, just where the general line of coast takes a southerly direction. Immediately south, a promontory ran out towards the east, effectually screening the town and its little harbor Capros (formed by the island of the same name), from the violence of the squalls coming up the Ægean. "In the terraced windings too, by which the visitor climbs through the orange groves of Sorento, he may without any great violence imagine the narrow and steep paths by which an ancient historian and chorographer describes those who crossed the mountains out of Macedonia, as descending into the valley of Arethusa, where was seen the tomb of Euripides and the town of Stagira."*

Aristotle, losing his parents at an early age, was consigned to the care of a certain Proxenus, who had him instructed in all the physical knowledge of the time. Proxenus died, and Aristotle then fulfilled his desire of seeing Athens.

During the three years of Plato's absence Aristotle was not idle. He prepared himself to be a worthy pupil. His wealth enabled him to purchase those costly luxuries, Books—there was no cheap Literature in those days—and in them he studied the speculations of the early thinkers, with a zeal and intelligence of which his own writings bear ample evidence. There were also some friends and followers of Socrates and Plato still at Athens: men who had listened to the entrancing conversation of the "old man eloquent," who could still remember with a smile his keen and playful irony; and others who were acquainted with some of the deep thoughts brooding in the melancholy soul of Plato. These Aristotle eagerly questioned, and from them prepared himself to receive the lessons of his future teacher.

Plato returned. His school was opened, and Aristotle joined the crowd of his disciples, amongst whom the penetrating glance of the master soon detected the immortal pupil. Plato saw that the impetuous youth needed the curb; but there was promise of greatness in that very need. His restless activity was charac-

---

* Blakesley's *Life of Aristotle*, p. 12.

terized by Plato in an epithet: "Aristotle is the *Mind* of my school."

Aristotle continued to listen to Plato for seventeen years; that is, till the death of the latter. But he did not confine himself to the Platonic Philosophy: nor did he entirely agree with it. And from this disagreement has arisen the vulgar notion of a personal disagreement between Master and Pupil: a notion, to be sure, propped up with pretended anecdotes, and refuted by others equally authentic. Much has been written on this quarrel, and on what people call Aristotle's ingratitude. We place no reliance on it. The same thing was said of Plato with respect to Socrates; and we have excellent reasons for treating that as calumny. In his writings Aristotle doubtless combats the opinion of Plato; but he always mentions him with respect, sometimes with tenderness. If that be ingratitude, it is such as all pupils have manifested who have not been slavish followers.*

It was a wise thought of Macedonian Philip to give his son Alexander such a preceptor as Aristotle. For four years was the illustrious pupil instructed by the illustrious master in poetry, rhetoric, and philosophy; and, when Alexander departed on his Indian expedition, a scholar of Aristotle's, one Calisthenes, attended him.† Both from Philip and from Alexander, the Stagirite received munificent assistance in all his undertakings: especially in the collection of natural curiosities, which were selected from captured provinces, to form the materials of the *History of Animals.*

"The conqueror is said, in Athenæus, to have presented his master with the sum of eight hundred talents (about two hundred thousand pounds sterling) to meet the expenses of his *History of Animals*, and, enormous as the sum is, it is only in pro

---

* The question is discussed with ability by Mr. Blakesley in his *Life of Aristotle*, pp. 24-28. See also Stahr's article on Aristotle in the *Dictionary of Greek and Roman Biography.*

† The story that Aristotle himself accompanied Alexander is now universally discredited.

portion to the accounts we have of the vast wealth acquired by the plunder of the Persian treasures. Pliny also relates that some thousands of men were placed at his disposal for the purpose of procuring zoological specimens, which served as materials for this celebrated treatise."* However he acquired his materials, it is becoming daily more evident that his work was based on direct knowledge, on actual inspection and dissection, not, as in Pliny's case, on what others reported. Several of the most astonishing discoveries of modern naturalists are found to have been distinctly known to Aristotle; and even on such subtle questions as the affinities of animals, we are sometimes forced to come round to his classification. "Thus, in the end," says Professor Forbes, in summing up his discussion on the classification of Acalephs, "we revert curiously enough to the views of the affinities of these Animals proposed by Aristotle, who plainly included under the designation of ἀκαλήφη, both Actiniæ and Medusæ: not from any vague guess, or in compliance with the popular recognition of their resemblance, but from a careful study of their structure and habits, as the varied notices preserved to us in the first, fourth, and fifth, eighth, and ninth books of the *History of Animals* prove beyond question."†

After a long interval Aristotle returned to Athens and opened a school in the Lyceum: a school which eclipsed all the others both in numbers and importance. It is curiously illustrative of his restless vivacious temperament that he could not stand still and lecture, but delivered his opinions whilst walking up and down the shady paths of the Lyceum, attended by his eager followers. Hence his disciples were called the Walking Philosophers—Peripatetics.

Mr. Blakesley thinks that it was Aristotle's delicate health which, combined with the wish to economize time, induced him

---

* Blakesley, p. 68.
† Forbes, *Monograph of the Naked-Eyed Medusæ*, p. 88. On the subject of Aristotle's zoological knowledge generally, see Meyer, *Aristotelis Thierkunde*, 1855, and De Blainville, *Histoire des Sciences de l'Organisation*, 1845.

to lecture while walking. Diogenes Laertius attributes its origin to a regard for the health of his pupil, Alexander. The point is unimportant; enough for us to know that he did lecture while walking to and fro along the shady paths of the Lyceum. Protagoras, as Mr. Blakesley reminds us, is represented by Plato as teaching in the same way; although not perhaps so systematically as Aristotle.

His lectures were of two kinds, scientific and popular—*acroamatic* or *acroatic*, and *exoteric*. The former were for the more advanced students, and those who were capable of pursuing scientific subjects: he delivered these in the morning. The latter were afternoon lectures to a much larger class, and treated of popular subjects—rhetoric, politics, and sophistics. Much learning and ingenuity has been thrown away in the endeavor to determine the precise nature of these two kinds of instruction; but we cannot here discuss it. Those who conclude that the distinction between the esoteric and exoteric was a distinction of doctrine seem to us in error; the distinction was, as above stated, purely that of subject-matter. Dialectics and Poetics are not addressed to the same hearers.

He spent a long laborious life in the pursuit of knowledge, and wrote an incredible number of works, about a fourth of which it is calculated are extant; the division, arrangement, and authenticity of which has long been a pet subject of contention among scholars; but, as no agreement has yet been effected, we should have to swell our pages with arguments rather than results.

The influence these works, spurious as well as genuine, have exercised on European culture, is incalculable, and we shall hereafter have to speak of the tyranny of this influence. Nor was it alone over European culture they exercised a despotic sway. "Translated in the fifth century of the Christian era into the Syriac language by the Nestorians who fled into Persia, and from Syriac into Arabic four hundred years later, his writings furnished the Mohammedan conquerors of the East with a germ of science which, but for the effect of their religious and political institutions, might have shot up into as tall a tree as it did produce in the west; while his logical works, in the Latin translation which Boethius, 'the last of the Romans,' bequeathed as a legacy to posterity, formed the basis of that extraordinary phenomenon, the Philosophy of the Schoolmen. An empire like this, extending over nearly twenty centuries of time, sometimes more, sometimes less despotically, but always with great force, recognized in Bagdad and in Cordova, in Egypt and in Britain, and leaving abundant traces of itself in the language and modes of thought of every European nation, is assuredly without a parallel."*

§ II. Aristotle's Method.

Plato and Aristotle may be said to contain all the speculative philosophy of Greece: whoso knows them, knows all that Greece had to teach. It is not our plan to draw comparisons between the greatness of two great men, otherwise these two would furnish a happy subject. We have endeavored to point out in what way Plato advanced the Philosophy of his age. We have now to do the same by Aristotle.

Aristotle was the most learned man of antiquity, but this learning did not enervate the vigor of his mind. He studiously sought, both in books and in external nature, for materials wherewith to build a doctrine. Before laying down his own views he always examines the views of his predecessors with tedious minuteness; and his own opinions often seem brought out in his criticisms rather than dogmatically affirmed. Hence some have declared his Method to be the historical Method; a misconception not to be wondered at when we consider the abundance of historical detail, and the absence of any express definition of his Method in his writings.

Unlike Plato, Aristotle never mentions the nature of his Meth-

---

* Blakesley, p. i.

od; but he has one, and we must detect it. We may expect to find it somewhat resembling that of his master, with some modifications of his own. Plato, as Van Heusde, in the *Initia Platonicæ* remarks, stands a middle point between Socrates and Aristotle. The Method of Socrates was one of Investigation; that of Aristotle was one of Demonstration. The Definition and Induction of Socrates were powerful, but vague; the syllogism of Aristotle rendered them powerful and precise. Plato, as it were, fills up the gap between these two thinkers; by the addition of Analysis and Classification he reduced the Socratic Method to a more systematic form, and gave it precision. Where Plato left it, Aristotle took it up; and, by still further modifications, all of which had but one aim,—*i. e.* greater precision,—he gave it a solidity which enabled it to endure for centuries.

Wherein did Plato and Aristotle fundamentally differ? Until the time of Hegel the general explanation of this difference was briefly to this effect: Plato is an Idealist, Aristotle a Materialist; the one a Rationalist, the other an Empiric: one trusting solely to Reason, the other solely to Experience. This explanation Hegel refuted by showing, that although Aristotle laid more stress upon experience than did Plato, yet he also expressly taught that Reason alone could form science.*

Let us, then, try if we can penetrate the real difference. And to do so, we must first ask, What was the fundamental position of the Platonic doctrine? That question admits of but one answer. The root of Plato's philosophy is the theory of Ideas, whereby Dialectics became science. If here Aristotle be found to agree with his master, there can be no fundamental difference between them; if here he be found to differ, we may be able to deduce from it all other differences.

Aristotle radically opposed the Ideal theory; and the greater part of his criticisms of Plato are criticisms of that theory. He does not deny to Ideas a *subjective* existence: on the contrary,

---

* Hegel, *Geschichte der Philos.* ii. 811 *sq.*

he makes them the materials of science; but he is completely opposed to their *objective* existence, calling it an empty and poetical metaphor. He says, that on the supposition of Ideas being Existences and Models, there would be several Models for the same Thing; since the same thing may be classed under several heads. Thus, Socrates may be classed under the Ideas of Socrates, of Man, of Animal, and of Biped; or Philosopher, General, and Statesman. The "stout Stagirite" not only perceived the logical error of the Ideal theory, but also saw how the error originated. He profoundly remarked, that Ideas are nothing but productions of the Reason, separating, by a logical abstraction, the particular objects from those relations which are common to them all. He saw that Plato had mistaken a subjective distinction for an objective one; had mistaken a relation, which the understanding perceived between two objects, for the evidence of a separate existence. The partisans of the theory of Ideas, Aristotle likens to those who, having to enumerate the exact number of things, commence by increasing the number, as a way of simplifying the calculation. In this caustic illustration we may see the nature of his objection to the Platonic doctrine. What, indeed, was the Ideal theory, but a multiplication of the number of Existences? Men had before imagined that things were great, and heavy, and black or brown. Plato separated the qualities of greatness, weight, and color, and made these qualities new existences.

Having disproved the notion of Ideas being Existences,—in other words, of General Terms being any thing more than the expressions of the Relations of individual things,—Aristotle was driven to maintain that the Individual Things alone *existed*. But, if only individuals exist, only by sensation can they be known; and, if we know them by sensation, how is the universal, τὸ καθόλου, ever known—how do we get abstract ideas? This question was the more pertinent because science could only be a science of the Universal, or, as we moderns say, a science of general truths; now inasmuch as Aristotle agreed with Plato in mainaining that sense cannot furnish us with science,* which is always founded on general truths (Universals), it was needful for him to show how we could gain scientific knowledge.

Plato's solution of the problem has already been exhibited; it was the ingenious doctrine of the soul's *reminiscence* of a former apprehension of truth, awakened by those traces of Ideas which sensation discovered in Things. This solution did not satisfy Aristotle. He, too, was aware that reminiscence was indispensable; but by it he meant reminiscence of previous experience, not of an anterior state of existence in the world of Ideas. By sensation we perceive particular things; by *induction* we perceive the general in the particular. Sensation is the basis of all knowledge: but we have another faculty besides that of sensation; we have Memory. Having perceived many things, we remember our sensations, and by that remembrance we are enabled to discern wherein things resemble and wherein they differ; and this Memory then becomes an *art* whereby a general conception is formed: this art is Induction. The natural method of investigation, he says, is to collect all the facts or particulars, and afterwards deduce from these the general causes of all things and their actions.† This is accomplished by Induction, which he aptly calls the pathway from particulars to generals—ἐπαγωγὴ δή ἡ ἀπὸ τῶν καθέκαστα ἐπὶ τὰ καθόλου ἔφοδος.‡ Man alone has this art. The distinction between brutes and men is, that the former, although they have Memory, have no Experience; that is to say, have not the art which converts Memory into Experience—the art of Induction. Man is the reasoning animal.

That Aristotle meant Induction by the art of which he speaks as furnished by experience, may be proved by one luminous passage of the *Metaphysics*. "Art commences when, from a great number of Experiences, one general conception is formed

---

* *Analyt. Post.* i. 81.
† *Ibid.*; comp. also *Hist. Animal.* i. 6.
‡ *Topic.* i. 10. comp. what Coleridge says on Method as a path of Transit, *Discourse on Method* affixed to *Encyclop. Metropolitana*.

which will embrace all similar cases.* And, lest there should be any misunderstanding of his definition, he proceeds to illustrate it. "Thus, if you know that a certain remedy has cured Callias of a certain disease, and that the same remedy has produced the same effect on Socrates, and on several other persons, that is *Experience;* but to know that a certain remedy will cure all persons attacked with that disease is *Art:* for Experience is the knowledge of individual things (τῶν καθέκαστα); Art is that of Universals (τῶν καθόλου)."

The commencement of Positive Science—the awakening to an appreciation of the nature and processes of Science—lies in that passage. In the Socratic conception of Induction we saw little more than Analogical Reasoning; but in this Aristotelian conception we see the Collection of Instances, and the generalization from those Instances which Science claims as part of its Method. Nor was this a random guess of the old Stagirite's: it was the logical deduction from his premises respecting knowledge. Hear him again: "Experience furnishes the principles of every science. Thus Astronomy is grounded on observation; for, if we were *properly to observe* the celestial phenomena, we might *demonstrate the laws* which regulate them. The same applies to other sciences. *If we omit nothing that observation can afford us respecting phenomena*, we could easily furnish the demonstration of all that admits of being demonstrated, and illustrate that which is not susceptible of demonstration."† And, in another place, when abandoned in his investigation by phenomena, he will not hazard an assertion. "We must wait," he says, "for further phenomena, since phenomena are more to be trusted than the conclusion of reason."

Looked at in a general way, the Aristotelian Method seems to be the Method of positive Science; but on closer meditation we shall detect their germinal difference to be the omission in Aris-

---

* Γίνεται δὲ τέχνη ὅταν ἐκ πολλῶν τῆς ἐμπειρίας ἐννοημάτων καθόλου μία γένηται περὶ τῶν ὁμοίων ὑπόληψις, *Met.* i. 1.

† *Analyt. Prior.* i. 30.

totle of the principle, so much insisted on in the Introduction to this History, namely, the rigorous Verification of each inductive step. The value of the truth expressed by a syllogism does not consist solely in its accurate distribution, but also in the accuracy of its major premise: we may form unexceptionable Syllogisms which shall be absurdly erroneous, as when we say, All black birds are crows; This bird is black: *ergo*, This bird is a crow. In the physical and metaphysical speculations of the ancients, we are constantly meeting with syllogisms as perfect as this,— and as absurd; because the ancients generally threw their ingenuity into logical deduction, and scarcely ever into preliminary verification. When Aristotle therefore lays down as a canon the necessity of ascertaining generals from an examination of particulars, his canon, admirable indeed, needs to be accompanied by a distinct recognition of the equal necessity of verification. Contrasted with the Platonic Method, Aristotle's is seen to great advantage. Plato, believing that the stimulus awakened by a single idea would enable a man to arrive at the knowledge of all ideas, in consequence of the necessary connection supposed to exist between them, could very well dispense with Induction. But Aristotle maintained that the completeness of knowledge is only obtainable through completeness of experience; every single idea is awakened in us by a separate sensation, and only on a comparison of like and unlike in phenomena are differences perceived. He complains of Plato very justly, for neglecting details in haste to judge of universals.

Aristotle had, therefore, a novel and profound conception of scientific Method; but because he did not—and, indeed, in that age *could* not—confine himself to Experience and the generalizations of Experience, he could not effectually carry out his own scheme. His conception was just; but the application of such a Method could have led him only a short way, because there was not sufficient Experience then accumulated, from which to generalize with any effect. Hence his speculations are not always carried on upon the Method which he himself laid down. Impatient at the insufficiency of facts, he jumps to a conclusion. Eager, as all men are, to solve the problems which present themselves, he solved them *à priori*. He applied his syllogism before he had verified the exactitude of his premises.

The distinction between Aristotle and Plato is, that while both admitted that science could only be formed from Universals, τὰ καθόλου, Aristotle contended that such Universals had purely a subjective existence, *i. e.* that they were nothing more than the *inductions* derived from particular facts. He, therefore, made Experience the basis of all Science, and Reason the Architect. Plato made Reason the basis. The tendency of the one was to direct man to the observation and interrogation of Nature; that of the other was to direct man to the contemplation of Ideas.

The distinction between Aristotle and Bacon is, that while they both insist upon the observation and generalization of facts, as alone capable of furnishing correct ideas, Aristotle believed that he could observe those primary facts of Existence and Cause, which Bacon wisely declared beyond the human ken. While both insisted on the necessity of experience, while both saw that the science of the "general" must be framed from the inductions of the particular, they differed profoundly as to the nature of that "general." Bacon endeavored in particular facts to trace the general *laws;* Aristotle endeavored in particular facts to trace the general *ideas.*

To understand this, we must cast a glance at Aristotle's Logic.

§ III. Aristotle's Logic.

It is often remarked, that Aristotle's use of the word Dialectics differs from Plato's use of it. Indeed, with Plato, dialectics was the science of Being; with Aristotle, it was no more than the instrument of Thought. But it is highly necessary that we should clearly understand the position occupied by Logic in the Aristotelian philosophy; the more so as after-ages prized the *Logic* above all his other works.

Logic is the science of Affirmation; Affirmation is the active operation of the Mind on that which sensation has presented to it; in other words, Affirmation is Thought. Affirmations may be true or false : there can be no falsehood in Sensation. If you have a sensation of an object, it must be a true sensation; but you may affirm something false of it. Every single thought is true, but when you connect two thoughts together, that is, when you affirm something of another thing, you may affirm that which is false. Every thing, therefore, that you think about may be reduced to a Proposition; in fact, thoughts are a series of Propositions. To understand the whole nature of Propositions—to understand the whole Art of Thinking—is the province of Logic.

By a very natural confusion, Aristotle, thus convinced of the importance of language, was led to maintain that truth or falsehood did not depend upon things, but upon words, or rather upon combinations of words—upon Propositions. Logic, therefore, to him, as to Plato, though in a different way, became the real Organon of Science. But, as John Mill remarks, "the distinction between real and nominal definitions, between definitions of words and what are called definitions of things, though conformable to the ideas of most Aristotelian logicians, cannot, as it appears to us, be maintained. We apprehend that no definition is ever intended to explain and unfold the nature of the thing. It is some confirmation of our opinion that none of those writers who have thought that there were definitions of things have ever succeeded in discovering any criterion by which the definition of a thing can be distinguished from any other proposition relating to that thing. The definition, they say, unfolds the nature of the thing: but no definition can unfold its whole nature; and every proposition in which any quality whatever is predicated of the thing unfolds some part of its nature. The true state of the case we take to be this: All definitions are of names, and of names only; but, in some definitions, it is clearly apparent that nothing is intended except to explain the meaning of the word; while, in others, besides explaining the meaning of the word, it is intended to be implied that there exists a thing corresponding to the word. Whether this be or be not implied in any given case, cannot be collected from the mere form of expression. 'A centaur is an animal with the upper parts of a man and the lower parts of a horse,' and 'a triangle is a rectilineal figure with three sides,' are, in form, expressions precisely similar; although, in the former, it is not implied that any *thing* conformable to the term really exists, while in the latter it is; as may be seen by substituting, in both definitions, the word means for *is*. In the first expression, 'a centaur *means* an animal,' etc., the sense would remain unchanged: in the second, 'a triangle means,' etc., the meaning would be altered, since it would be obviously impossible to deduce any of the truths of geometry from a proposition expressive only of the manner in which we intend to employ a particular sign.

"There are, therefore, expressions commonly passing for definitions which include in themselves more than the mere explanation of the meaning of a term. But it is not correct to call an expression of this sort a peculiar kind of definition. Its difference from the other kind consists in this, that it is not a definition, but a definition and something more. The definition given above of a triangle, obviously comprises not one, but two propositions, perfectly distinguishable. The one is, 'There may exist a figure bounded by three straight lines;' the other, 'and this figure may be termed a triangle.' The former of these propositions is not a definition at all; the latter is a mere nominal definition or explanation of the use and application of a term. The first is susceptible of truth or falsehood, and may therefore be made the foundation of a train of reasoning. The latter can neither be true nor false; the only character it is susceptible of, is that of conformity or disconformity to the ordinary usage of language.

"There is a real distinction, then, between definitions of names and what are erroneously called definitions of things; but it is that the latter, along with the meaning of a name, covertly asserts a matter of fact. This covert assertion is not a definition, but a postulate. The definition is a mere identical proposition, which gives information only about the use of language, and from which no conclusions respecting matters of fact can possibly be drawn. The accompanying postulate, on the other hand, affirms a fact which may lead to consequences of every degree of importance. It affirms the real existence of things possessing the combination of attributes set forth in the definition; and this, if true, may be foundation sufficient to build a whole fabric of scientific truth."*

This profound and luminous distinction was not seen by Aristotle, and his whole system was vitiated in consequence of the oversight. He thought that Logic was not only the Instrument of Thought, but, as such, the Instrument of investigating Causes. In his Logic the first place was occupied by the celebrated *Categories*. They are ten in number, and are as follows:

Οὐσία	Substance.
Πόσον	Quantity.
Ποῖον	Quality.
Πρός τι	Relation.
Ποιεῖν	Action.
Πάσχειν	Passion.
Ποῦ	The where.
Πότε	The when.
Κεῖσθαι	Position in space.
Ἔχειν	Possession.

These Categories, or, as the Latin writers say, Predicaments, were intended to be an enumeration of those classes or *genera*, under some of which every thing was to be reduced. They were held to be the most universal expressions for the various relations of things; they could not further be analyzed, but remained the fundamental definitions of things. It is, however, as has been remarked,† a mere catalogue of the distinctions rudely marked out by the language of familiar life, with little or no attempt to penetrate, by philosophic analysis, to the *rationale* even of those common distinctions. Such an analysis, however

---

* *System of Logic*, i. 195–7.   † Mill's *System of Logic*, i. 80.

superficially conducted, would have shown the enumeration to be both redundant and defective. Some objects are omitted, and others repeated several times under different heads. It is like a division of animals into men, quadrupeds, horses, asses, and ponies.

The remark is just, and would have been admitted as just by Aristotle himself, since he does not pretend the classification is complete, but confesses that the same object may, under different categories, be at once a quality and a relation. But Aristotle does not usually ascribe much importance to this enumeration of the most general notions; so that we may regard it as nothing more than an attempt to exhibit in a clear light the signification of words taken absolutely, in order to show how truth and falsehood consist in the right or wrong combination of these elements.*

However imperfect this attempt at classification may be, it was held to be a satisfactory attempt for many centuries; nor was any one bold enough to venture on another until Kant, who, as we shall see, had quite a different object. We have not here to criticise it, but to exhibit its historical position. The idea of examining the *forms* of thought could scarcely have originated earlier. Previous speculators had occupied themselves with inquiries into the origin and nature of knowledge: Aristotle saw that it was time to inquire into the necessary forms of thought. To do this, to analyze the various processes of the mind, and to exhibit the "art of thinking" in all its details, is the object of his Logic.

Some had declared sense-knowledge to be deceitful; others had declared that sense-knowledge was perfectly faithful, as far as it went, but that it was incapable of penetrating beneath phenomena. Skepticism was assuming a menacing attitude. Aristotle, in his way, endeavored to meet it, and he met it

---

* Ritter, iii. 66, where also will be found the authorities for the previous sentence.

thus: It is true that the knowledge derived from our senses is not always correct; true also that our senses are to be trusted, as far as they go. A sensation, as a sensation, is true; but any affirmation you may make about that sensation may be either true or false, according to the affirmation. If an oar dipped in the water appears to you to be broken, the sensation you have is accurate enough; you *have* that sensation. But if, on the strength of that sensation, you affirm that the oar is broken, your affirmation is false. Error lies not in false sensation, but in false affirmation.

Like Plato, he held it to be indispensable to understand words if we are to understand thoughts; a position which, as we saw in the teaching of Socrates, was both novel and at the time important, because it called attention to the extreme laxity of language under which men disguised the laxity of their reasoning. A word, he said, is in itself indifferent; it is neither true nor false: truth or falsehood must result from a combination of words into a proposition. No thought can be erroneous; error is only possible to propositions.

Hence the necessity of Logic, which is the science of affirmations; it is in the Enunciate Proposition, ἀποφαντικὸς λόγος, that we must seek truth or falsehood. This proposition is subdivided into Affirmative and Negative Propositions, which are mutually opposed, and give rise to Contradiction so soon as they are asserted in the same sense of one and the same thing: *e. g.* "It is impossible for the same thing to be and not to be."

The principle of Contradiction he declares to be the deepest of all; for on it all Demonstration is founded. Because, however, he confounded truth of Language with truth of Thought, and supposed that Thought was always the correlate of Fact, he fell into the mistake of maintaining truth of Language, or Propositions, to be identical with truth of Being. He did not recognize the fact that we can frame Propositions which shall be based on the principle of Contradiction, and which shall nevertheless be false.

Having erected Propositions, or the affirmative and negative combinations of Language, into such an exalted position, it became necessary to attend more closely to names, and thus we get the Predicables, a five-fold division of general Names, not grounded, as usual, upon a difference in their meaning, that is, in the attribute which they *con*note, but upon a difference in the kind of class which they *de*note. We may predicate of a thing five different varieties of class-name:

Γένος .... a Genus.
Εἶδος .... a Species.
Διαφορά .... a Difference
Ἴδιον .... a Property.
Συμβεβηκός .... an Accident.

"It is to be remarked of these distinctions that they express not what the predicate is in its own meaning, but what relation it bears to the subject on which it happens on the particular occasion to be predicated. There are not some names which are exclusively general and others which are exclusively species or differentiæ; but the same name is referred to one or another Predicable, according to the subject of which it is predicated on the particular occasion. *Animal*, for instance, is a genus with respect to Man or John; a species with respect to substance or Being. The words genus, species, etc., are therefore relative terms; they are names applied to certain predicates, to express the relation between them and some given subject: a relation grounded, not upon what the predicate *con*notes, but upon the class which it *de*notes, and upon the place which in some given classification that class occupies relatively to the particular subject."*

Induction and Syllogism are the two great instruments of his Logic. All knowledge must rest upon some antecedent conviction; and both in Induction and Syllogism we see how this takes place. Induction sets out, from particulars already known,

---

* Mill, *System of Logic*, i. 162.

to arrive at a conclusion; Syllogism sets out, from some general principle, to arrive at particulars.* There is this remarkable distinction, however, established by him between the two, namely, that the general principle from which the syllogism proceeds is *better known in itself* and in its own nature, while the particulars from which Induction proceeds are better known to us.† How came he by this surprising distinction? Thus: the particulars of Induction are derived from Sense, and are more liable on that account to error; whereas the general principle of the Syllogism is known in itself, is further removed from the fallacies of sense, and is κατὰ τὸν λόγον γνωριμώτερον. Do we not always doubt whether we have rightly understood any thing until we have demonstrated that it follows by necessity from some general principle? And does not this lead to the conviction that the Syllogism is the proper form of all science? Moreover, as the Syllogism proceeds from the general, the general must be better known than the particular, since the particular is proved by it.

Aristotle here lands us on a jagged reef of paradox: that which is better *known to us* is of less value than that which is *known in itself*. Sensations are less trustworthy than ideas. The particulars are sensibles, but in and for themselves they are nothing; they exist only in relation to us. Nevertheless we are forced to make them our point of departure. We begin with sensuous knowledge to reach ideal knowledge. In this manner we proceed from the world of experience to that higher world of cognition.

The various investigations into the nature of Propositions which Aristotle prosecuted, were necessary to form the basis of his theory of reasoning, *i. e.* the Syllogism. He defined the Syllogism to be an enunciation in which certain Propositions being 'aid down, a necessary conclusion is drawn, distinct from the

---

* *Analyt. Post.* i. 1.
† Φύσει μὲν οὖν πρότερος καὶ γνωριμώτερος ὁ διὰ τοῦ μέσου συλλογισμός, ἡμῖν δ' ἐναργέστερος ὁ διὰ τῆς ἐπαγωγῆς.—*Analyt. Prior.* ii. 24.

Propositions and without employing any idea not contained in the Propositions. Thus:

> All bad men are miserable;
> Every tyrant is a bad man:
> *ergo*
> All tyrants are miserable.

His examination of the sixteen forms of the Syllogism exhibits great ingenuity, and, as a dialectical exercise, was doubtless sufficient; but it must not detain us here. The theory of the Syllogism is succeeded by the theory of Demonstration. If all knowledge owes its existence to anterior knowledge, what is this anterior knowledge? It is the *major* proposition of a Syllogism. The conclusion is but the application of the general to the particular. Thus, if we know that Tyrants are miserable, we know it because we know that All bad men are miserable; and the middle term tells us that Tyrants are bad men. To know, is to be aware of the cause; to demonstrate, is to give the Syllogism which expresses the knowledge we have. It is therefore necessary that every scientific Syllogism should repose upon principles that are true, primitive, more evident in themselves than the conclusion, and *anterior* to the conclusion. These undemonstrable principles are Axioms, Hypotheses, etc., according as they are self-evident, or as they presuppose some affirmation or negation; they are Definitions when they limit themselves to an explanation of the essence of the thing defined, without affirming any thing respecting its existence.

The proper subjects of demonstration are those universal attributes of particular things which make them what they are, and which may be predicated of them. It is one thing to know *that* a thing is so; another thing to know *why* it is so: hence the two orders of demonstrations, the τοῦ ὅτι, "the demonstration of the cause from a consideration of the effect," and the τοῦ διότι, "the demonstration of the effect from the presence of the cause."

We close this exposition of the leading points of Aristotle's Logic with his own somewhat touching words, as he concludes his work: "We have had no works of predecessors to assist us in this attempt to construct a science of Reasoning; our own labors have done it all. If, therefore, the work appears to you not too inferior to the works on other sciences which have been formed with the assistance of successive laborers in the same department, you will show some indulgence for the imperfections of our work, and some gratitude for the discoveries it contains"

§ IV. ARISTOTLE'S METAPHYSICS.

The problem which the early thinkers had set themselves to solve was that of the First Cause. Aristotle maintained that there were Four Causes, not one, and each of these must be taken into consideration. The four Causes were as follows:—I. The Material Cause, the Essence, τὸ τί ἦν εἶναι,—the Invariable Existence, which philosophers so variously sought. Perhaps "*Essence*" is the best translation of the phrase. II. The Substantial Cause, ὑποκείμενον, the "*Substance*" of the Schoolmen. III. The Efficient Cause, ἀρχὴ τῆς κινήσεως, "the Principle of Motion." IV. The Final Cause, τὸ οὗ ἕνεκα καὶ τἀγαθόν, "the Purpose and End." These Causes were all recognized separately by the early speculators, but no one had recognized them as connected, and as all necessary.

Aristotle is right in his criticism on his predecessors; but his own theory is extremely vicious. It makes speculation subordinate to logical distinctions; it makes the Categories the great instrument of investigation; and it creates that spirit of useless and quibbling distinction which was the characteristic vice of the schoolmen, who were almost all fervent Aristotelians. In one word, the nearer Aristotle approached to systematic precision, the wider he wandered from sound principles of inquiry. And this because of his fundamental error in supposing that Logic was an Organon, *i. e.* that *subjective* distinctions must accord with *objective* distinctions. In consequence of which, instead of interrogating Nature he interrogated his own mind.

This may seem at variance with his notion of the necessity of sense-experience, and at variance with his Method; but, as we before observed, the rigorous application of his Method was barely possible; and, however excellent as a precept, it was so vague as to be almost inevitably vitiated in practice. The process of vitiation was this: Experience was necessary, as affording the materials for Reason to work with. Any reasoning not founded on a knowledge of phenomena must be false; but here was Aristotle's mistake: it by no means follows, that all reasoning founded on a knowledge of phenomena will be true. He thought that Experience could not deceive. But, to make his Method perfect, he should have laid down the rules for testing that Experience—for "interrogating" Nature—for discriminating what was pertinent to the question in hand—for establishing a proper "*experimentum crucis.*" Thus "facts," as they are called, are notoriously valuable in proportion only to the value of the verification to which they have been submitted. People talk of "facts" as if facts were to produce irresistible convictions; whereas facts are susceptible of very various explanations, and, in the history of science, we find the *facts* constant, but the *theories* changing: that is to say, Nature has preserved one uniform course, her ordinary operations are open to all men's inspection, and men have endeavored to explain these operations in an endless variety of ways. Now, from a want of a proper knowledge of the conditions of scientific inquiry, Aristotle's Method became fruitless. The facts collected were vitiated by a false theory: his sense-experience was wrongly interpreted.

It is time, however, to give his solution of the great metaphysical problem of Existence. Matter, he said, exists in a threefold form. It is,—I. Substance, perceptible by the senses, which is finite and perishable. This Substance is either the abstract substance, or the substance connected with form, εἶδος. II. The higher Substance, which, though perceived by the sense, is imperishable; such as are the heavenly bodies. Here the active principle (ἐνέργεια, *actus*) steps in, which, in so far as it contains that which is to be produced, is understanding (νοῦς). That which it contains is the *purpose* (τὸ οὗ ἕνεκα), which purpose is realized in the act. Here we have the two extremes of potentiality and agency, matter and thought. The celebrated *entelechie* is the relation between these two extremes, it is the point of transition between δύναμις and ἐνέργεια, and is accordingly the Cause of Motion, or *Efficient* Cause, and represents the Soul. III. The third form of Substance is that in which the three forms of power, efficient cause, and effect are united: the Absolute Substance: eternal, unmoved: God himself. God, as the Absolute Unmoved Eternal Substance, is Thought. The Universe is a thought in the Mind of God; it is "God passing into activity, but not exhausted in the Act." Existence, then, is Thought: it is the activity of the Divine Reason. In Man the thought of the Divine Reason completes itself, so as to become self-conscious. By it Man recognizes in the objective world his own nature again; for thought is the thinking of thought—ἔστιν ἡ νόησις, νοήσεως νόησις.

If we were occupied in this History with the particular opinions of Philosophers, rather than with their Methods and historical position in the development of speculation, we should dwell at some length on Aristotle's distinction between the *primary* and *secondary* qualities of bodies, which, according to Sir William Hamilton, he was the first to establish,[*] as also on the doctrine of Substantial Forms, which Hamilton says he did *not* teach (it was the Arabian commentators who misinterpreted Aristotle on this point); nor should we omit the claim to the discovery of the doctrine of Association of Ideas, which Hamilton has set up for him, with a vast array of Aristotelian erudition, proving indeed that Aristotle did recognize the facts of Association, but by no means proving that he recognized Association as the grand law of intellectual action. Our limits forbid such discursive wanderings from the purpose of this work, and we are forced to leave untouched the very points which in our opinion

---

[*] Hamilton's *Reid*, p. 820.

constitute the pre-eminence of Aristotle. In a history of Science greater justice could be done to his encyclopædic knowledge and marvellous power of systematization.* Here we have but to consider him as the philosopher who, resuming in himself all the results of ancient speculation, so elaborated them into a co-ordinate system, that for twenty centuries he held the world a slave.

Plato was a great speculative genius, and a writer unapproached in the art of imaginary conversations having a polemical purpose; and in most *literary* minds he will ever remain a greater figure than his pupil, Aristotle. But while I concede Plato's immeasurable superiority as a writer, I conceive his inferiority as a thinker to be no less marked. Aristotle seems to me to have been the greatest intellect of antiquity, an intellect at once comprehensive and subtle, patient, receptive, and original. He wrote on Politics, and the treatise, even in the imperfect state in which it has reached us, is still in many respects one of the best works on the subject. He wrote on Poetry, and the few detached passages which survive are full of valuable details. He wrote on Natural History, and his observations are still valuable, his reflections still suggestive. He wrote on Logic, and for many centuries no one could suggest any improvement. "Aristotle," says Hegel, "penetrated into the whole universe of things, and subjected to the comprehension its scattered wealth; and the greatest number of the philosophical sciences owe to him their separation and commencement. While in this manner science separates itself into a series of definitions, the Aristotelian philosophy at the same time contains the most profound speculative ideas. He is more comprehensive and speculative than any one else." While, therefore, the majority will prefer Plato, who, in spite of his difficulties, is much easier to read than Aristotle, yet all must venerate the latter as a grand intellectual phenomenon, to which scarcely any parallel can be suggested.

---

* Should I ever be enabled to complete a long projected plan, of writing, as a companion to the present work, a *Biographical History of Science*, I will endeavor to present Aristotle in this light.

His vast learning, his singular acuteness, the wide range of his investigations, and the astonishing number and the excellence of his works, will always make him a formidable rival to his more fascinating master. "A student passing from the works of Plato," it has been well said, "to those of Aristotle, is struck first of all with the entire absence of that dramatic form and that dramatic feeling with which he has been familiar. The living human beings with whom he has conversed have passed away. Protagoras, and Prodicus, and Hippias are no longer lounging upon their couches in the midst of groups of admiring pupils; we have no walks along the walls of the city; no readings beside the Ilissus; no lively symposia, giving occasion to high discourses about love; no Critias recalling the stories he had heard in the days of his youth, before he became a tyrant of ancient and glorious republics; above all, no Socrates forming a centre to these various groups, while yet he stands out clear and distinct in his individual character, showing that the most subtle of dialecticians may be the most thoroughly humorous and humane of men. Some little sorrow for the loss of those clear and beautiful pictures will perhaps be felt by every one; but by far the greater portion of readers will believe, that they have an ample compensation in the precision and philosophical dignity of the treatise, for the richness and variety of the dialogue. To hear solemn disquisitions solemnly treated; to hear opinions calmly discussed without the interruptions of personalities; above all, to have a profound and considerate judge, able and not unwilling to pronounce a positive decision upon the evidence before him; this they think a great advantage, and this and far more than this they expect, not wrongly, to find in Aristotle."*

---

* Maurice, *Moral and Metaphysical Philosophy.*

CHAPTER II.
SUMMARY OF THE SOCRATIC MOVEMENT.

For the sake of historical clearness we may here place a few words respecting the position of the Socratic Movement (as we may call the period from the Sophists down to Aristotle) in the history of Speculation.

What Socrates himself effected we have already seen. He appeared during the reign of utter skepticism. The various tentatives of the early thinkers had all ended in a skepticism, which was turned to dexterous use by the Sophists. Socrates banished this skepticism by the invention of a new Method. He withdrew men from the metaphysical speculations about Nature, which had led them into the inextricable confusion of doubt. He bade them look inward. He created Moral Philosophy. The Cyrenaics and the Cynics attempted to carry out this tendency; but, as they did so in a one-sided manner, their endeavor was only partially successful.

Plato, the youngest and most remarkable of the disciples of Socrates, accepted the Method, but applied it more universally. Nevertheless Ethics formed the most important of his speculations. Physics were only subordinate and illustrative of Ethics. The Truth—the God-like existence—which he forever besought men to contemplate, that they might share it, had always an Ethical object: it was sought by man for his own perfection. How to live in a manner resembling the Gods was the fundamental problem which he set himself to solve. But there was a germ of scientific speculation in his philosophy, and this germ was developed by his pupil, Aristotle.

The difference between Socrates and Aristotle is immense: Plato, however, fills up the interval. In Plato, we see the transition-point of development, both in Method and in Doctrine. Metaphysical speculations are intimately connected with those of Ethics. In Aristotle, Ethics only form one branch of philosophy: Metaphysics and Physics usurp the larger share of his attention.

One result of Aristotle's labors was precisely this: he brought Philosophy round again to that condition from which Socrates had wrested it; he opened the world again to speculation.

Was then the advent of Socrates nullified? No. The Socratic Epoch conferred the double benefit on humanity of having first brought to light the importance of Ethical Philosophy, and of having substituted a new and incomparably better Method for that pursued by the early speculators. That Method sufficed for several centuries.

In Aristotle's systematization of the Socratic Method, and, above all, in his bringing Physics and Metaphysics again into the region of Inquiry, he paved the way for a new epoch,—the epoch of Skepticism; not the unmethodical Skepticism of helpless baffled guessers, like that which preceded Socrates, but the methodical and dogmatic exposure of the vanity of philosophy.

EIGHTH EPOCH.

SECOND CRISIS OF GREEK PHILOSOPHY: THE SKEPTICS, EPICUREANS, STOICS, AND THE NEW ACADEMY.

CHAPTER I.

THE SKEPTICS.

§ I. Pyrrho.

In the curious train which accompanied the expedition of Alexander into India, there was a serious, reflective man, who followed him with purely philosophical interest: that man was Pyrrho, the founder of the Skeptical philosophy. Conversing with the Gymnosophists of India, he must have been struck with their devout faith in doctrines so unusual to him; and this spectacle of a race of wise and studious men believing a strange creed, and acting upon their belief, may have led him to reflect on the nature of belief. He had already, by the philosophy of Democritus, been led to question the origin of knowledge: he had learned to doubt; and now this doubt became irresistible.

On his return to Elis he became remarked for the practical philosophy which he inculcated, and the simplicity of his life. The profound and absolute skepticism with which he regarded all speculative doctrines, had the same effect upon him as upon Socrates: it made him insist wholly on moral doctrines. He was resigned and tranquil, accepting life as he found it, and guiding himself by the general precepts of common-sense. Socrates, on the contrary, was uneasy, restless, perpetually questioning himself and others, despising metaphysical speculations, but eager for truth. Pyrrho, dissatisfied with all the attempts of his predecessors to solve the great problems they had set to themselves, declared the problems insoluble. Socrates was also dissatisfied; he too declared that he knew nothing; but his doubt was an active, eager, questioning doubt, used as a stimulus to investigation, not as a final result of all investigation. The doubt of Pyrrho was a reprobation of all philosophy; the doubt of Socrates was the opening through which a new philosophy was to be established. Their lives accorded with their doctrines. Pyrrho, the grand Priest of Elis, lived and died in happiness, peace, and universal esteem.* Socrates lived in perpetual warfare, was always misunderstood, was ridiculed as a sophist, and perished as a blasphemer.

The precise doctrines of Pyrrho it is now hopeless to attempt to recover. Even in antiquity they were so mixed up with those of his followers, that it was found impossible to separate them. We are forced, therefore, to speak of the skeptical doctrines as they are collected and systematized by that acute and admirable writer, Sextus Empiricus.

The stronghold of Skepticism is impregnable. It is this: There is no *Criterium* of Truth. After Plato had developed his Ideal Theory, Aristotle crushed it by proving it to be purely *subjective*. But then the theory of Demonstration, which Aristotle placed in its stead, was not that equally *subjective?* What was this boasted Logic, but the systematic arrangement of Ideas obtained originally through Sense? According to Aristotle, knowledge could only be a knowledge of phenomena; although he too wished to make out a science of Causes. And what are Phenomena? Phenomena are the Appearances of things. But where exists the *Criterium* of the truth of these Appearances?

---

* All the stories about him which pretend to illustrate the effects of his skepticism in real life are too trivial for refutation, being obviously the invention of those who thought Pyrrho ought to have been consistent in absurdity.

How are we to ascertain the exactitude of the accordance o these Appearances with the Things of which they are Appearances? We know full well that Things appear differently to us at different times; appear differently to different individuals; appear differently to different animals. Are any of these Appearances true? If so, *which* are? and *how* do you know which are true?

Moreover, reflect on this: We have five senses, each of which reveals to us a different quality in the object. Thus an Apple is presented to us: we see it, smell it, feel it, taste it, hear it bitten; and the sight, smell, feeling, taste, and sound, are five different Appearances—five different Aspects under which we perceive the Thing. If we had three Senses more, the Thing would have three qualities more; it would present three more Appearances: if we had three Senses less, the Thing would have but three qualities less. Are these qualities *wholly and entirely dependent upon our Senses*, or do they really *appertain to the Thing?* And do they *all* appertain to it, or only some of them? The differences of the impressions made on different people seem to prove that the qualities of things are dependent on the Senses. These differences at any rate show that things do not present one uniform series of Appearances.

All we can say with truth is, that Things appear to us in such and such a manner. That we have Sensations is true; but we cannot say that our Sensations are *true images of the Things.* That the Apple we have is brilliant, round, odorous, and sweet, may be very true, if we mean that it appears such to our senses; but, to keener or duller vision, scent, tact, and taste, it may be dull, rugged, offensive, and insipid.

Amidst this confusion of sensuous impressions, Philosophers pretend to distinguish the true from the false; they assert that Reason is the Criterium of Truth: Reason distinguishes. Plato and Aristotle are herein agreed. Very well, reply the Skeptics, Reason is your Criterium. But what proof have you that this Criterium itself distinguishes truly? You must not return to

Sense: that has been already given up; you must rely upon Reason, and we ask you what proof have you that your Reason never errs? what proof have you that it is *ever* correct? A Criterium is wanted for your Criterium; and so on *ad infinitum*.

The Skeptics maintain, and justly, that because our knowledge is only the knowledge of Phenomena, and not at all of Noumena, —because we only know Things as they *appear* to us, not as they really *are*,—all attempt to penetrate the mystery of Existence must be vain; for the attempt can only be made on appearances. But, although *absolute* Truth is not attainable by man, although there cannot be a science of Being, there can be a science of Appearances. The Phenomena, they admit, are true as Phenomena. What we have to do is therefore to observe and classify Phenomena; to trace in them the resemblances of coexistence and succession, to trace the connections of cause and effect; and, having done this, we shall have founded a Science of Appearances adequate to our wants.

But the age in which the Skeptics lived was not ripe for such a conception: accordingly, having proved the impossibility of a science of Being, they supposed that they had established the impossibility of all Science, and had destroyed all grounds of certitude. It is worthy of remark that modern Skeptics have added nothing which is not implied in the principles of the Pyrrhonists. The arguments by which Hume thought he destroyed all the grounds of certitude are differently stated from those of Pyrrho, but not differently founded; and they may be answered in the same way.

The Skeptics had only a negative doctrine; consequently, only a negative influence. They corrected the tendency of the mind towards accepting in conclusions as adequate *expressions of the facts;* they served to moderate the impetuosity of the speculative spirit; they showed that the pretended Philosophy of the day was not so firmly fixed as its professors supposed. It is curious, indeed, to have witnessed the gigantic efforts of a Socrates, a Plato, and an Aristotle, towards the reconstruction of Philosophy, which the Sophists had brought to ruins—a reconstruction, too, on different ground—and then to witness the hand of the iconoclast smiting down that image, to witness the pitiless logic of the Skeptic undermining that laboriously constructed edifice, leaving nothing in its place but another heap of ruins, like that from which the edifice was built; for, not only did the Skeptics refute the notion that a knowledge of Appearances could ever become a knowledge of Existence, not only did they exhibit the fallacious nature of sensation, and the want of certitude in the affirmations of Reason, they also attacked and destroyed the main positions of that Method which was to supply the ground of certitude; they attacked Induction and Definitions.

Of Induction, Sextus, in one brief, pregnant chapter, writes thus:—"Induction is the conclusion of the Universal from individual things. But this Induction can only be correct in as far as all the individual things agree with the Universal. This universality must therefore be verified before the Induction can be made: a single case to the contrary would destroy the truth of the Induction."*

We will illustrate this by an example. The whiteness of swans shall be the Induction. Swans are said to be white because all the individual swans we may have seen are white. Here the Universal (whiteness) seems induced from the particulars; and it is true in as far as all particular swans are white. But there are a few black swans; one of these particular black swans is sufficient to destroy the former Induction. If, therefore, says Sextus, you are not able to verify the agreement of the universal with every particular, *i. e.* if you are not able to prove that there is no swan not black, you are unable to draw a certain and accurate Induction. That you cannot make this verification is obvious.

In the next chapter Sextus examines Definitions. He pronounces them perfectly useless. If we know the thing we define,

---

* *Pyrrhon. Hypot.* vol. ii. c. xv. p. 94. The edition we use is the Paris folio of 1621, the first of the Greek text.

we do not comprehend it because of the definition, bu. we im
pose on it the definition because we know it; and if we are
ignorant of the thing we would define, it is impossible to define it.

Although the Skeptics destroyed the dogmatism of their predecessors, they did not substitute any dogmatism of their own
in its place. The nature of their skepticism is happily characterized by Sextus in his comparison of them with Democritus
and Protagoras. Democritus had insisted on the uncertainty of
sense-knowledge; but he concluded therefrom that objects had
no qualities at all resembling those known to us through sensation. The Skeptics contented themselves with pointing out the
uncertainty, but did not pronounce decisively whether the qualities existed objectively or not.

Protagoras also insisted on the uncertainty, and declared man
to be the measure of truth. He supposed that there was a constant relation between the transformations of matter and those of
sensation; but these suppositions he affirmed dogmatically; to
the Skeptic they are uncertain.

This general incertitude often betrayed the Skeptics into ludi-
crous dilemmas, of which many specimens have been preserved.
Thus they said, " We assert nothing—no, not even that we assert
nothing." But if the reader wishes to see this distinction between a thing *seeming* and a thing *being,* ridiculed with a truly
comic gusto, he should turn to Molière's *Mariage Forcé,* act i.
sc. 8. Such follies form no portion of our subject, and we leave
them with some pleasure to direct our attention to more worthy
efforts of human ingenuity.

CHAPTER II.

THE EPICUREANS.

§ I. Epicurus.

The Epicureans are condemned in their names. We before noticed how the meaning attached to the name of Sophist inadvertently gives a bias to every judgment of the Sophist School, and renders it extremely difficult to conceive the members of that School otherwise than as shameless rogues. Equally difficult is it to shake off the influence of association with respect to the Epicureans; although historians are now pretty well agreed in believing Epicurus to have been a man of pure and virtuous life, and one whose doctrines were moderate and really inculcating abstemiousness.

Epicurus was born Ol. 109 (B. C. 342), at Samos, according to some; at Gargettus, in the vicinity of Athens, according to others. His parents were poor, his father a teacher of grammar. At a very early age, he tells us, his philosophical career began: so early as his thirteenth year. But we must not misunderstand this statement. He dates his career from those first questionings which occupy and perplex most young minds, especially those of any superior capacity. He doubtless refers to that period when, boy-like, he puzzled his teacher with a question beyond that teacher's power. Hearing the verse of Hesiod wherein all things are said to arise from Chaos, Epicurus asked, "And whence came Chaos?"

"Whence came Chaos?" Is not this the sort of question to occupy the active mind of a boy? Is it not by such questions that we are all led into philosophy? To philosophy he was referred for an explanation. The writings of Democritus fell in his way, and were eagerly studied; the writings of others followed; and, his vocation being fixed, he sought instruction from many masters. But from all these masters he could gain no solid convictions. They gave him hints; they could not give him Truth; and working upon the materials they furnished, he produced a system of his own, by which we presume he justified his claim to being self-taught.

His early years were agitated and unsettled. He visited Athens at eighteen, but remained there only one year. He then passed to Colophon, Mitylene, and Lampsacus. He returned to Athens in his six-and-thirtieth year, and there opened a school, over which he presided till his death, Ol. 127 (B. C. 272).

The place he chose for his school was the famous Garden, a spot pleasantly typical of his doctrine. The Platonists had their Academic Grove; the Aristotelians walked along the Lyceum; the Cynics growled in the Cynosarges; the Stoics occupied the Porch; and the Epicureans had their Garden.

Here, in the tranquil Garden, in the society of his friends, he passed a peaceful life of speculation and enjoyment. The friendship which existed amongst them is well known. In a time of general scarcity and famine they contributed to each other's support, showing that the Pythagorean notion of community of goods was unnecessary amongst friends, who could confide in each other. At the entrance of the Garden they placed this inscription: "The hospitable keeper of this mansion, where you will find pleasure the highest good, will present you liberally with barley-cakes and water fresh from the spring. The gardens will not provoke your appetite by artificial dainties, but satisfy it with natural supplies. Will you not be well entertained?"

The Garden has often been called a sty; and the name of Epicurean has become the designation of a sensualist. But, in spite of his numerous assailants, the character of Epicurus has been rescued from contempt, both by ancient and by modern critics. Diogenes Laertius, who gives some of the accusations in detail, easily refutes them by an appeal to facts; and the modern writers have been at no loss to discover the motive of the ancient calumnies, which mostly proceeded from the Stoics. A doctrine like that of Epicurus would, at all times, lend itself to gross misrepresentation; but in an epoch like that in which it appeared, and contrasted with a doctrine so fiercely opposed to it as the doctrine of the Stoics, we cannot wonder if the bitterness of opposition translated itself into bitter calumny. It is one of the commonest results of speculative differences to make us attribute to our opponent's opinions the consequences which *we* deduce from them, as if they were indubitably the consequences he deduces for himself. Our opinions are conducive to sound morality; of *that* we are convinced; and being so convinced, it is natural for us to believe that contrary opinions must be immoral. Our opponent holds contrary, *ergo* immoral opinions; and we proclaim his immorality as an unquestionable fact. In this, however, there is a slight forgetfulness, namely, that our opponent occupies exactly *similar* ground, and what we think of him, he thinks of us.

The Stoics had an ineffable contempt for the weakness and effeminacy of the Epicureans. The Epicureans had an ineffable contempt for the spasmodic rigidity and unnatural exaggeration of the Stoics. They libelled each other; but the libels against the Epicureans have met with more general credit than those against the Stoics, from the more imposing character of the latter, both in their actions and doctrines.

Epicurus is said to have been the most voluminous of all Greek Philosophers, except Chrysippus; and although none of these works are extant, yet so many fragments are preserved here and there, and there is such ample testimony as to his opinions, that there are few writers of whose doctrine we can speak with greater certainty; the more so as it does not in itself present any difficulties of comprehension.

Nothing can be more unlike Plato and Aristotle than Epicurus; and this difference may be characterized at the outset by their fundamental difference in the conception of Philosophy, which Epicurus regarded as the Art of Life, and not the Art of Truth. Philosophy, he said, was the power (ἐνέργεια) by which Reason conducted man to happiness. The investigations of Philosophy he despised: they were not only uncertain, but contributed nothing towards happiness; and of course Logic, the instrument of Philosophy, found no favor in his sight. His system was, therefore, only another form of Skepticism, consequent on his dissatisfaction with previous systems. Socrates had taught men to regard their own nature as the great object of investigation; but man does not interrogate his own nature out of simple curiosity, or for simple erudition: he studies his nature in order that he may improve it; he learns the extent of his capacities in order that he may properly direct them. The aim, therefore, of all such inquiries must be Happiness. And what constitutes Happiness? Upon this point systems differ: all profess to teach the road to Happiness, and all point out divergent roads. There can be little dispute as to what is Happiness, but infinite disputes as to the way of securing it.* In the Cyrenaic and Cynic Schools we saw this question leading to very opposite results; and the battle we are now to see renewed on similar ground between the Epicureans and the Stoics.

Epicurus, like Aristippus, declared that Pleasure constituted Happiness; all animals instinctively pursue it, and as instinctively avoid Pain. Man should do deliberately that which animals do instinctively. Every Pleasure is in itself good; but, in comparison with another, it may become an evil. The Philosopher differs from the common man in this: That while they both seek Pleasure, the former knows how to forego certain enjoyments which will cause pain and vexation hereafter; whereas, the common man seeks only the immediate enjoyment. The

---

* At a meeting of Socialists in London, to discuss in a friendly way the means of reforming the world, M. Pierre Leroux rose and addressed his brethren thus: "*Nous voulons arriver au Paradis, n'est-ce pas? n'est-ce pas? Eh bien! il ne s'agit que d'y arriver! Voilà!*"

Philosopher's art enables him to foresee what will be the result of his acts; and, so foreseeing, he will not only avoid those enjoyments which occasion grief, but know how to endure those pains from which surpassing pleasure will result.

True happiness, then, is not the enjoyment of the moment, but the enjoyment of the whole life. We must not seek to intensify, but to equalize; not debauchery to-day and satiety to-morrow, but equable enjoyment all the year round. No life can be pleasant except a virtuous life; and the pleasures of the body, although not to be despised, are insignificant when compared with those of the soul. The former are but momentary; the latter embrace both the past and future. Hence the golden rule of Temperance. Epicurus not only insisted on the necessity of moderation for continued enjoyment, he also slighted, and somewhat scorned, all exquisite indulgences. He fed moderately and plainly. Without interdicting luxuries, he saw that Pleasure was purer and more enduring if luxuries were dispensed with. This is the ground upon which Cynics and Stoics built their own exaggerated systems. They also saw that simplicity was preferable to luxury; but they pushed their notion too far. Contentedness with a little, Epicurus regarded as a great good; and he said, wealth consisted not in having great possessions, but in having small wants. He did not limit man to the fewest possible enjoyments: on the contrary, he wished him in all ways to multiply them; but he wished him to be able to live upon little, both as a preventive against ill fortune, and as an enhancement of rare enjoyments. The man who lives plainly has no fear of poverty, and is better able to enjoy exquisite pleasures.

Virtue rests upon Free Will and Reason, which are inseparable: since, without Free Will our Reason would be passive, and without Reason our Free Will would be blind. Every thing, therefore, in human actions which is virtuous or vicious depends on man's *knowing* and *willing*. Philosophical education consists in accustoming the Mind to judge accurately, and the Will to choose manfully.

From this slight outline of his Ethical doctrine may be seen how readily it furnished arguments both to assailants and to defenders. We may also notice its vagueness and elasticity, which would enable many minds to adapt it to their virtues or to their vices. The luxurious would see in it only an exhortation to their own vices; the temperate would see in it a scientific exposition of temperance.

Epicureanism, in leading man to a correct appreciation of the moral end of his existence, in showing him how to be truly happy, has to combat with many obstructions which hide from him the real road of life. These obstructions are his illusions, his prejudices, his errors, his ignorance. This ignorance is of two kinds: first, ignorance of the laws of the external world, which creates absurd superstitions, and troubles the soul with false fears and false hopes; hence the necessity of some knowledge of Physics. The second kind of ignorance is that of the nature of man; hence the necessity of the Epicurean Logic called *Canonic*, which is a collection of rules respecting human reason and its application.

The Epicurean psychology and physics were derived from the Democritean. The atoms of which the universe is formed are supposed to be constantly throwing off some of their parts, ἀπορροαί: and these, in contact with the senses, produce sensation, αἴσθησις. But Epicurus did not maintain that these ἀπορροαί were *images* of the atoms; he believed them to have a certain resemblance to their atoms, but was unable to point out where, and in how far this resemblance exists. Every sensation must be true as a sensation; and, as such, it can neither be proved nor contradicted; it is ἄλογος. The sensations of the insane and the dreaming are also true; and, although there is a difference between their sensations and those of sane and waking men, yet Epicurus confessed himself unable to determine in what the difference consists. Sensations, however, do not alone constitute knowledge; man has also the faculty of conception, πρόληψις, which arises from the repeated iteration of sensation: it is recollection of various sensations; or, as Aristotle would say, the general idea gathered from particular sensations. It is from these conceptions that the general ideas, δόξαι, are formed, and it is in these general ideas that error resides. A sensation may be considered either in relation to its object or in relation to him who experiences it; in the latter case it is agreeable or disagreeable, and renders the sentiments, τὰ πάθη, the basis of all morality.

With such a basis, we may readily anticipate the nature of the superstructure. If agreeable and disagreeable sensations are the origin of all moral phenomena, there can be no other moral rule than to seek the agreeable and to avoid the disagreeable; and whatever is pleasant becomes the great object of existence.

The Physics of Epicurus are so similar to the Physics of Democritus that we need not occupy our space with them.*

On reviewing the whole doctrine of Epicurus, we find in it that skepticism which the imperfect Philosophy of the day necessarily brought to many minds, in many different shapes; and the consequence of that skepticism was the effort to find a refuge in Morals, and the attempt to construct Ethics on a philosophic basis. The attempt failed because the basis was not broad enough; but the attempt itself is worthy of notice, as characteristic of the whole Socratic movement; for, although the Socratic Method was an attempt at reconstructing Philosophy, yet that reconstruction itself was only attempted with a view to morals. Socrates was the first to bring Philosophy down from the clouds; he was the first to make it the basis of Morality, and in one shape or other all his followers and all the schools that issued from them, kept this view present to their minds. The Epicureans are therefore to be regarded as men who ventured on a solution of the great problem, and failed because they only saw a part of the truth.

---

* They are expounded by Lucretius, who claims a rebellious originality for Epicurus which history cannot endorse. I. 67, *sqq.*

CHAPTER III.

THE STOICS.

§ I. Zeno.

The Stoics were a large sect, and of its members so many have been celebrated, that a separate work would be needed to chronicle them all. From Zeno, the founder, down to Brutus and Marcus Antoninus, the sect embraces many Greek and Roman worthies, and not a few solemn mountebanks. Some of these we would willingly introduce; but we are forced to confine ourselves to one type, and the one we select is Zeno.

He was born at Citium, a small city in the island of Cyprus, of Phœnician origin, but inhabited by Greeks. The date of his birth is uncertain. His father was a merchant, in which trade he himself engaged, until his father, after a voyage to Athens, brought home some works of Socratic Philosophers; these Zeno studied with eagerness and rapture, and determined his vocation.

When about thirty, he undertook a voyage, both of interest and pleasure, to Athens, the great mart both for trade and philosophy. Shipwrecked on the coast, he lost the whole of his valuable cargo of Phœnician purple; and, thus reduced to poverty, he willingly embraced the doctrine of the Cynics, whose ostentatious display of poverty had captivated many minds.

There is an anecdote of his having one day read Xenophon's *Memorabilia*, in a bookseller's shop, with such delight that he asked where such men were to be met with. At that moment Crates the Cynic passed by: the bookseller pointed him out to Zeno, and bade him follow Crates. He did so; and he became a disciple. But he could not long remain a disciple. The gross manners of the Cynics, so far removed from true simplicity, and their speculative incapacity, soon caused him to seek a master elsewhere. Stilpo, of Megara, became his next instructor; and from him he learned the art of disputation, which he subsequently practised with such success.

But the Megaric doctrine was too meagre for him. He was glad to learn from Stilpo; but there were things which Stilpo could not teach. He turned, therefore, to the expositors of Plato—Xenocrates and Polemo. In the philosophy of Plato there is, as before remarked, a germ of Stoicism; but there is also much that contradicts Stoicism, and so we presume, Zeno grew discontented with that also.

After twenty years of laborious study in these various schools, he opened one for himself, wherein to teach the result of all these inquiries. The spot chosen was the Stoa, or Porch, which had once been the resort of the Poets, and was decorated with the pictures of Polygnotus. From this Stoa the school derived its name.

As a man, Zeno appears deserving of the highest respect. Although sharing the doctrines of the Cynics, he did not share their grossness, their insolence, or their affectation. In person he was tall and slender; and although of a weakly constitution, he lived to a great age, being rigidly abstemious, feeding mainly upon figs, bread, and honey. His brow was furrowed with thought; and this gave a tinge of severity to his aspect, which accorded with the austerity of his doctrines. So honored and respected was he by the Athenians, that they intrusted to him the keys of the citadel; and when he died they erected to his memory a statue of brass. His death is thus recorded:—In his ninety-eighth year, as he was stepping out of his school, he fell and broke his finger. He was so affected at the consciousness of his infirmity, that, striking the earth, he exclaimed, "Why am I thus importuned? Earth, I obey thy summons!" He went home and strangled himself.

In the history of humanity there are periods when society

seems fast dissolving; when ancient creeds have lost their majesty, and new creeds want disciples; when the onlooker sees the fabric tottering, beneath which his fellow-men are crowded either in sullen despair or in blaspheming levity, and, seeing this, he feels that there is safety still possible, if men will but be bold; he raises a voice of warning, and a voice of exhortation; he bids them behold their peril and tremble, behold their salvation and resolve. He preaches to them a doctrine they have been unused to hear, or, hearing it, unused to heed; and by the mere force of his own intense conviction he gathers round him some believers who are saved. If the social anarchy be not too widely spread, he saves his country by directing its energies in a new channel; if the country's doom is sealed, he makes a gallant effort, though a vain one, and "leaves a spotless name to after-times."

Such a man was Zeno. Greece was fallen; but hope still remained. A wide-spread disease was fast eating out the vigor of its life: Skepticism, Indifference, Sensuality, Epicurean softness were only counteracted by the magnificent but vague works of Plato, or the vast but abstruse system of Aristotle. Greek civilization was fast falling to decay. A little time, and Rome, the she-wolf's nursling, would usurp the place which Greece had once so proudly held—the place of vanguard of European civilization. Rome, the mighty, would take from the feeble hands of Greece the trust she was no longer worthy to hold. There was a presentiment of Rome in Zeno's breast. In him the manly energy and stern simplicity which were to conquer the world; in him the deep reverence for moral worth, which was the glory of Rome, before, intoxicated with success, she sought to ape the literary and philosophical glory of old Hellas. Zeno the Stoic had a Roman spirit; and this is the reason why so many noble Romans became his disciples: he had deciphered the wants of their spiritual nature.

Alarmed at the skepticism which seemed inevitably following speculations of a metaphysical kind, Zeno, like Epicurus, fixed his thoughts principally upon Morals. His philosophy boasted of being eminently practical, and connected with the daily practices of life. But, for this purpose, the philosopher must not regard pleasure so much as Virtue: nor does Virtue consist in a life of contemplation and speculation, but in a life of activity; for what is Virtue?—Virtue is manhood. And what are the attributes of Man? Are they not obviously the attributes of an *active* as well as of a *speculative* being? and can that be Virtue which excludes or neglects man's activity? Man, O Plato, and O Aristotle, was not made for speculation only; wisdom is not his only pursuit. Man, O Epicurus, was not made for enjoyment only; he was made also to *do* somewhat, and to *be* somewhat. Philosophy?—It is a great thing; but it is not all. Pleasure? —It is a slight thing; and, were it greater, could not embrace men's entire activity.

The aim, then, of man's existence is neither to be wise nor to enjoy, but to be virtuous—to realize his manhood. To this aim, Philosophy is a means, and Pleasure may also be one; but they are both subordinate. Before we can be taught to lead a virtuous life, we must be taught what Virtue is. Zeno thought, with Socrates, that Virtue was the knowledge of Good; and that Vice was nothing but error. If to *know* the good were tantamount to the pursuit and practice of it, then was the teacher's task easily defined: he had to explain the nature of human knowledge, and to explain the relations of man to the universe.

Thus, as with Socrates, does Morality find itself inseparably connected with Philosophy; and more especially with psychology. A brief outline of this psychology becomes, therefore, necessary as an introduction to the Stoical Morality.

Zeno utterly rejected the Platonic theory of knowledge, and accepted, though with some modifications, the Aristotelian theory. "Reminiscence" and "Ideas" were to him mere words. Ideas he regarded as the universal notions formed by the mind from a comparison of particulars. Sense furnished all the materials of knowledge; Reason was the plastic instrument whereby these materials were fashioned. But those who maintain that Sense furnishes us the materials of knowledge are hampered with this difficulty: By what process does Sense perceive? What relation is there between Sense and the sensible Thing? What proof have we of those sensations being conformable with the Things? This difficulty is a serious one, and early occupied speculators. Indeed, this question may be pronounced the vital question of all philosophy; upon its solution depends, to a great extent, the solution of all other questions. Let us state it more clearly in an illustration.

At the distance of fifty yards you descry a tower; it is round. What do you mean by saying, It is round? You mean that the impression made upon your sense of sight is an impression similar to that made by some other objects, such as trees, which you, and all men, call round. Now, on the supposition that you never approached nearer that tower, you would always believe it to *be* round, because it *appeared* so. But, as you are enabled to approach it, and as you *then* find that the tower is square, and not round, you begin to examine into this difference. It appeared round at that distance; and yet you say it really *is* square. A little knowledge of optics seems to explain the difference; but does not. At fifty yards, you say, it appears round; but it really is square. At fifty yards, we reply, it appears round, and at one yard *it appears* square: it *is* neither: both round and square are conceptions of the mind, not attributes of things: they have a subjective, not an objective existence.

Thus far the ancient skeptics penetrated; but, seeing herein an utter destruction of all certainty in sense-knowledge, and compelled to admit that Sense was the only source of knowledge, they declared all knowledge a deceit. The perception of the real issue whence to escape this dilemma—the recognition of the uncertainty of sense-knowledge, and the reconciliation of that theory with the natural wants of the speculative mind—reconciling skepticism with belief, and both with reason, was the work of after-times.

Those who believed that the senses gave true reports of the Things which affected them, were driven to invent some hypothesis explanatory of the relation subsisting between the object and the Subject, the Thing and the Sense. We have seen how *eidola*, airy Images affluent from Things, were invented to choke up the gap, and to establish a direct connection between the Subject and the Object. Zeno, acutely enough, saw that an Image detaching itself in an airy form from the Object, could only represent the superficies of that Object, even if it represented it correctly. In this way the hypothesis of *eidola* was shown to be no more than an hypothesis to explain Appearances; whereas the real question is not, How do we perceive Appearances? but how do we perceive Objects? If we only perceive their superficies, our knowledge is only a knowledge of phenomena, and we fall into the hands of the Skeptics.

Zeno saw the extent of the difficulty, and tried to obviate it. But his hypothesis, though more comprehensive, was as completely without foundation. He assumed that Sense *could* penetrate beneath Appearance, and perceive Substance itself.

As considerable confusion exists on this point, we shall confine ourselves to the testimony of Sextus Empiricus, the most satisfactory of all. In his book directed against the Logicians, he tells us, "the Stoics held that there was one criterium of truth for man, and it was what they called the *Cataleptic Phantasm*" (τὴν καταληπτικὴν φαντασίαν, *i. e.* the Sensuous Apprehension). We must first understand what they meant by the Phantasm or Appearance. It was, they said, an *impression on the mind* (τύπωσις ἐν ψυχῇ). But from this point commence their differences; for Cleanthus understood, by this impression, an impression similar to that made by the signet-ring upon wax, τοῦ κηροῦ τύπωσιν. Chrysippus thought this absurd; for, said he, seeing that thought conceives many objects at the same time, the soul must upon that hypothesis receive many impressions of figures. He thought that Zeno meant by *impression* nothing more than a *modification* (ἑτεροίωσις): likening the soul to the air, which when many voices sound simultaneously, receives simultaneously the various alterations, but without confounding them. Thus the Soul unites several perceptions which correspond with their several objects.

This is extremely ingenious, and the indication of Sensation as a *modification* of the Soul, opens a shaft deep down into the dark region of psychology. But, if it lets in some of the light of day, it also brings into notice a new obstacle. This soul, which is modified, does it not also in its turn exercise an influence? If wine be poured into water, it modifies the water; but the water also modifies the wine. There can be no action without reaction. If a stone is presented to my sight, it modifies my soul; but does the stone remain unmodified?—No; it receives from me certain attributes, certain form, color, taste, weight, etc., which my soul bestows on it, which it does not possess in itself.

Thus is doubt again spread over the whole question. The soul modifying the object *in sensation*, can it rely upon the truth of the sensation thus produced? Has not the wine become watery, no less than the water vinous? These consequences, however, Zeno did not foresee. He was intent upon proving that the soul really apprehended objects, not as *eidola*, not as the wax receives the impression of a seal, but in absolute truth. Let us continue to borrow from Sextus Empiricus.

The Phantasm, or Appearance, which causes that Modification of the Soul which we name Sensation, is also understood by the Stoics as we understand ideas; and in this general sense, they said that there were three kinds of Phantasms: those that were probable, those that were improbable, and those that were neither one nor the other. The first are those that cause a slight and equable motion in the soul: such as those which inform us that it is day. The second are those which contradict our reason: such as if one were to say during the day-time, "Now the sun is not above the earth;" or, during the night-time, "Now it is day." The third are those, the truth of which it is impossible to verify;

such as this, "The number of the stars is even;" or, "the number is odd."

Phantasms, when probable, are true or false, or both true and false at the same time, or neither true nor false. They are true when they can be truly affirmed of any thing; false if they are wrongly affirmed, such as when one believes an oar dipped in the water to be broken, because it appears so. When Orestes, in his madness, mistook Electra for a Fury, he had a Phantasm both true and false: true, inasmuch as he saw something, viz., Electra; false, inasmuch as Electra was not a Fury.

Of true Phantasms, some are cataleptic (apprehensive), and others non-cataleptic. The latter are such as arise from disease or perturbation of the mind: as, for instance, the innumerable Phantasms produced in frenzy and hypochondria. The cataleptic Phantasm is that which is impressed by an object which exists, which is a copy of that object, and can be produced by no other object. Perception is elsewhere said to be a sort of light, which manifests itself at the same time that it lights up the object from which it is derived.

Zeno distinctly saw the weakness of the theories proposed by others; he failed however in establishing any better theory in their place. Sextus Empiricus may well call the Stoical doctrine vague and undecided. How are we to distinguish the true from the false in appearances? Above all, how are we to learn whether an impression exactly coincides with the object? This is the main problem, and Zeno pretends to solve it by a circular argument. Thus: given the problem, how are we to distinguish the true impressions from the false impressions? The solution offered is, by ascertaining which of the impressions coincide with the real objects: in other words, by distinguishing the true impressions from the false.

Let us continue the exposition:—Having a perception of an object is not knowledge: for knowledge, it is necessary that reason should assent. Perception comes from without; assent from within: it is the free exercise of man's reason. Science is composed of perceptions so solidly established that no argumentation can shake them. Perceptions not thus established only constitute Opinion.

This is making short work with difficulties, it must be confessed; but the Stoics were eager to oppose something against the Skepticism which characterized the age; and, in their eagerness to build, they did not sufficiently secure their foundations. Universal doubt they felt to be impossible. Man must occasionally assent, and that too in a constant and absolute manner. There are perceptions which carry with them irresistible conviction. There would be no possibility of action unless there were some certain truth. Where then is conviction to stop? That all our perceptions are not correct, every one is willing to admit. But which are exact, and which are inexact? What *criterium* have we? The criterium we possess is *Evidence*. "Nothing can be clearer than evidence," they said; "and, being so clear, it needs no definition." This was precisely what it *did* want; but the Stoics could not give it.

In truth, the Stoics, combating the Skepticism of their age, were reduced to the same strait as Reid, Beattie, and Hutcheson, combating the Skepticism of Hume: reduced to give up Philosophy, and to find refuge in *Common-Sense*. The battle fought by the Stoics is very analogous to the battle fought by the Scotch philosophers, in the ground occupied, in the instruments employed, in the enemy attacked, and the object to be gained. They both fought for Morality, which they thought endangered.

We shall subsequently have to consider the Common-Sense theory: enough if we now call attention to the curious *ignoratio elenchi*—the curious misconception of the real force of the enemy, and the utter helplessness of their own position, which the Common-Sense philosophers displayed. The Skeptics had made an irresistible onslaught upon the two fortresses of philosophy, Perception and Reason. They showed Perception to be based upon Appearance, and Appearance to be only *Appearance*, but not *Certainty*. They showed also that Reason was unable to distinguish between Appearance and Certainty, because, in the first place, it had nothing but Phenomena (Appearances) to build upon; and, in the second place, because there is no criterium to apply to Reason itself. Having gained this victory, they proclaimed Philosophy no longer existent. Whereupon the Stoics valorously rise, and, taking their stand upon Common-Sense, believe they rout the forces of the Skeptics; believe they retake the lost fortresses by declaring that Perceptions are true as well as false, and that you may distinguish the true from the false, by—distinguishing them: and that Reason has its criterium in Evidence, which requires no criterium, it is so clear. This seems to us pretty much the same as if the French were to invade Great Britain, possess themselves of London, Edinburgh, and Dublin, declare England the subject of France, and patriots were then to declare that the French were to be driven home again by a party of volunteers taking their stand upon Hampstead Heath, displaying the banners of England, and with loud alarums proclaiming the invaders defeated.

But it is time to consider the Ethical doctrines of the Stoics; and to do this effectually we must glance at their conception of the Deity. There are two elements in Nature. The first is ὕλη πρώτη, or primordial matter; the passive element from which things are formed. The second is the active element, which forms things out of matter: Reason, Destiny (εἱμαρμένη), God. The divine Reason operating upon matter bestows upon it the laws which govern it, laws which the Stoics called λόγοι σπερματικοί, or productive causes. God is the Reason of the world.

With this speculative doctrine it is easy to connect their practical doctrine. Their Ethics are easily to be deduced from their theology. If Reason is the great creative law, to live conformably with Reason must be the practical moral law. If the universe be subject to a general law, every part of that universe must also be duly subordinate to it. The consequence is clear: there is but one formula for Morals, and that is, "Live harmoniously with Nature," ὁμολογομένως τῇ φύσει ζῆν.

This is easily said. An anxious disciple might however desire greater precision, and ask, Is it universal nature, or is it the particular nature of man, that I am to live in unison with? Cleanthes taught the former; Chrysippus the latter; or, we should rather say, taught that both individual and universal nature should be understood by the formula. And this appears to have been the sense in which it was usually interpreted.

The distinctive tendency of the formula cannot be mistaken: it is to reduce every thing to Reason, which, as it has supremacy in creation, must also have supremacy in man. This is also the Platonic conception. It makes Logic the rule of life; and assumes that there is nothing in man's mind which cannot be reduced within the limits of Logic; assumes that man is all intellect. It follows, that every thing which interferes with a purely intellectual existence is to be eliminated as dangerous. The pleasures and the pains of the body are to be despised: only the pleasures and the pains of the intellect are worthy to occupy man. By his passions he is made a slave; by his intellect he is free. His senses are passive; his intellect is active. It is his duty therefore to surmount and despise his passions and his senses, that he may be free, active, virtuous.

We have here the doctrine of the Cynics, somewhat purified, but fundamentally the same; we have here also the anticipation of Rome; the forethought of that which was subsequently realized in act. Rome was the fit theatre of Stoicism, because Rome was peopled with soldiers: these soldiers had their contempt of death formed in perpetual campaigns. How little the Romans regarded the life of man their history shows. The gladiatorial combats, brutal and relentless, must have hardened the minds of all spectators; and there were no softening influences to counteract them. How different the Greeks! They did not pretend to despise this beautiful life; they did not affect to be above humanity. Life was precious, and they treasured it: treasured it not with petty fear, but with noble ingenuousness. They loved life, and wept on quitting it; and they wept without shame.

They loved life, and they said so. When the time came for them to risk it, or to give it for their country, or their honor,—when something they prized higher was to be gained by the sacrifice,—then they died unflinchingly. The tears shed by Achilles and Ulysses did not unman them: these heroes fought terribly, as they loved tenderly. Philoctetes, in agony, howls like a wild beast, because he feels pain, and feels no shame in expressing it. But these shrieks have not softened him: he is still the same stern, terrible, implacable Philoctetes.

The Stoics, in their dread of becoming effeminate, became marble. They despised pain; they despised death. To be above pain was thought manly. They did not see, that, in this respect, instead of being above Humanity, they sank miserably below it. If it is a condition of our human organization to be susceptible of pain, it is only affectation to conceal the *expression* of that pain. Could silence stifle pain, it were well; but to stifle the cry, is not to stifle the feeling; and to have a feeling, yet affect not to have it, is pitiful. The Savage soon learns that philosophy; but the civilized man is superior to it. You receive a blow, and you do not wince? so much of heroism is displayed by a stone. You are face to face with Death, and you have no regrets? then you are unworthy of life. Real heroism feels the pain it conquers, and loves the life it surrenders in a noble cause.

As a reaction against effeminacy, Stoicism may be applauded; as a doctrine it is one-sided. It ends in apathy and egoism. Apathy, indeed, was considered by the Stoics as the highest condition of humanity; whereas, in truth, it is the lowest.

CHAPTER IV.
THE NEW ACADEMY.

§ I. Arcesilaus and Carneades.

THE New Academy would solicit our attention, were it only for the celebrity bestowed on it by Cicero and Horace; but it has other and higher points of interest than those of literary curiosity. The combat of which it was the theatre was, and is, of singular importance. The questions connected with it are those vital questions respecting the origin and certitude of human knowledge, which so long have occupied the ingenuity of thinkers; and the consequences which flow from either solution of the problem are of the utmost importance.

The Stoics endeavored to establish the certitude of human knowledge, in order that they might establish the truth of moral principles. They attacked the doctrines of the Skeptics, and believed they triumphed by bringing forward their own doctrine of Common-Sense. But the New Academicians had other arguments to offer. They too were Skeptics, although their skepticism differed from that of the Pyrrhonists. The nature of this difference Sextus Empiricus has noted. "Many persons," says he, "confound the Philosophy of the Academy with that of the Skeptics. But although the disciples of the New Academy declare that all things are incomprehensible; yet they are distinguished from the Pyrrhonists in this very dogmatism: they affirm that all things are incomprehensible—the Skeptics do not affirm that. Moreover, the Skeptics consider all perceptions perfectly equal as to the faithfulness of their testimony; the Academicians distinguish between probable and improbable perceptions: the first they class under various heads. There are some, they say, which are merely probable, others which are also confirmed by reflection, others which are subject to no doubt. Assent is of two kinds: simple assent, which the mind yields without repugnance as without desire, such as that of a child following its master; and the assent which follows upon conviction and reflection. The Skeptics admitted the former kind; the Academicians the latter."

These differences are of no great moment; but in the history of sects we find the smallest variation invested with a degree of importance; and we can understand the pertinacity with which the Academicians distinguished themselves from the Skeptics, even on such slight grounds as the above.

In treating of the Academicians we are forced to follow the plan pursued with the Skeptics, namely to consider the doctrines of the whole sect, rather than to particularize the share of each individual member. The Middle Academy and the New Academy we thus unite in one; although the ancients drew a distinction between them, it is difficult for moderns to do so. Arcesilaus and Carneades, therefore, shall be our types.

Arcesilaus was born at Pitane in the 116th Olympiad (B. C. 316). He was early taught mathematics and rhetoric, became the pupil of Theophrastus, afterwards of Aristotle, and finally of Polemo the Platonist. In this last school he was contemporary with Zeno, and probably there began that antagonism which was so remarkable in their subsequent career. On the death of Crates, Arcesilaus filled the Academic chair, and filled it with great ability and success. His fascinating manners won him general regard. He was learned and sweet-tempered, and generous to a fault. Visiting a sick friend, who, he saw, was suffering from privation, he slipped, unobserved, a purse of gold underneath the sick man's pillow. When the attendant discovered it, the sick man said with a smile, "This is one of Arcesilaus's generous frauds." He was of a somewhat luxurious temper, but he lived till the age of seventy-five, when he killed himself by hard drinking.

Carneades, the most illustrious of the Academicians, was born at Cyrene, in Africa, Ol. 141, 4 (b. c. 213). He was a pupil of Diogenes the Stoic, who taught him the subtleties of disputation. This made him sometimes exclaim in the course of a debate: " If I have reasoned rightly, you are wrong; if not, O Diogenes, return me the *mina* I paid you for my lessons." On leaving Diogenes he became the pupil of Hegesinus, who then held the Academic chair; by him he was instructed in the skeptical principles of the Academy, and on his death he succeeded to his chair. He also diligently studied the voluminous writings of Chrysippus. These were of great value to him, exercising his subtlety, and trying the temper of his own metal. He owed so much to this opponent that he used to say, "Had there not been a Chrysippus, I should not be what I am:" a sentiment very easy of explanation. There are two kinds of writers: those who directly instruct us in sound knowledge, and those who indirectly lead us to the truth by the very opposition they raise against their views. Next to exact knowledge, there is nothing so instructive as exact error: an error clearly stated, and presented in somewhat the same way as it at first presented itself to the mind which now upholds it, enables us to see not only that it is an error, but by what process it was deduced from its premises, and thus is among the most valuable modes of instruction. It is better than direct instruction: better, because the learner's mind is called into full activity, and apprehends the truth for itself, instead of passively assenting to it.

Carneades was justified in his praise of Chrysippus. He felt how much he owed to his antagonist. He felt that to him he owed a clear conception of the Stoical error, and a clear conviction of the truth of the Academic doctrine; and owed also no inconsiderable portion of that readiness and subtlety which marked him out amongst his countrymen as a fitting Ambassador to send to Rome.

Carneades in Rome—Skepticism in the Stoic city—presents an interesting picture. The Romans crowded round him, fascinated by his subtlety and eloquence. Before Galba—before Cato the Censor—he harangued with marvellous unction in praise of Justice; and the hard brow of the grim Stoic softened; an approving smile played over those thin firm lips. But the next day the brilliant orator undertook to exhibit the uncertainty of all human knowledge; and, as a proof, he refuted all the arguments with which the day before he had supported Justice. He spoke against Justice as convincingly as he had spoken for it. The brow of Cato darkened again, and with a keen instinct of the dangers of such ingenuity operating upon the Roman youth, he persuaded the Senate to send back the Philosophers to their own country.

Carneades returned to Athens, and there renewed his contest with the Stoics. He taught with great applause, and lived to the advanced age of ninety.

That the Academicians should have embraced Skepticism is not strange: indeed, as we have said, Skepticism was the inevitable result of the tendencies of the whole epoch; and the only sect which did not accept it was forced to find a refuge in Common-Sense: that is to say, was forced to find refuge in the abdication of Philosophy, which abdication was in itself a species of Skepticism. But it may seem strange that the Academy should derive itself from Plato; it may seem strange that Arcesilaus should be a continuer and a warm admirer of Plato. The ancients themselves, according to Sextus Empiricus, were divided amongst each other respecting Plato's real doctrine; some considering him a skeptic, others a dogmatist. We have already explained the cause of this difference of opinion, and have shown how very little consistency and precision there is in the ideas of Plato upon all subjects except Method. Skepticism, therefore, might very easily result from a study of his writings. But this is not all. Plato's attack upon the theories of his predecessors, which were grounded upon sense-knowledge, is constant, triumphant. The dialogue of the *Theætetus*, which is devoted to the subject of Philosophy, is an exposition of the incapacity of sense to furnish materials for Philosophy. All that sense can furnish the materials for, is *Opinion*, and Opinion, as he frequently declares, even when it is Right Opinion, never can be Philosophy. Plato, in short, destroyed all the old foundations upon which theories had been constructed. He cleared the ground before commencing his own work. By this means he obviated the attacks of the Sophists, and yet refused to sustain the onus of errors which his predecessors had accumulated. The Sophists saw the weakness of the old belief, and attacked it. Having reduced it to ruins, they declared themselves triumphant. Plato appeared, and admitted the fact of the old fortress being in ruins, and its deserving to be so; but he denied that the city of Truth was taken. "Expend," said he, "your wrath and skill in battering down such fortresses; I will assist you; for I too declare them useless. But the real fortress you have not yet approached; it is situate on far higher ground." Sense-knowledge and Opinion being thus set aside, the stronghold of Philosophy was the Ideal theory: in it Plato found refuge from the Sophists. Aristotle came and destroyed that theory. What then remained? Skepticism.

Arcesilaus admitted, with Plato, the uncertainty of Opinion; but he also admitted with Aristotle the incorrectness of the Ideal theory. He was thus reduced to absolute Skepticism. The arguments of Plato had quite destroyed the certitude of Opinion; the arguments of Aristotle had quite destroyed the Ideal theory. And thus, by refusing to accept one argument of the Platonic doctrine, Arcesilaus could from Plato's works deduce his own theory of the Incomprehensibility of all things; the *acatalepsy*.

The doctrine of *acatalepsy* recalls to us the Stoical doctrine of *catalepsy* or Apprehension, to which it is the antithesis. The *Cataleptic Phantasm* was the True Perception, according to the Stoics; and, according to the Academicians, all Perceptions were *acataleptic*, *i.e.* bore no conformity to the objects perceived; or, if they did bear any conformity thereto, it could never be known.

Arcesilaus saw the weak point of the Stoical argument. Zeno pretended that there was a Criterium, which decided between science and opinion, which decided between true and false perceptions, and this was the *Assent* which the mind gave to the truth of certain perceptions: in other words, Common-Sense was the Criterium. "But," said Arcesilaus, "what is the difference between the Assent of a wise man, and the Assent of a madman? —There is no difference but in name." He felt that the criterium of the Stoics was itself in need of a Criterium.

Chrysippus the Stoic combated Arcesilaus, and was in urn combated by Carneades. The great question then pending was this:—

What Criterium is there of the truth of our knowledge?

The Criterium must reside either in Reason, in Conception, or in Sensation. It cannot reside in Reason, because Reason itself is not *independent* of the other two: it operates upon the materials furnished by them, and is dependent upon them. Our knowledge is derived from the senses, and every object presented to the mind must consequently have been originally presented to the senses: on their accuracy the mind must depend.

Reason cannot therefore contain within itself the desired Criterium. Nor can conception; for the same arguments apply to it. Nor can the Criterium reside in Sense; because, as all admit, the senses are deceptive, and there is no perception which cannot be false. For what is Perception? Our Senses only inform us of the presence of an object in so far as they are affected by it. But what is this? Is it not *we* who are affected—*we* who are modified? Yes; and this modification reveals both itself and the object which causes it. Like Light, which in showing itself, shows also the objects upon which it is thrown; like light also, it shows objects in *its own colors*. Perception is a peculiar *modification of the soul*. The whole problem now to solve is this:—

Does every modification of the soul exactly correspond with the external object which causes that modification?

This is a problem presented by the Academicians. They answered, but they did not solve it; they left to their adversaries the task of proving the *correspondence* between the object and subject. We may here venture to carry out their principles, and endeavor to solve the problem, as it is one still agitating the minds of metaphysicians.

In nowise does the Sensation correspond with the object; in nowise does the modification correspond with the external cause, except in the relation of cause and effect. The early thinkers were well aware that, in order to attribute any certainty to sensuous knowledge, we must assume that the Senses transmit us *Copies* of things. Democritus, who was the first to see the necessity of such an hypothesis, suggested that our Ideas were *Eidola*, or Images of the Objects, of an extremely airy texture, which were thrown off by the objects in the shape of effluvia, and entered the brain by the pores. Those who could not admit such an explanation substituted the hypothesis of *Impressions*. Ask any man, not versed in such inquiries, whether he believes his perceptions to be *copies* of objects—whether he believes that the flower he sees before him exists quite independently of him, and of every other human being, and exists with the same attributes of shape, fragrance, taste, etc., his answer is sure to be in the affirmative. He will regard you as a madman if you doubt it. And yet so early as the epoch of which we are now sketching the history, thinking men had learned in somewise to see that our Perceptions were *not* copies of Objects, but were simply modifications of our minds, caused by the objects. Once admit this, and sensuous knowledge is forever pronounced not only uncertain, but absolutely false. Can such a modification be a *copy* of the cause which modifies? As well ask, Is the pain, occasioned by a burn, a copy of the fire? Is it at all like the fire? Does it at all express the essence of fire? Not in the least. It only expresses one relation in which we stand to the fire; one effect upon us which fire will produce. Nevertheless fire is an Object, and a burn is a sensation. The way in which we perceive the existence of the Object (fire) is similar to that in which we perceive the existence of other objects: and that way is in the modifications they occasion; *i. e.* in the Sensations.

Let us take another instance. We say that we hear Thunder: in other words, we have a Perception of the Object called Thunder. Our sensation really is of a sound, which the electrical phenomena we call Thunder have caused in us, by acting on the aural nerve. Is our sensation of this sound any copy of the Phenomena? Does it in any degree express the nature of the Phenomena? No; it only expresses the sensation we receive from a certain electrical state of the atmosphere.

In these cases most people will readily acquiesce; for, by a very natural confusion of ideas, whenever they speak of perceptions, they mostly mean visual perceptions; because with sight the clearest knowledge is associated; because also the hypothesis of our perceptions being copies of Things, is founded upon sight. The same persons who would willingly admit that Pain was not a copy of the Fire, nor of any thing in the nature of Fire, except in its effect on our nerves, would protest that the appearance of Fire *to the Eye* was the *real* appearance of the Fire, all Eyes apart, and quite independent of human vision. Yet if all sentient beings were at once swept from the face of the earth, the fire would have no attribute at all *resembling* Pain; because Pain is a modification, not of Fire, but of a sentient being. In like manner, if all sentient beings were at once swept from the face of the earth, the Fire would have no attributes at all *resembling* light and color; because light and color are modifications of the sentient being, caused by *something* external, but no more resembling its cause than the pain inflicted by an instrument resembles that instrument.

Pain and color are modifications of the sentient being. The question at issue is, Can a modification of a sentient being be a copy of its cause? The answer is clearly a negative. We may imagine that when we see an Object, our sensation is a copy of it; because we believe that the Object paints itself upon the retina; and we liken perception to a mirror, in which things are reflected. It is extremely difficult to divest ourselves of this prejudice; but we may be made aware of the fallacy if we attend to those perceptions which are not visual—to the perceptions of sound, fragrance, taste, or pain. These are clearly nothing but modifications of our sentient being, *caused* by external objects, but in nowise *resembling* them. We are all agreed that the heat is not in the fire, but in us; that sweetness is not in the sugar, but in us; that fragrance is but the particles which, impinging on the olfactory nerve, cause a sensation in us. In all beings similarly constituted these things would have similar effects, would cause pain, sweetness, and fragrance; but on all other beings the effects would be different. Fire would burn paper, but not pain it; sugar would mix with water, but not give it the sensation of sweetness.

The radical error of those who believe that we perceive things *as they are*, consists in mistaking a metaphor for a fact, and believing that the mind is a mirror in which external objects are reflected. But, as Bacon finely says, "The human understanding is like an *unequal* mirror to the rays of things, *which, mixing its own nature with the nature of things, distorts and perverts them.*" We attribute heat to the fire, and color to the flower; heat and color really being *states of our consciousness*, occasioned by the fire and the flower under certain conditions.

Perception is nothing more than *a state of the percipient; i. e.* a state of consciousness. This state may be occasioned by some external cause, and may be as complex as the cause is complex, but it is still nothing more than a state of consciousness—an effect produced by an adequate cause. Of every change in our Sensation we are conscious, and in time we learn to give definite names and forms to the causes of these changes. But in the fact of Consciousness there is nothing *beyond* consciousness. In our perceptions we are conscious only of the changes which have taken place within us: we can never transcend the sphere of our own consciousness; we can never go out of ourselves, and become aware of the objects which caused those changes. All we can do is to identify certain *external appearances* with certain *internal changes*, e. g. to identify the appearance we name "fire," with certain sensations we have known to follow our being placed near it. Turn the fact of Consciousness how we will, we can see nothing in it but the change of a sentient being operated by some external cause. Consciousness is no mirror of the world; it gives no faithful reflection of things as they are *per se;* it only gives a faithful report of its own modification *as excited* by external things.

The world, apart from our consciousness, *i. e.* the non-ego *quâ* non-ego—the world *per se*—is, in all likelihood, something utterly different from the world as we know it; for all we know of it is derived through our consciousness of what its effects are on *us*, and our consciousness is obviously only a *state of ourselves*, not a copy of external things.

It may be here asked, How do you infer that the world is different from what it appears to us?

The question is pertinent, and may be answered briefly. The world *per se* must be different from what it appears to us through consciousness, because to us it is only known in the relation of cause and effect. World is the Cause; our Consciousness the Effect. But the same Cause operating on some other organization would produce a very different effect. If all animals were blind, there would be no such thing as *light* (*i. e.* light as we know it), because light is a *phenomenon* made up out of the operation of some unknown thing on the retina. If all animals were deaf, there would be no such thing as *sound*, because sound is a *phenomenon* made up out of the operation of some unknown thing on the tympanum. If all men were without their present nervous system, there would be no such thing as *pain*, because pain is a *phenomenon* made up out of the operation of some external thing on the specialized nervous system.

Light, color, sound, taste, smell, are all states of Conscious ness; what they are beyond Consciousness, as existences *per se*, we cannot know, we cannot imagine, because we can only conceive them *as* we know them. Light, with its myriad forms and colors—Sound, with its thousand-fold life—make Nature what Nature appears to us. But they do not exist *as such* apart from our consciousness; they are the investitures with which we clothe the world. Nature in her insentient solitude is an eternal Darkness—an eternal Silence.

We conclude, therefore, that the world *per se* in nowise resembles the World as it appears to us. Perception is an Effect; and its truth is not the truth of *resemblance*, but of *relation, i. e.* it is the true operation of the world on us, the true operation of Cause and Effect. But perception is not the true resemblance of the world: Consciousness is no mirror reflecting external things.

Let us substitute for the metaphor of a mirror the more abstract expression, " Perception is the Effect of an external Object acting on a sentient being," and much of the confusion darkening this matter will be dissipated. An Effect, we know, agrees with its Cause, but it does not necessarily *resemble* it. An Effect is no more a Copy of the Cause than pain is a copy of the application of fire to a finger: *ergo*, Perception can never be an accurate report of what things are *per se*, but only of what they are in relation to us.

It has been said that, although no single sense does actually convey to us a correct impression of any thing, nevertheless we are enabled to confirm or modify the report of one sense by the report of another sense, and that the result of the whole activity of the five senses is a true impression of the external Thing. This is a curious fallacy: it pretends that a number of *false* impressions are sufficient to constitute a true one!

The conclusion to be drawn from the foregoing premises is this: There is no correspondence between the object and the sensation, except that of Cause and Effect. Sensations are not Copies of Objects; do not at all resemble them. As we can only know objects through sensation—*i. e.* as we can only know our sensations—we can never ascertain the truth respecting objects.

This brings us back to the New Academy, the disciples of which strenuously maintained that Perception, being nothing but a modification of the Soul, could never reveal the real nature of things.

Do we then side with the Academicians in proclaiming all human knowledge deceptive? No: to them, as to the Pyrrhonists, we answer: You are quite right in affirming that man cannot transcend the sphere of his own consciousness, cannot penetrate the real essences of things, cannot know causes, can only know phenomena. But this affirmation—though it crushes Metaphysics—though it interdicts the inquiry into *noumena*, into essences and causes, as frivolous because futile—does not touch Science. If all our knowledge is but a knowledge of phenomena, there can still be a Science of Phenomena adequate to all man's true wants. If Sensation is but the effect of an External Cause, we, who can never know that Cause, know it in its relation to us, *i. e.* in its Effect. These Effects are as constant as their Causes; and, consequently, there can be a Science of Effects. Such a Science is that named Positive Science, the aim of which is to trace the Co-existences and Successions of Phenomena, *i. e.* to trace the relation of Cause and Effect throughout the universe submitted to our inspection.

But neither the Pyrrhonists nor the Academicians saw this refuge for the mind; they consequently proclaimed Skepticism as the final result of inquiry.

CHAPTER V.

SUMMARY OF THE EIGHTH EPOCH.

We have now brought our narrative to the second crisis in the history of speculation. The Skepticism which made the Sophists powerful, and which closed the first period of this history, we now behold once more usurping the intellects of men, and this time with far greater power. A Socrates appeared to refute the Sophists. Who is there to refute and to discredit the Skeptics?

The Skeptics, and all thinkers during the epoch we have just treated were such, whether they called themselves Epicureans, Stoics, Pyrrhonists, or New Academicians—the Skeptics, we say, were in possession of the most formidable arms. From Socrates, from Plato, and from Aristotle, they had borrowed their best weapons, and with these had attacked Philosophy, and attacked it with success.

All the wisdom of the antique world was powerless against the Skeptics. Speculative belief was reduced to the most uncertain "probability." Faith in philosophic Truth was extinct. Faith in human endeavor that way was gone. Philosophy was impossible.

But there was one peculiarity of the Socratic doctrine which was preserved even in the midst of skepticism. Socrates had made Ethics the great object of his inquiries: and all subsequent thinkers had given it a degree of attention which before was unknown. Philosophy contented itself with the Common-Sense doctrine of the Stoics, and the Probabilities of the Skeptics, which, however futile as philosophic principles, were efficacious enough as moral principles. Common-Sense may be a bad basis for metaphysical or scientific reasoning; but it is not so bad a basis for a system of morals.

The protest, therefore, which Skepticism made against all Philosophy was not so anarchical in its tendency as the protest made by the Sophists; but it was more energetic, more terrible. In the wisdom of that age there lay no cure for it. The last cry of despair seemed to have been wrung from the baffled thinkers, as they declared their predecessors to have been hopelessly wrong, and declared also that their error was without a remedy.

It was, indeed, a saddening contemplation. The hopes and aspirations of so many incomparable minds thus irrevocably doomed; the struggles of so many men, from Thales, who first asked himself, Whence do all things proceed? to the elaborate systematization of the forms of thought which occupied an Aristotle—the struggles of all these men had ended in Skepticism. Little was to be gleaned from the harvest of their endeavors but arguments against the possibility of that Philosophy they were so anxious to form. Centuries of thought had not advanced the mind one step nearer to a solution of the problems with which, child-like, it began. It began with a child-like question; it ended with an aged doubt. Not only did it doubt the solutions of the great problem which others had attempted; it even doubted the possibility of any solution. It was not the doubt which begins, but the doubt which ends inquiry: it had no illusions.

This was the second crisis of Greek Philosophy. Reason thus assailed could only find a refuge in Faith; and the next period opens with the attempt to construct a Religious Philosophy

NINTH EPOCH.

PHILOSOPHY ALLIES ITSELF WITH FAITH: THE ALEXAN-
DRIAN SCHOOLS.

CHAPTER I.
RISE OF NEO-PLATONISM.

§ I. ALEXANDRIA.

PHILOSOPHY no longer found a home in Greece; it had no longer any worshippers in its native country, and was forced to seek them elsewhere. A period had arrived when all problems seemed to have been stated, and none seemed likely to be solved. Every system which human ingenuity could devise had been devised by the early thinkers; and not one had been able to withstand examination. In the early annals of speculation, a new and decisive advance is made whenever a new question is asked; to suggest a doubt, is to exercise ingenuity; to ask a question, is to awaken men to a new view of the subject. But now all questions had been asked; old questions had been revived under new forms; nothing remained to stimulate inquiry, nothing to give speculators a hope of success.

Unable to ask new questions, or to offer new answers to those already asked, the Philosophers readily seized on the only means which enabled them to gain renown: they travelled. They carried their doctrines into Egypt and to Rome; and in those places they were listened to with wonder and delight. Their old doctrines were novelties to a people who had no doctrines of its own; and, from the excessive cost of books in those days, almost all instruction being oral, the strangers were welcomed warmly, and the doctrines imported were as novel as if they had been just invented.

Philosophy, exiled from Greece, was a favored guest in Alexandria and Rome: but in both cases it was a stranger, and could not be naturalized. In Alexandria, however, it made a brilliant display; and the men it produced gave it an originality and an influence which it never possessed in Rome.

Roman Philosophy was but a weak paraphrase of the Grecian; and we, therefore, give it no place in this history. To speak Greek, to write Greek, became the fashionable ambition of Rome. The child was instructed by a Greek slave. Greek Professors taught Philosophy and Rhetoric to aspiring youths. Athens had become the necessary "*tour*" which was to complete a man's education. It was there that Cicero learned those ideas which he delighted in setting forth in charming dialogues. It was there Horace learned that light and careless philosophy, which shines through the sparkling crystal of his verse. Wandering from the Academy to the Porch, and from the Porch to the Garden, he became imbued with that skepticism which checks his poetical enthusiasm; he learned to make a system of that pensive epicureanism which gives so peculiar a character to his poems; a character which, with a sort of after-dinner freedom and *bonhomie*, recommends him to men of the world.

In Rome, Philosophy might tinge the poetry, give weight to oratory, method to jurisprudence, and supply some topics of conversation; but it was no Belief filling the minds of serious men: it took no root in the national existence; it produced no great Thinkers.

In Alexandria the case was different. There several schools were formed, and some new elements introduced into the doctrines then existent. Great thinkers—Plotinus, Proclus, Porphyry—made it illustrious; and it had a rival, whose antagonism alone would confer immortal renown upon it: that rival was Christianity.

In no species of grandeur was the Alexandrian school deficient, as M. Saisset justly observes :* genius, power, and duration, have consecrated it. Reanimating, during an epoch of decline, the fecundity of an aged civilization, it created a whole family of illustrious names. Plotinus, its real founder, resuscitated Plato; Proclus gave the world another Aristotle; and, in the person of Julian the Apostate, it became master of the world. For three centuries it was a formidable rival to the greatest power that ever appeared on earth—the power of Christianity; and, if it succumbed in the struggle, it only fell with the civilization of which it had been the last rampart.

Alexandria, the centre of gigantic commerce, soon became a new metropolis of science, rivalling Athens. The Alexandrian Library is too celebrated to need more than a passing allusion: to it, and to the men assembled there, we owe the vast labors of erudition in philosophy and literature which were of such service to the world. We cannot here enumerate all the men of science who made it illustrious; enough if we mention Euclid, for Mathematics; Conon and Hipparchus, for Astronomy; Eratosthenes, for Geography; and Aristarchus, for literary Criticism. Besides these, there were the Philosophers; and Lucian, the witty Skeptic; and the Poets, Apollonius Rhodius, Callimachus, Lycophron, Tryphiodorus, and, above all, the sweet idyllic Theocritus.

It is a curious spectacle. Beside the Museum of Alexandria there rises into formidable importance the Didascalia of the Christians. In the same city, Philo the Jew, and Œnesidemus the Pyrrhonist, founded their respective schools. Ammonius Saccas appears there. Lucian passes through at the same time that Clemens Alexandrinus is teaching. After Plotinus has taught, Arius and Athanasius will also teach. Greek Skepticism, Judaism, Platonism, Christianity—all have their interpreters within so small a distance from the temple of Serapis!

---

* *Revue des Deux Mondes*, 1844, tome iii. p. 783; an admirable article on the Alexandrian Schools.

§ II. Philo.

Alexandria, as we have seen, was the theatre of various struggles: of these we are to select one, and that one the struggle of the Neo-Platonists with the Christian Fathers.

Under the name of the Alexandrian School are designated, loosely enough, all those thinkers who endeavored to find a refuge from Skepticism in a new Philosophy, based on altogether new principles. Now, although these various Thinkers by no means constitute a School, they constitute a Movement, and they form an Epoch in the history of Philosophy. We may merely observe that the "Alexandrian School" and the "Neo-Platonists" are not convertible terms: the former designates a whole movement, the latter designates the most illustrious section of that movement.

Philo the Jew is the first of these Neo-Platonists. He was born at Alexandria, a few years before Christ. The influence of Greek ideas had long been felt in Alexandria, and Philo, commenting on the writings of the Jews, did so in the spirit of one deeply imbued with Greek thought. His genius was Oriental, his education Greek; the result was a strange mixture of mysticism and dialectics.* To Plato he owed much: but to the New Academy, perhaps more. From Carneades he learned to distrust the truth of all sensuous knowledge, and to deny that Reason had any criterium of truth.

Thus far he was willing to travel with the Greeks; thus far had dialectics conducted him. But there was another element in his mind besides the Greek: there was the Oriental or mystical element. If human knowledge is a delusion, we must seek for truth in some higher sphere. The Senses may deceive; Reason may be powerless; but there is still a faculty in man—

---

* St. Paul thus comprehensively expresses the national characteristic of the Jews and Greeks: "The Jews require a sign (*i. e.* a miracle), and the Greeks seek after wisdom (*i. e* philosophy)."—1 *Corinth.* i. 22.

there is Faith. Real Science is the gift of God: its name is Faith: its origin is the goodness of God: its cause is Piety.

This conception is not Plato's, yet is nevertheless Platonic. Plato would never have thus condemned Reason for the sake of Faith; and yet he, too, thought that the nature of God could not be known, although his existence could be proved. In this respect he would have agreed with Philo. But, although Plato does not speak of Science as the gift of God, he does in one place so speak of Virtue; and he devotes the whole dialogue of the *Meno* to show that Virtue cannot be taught, because it is not a thing of the understanding, but a gift of God. The reasons he there employs may easily have suggested to Philo their application to Philosophy.

From this point Philo's Philosophy of course becomes a theology. God is ineffable, incomprehensible: his existence may be known; his nature can never be known; ὁ δ' ἄρα οὐδὲ τῷ νῷ καταληπτός, ὅτι μὴ κατὰ τὸ εἶναι μόνον. But to know that he exists, is in itself the knowledge of his being one, perfect, simple, immutable, and *without attribute*. This knowledge is implied in the simple knowledge of his existence: he cannot be otherwise, if he exist at all. But to know this, is not to know in what consists his perfection. We cannot penetrate with our glance the mystery of his essence. We can only believe.

If however we cannot know God in his essence, we can obtain some knowledge of his Divinity: we know it in *The Word*. This λόγος—this *Word* (using the expression in its Scriptural sense)—fills a curious place in all the mystical systems. God being incomprehensible, inaccessible, an intermediate existence was necessary as an interpreter between God and Man, and this intermediate existence the Mystics called *The Word*.

The Word, according to Philo, is God's Thought. This Thought is two-fold: it is λόγος ἐνδιάθετος, the Thought as embracing all Ideas (in the Platonic sense of the term Idea), *i. e* Thought *as* Thought; and it is λόγος προφορικός, the Thought *realized*: Thought become the World.

In these three *hypostases* of the Deity we see the Trinity of Plotinus foreshadowed. There is, first, God the Father; secondly the Son of God, *i. e.* the λόγος; thirdly, the Son of the λόγος, *i. e.* the World.

This brief outline of Philo's Theology will sufficiently exemplify the two great facts which we are anxious to have understood:—1st, the union of Platonism with Oriental mysticism; 2dly, the entirely new direction given to Philosophy, by uniting it once more with Religion. It is this direction which characterizes the Movement of the Alexandrian School. Reason had been shown to be utterly powerless to solve the great questions of Philosophy then agitated. Various Schools had pursued various Methods, but all with one result. Skepticism was the conclusion of every struggle. "And yet," said the Mystics, "we have an idea of God and of his goodness; we have an ineradicable belief in his existence, and in the Perfection of his nature, consequently, in the beneficence of his aims. Yet these ideas are not innate; were they innate, they would be uniformly entertained by all men, and amongst all nations. If they are not innate, whence are they derived? Not from Reason; not from experience: then from Faith."

Now, Philosophy, conceive it how you will, is entirely the offspring of Reason: it is the endeavor to explain by Reason the mysteries amidst which we "move, live, and have our being." Although it is legitimate to say, "Reason is incapable of solving the problems proposed to it," it is not legitimate to add, "*therefore* we must call in the aid of Faith." In Philosophy, Reason must either reign alone, or abdicate. No compromise is permissible. If there are things between heaven and earth which are not dreamt of in our Philosophy—which do not come within the possible sphere of our Philosophy—we may believe in them, indeed, but we cannot christen that belief philosophical.

One of two things,—either Reason is capable of solving the problems, or it is incapable: in the one case its attempt is phi losophical; in the second case its attempt is futile. Any attempt to mix up Faith with Reason, in a matter exclusively addressed to the Reason, must be abortive. We do not say that what Faith implicitly accepts, Reason may not explicitly justify; but we say, that to bring Faith to the aid of Reason, is altogether to destroy the *philosophical* character of an inquiry. Reason may justify Faith; but faith must not furnish conclusions *for* Philosophy. Directly Reason is abandoned, Philosophy ceases; and every explanation then offered is a theological explanation, and must be put to altogether different tests from what a philosophical explanation would require.

All speculation must originally have been theological: but in process of time Reason timidly ventured upon what are called "natural explanations;" and from the moment that it felt itself strong enough to be independent, Philosophy was established. In the early speculations of the Ionians we saw the pure efforts of Reason to explain mysteries. As Philosophy advanced, it became more and more evident that the problems attacked by the early thinkers were, in truth, so far from being nearer a solution, that their extreme difficulty was only just becoming appreciated. The difficulty became more and more apparent, till at last it was pronounced insuperable: Reason was declared incompetent. Then the Faith which had so long been set aside was again called to assist the inquirer. In other words, Philosophy, discovering itself to be powerless, resigned in favor of Theology.

When, therefore, we say that the direction given to the human mind by the Alexandrian School, in conjunction with Christianity—the only two spiritual movements which materially influenced the epoch we are speaking of—was a theological direction, the reader will at once see its immense importance, and will be prepared to follow us in our exposition of the mystical doctrines of Plotinus.

CHAPTER II.

ANTAGONISM OF CHRISTIANITY AND NEO-PLATONISM.

§ I. Plotinus.

WHILE Christianity was making rapid and enduring progress in spite of every obstacle; while the Apostles wandered from city to city, sometimes honored as Evangelists, at other times insulted and stoned as enemies, the Neo-Platonists were developing the germ deposited by Philo, and not only constructing a theology, but endeavoring on that theology to found a Church. Whilst a new religion, Christianity, was daily usurping the souls of men, these philosophers fondly imagined that an old Religion could effectually oppose it.

Christianity triumphed without much difficulty. Looking at it in a purely moral view, its immense superiority is at once apparent. The Alexandrians exaggerated the vicious tendency of which we have already seen the fruits in the Cynics and Stoics—the tendency to despise Humanity. Plotinus blushed because he had a body: contempt of human personality could go no further. What was offered in exchange? The ecstatic perception; the absorption of personality in that of the Deity—a Deity inaccessible to knowledge as to love—a Deity which the soul can only attain by a complete annihilation of its personality.

The attempt of the Neo-Platonists failed, as it deserved to fail; but it had great talents in its service, and it made great noise in the world. It had, as M. Saisset remarks, three periods. The first of these, the least brilliant but the most fruitful, is that of Ammonius Saccas and Plotinus. A porter of Alexandria becomes the chief of a School, and men of genius listen to him; amongst his disciples are Plotinus, Origen, and Longinus. This School is perfected in obscurity, and receives at last a solid basis by the development of a metaphysical system. Plotinus, the author of this system, shortly after lectures at Rome with amazing success. It is then that the Alexandrian School enters upon its second period. With Porphyry and Iamblicus it becomes a sort of Church, aud disputes with Christianity the empire of the world. Christianity had ascended the throne in the person of Constantine; Neo-Platonism dethrones it, and usurps its place in the person of Julian the Apostate. But now mark the difference. In losing Constantine, Christianity lost nothing of its real power; for its power lay in the might of convictions, and not in the support of potentates; its power was a spiritual power, ever active, ever fruitful. In losing Julian, Neo-Platonism lost its power, political and religious. The third period commences with that loss: and the genius of Proclus bestows on it one last gleam of splendor. In vain did he strive to revive the scientific spirit of Platonism, as Plotinus had endeavored to revive the religious spirit of Paganism: his efforts were vigorous, but sterile. Under Justinian the School of Alexandria became extinct.

Such is the outward history of the School: let us now cast a glance at the doctrines which were there elaborated. In the writings of thinkers professedly eclectic, such as were the Alexandrians, it is obvious that the greater portion will be repetitions and reproductions of former thinkers; and the historian will therefore neglect such opinions to confine himself to those which constitute the originality of the School. The originality of the Alexandrians consists in having employed the Platonic Dialectics as a guide to Mysticism and Pantheism; in having connected the doctrine of the East with the dialectics of the Greeks; in having made Reason the justification of Faith.

There are three essential points to be here examined: their Dialectics, their theory of the Trinity, and their principle of Emanation. By their Dialectics they were Platonists; by their theory of the Trinity they were Mystics; by their principle of Emanation they were Pantheists.

§ II. The Alexandrian Dialectics.

The nature of the Platonic Dialectics we hope to have already rendered intelligible; so that in saying Plotinus employed them we are saved from much needless repetition. But although Dialectics formed the basis of Alexandrian philosophy, they did not, as with Plato, furnish the grounds of *belief*. As far as human philosophy went, Dialectics were efficient; but there were problems which did not come within the sphere of human philosophy, and for these another Method was requisite.

Plotinus agreed with Plato that there could only be a science of Universals. Every individual thing was but a phenomenon, passing quickly away, and having no real existence; it could not therefore be the object of philosophy. But these universals—these Ideas which are the only real existences—are they not also subordinate to some higher Existence? Phenomena were subordinate to Noumena; but Noumena themselves were subordinate to the One Noumenon. In other words, the Sensible world was but the Appearance of the Ideal World, and the Ideal World in its turn was but the mode of God's existence.

The question then arises: How do we know any thing of God? The sensible world we perceive through our senses; the Ideal World we gain glimpses of through the *reminiscence* which the sensible world awakens in us; but how are we to take the last step—how are we to know the Deity?

I am a finite being; but how can I comprehend the Infinite? As soon as I comprehend the Infinite, I am Infinite myself; that is to say, I am no longer myself, no longer that finite being, having a consciousness of his own separate existence.* If, therefore, I attain to a knowledge of the Infinite, it is not by my Rea-

---

* Τίς ἂν οὖν τὴν δύναμιν αὐτοῦ ἴλοι ὁμοῦ πᾶσαν; εἰ γὰρ ὁμοῦ πᾶσαν, τί ἂν τις αὐτοῦ διαφέροι.—*Plotinus, Enn.* v. lib. 5. c. 10.

son, which is finite and embraces only finite objects, but by some higher faculty, a faculty altogether impersonal, which *identifies itself with its object.*

The identity of Subject and Object—of the thought with the thing thought of—is the only possible ground of knowledge. This position, which some of our readers will recognize as the fundamental position of modern German speculation, is so removed from all ordinary conceptions, that we must digress awhile in order to explain it. Neo-Platonism is a blank without it.

Knowledge and Being are Identical; to know more is to *be* more. This is not, of course, maintaining the absurd proposition that to know a horse is to be a horse: all we know of that horse is only what we know of the changes in ourselves occasioned by some external cause, and identifying our internal change with that external cause, we call it a horse. Here knowledge and being are identical. We really know nothing of the external cause (horse), we only know our own state of being; and to say, therefore, that "in our knowledge of the horse we are the horse," is only saying, in unusual language, that our knowledge is a state of our being, and nothing more. The discussion in the fourth Chapter of the foregoing Epoch respecting perception, was an attempt to prove that knowledge is only a state of our own consciousness, excited by some unknown cause. The cause *must* remain unknown, because knowledge is effect, not cause.

An apple is presented to you; you see it, feel it, taste it, smell it, and are said to know it. What is this knowledge? Simply a consciousness of the various ways in which the apple *affects you.* You are blind and cannot see it: there is one quality less which it possesses, *i. e.* one mode less in which it is possible for you to be affected. You are without the senses of smell and taste: there are two other deficiencies in your knowledge of the apple. So that, by taking away your senses, we take away from the apple each of its qualities: in other words, we take away the means of your being affected. Your knowledge of the apple is reduced to nothing. In a similar way, by endowing you with more senses we increase the qualities of the apple; we increase your knowledge by enlarging your being. Thus are Knowledge and Being identical; knowledge is a state of Being as knowing.

"If," said Plotinus, "knowledge is the same as the thing known, the Finite, as Finite, never can know the Infinite, because it cannot *be* the Infinite. To attempt, therefore, to know the Infinite by Reason is futile, it can only be known in immediate presence, παρουσία. The faculty by which the mind divests itself of its personality is *Ecstasy*. In this Ecstasy the soul becomes loosened from its material prison, separated from individual consciousness, and becomes absorbed in the Infinite Intelligence from which it emanated. In this Ecstasy it contemplates real existence; it identifies itself with that which it contemplates."

The enthusiasm upon which this Ecstasy is founded is not a faculty which we constantly possess, such as Reason or Perception: it is only a transitory state, at least so long as our *personal* existence in this world continues. It is a flash of rapturous light, in which *reminiscence* is changed into *intuition*, because in that moment the captive soul is given back to its parent, its God. The bonds which attach the soul to the body are mortal; and God, our father, pitying us, has made those bonds, from which we suffer, fragile and delicate, and in his goodness he gives us certain intervals of respite: Ζεὺς δὲ πατὴρ ἐλέησας πονουμένας, θνητὰ αὐτῶν τὰ δεσμὰ ποιῶν περὶ ἃ πονοῦνται, δίδωσιν ἀναπαύλας ἐν χρόνοις.

The Oriental and mystical character of this conception is worth remarking; at the same time there is a Platonic element in it, which may be noticed. Plato, in the *Ion*, speaks of a chain of inspiration, which descends from Apollo to poets, who transmit the inspiration to the rhapsodists; the last links of the chain are the souls of lovers and philosophers, who, unable to transmit the divine gift, are nevertheless agitated by it. The Alexandrians also admit the divine inspiration: not that inspiration which only warms and exalts the heart, but that inspiration revealing the Truth which Reason can neither discern nor comprehend.

Whether, in ascending through the various sciences and laboriously mounting all the degrees of Dialectics, we finally arrive at the summit, and tear away the veil behind which the Deity is hidden; or, instead of thus slowly mounting, we arrive at the summit by a sudden spring, by the force of virtue or by the force of love, the origin of this revelation is the same: the Poet, the Prophet, and the Philosopher only differ in the point of departure each takes. Dialectics, therefore, though a valuable method, is not an infallible one for arriving at Ecstasy. Every thing which purifies the soul and makes it resemble its primal simplicity, is capable of conducting it to Ecstasy. Besides, there are radical differences in men's natures. Some souls are ravished with Beauty; and these belong to the Muses. Others are ravished with Unity and Proportion; and these are Philosophers. Others are more struck with Moral perfections; and these are the pious and ardent souls who live only in religion.

Thus, then, the passage from simple Sensation, or from Reminiscence, to Ecstasy, may be accomplished in three ways. By Music (in the ancient and comprehensive sense of the term), by Dialectics, and by Love or Prayer. The result is always the same,—the victory of the Universal over the Individual.

Such is the answer given by the Alexandrians to that world-old question, How do we know God? The Reason of man is incompetent to such knowledge, because Reason is finite, and the finite cannot embrace the infinite. But, inasmuch as Man has a knowledge of the Deity, he must have obtained it in some way: the question is, In what way? This question, which the Christian Fathers were enabled to answer satisfactorily by referring to Revelation, the Alexandrians could only answer most unsatisfactorily by declaring Ecstasy to be the medium of communication, because in Ecstasy the soul lost its personality and became absorbed in the Infinite Intelligence.

We may read in this philosophy an instructive lesson respecting the vicious circle in which all such reasonings are condemned to move:

"The one poor finite being in the abyss
Of infinite being twinkling restlessly."

This finite being strives to comprehend that which includes it, and in the impossible attempt exerts its confident ingenuity. Conscious that the finite *as* finite cannot comprehend the infinite, the Alexandrian hypothesis is at least consistent in making the finite become, for an instant, infinite. The grounds however upon which this hypothesis is framed are curious. The axiom is this:—The finite *cannot* comprehend the infinite. The problem is this:—How *can* the finite comprehend the infinite? And the solution is: The finite must *become* the infinite.

Absurd as it is, it is the conclusion deduced by a vigorous intellect from premises which seemed indisputable. It is only one of the absurdities inseparable from the attempted solution of insoluble problems.

§ III. The Alexandrian Trinity.

We have said that the philosophy of the Alexandrians was a theology; their theology may be said to be concentrated in the doctrine of the Trinity. Nearly allied to the mystery of the Incarnation, which was inseparable from the mystery of Redemption, the dogma of the Holy Trinity was, as M. Saisset remarks, the basis of all the Christian metaphysics. The greater part of the important heresies, Arianism, Sabellianism, Nestorianism, etc., resulted from differences respecting some portion of this doctrine. It becomes, therefore, a matter of high historical interest to determine its parentage. Some maintain that the Trinity of the Christians was but an imitation of that of the Alexandrians; others accuse the Alexandrians of being the imitators. The dispute has been angrily conducted on both sides. It is not our purpose to meddle with it, as our history steers clear of such matters; but we think it right to indicate the quarrel.*

---

* Such of our readers as may desire a compendious statement of the question are referred to M. Jules Simon, *Histoire de l'École d'Alexandrie*, vol. i. pp. 308–341, and to the article by M. Saisset, in the *Revue des Deux Mondes*, before referred to.

The Alexandrian Trinity is as follows :—God is triple, and, at the same time, one. His nature contains within it three distinct *Hypostases* (Substances, *i. e.* Persons), and these three make one Being. The first is the Unity : not The One Being, not Being at all, but simple Unity. The second is the Intelligence, which is identical with Being. The third is the Universal Soul, cause of all activity and life.

Such is the formula of the dogma. Let us now see how their Dialectics conducted them to it. On looking abroad upon the world, and observing its constant transformations, what is the first thing that presents itself to our minds as the cause of all these changes? It is Life. The whole world is alive; and, not only alive, but seemingly participating in a life similar to our own. On looking deeper, we discover that life itself is but an effect of some higher cause; and this cause must be the "Universal," which we are seeking to discover. Our logic tells us that it is Activity—Motion. But with this Motion we cannot proceed far. It soon becomes apparent to us that the myriad ongoings of nature are not merely activities, but *intelligent* activities. No hazard rules this world. Intelligence is everywhere visible. The Cause, then, we have been seeking is at last discovered : it is an Intelligent Activity. Now, what is this, but that mysterious force residing within us, directing us, impelling us? What is this Intelligent Activity but a soul? The soul which impels and directs us is an image of the Soul which impels and directs the world. God, therefore, is the eternal Soul, the $\psi\nu\chi\acute{\eta}$. We have here the first Hypostasis of the Alexandrians. On a deeper inspection this notion turns out less satisfactory. The dialectician, whose whole art consists in dividing and subdividing, in order to arrive at pure unity—who is always unravelling the perplexed web of speculation, to lay bare at last the unmixed One which had become enveloped in the Many—the dialectician, bred up in the Schools of Plato and Aristotle, could not rest satisfied with so complex an entity as an Intelligent Activity. There are at least two ideas here, and two ideas entirely distinct in nature, viz., In telligence and Motion. Now, although these might be united in some idea common to both, yet superior to both, neither of them could be considered as the last term in an analysis. The Intelligence, when analyzed, is itself the activity of some intelligent being, of Mind, λόγος.

God, therefore, is Mind, absolute, eternal, immutable. We have here the second Hypostasis. Superior to the Divine Soul, ψυχὴ τοῦ παντός, which is the cause of all activity, and king of the sensible world, χορηγὸς τῆς κινήσεως, βασιλεὺς τῶν γιγνομένων, we find the Divine Mind, νοῦς, the magnificence of which we may faintly conceive by reflecting on the splendors of the sensible world, with the Gods, Men, Animals, and Plants, which adorn it: splendors which are but imperfect images of the incomparable lustre of eternal truth. The Divine Mind embraces all the intelligible Ideas which are without imperfection, without movement. This is the Age of Gold, of which God is the Saturn. For Saturn, of whom the Poets have so grandly sung, is the Divine Intelligence; that perfect world which they have described, when

> "Ver erat æternum: placidique tepentibus auris
> Mulcebant Zephyri natos sine semine flores.
> Mox etiam fruges tellus inarata ferebat;
> Nec renovatus ager gravidis canebat aristis.
> Flumina jam lactis, jam flumina nectaris ibant;
> Flavaque de viridi stillabant ilice mella."*

That golden age is the Intelligible World, the eternal Thought of eternal Intelligence.

A word or two on this Alexandrian νοῦς. It is Thought abstracted from all thinking: it does not reason; for to reason is to acquire a knowledge of something: he who reasons, arrives at a consequence from his premises, which he did not see in those premises without effort. But God sees the consequence

---

* "The flowers unsown in fields and meadows reigned;
  And western winds immortal spring maintained.
  In following years the bearded corn ensued
  From earth unasked; nor was that earth renewed.
  From veins of valleys milk and nectar broke,
  And honey sweating from the pores of oak."—DRYDEN'S *Ovid*.

simultaneously with the premises. His knowledge resembles our knowledge as hieroglyphic writing resembles our written language: that which we discursively develop, he embraces at once.

This νοῦς is at the same time the eternal existence, since all Ideas are united in it. It is the νόησις νοήσεως νόησις of Aristotle,— or, to use the language of Plotinus, is the Sight Seeing, the identity of the act of seeing with the object seen: ἔστι γὰρ ἡ νόησις ὅρασις ὁρῶσα, ἄμφω τὸ ἕν,—a conception which will at once be understood by recurring to our illustration of the identity of Knowledge and Being, given above.

One would fancy that this was a degree of abstraction to satisfy the most ardent dialectician ; to have analyzed thus far, and to have arrived at pure Thought and pure Existence—the Thought apart from Thinking and the Existence apart from its modes— would seem the very limit of human ingenuity, the last abstraction possible. But no: the dialectician is not yet contented: he sees another degree of abstraction still higher, still simpler: he calls it Unity. God, as Existence and Thought, is God as conceived by human intelligence: but, although human intelligence is unable to embrace any higher notion of God, yet is there in human intelligence a hint of its own weakness and an assurance of God's being something ineffable, incomprehensible. God is not, *en dernière analyse*, Existence and Thought. What is Thought? What is its type? The type is evidently human reason. What does an examination of human reason reveal? This :—To think is to be aware of some object from which the thinker distinguishes himself. To think is to have a self-consciousness, to distinguish one's personality from that of all other objects, to determine the relation of self to not-self. But nothing is external to God : in him there can be no distinction, no determination, no relation. Therefore God, in his highest hypostasis, cannot think, cannot be thought, but must be something superior to thought. Hence, the necessity for a third hypostasis, which third in the order of discovery is first in the order of being: it is Unity,— τὸ ἕν ἁπλοῦν.

The Unity is not Existence, neither is it Intelligence—it is superior to both: it is superior to all action, to all determination, to all knowledge; for, in the same way as the *multiple* is contained in the *simple*, the many in the one, in the same way is the simple contained in the unity; and it is impossible to discover the truth of things until we have arrived at this absolute unity; for, how can we conceive any existing thing except by unity? What is an individual, an animal, a plant, but that unity which presides over multiplicity? What even is multiplicity—an army, an assembly, a flock—when not brought under unity? Unity is omnipresent; it is the bond which unites even the most complex things. The Unity which is absolute, immutable, infinite, and self-sufficing is not the numerical unit, not the indivisible point. It is the absolute universal *One* in its perfect simplicity. It is the highest degree of perfection—the ideal Beauty, the supreme Good, πρῶτον ἀγαθόν.

God therefore in his absolute state—in his first and highest Hypostasis—is neither Existence nor Thought, neither moved nor mutable: he is the simple Unity, or, as Hegel would say, the Absolute Nothing, the Immanent Negative. Our readers will perhaps scarcely be patient under this infliction of dialectical subtlety; but we beg them to remember that the absurdities of genius are often more instructive than the discoveries of common men, and the subtleties and extravagances of the Alexandrians are fraught with lessons. If rigorous logic conducted eminent minds to conceptions which appear extravagant and sterile, they may induce in us a wholesome suspicion of the efficacy of that logic to solve the problems it is occupied with. Nor is the lesson inapplicable to our age. The present enthusiasm for German Literature and German Philosophy will of course turn the attention of many young minds to the speculations in which Germany is so rife; we are consequently more interested in Plotinus, because he agitates similar questions and affords very similar answers. The German Metaphysicians resemble Plotinus more than Plato or Aristotle: nor is the reason difficult of discovery. Plotinus, coming after all the great thinkers had asked almost every metaphysical question and given almost every possible answer, was condemned either to skepticism or to accept any consequences of his dialectics, however extreme. Philosophy was in this dilemma—either to abdicate, or to be magnificently tyrannical: it chose to be the latter. Plotinus therefore shrank from no extravagances: where Reason failed, there he called upon Faith. The Germans, coming after the secure establishment of Positive Science, found Philosophy in a similar dilemma: either to declare itself incapable, or to proclaim its despotism and infallibility: what Logic demonstrated must be absolutely true.

This faith in logic is remarkable, and may be contrasted with the Alexandrian faith in Ecstasy. Of the *possibility* of human logic not being the standard of truth, the Germans have no suspicion; they are without the Greek skepticism as to the Criterium. They proceed with peaceable dogmatism to tell you that God is this, or that; to explain how the Nothing *becomes* the Existing world, to explain many other inexplicable things; and, if you stop them with the simple inquiry, How do you know this? what is your ground of certitude? they smile, allude blandly to *Vernunft*, and continue their exposition.

Plotinus was wiser, though less consequent. He said, that although Dialectics raise us to some conviction of the existence of God, we cannot speak of his nature otherwise than negatively: ἐν ἀφαιρέσει πάντα τὰ περὶ τοῦτον λεγόμενα. We are forced to admit his existence, though it is not correct to speak even of his existence. To say that he is superior to Existence and Thought, is not to define him; it is only to distinguish him from what he is not. What he is we cannot know; it would be ridiculous to endeavor to comprehend him. This difference apart, there is remarkable similarity in the speculations of the Alexandrians and the modern Germans: a similarity which all will detect who are capable of detecting identity of thought under diversity of language.

To return to the Alexandrian Trinity, we see in it the Perfect Principle, the One, τὸ ἕν ἁπλοῦν, which generates, but is ungenerated; the Principle generated by the Perfect, is of all generated things the most perfect: it is therefore Intelligence—νοῦς. In the same way as Intelligence is *the Word* (λόγος) of the One and the manifestation of its power, so also the Soul is *the Word* and manifestation of the Intelligence, οἷον καὶ ἡ ψυχὴ λόγος νοῦ. The three Hypostases of the Deity are therefore, 1st, the Perfect, the Absolute Unity, τὸ ἕν ἁπλοῦν; 2d, the First Intelligence, τὸ νοῦν πρώτως; 3d, the Soul of the world.

This Trinity is very similar to the threefold nature of God in Spinoza's system. Spinoza says, that God is the infinite Existence, having two infinite Attributes—Extension and Thought. Now this Existence, which has neither Extension nor Thought, except as Attributes, although verbally differing from the Absolute Unconditioned, the One, of Plotinus, is, in point of fact, the same: it is the last abstraction which human logic can make: it is that *of which* nothing can be predicated, and yet which must be the final predicate of every thing: division and subdivision, however prolonged, stop there, and admit as final the Unconditioned Unconditional Something; that which Proclus calls the Non-Being, μὴ ὄν, although it is not correct to call it nothing, μηδέν.

This conception, which it is impossible to state in words without stating gross contradictions, is the result of rigorous logic, reasoning from false premises. The process is this: I have to discover that which is at the bottom of the mystery of existence—the great First Cause; and to do this, I must eliminate, one by one, every thing which does not present itself as self-existing, self-sufficing, as necessarily the *first* of all things, the ἀρχή.

The ancients began their speculations in the same way, but with less knowledge of the conditions of inquiry. Hence, Water, Air, Soul, Number, Force, were severally accepted as *Principia*. In the time of the Alexandrians something more subtle was required. They asked the same question, but they asked it with a full consciousness of the failure of their predecessors. Even Thought would not satisfy them as a *Principium*; nor were they better satisfied with abstract Existence. They said there is something beyond Thought, something beyond Existence: there is *that which* thinks, *that which* exists. This "*that*," this Indeterminate Ineffable, is the Principium. It is self-sufficing, self-existent; nothing can be conceived beyond it. In the old Indian hypothesis of the world being supported by an elephant, who stood on the back of a tortoise, the tortoise standing on nothing, we see a rude solution of the same problem: the mind is forced to arrest itself somewhere, and wherever it arrests itself it is forced to declare, explicitly or implicitly, that it stops at Nothing; because, as soon as it predicates any thing of that at which it stops, it is forced to admit *something* beyond: if the tortoise stands on the back of some other animal, *upon what* does that other animal stand?

Human logic, when employed upon this subject, necessarily abuts upon Nothing, upon absolute Negation; the terms in which this conception is clothed may differ, but the conception remains the same: Plotinus and Hegel shake hands.

In reviewing the history of Greek speculation, from the "Water" of Thales to the "Absolute Negation" of Plotinus, what a reflection is forced upon us of the vanity of metaphysics! So many years of laborious inquiry, so many splendid minds engaged, and, after the lapse of ages, the inquiry remains the same, the answer only more ingeniously absurd! Was, then, all this labor vain? Were those long, laborious years, all wasted? Were those splendid minds all useless? No: earnest endeavor is seldom without result. Those centuries of speculation were not useless, they were the education of the human race. They taught mankind this truth, at least: the Infinite cannot be known by the finite; and man, as finite, can only know phenomena. Those labors, so fruitless in their immediate object, have indirect lessons. The speculations of the Greeks preserve the same privilege as the glorious products of their art and literature; they are the models from which the speculations of posterity are reproductions. The history of modern metaphysical philosophy, is but the narrative of the same struggles which agitated Greece. The same problems are revived, and the same answers offered.

§ IV. The Doctrine of Emanation.

Metaphysics propounds three questions: Has human knowledge any absolute certainty? What is the nature of God? What is the origin of the World?

Our review of the various attempts to answer these questions, has ended in the Alexandrian School, which answered them as follows: 1st. Human knowledge is necessarily uncertain; but this difficulty is got over by the hypothesis of an Ecstasy, in which the soul becomes identified with the Infinite. 2d. The Nature of God is a triple Unity—three hypostases of the One Being. 3d. The origin of the world is the law of *Emanation*.

This third answer is of course implied in the second. God, as Unity, *is* not Existence; but he becomes Existence by the Emanation from his Unity (Intelligence), and by the second emanation from his Intelligence (Soul), and this Soul, in its manifestations, is the World.

Hitherto dualism has been the universal creed of those who admitted any distinction between the world and its creator. Jupiter, organizing Chaos; the God of Anaxagoras, whose force is wasted in creation; the δημιουργός of Plato, who conquers and regulates Matter and Motion; the immovable Thought of Aristotle: all these creeds were dualistic; and, indeed, to escape dualism was no easy task.

If God is distinct from the World, dualism is at once assumed. If he is distinct, he must be distinct in Essence. If distinct in essence, the question of Whence came the world? is not answered; for the world must have existed contemporaneously with him.

THE DOCTRINE OF EMANATION.

Here lies the difficulty: either God made the world, or he did not. If he made it, whence did he make it? He could not, said logic, make it out of Nothing; for nothing can come of Nothing; he must, therefore, have made it out of his own substance. If it is made out of his own substance, then it is identical with him : it must, then, have existed already in him, or he could not have produced it. But this identification of God with the world is Pantheism; and begs the question it should answer.

If he did not make it out of his own substance, he must have made it out of some substance already existing; and thus, also, the question still remains unanswered.

This problem was solved by the Christians and Alexandrians in a similar, though apparently different, manner. The Christians said that God created the world out of Nothing by the mere exercise of his omnipotent will; for to Omnipotence every thing is possible; one thing is as easy as another. The Alexandrians said that the world was distinct from God *in act* rather than *in essence:* it was the manifestation of his will or of his intelligence.

Thus the world is God; but God is not the world. Without the necessity of two principles, the distinction is preserved between the Creator and the Created. God is not confounded with Matter; and yet Philosophy is no longer oppressed with the difficulty of accounting for two eternally existing and eternally distinct principles.

Plotinus had by his Dialectics discovered the necessity of Unity as the basis of existence: he had also by the same means discovered that the Unity could not possibly remain alone : otherwise there would never have been the Many. If the Many implies the One, the One also implies the Many. It is the property of each principle to engender that which follows it : to engender it in virtue of an ineffable power which loses nothing of itself. This power, ineffable, inexhaustible, exercises itself without stopping, from generation to generation, till it attains the limits of possibility.

By this law, which governs the world, and from which God himself cannot escape, the totality of existences, which Dialectics teach us to arrange in a proper hierarchy from God to sensible Matter, appear to us thus united in one indissoluble chain, since each being is the necessary product of that which precedes it, and the necessary producer of that which succeeds it.

If asked why Unity should ever become Multiplicity—why God should ever manifest himself in the world? the answer is ready: The One, as conceived by the Eleatics, had long been found incomplete; for a God who had no intelligence could not be perfect: as Aristotle says, a God who does not think is unworthy of respect. If, therefore, God is Intelligent, he is necessarily active: a force that engenders nothing, can that be a real force? It was, therefore, in the very nature of God a necessity for him to create the world: ἐν τῇ φύσει ἦν τὸ ποιεῖν.

God, therefore, is in his very essence a Creator, ποιητής. He is like a Sun pouring forth his rays, without losing any of its substance: οἷον ἐκ φωτὸς, τὴν ἐξ αὐτοῦ περίλαμψιν. All this flux—this constant change of things, this birth and death—is but the restless manifestation of a restless force. These manifestations have no absolute truth, no duration. The individual perishes, because individual: it is only the universal that endures. The individual is the finite, the perishable; the universal is the infinite, immortal. God is the only existence: he is the real existence, of which we, and other things, are but the transitory phenomena. And yet timid ignorant man fears death! timid because ignorant. To die is to live the true life: it is to lose, indeed, sensation, passions, interests, to be free from the conditions of space and time,—to lose personality; but it is also to quit this world and to be born anew in God,—to quit this frail and pitiable individuality, to be absorbed in the being of the Infinite. To die is to live the true life. Some faint glimpses of it—some overpowering anticipations of a bliss intolerable to mortal sense, are realized in the brief moments of Ecstasy, wherein the Soul is absorbed in the Infinite, although it cannot long remain there. Those moments so exquisite yet so brief are sufficient to reveal to us the divinity, and to show us that deep imbedded in our personality there is a ray of the divine source of light, a ray which is always struggling to disengage itself, and return to its source. To die is to live the true life: and Plotinus dying, answered, in his agony, to friendly questions: "I am struggling to liberate the divinity within me."

This mysticism is worth attention, as indicative of the march of the human mind. In many preceding thinkers we have seen a very strong tendency towards the desecration of personality. From Heraclitus to Plotinus there is a gradual advance in this direction. The Cynics and the Stoics made it a sort of philosophical basis. Plato implicitly, and sometimes explicitly, gave it his concurrence. The conviction of man's insignificance, and of the impossibility of his ever in this world ascertaining the truth, seem to have oppressed philosophers with self-contempt. To curse the bonds which bound them to ignorance, and to quit a world in which they were thus bound, were the natural consequences of their doctrines; but, linked mysteriously as we are to life—even to the life we curse—our doctrines seldom lead to suicide. In default of suicide, nothing remained but Asceticism— a moral suicide. As man could not summon courage to quit the world, he would at least endeavor to lead a life as far removed from worldly passion and worldly condition as was possible; and he would welcome death as the only true life.

CHAPTER III.

PROCLUS.

PLOTINUS attempted to unite Philosophy with Religion, attempted to solve by Faith the problems insoluble by Reason; and the result of such an attempt was necessarily mysticism. But, although the mystical element is an important one in his doctrine, he did not allow himself to be seduced into all the extravagances which naturally flowed from it. That was reserved for his successors, Iamblicus in particular, who performed miracles, and constituted himself High Priest of the Universe.

With Proclus the Alexandrian School made a final effort, and with him its defeat was entire. He was born at Constantinople, A. D. 412. He came early to Alexandria, where Olympiodorus was teaching. He passed onwards to Athens, and from Plutarch and Syrianus he learnt to comprehend the doctrines of Plato and Aristotle. Afterwards, becoming initiated into the Theurgical mysteries, he was soon made a High Priest of the Universe.

The theological tendency is still more visible in Proclus than in Plotinus. He regarded the Orphic poems and the Chaldean oracles as divine revelations, and, therefore, as the real source of philosophy, if properly interpreted; and in this allegorical interpretation consisted his whole system.

> "The intelligible forms of ancient poets,
> The fair humanities of old religion,
> The Power, the Beauty, and the Majesty,
> That had her haunts in dale, or piny mountain,
> Or forest by slow stream, or pebbly spring,
> Or chasms and wat'ry depths; all these have vanish'd,
> They live no longer in the faith of reason!
> But still the heart doth need a language, still
> Doth the old instinct bring back the old names.
> And to yon starry world they now are gone,

> Spirits or Gods that used to share this earth
> With man as with their friend."*

To breathe the breath of life into the nostrils of these defunct deities, to restore the beautiful Pagan creed, by interpreting its symbols in a new sense, was the aim of the whole Alexandrian School.

Proclus placed Faith above Science. It was the only faculty by which The Good, that is to say, The One, could be apprehended. "The Philosopher," said he, "is not the Priest of one Religion, but of all Religions;" that is to say, he is to reconcile all modes of Belief by his interpretations. Reason is the Expositor of Faith. But Proclus made one exception: there was one Religion which he could not tolerate, which he would not interpret,—that was the Christian.

With this conception of his mission, it is easy to see that his method must be eclectic. Accordingly, in making Philosophy the expositor of Religion, he relied upon the doctrines of his predecessors without pretending to discover new ones for his purpose. Aristotle, whom he called "the Philosopher of the understanding," he regarded as the man whose writings formed the best introduction to the study of wisdom. In him the student learnt the use of his Reason; learnt also the forms of thought. After this preparatory study came the study of Plato, whom he called the "Philosopher of Reason," the sole guide to the region of Ideas, that is, of Eternal Truths. The reader will probably recognize here the distinction between Understanding and Reason, revived by Kant, and so much insisted on by Coleridge and his followers.

Plato was the idol of Proclus; and the passionate disciple thought every word of the master an oracle; he discovered every where some hidden and oracular meaning, interpreting the simplest recitals into sublime allegories. Thus the affection of Socrates for Alcibiades became the slender text for a whole volume of mystical exposition.

---

* Coleridge, in his translation of the *Piccolomini*.

It is curious to notice the transformations of philosophy in the various schools. Socrates interpreted the inscription on the temple at Delphi, "Know thyself," as an exhortation to psychological and ethical study. He looked inwards, and there discovered certain truths which skepticism could not darken; and he discoursed, says his biographer, on Justice and Injustice, on things holy and things unholy.

Plato also looked inwards, hoping to find there a basis of philosophy; but his "Know thyself" had a different signification. Man was to study himself, because, by becoming thoroughly acquainted with his mind, he would become acquainted with the eternal Ideas of which sense awakened Reminiscence. His self-knowledge was Dialectical, rather than Ethical. The object of it was the contemplation of eternal Existence, not the regulation of our worldly acts.

The Alexandrians also interpreted the inscription; but with them the Socratic conception was completely set aside, and the Platonic conception carried to its limits. "Know thyself," says Proclus, in his commentary on Plato's *First Alcibiades*, "that you may know the essence from whose source you are derived. Know the divinity that is within you, that you may know the divine One of which your soul is but a ray. Know your own mind, and you will have the key to all knowledge." These are not the words of Proclus, but they convey the meaning of many pages of his enthusiastic dialectics.

We are struck in Proclus with the frank and decided manner in which Metaphysics is assumed to be the only possible science; we are struck with the *naïve* manner in which the fundamental error of metaphysical inquiry is laid open to view, and presented as an absolute truth. In no other ancient system is it stated so nakedly. If we desired an illustration of the futility of metaphysics we could not find a better than is afforded by Proclus, who, be it observed, only pushed the premises of others to their rigorous conclusions.

He teaches that the hierarchy of ideas, in which there is a

gradual generation from the most abstract to the most concrete, exactly corresponds with the hierarchy of existences, in which there is a constant generation from the most abstract (Unity) to to the most concrete (phenomena): so that the relations which these ideas bear to each other, the laws which subordinate one to the other—in a word, the forms of the nomenclature of human conceptions—express the real causes, their action, their combinations; in fact, the whole system of the universe.*

This is frank. The objection to the metaphysician has been that he looks *inwards* to discover that which lies *without* him, hoping, in his own conceptions of that which he is seeking to know, to find the thing he seeks. We "philosophers of the Understanding" aver that to analyze your mind is to learn the nature of your mind: nothing else. Proclus boldly assumes that to know the nature of your own mind is to know the whole universe. This is at least consistent. But one might reasonably ask how this knowledge is to be gained? not simply by looking inwards, or else all philosophers would have gained it; not even by meditation. How then? Listen:

"Mercury, the Messenger of Jove, reveals to us Jove's paternal will, and thus teaches us science; and, as the author of all investigation, transmits to us, his disciples, the genius of invention. The Science which descends into the soul from above is more perfect than any science obtained by investigation; that which is excited in us by other men is far less perfect. Invention is the energy of the soul. The Science which descends from above fills the soul with the influence of the higher Causes. The Gods announce it to us by their presence and by illuminations, and discover to us the order of the universe."

Of course the Mystic who had revelations from above, dispensed with the ordinary methods of investigation; and here again we see Proclus consistent, though consistent in absurdity.

---

* This is also the doctrine of Hegel.

CONCLUSION OF ANCIENT PHILOSOPHY.

With Proclus the Alexandrian School expired; with him Philosophy ceased. Religion, and Religion only, seemed capable of affording satisfactory answers to the questions which perplexed the human race, and Philosophy was reduced to the subordinate office which the Alexandrians had consigned to the Aristotelian Logic. Philosophy became the servant of Religion, no longer reigning in its own right.

Thus was the circle of endeavor completed. With Thales, Reason separated itself from Faith; with the Alexandrians, the two were again united. The centuries between these epochs were filled with helpless struggles to overcome an insuperable difficulty.

The difference is great between the childlike question of the Ionian thinker, and the *naïve* extravagance of the Alexandrian Mystic: and yet each stands upon the same ground, and looks out upon the same troubled sea, hoping to detect a shore, ignorant that all philosophy

> "is an arch where through
> Gleams that untravelled world, whose margin fades
> Forever and forever as we move."

But, to the reflective student who thus sees these men, after centuries of endeavor, fixed on the self-same spot, the Alexandrian straining his eager eyes after the same object as the Ionian, and neither within the possible range of vision, there is something which would be unutterably sad, were it not corrected by the conviction that these men were fixed to one spot, because they had not discovered the only true pathway, a pathway which those who came after them securely trod.

Still, the spectacle of human failure, especially on so gigantic a scale, cannot be without some pain. So many hopes thwarted, so many great intellects wandering in error, are not to be thought of without sadness. But it bears a lesson which we hope those who have followed us thus far will not fail to read: a lesson on the vanity of Philosophy; a lesson which almost amounts to a demonstration of the impossibility of the human mind ever compassing those exalted objects which its speculative ingenuity suggests as worthy of its pursuit. It points to that profound remark of Auguste Comte, that there exists in all classes of our investigations a constant and necessary harmony between the extent of our real intellectual wants, and the efficient extent, actual or future, of our real knowledge.

But these great Thinkers, whose failures we have chronicled, did not live in vain. They left the great problems where they found them: but they did not leave Humanity as they found it. Metaphysics might be still a region of doubt; but the human mind, in its endeavors to explore that region, had learnt in some measure to ascertain its weakness and its force. Greek Philosophy was a failure; but Greek Inquiry had immense results. Methods had been tried and discarded; but great preparations for the real Method had been made.

Moreover, Ethics had become elevated to the rank of a science. In the Pagan Religion morality consisted in obeying the particular Gods: to propitiate their favor was the only needful art. Greek Philosophy opened men's eyes to the importance of human conduct—to the importance of moral principles, which were to stand in the place of propitiations. The great merit of this is due to Socrates. He objected to propitiation as impious: he insisted upon moral conduct as alone guiding man to happiness here and hereafter.

But the Ethics of the Greeks were at the best narrow and egoistical. Morality, however exalted or comprehensive, only seemed to embrace the *individual;* it was extremely incomplete as regards the family; and had scarcely any suspicion of what we call social relations. No Greek ever attained the sublimity of such a point of view. The highest point he could attain was to conduct *himself* according to just principles; he never troubled himself with others. By the introduction of Christianity, Ethics became Social, as well as Individual.

So far advanced are we in the right direction—so earnestly are we engaged in the endeavor to perfect Social as well as Individual Ethics—that we are apt to look down upon the progress of the Greeks as trivial; but it was immense, and in the history of Humanity must ever occupy an honorable place.

Ancient Philosophy expired with Proclus. Those who came after him, although styling themselves philosophers, were in truth Religious Thinkers employing philosophical formulæ. No one endeavored to give a solution of the three great problems: Whence came the world? What is the nature of God? What is the nature of human knowledge? Argue, refine, divide, and subdivide as they would, the Religious Thinkers only used Philosophy as a subsidiary process: for all the great problems, Faith was their only instrument.

The succeeding Epochs are usually styled the Epochs of Christian Philosophy; yet Christian Philosophy is a misnomer. A Christian may be also a Philosopher; but to talk of Christian Philosophy is an abuse of language. Christian Philosophy means Christian Metaphysics; and that means the solution of metaphysical problems upon Christian principles. Now what are Christian Principles but the Doctrines *revealed* through Christ; revealed because inaccessible to Reason; revealed and accepted by Faith, because Reason is utterly incompetent?

So that metaphysical problems, the attempted solution of which by Reason constitutes Philosophy, are solved by Faith, and yet the name of Philosophy is retained! But the very essence of Philosophy consists in reasoning, as the essence of Religion is Faith. There cannot, consequently, be a Religious Philosophy: it is a contradiction in terms. Philosophy may be occupied about the same problems as Religion; but it employs altogether different Methods, and depends on altogether different principles. Religion may, and should, call in Philosophy to its aid; but in so doing it assigns to Philosophy only the subordinate office of illustrating, reconciling, or applying its dogmas. This is not a Religious Philosophy; it is Religion *and* Philosophy, the latter stripped of its boasted prerogative of deciding for itself, and allowed only to employ itself in reconciling the decisions of Religion and of Reason.

From these remarks it is obvious that our History, being a narrative of the progress of Philosophy only, will not include any detailed account of the so-called Christian Philosophy, because that is a subject strictly belonging to the History of Religion.

Once more we are to witness the mighty struggle and the sad defeat; once more we are to watch the progress and development of that vast but ineffectual attempt which the sublime audacity of man has for centuries renewed. Great intellects and great hopes are once more to be reviewed; and the traces noted which they have left upon that Desert whose only semblance of vegetation is a mirage,—the Desert without fruit, without flower, without habitation: arid, trackless, and silent, but vast, awful, and fascinating. To trace the footsteps of the wanderers—to follow them on their gigantic journeys—to point again the moral of

"Poor Humanity's afflicted will
Struggling in vain with ruthless destiny,"

to bring home to the convictions of men the humble, useful truth that

"Wisdom is ofttimes nearer when we stoop,
Than when we soar,"

will be the object of our SECOND PART.

www.ingramcontent.com/pod-product-compliance
Lightning Source LLC
Chambersburg PA
CBHW020303240426
43673CB00039B/689